together Unbroken

Stories, Law, Practice, and Healing at the Intersection of Domestic Violence and Child Welfare

SARA B. BLOCK

ABA
AMERICAN BAR ASSOCIATION
ABA Publishing

Cover design by Amanda Fry/ABA Design

Printed in the United States of America.

26 25 24 23 5 4 3 2

Library of Congress Control Number: 2022910847

ISBN: 978-1-63905-140-3
e-ISBN: 978-1-63905-141-0

This book is dedicated

To the memory of A.K. and her daughter V.K., who experienced love, domestic violence, the child welfare system, and, tragically, murder; and

In honor of my parents for showing me the truest meaning of family, and my husband and daughters for being my most treasured family.

Contents

Preface: Story of these Stories, Stories of this Story

This book examines the intersection of child welfare and domestic violence by exploring the stories, laws, practices, and healing impacting families at this crossing. May the stories affect the hearts and minds of the readers. May the journeys of individuals—adults and children—and families illustrate the intricacies and complexities that are revealed through efforts to craft sound policy and implement effective practice. May the importance of critical research, statistics, laws, rules, regulations, and case law remain grounded in the human lives of those affected. Those lives are the soul of this exploration. Throughout these chapters, lawyers, advocates, child welfare workers, policymakers, and generally concerned, aware, and informed members of a community who believe in the dignity of every person, the right to be safe and well, and the value of every family, will journey alongside these stories in order to develop interest in, knowledge of, understanding about, and the capacity to effectuate progress alongside families experiencing both domestic violence and the child welfare system.

In this endeavor, the book shares the stories of those who have experienced domestic violence, childhood trauma, and the child welfare system, as well as those who have impacted the experience of families at such junctures. Each story imparted in this book is conveyed with the consent, active participation, and approval of the person to whom the story belongs. Many names, nonetheless, are changed to obscure identities for reasons of privacy and safety. In recounting the stories of researchers, leaders, and reformers who made invaluable marks on this intersection, their names have not been altered. Throughout these stories, the line often fades, and distinctions become one and the same between those impacted by and those impacting this intersection. In carrying these stories with shared power, this book attempts to avoid the "danger of a single story" in which the complexities of individuals and their experiences are flattened into a single narrative of good or bad, strength or weakness, catastrophe or triumph, impactor or the impacted.[1]

There is power in storytelling, in sharing lived truths and experiences. Through the human narrative, stories have the power to inspire, motivate, and expand the views of action, hope, strength, and unity. Stories are powerful data. Ending violence in families must be survivor centered and should remain historically survivor driven listening to stories educates and informs, revealing lessons, challenges, and opportunities. Survivor voices rise up through their stories and when heard, inform interventions that are culturally responsive, inclusive, and effective.

Stories are equally powerful to the storyteller. On the healing journey, stories lead to resilient reclamation that transforms traumatic experiences. Sharing stories can be liberating and transformative, lifting the burden of silence, pain, isolation, stigma, and shame in exchange for a renewed sense of peace, possibility, and hopefulness. There is power in storytelling, in being a catalyst for impactful support and lasting inspiration. Stories touch and linger, threading connections from one to another across distance, time, and tradition, drawing on common experiences and familiar feelings to come to a place of compassion, respect, knowledge, and understanding.

And you, the reader, become a partner in the journey of healing and inspiration through the—indeed your own—"revolutionary act

---

1 Chimamanda Ngozi Adichie, Novelist, *The Danger of a Single Story,* TED Talk at TEDGlobal 2009 (July 2009). ("The single story creates stereotypes, and the problem with stereotypes is not that they are untrue, but that they are incomplete. They make one story become the only story. The consequence of the single story is this: it robs people of dignity. It makes our recognition of our equal humanity difficult. It emphasizes how we are different rather than how we are similar . . . Stories matter. Many stories matter. Stories have been used to dispossess and to malign, but stories can also be used to empower and to humanize. Stories can break the dignity of people, but stories can also repair that broken dignity . . . When we reject the single story, when we realize that there is never a single story, we regain a kind of paradise)."

of listening."[2] The stories here are much more than tales of adversity. The stories here reveal our shared humanity.[3]

> Empathy is the most radical of human emotions.
> —Gloria Steinem

> Someday soon I would love to hand over the files in my basement, filled with notes and minutes from the 1970s and '80s, to the next generation of activists and writers interested in the history of the battered women's movement. It deserves at least several more tellings. Personally, it is a history filled with great satisfaction and sometimes heartache. As I work within the movement today, I am still amazed at what has been accomplished, surprised and disappointed by what we fail to foresee, and awed by the passion, pain, and renewal in the work of liberating women from tyranny and violence. Luckily for me, revelation continued. May they also continue for those who come next![4]
> —Susan Schechter, 1946-2004

---

2 Gloria Steinem coined this phrase. Gloria Steinem, My Life on the Road (2016).

3 This description of the power of storytelling is adapted from the publication, *From the Front of the Room: A Public Speaking Guide for Domestic Violence Survivors & Advocates* (December 2017) by the National Resource Center on Domestic Violence.

4 Raquel Kennedy Bergen, Jeffrey L. Edleson, & Claire M. Renzetti, *Susan Schechter, Reflections: Women and Male Violence*, Violence Against Women, Classic Papers (2005), 219, https://docs.wixstatic.com/ugd/1e71bb_41fe0a1669be413bb318e099bb25d02f.pdf.

1
Introduction: The Angels Are Always Behind Us

The flames from the candles grace light and cast dusky shadows onto the handwritten words in the notebook she grasps in her hands.

"My name is Isabel Rodriguez. Four years ago, I left a five-year abusive relationship where I suffered from sexual, physical, verbal emotional and mental abuse. From this relationship I became a teen mom at the age of fifteen. The only blessing from this harmful relationship was a beautiful baby boy.

"In the midst of all the painful memories, there are things I wish I could have changed, one being that I believed his lies. I believed I wasn't good enough, I believed I wasn't going to be anyone without him, and that there was no way out. His lies manipulated me to the point where they filtered through my heart, mind and soul."

The group gathering in vigil continued listening as she spoke,

"Until one day I had enough! I remember I started looking at myself in the mirror each day telling myself, 'I am beautiful.' I started telling myself, 'I am worthy!' *Aren't we all worthy of respect? We are the definition of worthy.*

"When I left this toxic relationship, it took two years with the help and the support from people who believed in me to fix my broken wounds. Now I know I am worthy. Do not let anyone tell you differently. You are worthy!"

• • •

Isabel Rodriguez was born in Mexico to two parents who always envisioned a life for their family filled with greater opportunity than their rural town could offer. To fulfill this dream, four-year-old Isabel and her *mamá* embarked upon the perilous journey of crossing into America. One night in the desert, while lying next to her mother, Isabel said, "Mama, I see an angel behind me." Each harrowing step, Isabel repeated, "*Mamá, los ángeles siempre están detrás de nosotros.*" Believing the angels were always behind them, Isabel and her *mamá* reached the border and safely crossed to join Isabel's father, avoiding both apprehension and the violence often inflicted upon a woman traveling alone with her daughter.

From American cartoons, Isabel learned English and soon was translating for both of her parents. She became a conscientious, hardworking student. In junior high, two girls bullied Isabel for being too nice, too polite, too studious, and too committed to doing right by others. Isabel was confused and embarrassed, holding this secret close.

In the aftermath of losing faith in the version of herself that made her proud, Isabel met Jason Galvez. By the time he was regularly walking Isabel home from school, Jason was Isabel's boyfriend. While the bullies had treated her with mockery and scorn for being who she was, Jason told Isabel how much he loved her. Isabel's eighth-grade year came to an end with both impressive grades and a sexually active relationship with Jason. One day over the summer, however, they began arguing, and Jason grabbed Isabel's wrist a little too tight and for a little too long. Isabel thought that Jason must have had a "bad day." As the summer progressed, Jason would go days without calling Isabel. By the start of high school, Jason had another girlfriend.

At the beginning of freshman year, Isabel discovered she was pregnant with Jason's child. The first time Isabel heard the sound of her son's heart beating on the ultrasound, she was flooded with many feelings—fear, uncertainty, desperation, shame—but the sound of that tiny heartbeat reverberated throughout her own heart. Isabel remained determined to finish her freshman year on time and with good grades, all for the son she already loved.

Toward the end of Isabel's pregnancy, Jason told her everything she wanted to hear, promising commitment and love. In the spring, Nathan, a beautiful baby boy, was born, and Jason was there. Isabel moved to Jason's parents' home so they could live as a family. When she returned to school, Isabel brought Nathan to the in-school day care each morning, which enabled her to focus on her classes and visit Nathan during free periods. She also registered Nathan at the county-run health clinic in the school, which provided physical and mental health services to the student body.

In the months that followed, Jason's behavior worsened, and Isabel came to realize that she could no longer explain his behavior merely by believing he was having a "bad day." He smashed her phone and her head onto the sidewalk when she asked him where he had been late at night. Every request for Jason to buy diapers was met with a slap. Every suggestion for him to make a bottle brought a shove. The slaps and hits turned into chokings. Accusing Isabel of having an affair with a coworker, Jason pushed her onto the bed and put his hands around her throat, choking the air from her lungs. As she gasped to breathe, Jason dug his nails into her neck and threated, "If you ever cheat on me, I will kill you." Isabel believed he could.

Isabel's very existence became shrouded in fear. She was scared when Jason was around and when he was not. But each morning, Isabel got out of bed, got her son ready, took him to school, visited him in the day care during breaks between classes, completed her schoolwork at night, and received high grades in her courses.

Then one evening, seemingly out of nowhere, Jason slapped Isabel across the face. Isabel quickly stood up, put Nathan in his bed, and returned to the living room, telling Jason to never slap her in front of her son again. Pulling her into the bedroom, Jason held Isabel down and tore off her clothes. "No," Isabel mustered countless times, but Jason did not stop. Isabel listlessly stared at the ceiling; a crack looked like the wing of an angel, yet deliverance to safety did not follow like it had in the desert.

After this rape, Isabel felt worthless. Jason's escalating violence continued to diminish her fading self-worth. One time, after she rejected his sexual advances, Jason put his arms around Isabel's neck, strangling not only the air but nearly all the life from her body. Isabel's tongue hung from her mouth, the veins in her head throbbed, and the pressure in her eyes became overwhelming. Unable to cry out for help, Isabel feared he would kill her. Who then would be there for Nathan? Jason released his hold before the question would need to be answered.

Then one day, as senior year began, Jason came home with a dog. Bella was a beautiful pit bull, only a couple of months old, with green eyes and tiger-striped fur. One afternoon after school, Jason came home to an accident and slammed Bella's face in her own urine. From then on, Isabel raced home every day after school so she could be the first to open the door to Bella's room and clean up any mess that Bella may have made before Jason came home. Jason was no longer hurting Isabel but instead was abusing her beloved Bella, thereby magnifying Isabel's fear and anger each day she was spared at the expense of Bella's suffering.

Every morning, Isabel woke up thinking that this would be the day she would leave—leave for good with Nathan and never come back; if only she could ride the wings of an angel to freedom. She began devising a plan with Marta, her school counselor. Isabel packed bags with clothes and important documents and gave Nathan's Social Security number to Marta in case anything happened to her. Isabel wanted to escape to her parents, but she was deeply ashamed. A domestic violence shelter, farther than walking distance from school, became the only option, but without a car, Isabel did not know how she would get to school. Graduating high school to give her son a better life continued to be Isabel's motivating mantra. Leaving seemed scarier than remaining in the relationship with Jason because Isabel feared she would miss too much school to graduate.

One evening, when Isabel returned from school, Bella was not there. Isabel frantically searched for her, inside and outside. Late that night, Jason returned. He stood in the hallway, with blood splattered on his boots and a hammer, axe, knife, and shovel in his hands. Isabel's desperate inquiries about Bella were met with a combination of eerie silence and wicked, detached laughter. Knowing she needed to live through this night, Isabel calmly pulled Jason into their bedroom. She sat him on the edge of the bed. He dropped the tools to the ground, and Isabel discretely pushed them out of his reach.

"I killed Bella. I killed our dog." Jason then told Isabel the details of how he mutilated and dismembered Bella and where he disposed of her body. Rather than screaming aloud, Isabel cried silently in her head. "If you tell anyone, I will kill you, like I killed her." Isabel believed he could and would.

It then began to snow.

For the next week, Isabel felt omnipresent fear. Nathan stayed at Isabel's parents' house, even though they wondered why. Isabel knew she would leave, but how and when? Then Jason came home with a new dog. Ruby was another pit bull Jason rescued from dog fighting, only for her to have to continue fighting for her life when with him. Like Bella, Ruby became Isabel, too, as Jason abused them both. Jason pushed Isabel to the ground and dragged her by her hair, shoving her into Ruby's urine-filled kennel. The next time Jason kicked and punched Ruby, Isabel tried to protect her. In response, Jason grabbed Isabel's arm and bent it all the way behind and up her back. Isabel heard her arm creak, as her bones were about to break. Jason shoved her face into the pillow and Isabel struggled to breath. Creak. He ripped off her pants. Creak. Isabel shouted for help. Creak. When Jason finished raping Isabel, she felt the cold breeze from the open window traverse her face, as though the feathers of an angel's wing had grazed her wet cheeks.

At school, Isabel told her school counselor, Marta, everything that Jason threatened to kill her over if she shared. Marta supported Isabel in devising a plan to leave that evening. Isabel would return home after school, get her bags, pick up Nathan, and return to school, and Marta would drive them to the domestic violence shelter. That afternoon, Isabel returned home as planned. Unexpectedly, Jason was there. Jason shouted that he would kill himself if Isabel left and stormed out of the house, taking Ruby with him. Paralyzed, Isabel did not make it to back to school as planned. When Isabel did not return, Marta feared the worst and called the state's child abuse and neglect Hotline to report that a minor and her son were in danger.

Within an hour, there was a knock on the door. Isabel opened the door to a child welfare investigator. The investigator told Isabel to collect her belongings. Already ready with Nathan at Isabel's parents house, Isabel walked out of the door for the very last time, with her four prepacked duffle bags dragging behind her. The investigator drove Isabel to her parents' house and informed them about the violence and terror Isabel had endured.

The investigator implemented a safety plan that required Isabel and Nathan to stay at Isabel's parents' house and prohibited contact with Jason. The safety plan also prohibited Isabel from being with Nathan alone. Despite the uninterrupted love, care, and protection she had given to Nathan even when her life was at risk, she now could only be alone with her son unsupervised when she took him to school. Isabel felt judged and misunderstood.

Feeling safer in her parents' home, Isabel needed and wanted to heal. Marta helped Isabel find domestic violence counseling. Isabel reported Jason's crimes to the police. She took the police to the location where Jason had said he killed Bella; each of her parts were found, just like Jason had described, preserved in the cold of the snow. Isabel also reported the rape that occurred just before Isabel left Jason's home.

The child welfare investigation concluded days after Isabel's eighteenth birthday and Isabel entered adulthood with a finding of child neglect against her. The child welfare agency had determined that Isabel neglected her son because of the domestic violence perpetrated against her. After all she had borne, the finding of neglect—a designation that she was a "bad mother"—nearly destroyed her. The investigator had told her to be prepared to give Jason visitation if she ever wanted child support from him. She wondered how she could be a "bad mother" for letting her son live with a person a judge would allow to visit her son. How could the designation that she had neglected her son be justified? Could the child welfare intervention have done more to help her and Nathan, rather than making it harder for them?

Determined to still graduate from high school, Isabel would often have to suddenly leave class as a flashback of the abuse took control of her mind and body—but she always returned. Graduation was one of her proudest moments. Surrounded by her son and parents, Isabel realized that, even in the hardest of moments, the faith-filled, kind, and brave girl who crossed the desert to reach a better future over a decade ago had not been destroyed; she was always within her. Isabel found her way back to herself.

Since graduation, the finding of neglect against her was removed through the help of a legal aid organization. Isabel aspires to go to college. Nathan is a happy, energetic, and engaging boy who loves to walk their new puppy.

• • •

There are millions of women, children, and men like Isabel,[1] Nathan,[2] and Jason, whose lives are impacted by domestic violence.[3] Three to fifteen million children are exposed to domestic violence per year.[4] One in every three or four children will witness domestic violence in their lifetimes.[5] Domestic violence occurs in homes

---

1 On average, nearly twenty people per minute are physically abused by an intimate partner in the United States, equating to more than ten million men and women each year. M.C. Black et al., Centers for Disease Control and Prevention, National Intimate Partner and Sexual Violence Survey: 2010 Summary Report (2010), http://www.cdc.gov/violenceprevention/pdf/nisvs_report2010-a.pdf.

2 Thirty million children in the United States will be exposed to some type of family violence before the age of 17. Kristen Selleck, Jeannie Newman & Debra Gilmore, U.S. Dep't of Health and Human Servs., Child Protection in Families Experiencing Domestic Violence 11 (2nd ed. 2018), https://www.childwelfare.gov/pubPDFs/domesticviolence2018.pdf; *Abuse Hurts: Definitions,* University of Michigan (Nov. 2, 2018), 63, http://www.stopabuse.umich.edu/resources/definitions.html. Studies estimate that 10 to 20% of all children are at risk for exposure to domestic violence. H. Lien Bragg, U.S. Dep't of Health and Human Servs., Child Protection in Families Experiencing Domestic Violence 5 (2nd ed. 2003), https://www.childwelfare.gov/pubPDFs/domesticviolence.pdf.

3 One in four women and one in seven men experience severe domestic violence in their lifetimes. Sharon G. Smith et al., Centers for Disease Control and Prevention, The National Intimate Partner and Sexual Violence Survey (NISVS): 2010-2010 State Report (April 2017), https://www.cdc.gov/violenceprevention/pdf/NISVS-StateReportBook.pdf; *see also National Statistics,* National Coalitional Against Domestic Violence (2018), https://ncadv.org/learn-more/statistics.

4 H. Davidson, The Impact of Domestic Violence on Children, A Report to the President of the American Bar Association (1994), https://www.ojp.gov/ncjrs/virtual-library/abstracts/impact-domestic-violence-children-report-president-american-bar; *see also* Jeffrey L. Edleson, *Children's Witnessing of Adult Violence*, 14 J. of Interpersonal Violence 839, 843 (1999). Edleson explains the research sources underlying the varying estimates of the number of children exposed to domestic violence each year, citing Bonnie Carlson's 1984 calculation and Murray Straus's 1992 study.

5 Murray Strauss, *Children as Witnesses to Marital Violence: A Risk Factor for Lifelong Problems Among a Nationally Representative Samples of American Men and Women,* Report of the Twenty-Third Ross Round Table 98 (1992); David Finkelhor, Heather Turner, Anne Shattuck & Sherri Hamby, *Prevalence of Childhood Exposure to Violence, Crime, and Abuse*, 169 JAMA Pediatrics 746, 746 (2015). One in nine (11%) youth were exposed to some form of family violence in the past year. Sherri Hamby, David Finkelhor & Heather Turner, *Intervention Following Family Violence: Best Practices and Helpseeking Obstacles in*

and relationships in every neighborhood, among all races, within all religions, regardless of sexual orientation or gender identity, amid any social-economic level around the world.[6] Women are the targets of domestic violence at higher rates than men such that around 80 percent of victims of domestic violence are women.[7] Many of these women are also mothers.[8] One in every fifteen children, like Nathan, live in homes in which domestic violence is occurring.[9] In about half of families in which a child is abused, a mother is also abused.[10] Homes also exist in which a violent partner does not equate to an abusive father.[11] Weaponizing the child welfare system can be a tool

---

a Nationally Representative Sample of Families with Children, 5 PSYCHOLOGY OF VIOLENCE 325, 324 (2014).

6 LENORE F. WALKER, TERRIFYING LOVE: WHY BATTERED WOMEN KILL AND HOW SOCIETY RESPONDS, 101-102 (1989) ("Battered women from all types of economic, cultural, religious, and racial backgrounds . . . They are women like you. Like me. Like those whom you know and love); MURRAY A. STRAUS ET AL., BEHIND CLOSED DOORS: VIOLENCE IN THE AMERICAN FAMILY, 31 (1980); NATIONAL DOMESTIC VIOLENCE HOTLINE, https://www.theHotline.org/is-this-abuse/abuse-defined (last visited on Feb. 11, 2022); NATIONAL NETWORK TO END DOMESTIC VIOLENCE, https://nnedv.org/content/domestic-violence-doesnt-discriminate (last visited on Feb. 11, 2022); *see also Domestic Violence*, U.S. DEP'T OF JUSTICE, OFFICE ON VIOLENCE AGAINST WOMEN (2017), https://www.justice.gov/ovw/domestic-violence.

7 From 1994 to 2010, about four out of five victims of domestic violence were women. SHANNON M. CATALANO, PH.D., BUREAU OF JUSTICE STATISTICS, INTIMATE PARTNER VIOLENCE, (Feb. 2, 2019), http://www.bjs.gov/index.cfm?ty=pbdetail&iid=4536.

8 *Get the Facts*, PROMISING FUTURES WITHOUT VIOLENCE (Oct. 31. 2018), http://promising.futureswithoutviolence.org/what-do-kids-need/get-the-facts.

9 SHERRY HAMBY, DAVID FINKELHOR, RICHARD ORMROD & HEATHER TURNER, U.S. DEP'T OF JUSTICE, CHILDREN'S EXPOSURE TO INTIMATE PARTNER VIOLENCE AND OTHER FAMILY VIOLENCE, 3 (Oct. 2011), https://www.ncjrs.gov/pdffiles1/ojjdp/232272.pdf.

10 NATIONAL COUNCIL OF JUVENILE AND FAMILY COURT JUDGES, EFFECTIVE INTERVENTION IN DOMESTIC VIOLENCE AND CHILD MALTREATMENT CASES: GUIDELINES FOR POLICY AND PRACTICE, 9 (1999), https://www.futureswithoutviolence.org/greenbook-effective-interventions-in-domestic-violence-and-child-maltreatment-guidelines-for-policy-and-practice/ ; CHIC DABBY & ANGELA AUTRY, FAMILY VIOLENCE PREVENTION FUND, ACTIVIST DIALOGUES: HOW DOMESTIC VIOLENCE AND CHILD WELFARE SYSTEMS IMPACT WOMEN OF COLOR AND THEIR COMMUNITIES, 12 (2005).

11 INSTITUTE ON DOMESTIC VIOLENCE IN THE AFRICAN AMERICAN COMMUNITY, CO-PARENTING CONCERNS OF AFRICAN AMERICAN BATTERED WOMEN (2003).

of power and control along with physical, sexual, emotional, psychological, and financial abuse.

Domestic violence is often a secret that is kept, as best its secret holders can, within walls and behind closed doors. Other times, mothers, children, and men find themselves at the intersection of systemic—governmental, judicial, social service, and community—responses to the domestic violence that has occurred. Families may experience none, some, or all of these responses today, tomorrow, or in the future; in other words, the responses to domestic violence in a family are as unique as the family's experience with domestic violence itself. Some of these responses are sought out by the individuals impacted, others are initiated by one of the individuals, and some are thrust somewhat or wholly involuntarily upon the family.

A family's unique experience with domestic violence mirrors the uniqueness and particularity of the sought resources and responses to their experiences. A mother may apply for public benefits or housing assistance after leaving an abusive breadwinning partner. A mother on Medicaid may bring her children to their pediatrician to seek help with the night terrors and anxiety her children are exhibiting. A woman may call the police after her boyfriend punched her and threw her down the stairs. A mother and her three children may seek refuge in a domestic violence shelter in a nearby town. A woman victimized by domestic violence may reside at an inpatient drug treatment center with her children. A person who uses violence and coercive control may attend a batterer's intervention program at a nonprofit organization while a domestic violence agency provides group and individual counseling to his girlfriend and children. That same girlfriend may petition for a civil protection order to prohibit her boyfriend from having any contact with her and her children and to prevent him from coming close to her work and the children's school. A husband may file for divorce, seeking custody of his two children from a woman he abused. The state may prosecute an offender for crimes related to the abuse he perpetrated against his girlfriend and her children. A man may be sent to prison for raping his wife. An ex-husband may make false allegations of abuse or neglect against the mother of his children, threaten to call the child welfare agency, or indeed call as a way of further perpetrating coercive control against his ex-wife. The state's child abuse and neglect

Hotline may receive a call from a school counselor like Marta or from anyone about children living in a home where domestic violence is occurring.

The child welfare system is one of the many systems that can intersect with families experiencing domestic violence. Each state (and, sometimes, city or county) has its own child welfare system that consists of a government agency governed by laws and regulations that is charged with responding to the maltreatment of children, along with the court system and social service agencies. The workers in this "system" often usurp and replace the rights and ability of parents to make decisions regarding their children.

Rather than child *protection* system, the term child *welfare* system is intentionally used in this book to capture the breadth of considerations that should influence decisions others make about the lives of children and families. Safety is only one, albeit important, factor affecting the overall welfare of children. The welfare of children is indeed multifaceted, encompassing children's safety *and* overall needs, and is unavoidably impacted by the collision of outside systems into their lives. Limiting the purview of the system designed to respond to families in need to only protection dangerously ignores how decisions regarding safety may impact children's welfare—including their stability, well-being, and healing. Preserving and ensuring children's welfare from the start should be the spirt and aim of the child welfare system. Importantly, insisting—albeit demanding—that the child welfare system not only avoid harm to children and families but also meet the holistic needs of children within their families does not invite intrusion of the child welfare system into the lives of families nor endorse the expansion of a system in which possible support carries the cost of surveillance, mandates, and separation.

The aspiration to center children's welfare does not change the reality of the legal mandates at each phase of the child welfare process, nor does it intend to place an additional unattainable burden onto an already taxed system, but it does establish a critical mindset and philosophical foundation. While the initiation of the child welfare system into the lives of families focuses on protecting children and their safety, the longer the case persists in the system, especially through a dependency case in juvenile court, the more the scope expands and morphs into determinations of a child's best interest.[12] In other words, if the point of entry is protection, but the point of exit is an expanded view of the child's welfare governed by the best interest framework, that which happens in the middle is often confused about its bearings.

This functional ambiguity is nowhere more apparent than when a family is experiencing domestic violence. The best interest standard is inherently subjective, but by definition encompasses children's overall welfare, not merely safety. Safety is indeed only one of the many enumerated factors to consider in determining what is in the best interest of a child. Although the best interest standard often attains fallacious mythological status in positing that there is one ideal scenario that child welfare system workers need to uncover and actualize, it is a reminder than many factors impact a child's welfare. While the mandate to initiate child welfare interventions should remain limited, considering children's overall welfare from the start will increasingly lead to interventions that are effective and impactful, which is ever more relevant and important when domestic violence is present.

This book uses other specific terms that carry important significance that sometimes belie their conventional meanings. "Domestic violence" is a pattern of assaultive and controlling behaviors perpetrated by one intimate partner against another.[13] Here, domestic violence does not include violence in a home between siblings, abuse by a child against a parent or caregiver, or mutual aggression or violence between two adults who have equal power; rather, "intimate partner violence" is interchangeable with "domestic violence." As a cornerstone of domestic violence, imbalance of power exists between the person perpetrating the abuse against the other, and this imbalance remains constant and unchanging as the abuse cycles and escalates, regardless of the protective, defensive, reactive, or preventative actions of the other.

Throughout this book, intentional yet constraining terms and pronouns are used to describe the individuals involved in the dynamics

---

12 *Determining the Best Interests of the Child: State Statues Current Through June 2020,* Child Welfare Information Gateway, 1, https://www.childwelfare.gov/pubPDFs/best_interest.pdf#page=1&view=Introduction.

13 *The Greenbook, supra* note 10. Intimate partners are current or former spouses or dating partners.

of domestic violence. The person who perpetrates domestic violence, in other words, someone who deploys a pattern aimed at coercively and abusively controlling an intimate partner,[14] is referred to as the offender and/or person using violence and coercive control, and male pronouns are used.[15] While both men and women perpetrate and experience domestic violence, men perpetrate at higher rates than women.[16] In the 2009 National Crime Victimization Survey, men perpetrated over 85 percent of domestic violence incidents,[17] and one out of five men reported perpetrating domestic violence against an intimate partner over his lifetime.[18] The person against whom the domestic violence is perpetrated is referred to as the adult survivor or nonoffending parent, and female pronouns are used, and because this book focuses on the response of the child welfare system, all of these women are mothers.[19] The majority of those victimized by domestic

---

[14] Fernando Mederos, *Accountability and Connection with Abusive Men: The New Child Protection Response to Increasing Family Safety*, FAMILY VIOLENCE PREVENTION FUND, 6 (2004), http://www.futureswithoutviolence.org/userfiles/file/Children_and_Families/Accountability_Connection.pdf. A batterer is a person who exercises a pattern of coercive control in a partner relationship predominantly through psychological, economic, or sexual intimidation, punctuated by one or more acts of intimidating physical violence, sexual assault, or credible threat of physical violence. LUNDY BANCROFT & JAY SILVERMAN, THE BATTERER AS PARENT (2002) at 3.

[15] Sarah E. Romans, Marion R. Poore & Judy L. Martin, *The Perpetrators of Domestic Violence,* 174 MED J. AUST. 484, 485 (2000).

[16] Murray A. Straus, *Children as Witness to Marital Violence: A Risk Factor for Lifelong Problems Among a Nationally Representative Sample of American Men and Women, in* CHILDREN AND VIOLENCE: REPORT OF THE TWENTY-THIRD ROSS ROUNDTABLE ON CRITICAL APPROACHES TO COMMON PEDIATRIC PROBLEMS 98–104 (D. F. Schwarz, ed., 1992).

[17] Sherri Hamby, Richard Ormrod & David Finkelhor, Victim Gender, Perpetrator Gender and Victim-Offender Relationship in a Nationally Representative Study of Youth Victimization (July 10–13, 2005) (paper presented at the Ninth International Family Violence Research Conference, Portsmouth, NH, citing the results from the 2009 National Survey of Children's Exposure to Violence).

[18] Vijay Singh, Richard Tolman, Maureen Walton, Stephen Chermack & Rebecca Cunningham, *Characteristics of Men Who Perpetrate Intimate Partner Violence,* 27 J. AM. BOARD FAM. MED., 661, 662 (2014).

[19] *See* "Many of the families receiving child protective and family preservation services are also single-parent, woman-headed households." Susan Schechter & Jeffrey L. Edleson, *In the Best Interest of Women and Children: A Call for Collaboration Between Child Welfare and Domestic Violence Constituencies,* 11 PROTECTING CHILDREN 6, 7 (1995).

violence are women.[20] The targets of the domestic violence who are also parenting are designated as "survivors" rather than "victims"[21] in order to capture the active protective roles they take despite the abuse they experience.[22] The term "nonoffending parent" distinguishes their role from the perpetrator of the domestic violence.[23] Children, along with their mothers, are survivors, too.

The word "family" is used throughout this book to describe the group of people at the center of the domestic violence—the person using violence and coercive control, the adult survivor, and the child survivor. The conventional sense of a traditional family is not implied here. Instead, for ease of a group designation, the term "family" is used to convey the individuals who are connected to each other because of the domestic violence, accepting of self-defined families,[24] even if those individuals may not be considered a family by law or relations. Sometimes specific members are not considered part of the family unit for child welfare purposes. Indeed, as Judge Jack

---

20 James Cameron, *Domestic Violence Among Homosexual Partners,* 93 Psychological Reports 410, 410 (2003). In 1976, the Lafayette, Louisiana Task Force on Domestic Violence found that of the 2,000 domestic violence calls that year, 95% were from women victims, in both heterosexual and homosexual relationships. Susan Schechter, Women and Male Violence, 214 (1982); James Cameron, *Domestic Violence Among Homosexual Partners,* 93 Psychological Reports 410, 410 (2003).

21 As Susan Schechter wrote in 1982, "victim is also a label that many shelter residents reject." Susan Schechter, Women and Male Violence, 252 (1982).

22 ". . . studies show that many battered women take active steps to protect their children despite the unpredictability of the violence and the effects such violence has on them." Susan Schechter & Jeffrey L. Edleson, *In the Best Interest of Women and Children: A Call for Collaboration Between Child Welfare and Domestic Violence Constituencies,* 11 Protecting Children 6, 9 (1995).

23 Kristen Selleck, Jeannie Newman & Debra Gilmore, U.S. Dep't of Health and Human Servs., Child Protection in Families Experiencing Domestic Violence, 11 (2nd ed. 2018), https://www.childwelfare.gov/pubPDFs/domesticviolence2018.pdf; *Abuse Hurts: Definitions,* University of Michigan (Nov. 2, 2018), http://www.stopabuse.umich.edu/resources/definitions.html.

24 The experiences of families impacted by domestic violence vary and are not restricted to traditional and binary genders and family constructions., as federal judge Jack B. Weinstein of the Eastern District of New York opined, "in a heterogeneous, non-theocratic and democratic society such as ours, there is enormous diversity in domestic relationships and in the degree that they are founded on mutual respect and love (the norm) or malevolence." Nicholson v. Williams, 203 F. Supp. 2d 153, 164 (2002).

Weinstein opined, family "... is the most basic social unit—and even in modern times it upholds the very fabric of [society]. It makes each of us stronger, more resilient, more productive and better at being human."[25] Within the inherent importance and necessity of "family," domestic violence regularly fractures families. Many families desire to remain intact, and others do not.

While domestic violence does not discriminate, the faces of the child welfare system are often families of color and those living in poverty.[26] The races of children and their parents impact their experience in the child welfare system from beginning to end.[27] Over 50 percent of African American children will experience a child welfare investigation by age 18.[28] African American and Native American children are more likely to be the subject of calls to an abuse and neglect Hotline,[29] to be removed from their parents, to be placed in foster care,[30] and to be kept in foster care longer, and they are less likely to be adopted.[31] One in every six Hispanic children will be referred to a child welfare agency before they turn seven years old, and Hispanic families are twice as likely as white families to live in poverty.[32] Often coupled with race, poverty is one of the greatest

---

25 *Id.*

26 Chic Dabby & Angela Autry, Family Violence Prevention Fund, Activist Dialogues: How Domestic Violence and Child Welfare Systems Impact Women of Color and Their Communities, 22 (2005).

27 Dorothy Roberts, Shattered Bonds (2002); Child Welfare Information Gateway, Child Welfare Practice to Address Racial Disproportionality and Disparity, 2 (2021), https://www.childwelfare.gov/pubPDFs/racial_disproportionality.pdf.

28 Hyunil Kim, Christopher Wildeman, Melissa Jonson-Reid & Brett Drake, *Lifetime Prevalence of Investigating Child Maltreatment Among US Children,* 108 Am. J. of Public Health, 275–90 (2017). By age 18, over half of African American children (53%) are investigated for child abuse or neglect.

29 *Id.* at 9.

30 Over 10% of African American children will spend part of their childhood in foster care. Christopher Wildeman & Natalia Emanuel, *Cumulative Risks of Foster Care Placement by Age 18 for U.S. Children, 2000-2011,* 9 PLoS One (March 2014).

31 Joshua Padilla & Alicia Summers, *Disproportionality Rates for Children of Color in Foster Care,* 1, National Council of Juvenile and Family Court Judges (May 2011), http://www.nrc4tribes.org/files/CCC%20Disproportionality%20Rates%20&%20Maps%20(Tribal%20Only).pdf.

32 Jill Duerr Berrick, The Impossible Imperative 27 (2017); Megan Martin & Alexandra Citrin, *Prevent, Protect, & Provide: How Child Welfare Can*

predictors of whether a family will come to the attention of child welfare.[33] Poverty impacts the conditions in which children live and limits the viable options parents have to change these conditions.[34] The exposure of children to domestic violence reinforces, rather than ameliorates, these disparities.

At the heart of the intersection of child welfare and domestic violence are mothers—often women of color and living in poverty. In other words, child welfare interventions into the lives of families experiencing domestic violence mostly target and impact mothers, like Isabel, Kathlene, Sharwline, Karen, Heather, and Patricia, and their children, whom the reader will meet soon enough. Like these women experienced, mothers are often held responsible for the violence perpetrated against them. Interventions often place blame on the mother, and as the more compliant parent, hold her responsible for changing circumstances that by definition she cannot control. As a result, mothers are oftentimes held even more responsible than the person perpetrating the violence, an example of applying "gender-biased standards" upon mothers regarding the care of their children.[35] In reality, the vast majority of nonoffending mothers care deeply about their children and their safety,[36] having made countless

---

Better Support Low-Income Families, CENTER FOR THE STUDY OF SOCIAL POLICY 2 (Aug. 2014), http://childwelfaresparc.org/wp-content/uploads/2014/08/Prevent-Protect-Provide-Brief.pdf.

33 *Id.* at 1.

34 ANDREA J. SEDLAK ET AL., U.S. DEP'T OF HEALTH AND HUMAN SERVS., FOURTH NATIONAL INCIDENCE STUDY OF CHILD ABUSE AND NEGLECT (NIS–4): REPORT TO CONGRESS (2010), https://www.acf.hhs.gov/sites/default/files/documents/opre/nis4_report_congress_full_pdf_jan2010.pdf . Nearly half of families (47%) who have their children removed from their homes have trouble paying for basic necessities. U.S. DEP'T OF HEALTH AND HUMAN SERVS., NATIONAL SURVEY OF CHILD AND ADOLESCENT WELL-BEING, CPS SAMPLE COMPONENT WAVE 1 DATA ANALYSIS REPORT (2010), http://www.acf.hhs.gov/sites/default/files/documents/opre/cps_report_revised_090105.pdf.

35 Susan Schechter coined the term "gender-biased standards" to account for heightened scrutiny and blame that abused mothers receive for their children's exposure to domestic violence. Susan Schechter & Jeffrey L. Edleson, *In the Best Interest of Women and Children: A Call for Collaboration Between Child Welfare and Domestic Violence Constituencies,* 11 PROTECTING CHILDREN 6, 8 (1995).

36 *See* "In her study of [twenty] battered women, Hilton found many of the women deeply concerned for their children. In fact, a majority of those she interviewed left their abusers for the children's sake . . . Ironically, it was concerns for their

sacrifices to ensure their welfare amidst their own barrage of violence, intimidation, and fear.[37] In fact, their children's well-being controls the decisions most mothers make about the domestic violence they are enduring.[38] Child welfare systems every year intervene with millions of these mothers and children.

Across the United States, child welfare systems intersect with 7.5 million children each year.[39] Accurate and reliable data about the existence of domestic violence in child welfare caseloads are difficult to ascertain, and states report wide variability in the prevalence of domestic violence among families involved in their child welfare systems. Nonetheless, experts conservatively estimate that 30 to 60 percent of all families who come to the attention of child welfare systems are experiencing domestic violence.[40] These estimates capture the reality that some families come to the attention of the child welfare

---

children that led almost one-third of the women to remain with their abusive partners. Women stayed, despite the violence, in order to ensure necessary financial support for their children or because of threats by their violent partners to harm the children or wage lengthy custody battles if they did leave . . . Over half of the women she interviewed cited concern for their children as the major factor that led to re-evaluating their relationships." *See id.* At 9. *Citing* Zoe N. Hilton, *Battered Women's Concerns About Their Children Witnessing Wife Assault,* 7 J. of Interpersonal Violence 77 (1992).

37 Hilton, *Supra* note 36 at 77–86; Janice Humphries, *The Work of Worrying: Battered Women and Their Children*, 9 Scholarly Inquiry for Nursing Practice 127, 127–145 (1995).

38 As Susan Schechter and Jeffrey Edleson documented, "the decision to leave or stay often hinges on the mother's assessment of what will be in the best interests of her children." *Supra* note 19 at 9.

39 U.S. Dep't of Health & Human Servs., Child Maltreatment 2016, Administration for Children and Families, xii, (2017), https://www.acf.hhs.gov/sites/default/files/documents/cb/cm2017.pdf. These 7.5 million children are the subjects of 4.1 million referrals to child welfare agencies across the country; child welfare agencies receive almost 10,000 child maltreatment referrals a day—a rate of 55.1 per 1,000 children; 58% percent are screened into the child welfare system and 42% are screened out. *Id.* at xii.

40 Shellie Taggart, Child and Family Service Review Outcomes: Strategies to Improve Domestic Violence Responses in CFSC Program Improvement Plans, 6 (2011); Jeffrey L. Edleson, *Interventions and Issues in the Co-Occurrence of Child Abuse and Domestic Violence*, 4 Child Maltreat. 91–182 (1999). *See also* Anne E. Appel & George W. Holden, *The Co-Occurrence of Spouse and Physical Child Abuse: A Review and Appraisal*, 12 J. Fam. Psychol. 578–599 (1998).

system primarily because the children have been exposed to domestic violence, while others are experiencing additional issues of alleged maltreatment that are co-occurring with domestic violence. Despite, or maybe in spite of, this prevalence, many child welfare workers find domestic violence to be one of the most complicating circumstances affecting children and families who come to their attention.

The challenges many child welfare workers face are revealed through attempts to answer the following "hard questions." What can be done to stop the partner from abusing the adult survivor and harming or creating a risk of harm for the children? Are the children "neglected" under the law due to witnessing domestic violence? If so, who is deemed responsible under the law for causing this neglect: the parent using violence and coercive control or the victimized parent? How should the law and intervention respond when a nonoffending parent wants and tries to protect the children but is unable to do so? How can the adult and child survivors be kept safe? Do the children need to be removed from one or both parents? How can the intervention balance children's need for safety, stability, well-being, and healing? How have the children been impacted by the domestic violence and how can the system give them what they need to recover from any harm they have experienced? Can children be protected without re-victimizing and blaming their nonoffending parent? How can the offender be held accountable while encouraging safe engagement and reparation with his children? How can the child welfare system meet the complex and layered needs of the family together? Historically and traditionally, efforts to respond to these "hard questions" and the interventions that follow often weaken, rather than strengthen, families, thereby inhibiting families' ability to heal from the trauma they have experienced. But why are the answers to these questions so flummoxing, so alarming, so uncertain, and hard, even amidst well-intentioned actors?

Inadvertently, by design or through willful blindness, the moral construction surrounding the characteristics of families to which these "hard questions" pertain provides a critical perspective about the subsequent child welfare responses to the families at the center of these questions. The families coming to the attention of the child welfare system are most often poor, of color, and, in this context, experiencing domestic violence. And within the intersection of domestic violence and child welfare, the focus is often on the mother, the nonoffending parent, the adult survivor. Compounding the moral construction of each of these qualities—poverty, race, gender, and status as it relates to domestic violence—is the underbelly of a system that is predisposed to identifying individual fault, blame, and deficiencies, thus preserving the historical place in the child welfare system for such families and, as a by-product, obfuscating the inherent value these families possess.

Most families involved in the child welfare system are poor, and poverty is morally constructed. The moral construction of poverty is an individualistic explanation based upon the idea that people are poor because there is something wrong with them, rather than because of societal systems of oppression that foster impoverished economic states.[41] If there is something wrong with poor people—such that, they are lazy, irresponsible, promiscuous, and so on—then it follows that these failings or pathologies could put their children at increased risk, thus warranting, even necessitating, the child welfare system's protection.[42] Anthropologist and legal scholar Khiara Bridges outlines the purported logic that "if personal failures are the presumptive cause of poverty, then poor mothers [and families] ought to be supervised more closely, as their personal failures necessarily implicate children,"[43] thus explaining the place poor families predominantly occupy in the child welfare system. The state's interest in protecting children from abuse and neglect is not universally applied because, as Bridges explains, "even though wealthier women share the same histories and engage in the same behaviors as poor women, the government feels no need to occupy the wealthy in order to protect their children" because wealthy people do not share the supposed deficient character of poor families that the very existence of their poverty implicates.[44]

While this explanation may sit uncomfortably with those who value equality and attempt to practice within the bounds of equity, discourse, and action around poverty are further easily moralized when those who are "disproportionately impoverished are racial

---

41 Khiara M. Bridges, The Poverty of Privacy Rights at 38 (2017).

42 *Id.*

43 Bridges, *supra* note 41 at 38–39.

44 *Id.* at 136.

Others"[45] whose alleged inferiority is also based upon contrived deficiencies. Race is such an age-old example of a morally constructed attribute nearly so self-evident as not to require specificity, yet honed in part through the perceptions of color that slavery, Jim Crowe segregation, civil rights opposition, anti-immigration policies, and backlash against the Black Lives Matter movement have fomented. The moral construction of race is commonly known as racism. The history of the child welfare system confirms its role in the moralistic and systemic oppression of families of color.

Layering upon the moral construction of poverty and race, domestic violence is also morally constructed. "Wrongness" is ascribed to families experiencing domestic violence, thereby morally constructing each member of the family. Rather than asking what has happened to the person who uses violence and coercive control that causes him to abuse, most discourse centers on locating individual defects, weaknesses, shortcomings, failings—the phantom sources of perceived wrongness. Mothers who are experiencing domestic violence are viewed as the "immoral agents of their own misfortune," as Bridges coined.[46] Such mothers are moralized in countless judgment-laden ways as the breadth of their individual defects rests in choosing an abusive partner, allowing themselves to be abused, appearing helpless, becoming dependent, staying too long, leaving too late, returning too often, and even fighting back. And, if something is wrong with poor, minority mothers, then something is increasingly wrong with—and morally blameworthy about—poor, minority mothers who are victims of domestic violence. These deficiencies become insurmountable and endemic character flaws when abused mothers have children, who live in homes where domestic violence occurs and who may be at risk or mistreated too. Damage and harm are prescribed to children who have experienced domestic violence as the fault of their mother's shortcomings. Entrenched victim blaming leads the system to make conclusions about their mothers that the mothers cannot overcome by presuming they chose the abusive partners over their children, supposing that they will return to the abusive partners, and concluding that they are predisposed to future abusive relationships. As a result,

45 *Id.* at 138.
46 *Id.* at 249.

these children often lose the "crazy about them" or the home that holds their heart.

When faced with hard questions—those that do not have settled mandates or clear dictates, made murkier by the amorphous and idealistic "best interest" standard—decision makers are influenced by moral considerations when they fill in the gaps in order to make decisions.[47] As such, when grappling with the hard questions involving families who experience domestic violence and the child welfare system, filling the gap with morally constructed biases and judgments often leads to interventions that dismantle, rather than strengthen, families. Within the compounded moral construction of poverty, race, gender, and domestic violence that families confront, crafting child welfare interventions that competently meet the needs of families becomes further challenging within the reality of the burden child welfare workers singularly bear to keep children safe.

Child welfare workers are responsible for the safety of the children that come to their system's attention. Child welfare workers shoulder this mandate alone, and their work can be perilous.[48] No other professional—lawyer, advocate, counselor, psychologist, educator, doctor—would be held responsible under the law and public opinion if something dreadful happened if a child is harmed at the hands of another. While their legal liability does have limitations,[49] child welfare workers bear significant personal, moral, and public relations liability. Like domestic violence stories, child welfare stories often hit the media and usually only capture the public's attention when something really tragic happens,[50] such as when a

---

[47] Legal positivists disagree and argue that the law can be independent of morality. *Id.* at 100.

[48] Child welfare workers have been hurt and killed on home visits. *See* Kate Thayer, *DCFS Worker Beaten While Taking Child into Protective Custody Last Year Has Died, Officials Say,* Chicago Tribune (Feb. 9, 2018), https://www.chicagotribune.com/news/breaking/ct-met-dcfs-worker-dies-20180208-story.html; Mark Maxwell, *DCFS Worker Stabbed to Death During Home Visit*, WCIA (Jan. 5, 2022), https://www.wcia.com/news/local-news/dcfs-worker-stabbed-to-death-during-home-visit/.

[49] DeShaney v. Winnebago City. Dep't of Soc. Servs., 489 U.S. 189 (1989).

[50] Sarah Han, Laura Nixon, Pamela Mejia, Daphne Marvel & Lori Dorfman, *The Child Welfare System in the U.S. News: What's Missing?*, Berkeley Media

child dies.[51] Child welfare workers' mandate to keep children safe is magnified by the public's scrutiny if a mistake is made under their watch.[52] Yet the message that the public often consumes and pummels back is one of blame and distrust—toward both the family and the child welfare agency. The demands for increased vigilance that likely follow often result in panicked attempts to remove more children from their homes at the expense of family preservation, even though keeping children with their families often results in better outcomes.[53] The fear of public outcry often stymies decisions that consider the broad view of children's overall welfare,[54] yet ensuring children's overall welfare and protecting their safety are essential when children have been exposed to domestic violence. While acknowledging the burden of their isolating protective mandate, the systems responding to families experiencing domestic violence, especially child welfare, must be as courageous, knowledgeable, and creative as the adult and child survivors themselves.

Group (Jan. 2019), https://dvchildwelfare.org/wp-content/uploads/2019/04/QIC-DVCW-NewsAnalysis-FINAL-approved-1.30.19.pdf. In a study of media coverage of domestic violence and child welfare from July 1, 2016 to June 30, 2017, the authors conclude, "In short, the news framing of the child welfare system illustrates the double bind agencies find themselves in—they are publicly faulted for taking actions, as well as for failing to do so." *Id.* at 9.

51 *See, e.g.*, Alicia Fabbre, *One Year Ago Semaj Crosby's Death Sparked Outcry, Prompted Change—but Remains Unsolved*, The Chicago Tribune (April 25, 2018), https://www.chicagotribune.com/news/ct-met-semaj-crosby-joliet-girl-death-one-year-later-20180424-story.html; Steve Saden, *Coroner Says Knife Was Used in Fatal Attack on Deerfield Woman; Husband Charged with Murder*, Deerfield Review (Sept. 24, 2018), https://www.chicagotribune.com/suburbs/deerfield/news/ct-dfr-deerfield-murder-autopsy-tl-0927-story.html.

52 Jill Duerr Berrick, The Impossible Imperative 3 (2017).

53 In 1993, three-year-old Joseph Wallace was killed by his mother Amanda after a juvenile court judge returned him to her care. Richard Wexler, *Child Welfare in Illinois: The Children's Crusade Redux?*, National Coalition for Child Protection Reform (May 1, 2019), https://www.nccprblog.org/2019/05/child-welfare-in-illinois-childrens.html.

54 Judges interviewed for the Special Child Welfare Advisory Panel created pursuant to the settlement in Marisol v. Guiliani reported that "they felt that they could not risk making a mistake and having a child die" and "spoke of the withering media attention to decisions which turn out badly . . . noting the doctrine of the 'safer course.'" Nicholson v. Williams, 203 F. Supp. 2d 153, 222 (2002); *see* Marisol v. Giuliani, 929 F. Supp. 662 (S.D.N.Y. 1996).

The essence and intention of this book is to highlight and navigate the complexities that exist for the families who experience both domestic violence and the child welfare system, and for child welfare systems in responding effectively to families experiencing domestic violence. These complexities exist both when domestic violence is the predominant reason the child welfare system becomes involved and when other reasons prompt the child welfare intervention or when additional circumstances exist. Co-occurring struggles with substance abuse, mental health, housing instability, or poverty are often present in child welfare caseloads, and for many mothers, these struggles are connected to the domestic violence they have endured. Amidst these connected struggles, domestic violence often becomes the most challenging aspect of the intervention for child welfare and the reason why the case remains in the system even after the system deems the other struggles resolved. This book focuses on child welfare interventions where domestic violence is the primary reason for the family's involvement. The book's trauma-informed, strength-based, family-centered, equity-focused message would remain the same amidst additional struggles. As such, this book questions the appropriateness of using the traditional child welfare system as a primary way to respond to and service families experiencing domestic violence, offers strategies for less harmful and more effective interventions within child welfare systems, and offers that such interventions are possible and deserve investment and commitment so long as the system of child welfare exists.

This book enters the discourse at a time in which calls to abolish the child welfare system ring loudly.[55] Abolitionists ultimately envision the eradication of the child welfare system, connected to and united in arguments to end carceral responses, undo the criminal legal system, and defund the police. Child welfare abolitionists view the child welfare system as so endemically harmful as to be unreformable due to the historical and current systemic oppression it spews, its intentionality in destroying families of color and those living in poverty, and

[55] How We endUP: A Future Without Family Policing, UpEnd Movement (Oct 26–27, 2021) (virtual conference); Derecka Purnell, Becoming Abolitionists: Police, Protest, and the Pursuit of Freedom (2021); Dorothy Roberts, Torn Apart: How the Child Welfare System Destroys Black Families—And How Abolition Can Build a Safer World (2022).

the intergenerational detriment of systemic family regulation. Amidst these same observations, a more moderate reformist in the spectrum from endorsement to abolition utilizes strategies of harm reduction to limit the damage the system inflicts and tactics of radical transformation to render the system so different that it is no longer recognizable. While the child welfare system will persist into the foreseeable future, this book aims to provide a roadmap to transform the child welfare system in ways that both avoid harm and aspire higher.

Not outwardly radical but transformative in comparison to the current child welfare system, the messages here underscore the need for empathy, self-determination, partnership, adequate laws, and evidence-informed practices all focused on what children need in order to recover from any harm the domestic violence caused and to ultimately heal. Children need a strong, safe, and stable relationship with a competent, caring, positive adult, most often the survivor parent. Importantly, the safety and well-being of the child survivor are directly connected to the safety and well-being of the adult survivor. Child welfare interventions should therefore strengthen the adult survivor's ability to parent in safety and stability while promoting engagement and fostering opportunities for accountability with the person who uses violence and coercive control. Such child welfare interventions should not exist in a vacuum but rather within coordinated and consistent governmental, judicial, social service, and community responses to childhood exposure to domestic violence. Yet child welfare interventions still exist among inconsistent and conflicting systems and in a society replete with inequality, oppression, lack of resources, and countless "-isms."

Although their charge is significant and overbearing, child welfare systems cannot realistically overhaul the contexts in which families live. While a child welfare worker can help a mother and her four children find a bed in a domestic violence shelter, that same worker may not be able to find them permanent safe housing. Although a worker may help the mother get a protective order forbidding the offender from living in the home with their children, the child welfare worker may not be able to find a job for the offender that would enable the family to afford two rent payments. Even if a child welfare worker can secure domestic violence counseling for a mother and her children that helps them plan for their safety, in two years, when the relationship with the offender resumes, the child welfare worker may be unable to obtain affordable medical treatment for the mother's undocumented son in need of surgery. And even after a thorough investigation that permits children to remain with their mother, a child welfare worker is unable, nor should she be expected to be able, to prevent the offender who kidnaps and murders his children. Realistic expectations of child welfare systems, therefore, must surface and the child welfare system must not punish and separate families in the name of safety and protection for conditions that the system itself cannot alter. This book contemplates the bounds of those expectations and offers solutions for effectively and practically meeting those demands.

The trajectory of this book provides a thorough examination of the stories, law, practice, and healing at the intersection of domestic violence and child welfare. Within a national landscape, the book provides an overview of child welfare systems' purpose, history, functions, and structures. The book then synthesizes the social science research about the impact of domestic violence on children and the critical ingredients children need to recover from any harm they may have experienced. An examination of child welfare best practices as informed by the established and evolving social science research then ensues, positing that strength-based, family-centered, trauma-informed, and equity-focused child welfare interventions will sustainably enhance the safety, stability, well-being and healing of children and families experiencing domestic violence. Child welfare investigations related to domestic violence are then covered, with a thorough survey of child welfare laws and policies woven throughout. Discussion of court cases related to domestic violence and child welfare occurs in order to understand the dependency process in juvenile court for families experiencing domestic violence. An examination of the seminal *Nicholson* cases accordingly follows. Innovative and collaborative practices across the country are explored, and then a case study about one state's journey to improved practice is shared. The book then examines the process of healing from trauma and the insistence that all systems intervening into the lives of families experiencing domestic violence foster, rather than inhibit, the pathway toward healing for all members of the family. The book concludes with options for reform that unify the currently discordant responses of the various systems interacting with families experiencing domestic violence as well as limit the child welfare system's reach. Stories of those impacted by both domestic violence and child welfare, as well as those who have impacted this intersection as researchers, leaders, and reformers, are the soul of this exploration. Like the founding mothers of the "battered women's movement" and like Isabel, many of those who have been impacted have also become impactors.[56]

• • •

Isabel looks up from her notebook, first noticing the flames from the candles, then reflecting on the glowing faces looking at her, many of whom she recognizes as staff or clients of the domestic violence agency she has received counseling from for over two years. They stand in a circle of mutual support, waiting for her to continue.

"Here I am now. I'm happy now. I found someone who truly loves me and treats me with dignity and respect. I'm happy about the things I have accomplished—graduating high school, moving into my new apartment. I want to be an advocate one day. But most importantly I get to enjoy seeing my son grow up. His smile keeps me on my feet each day. What makes me proud is seeing all the milestones he achieves. He is my angel.

"Your beauty is within you; let it shine. Let the world see it. I know that it's been a difficult process for some of us. But I want to tell you that it doesn't define who you are because you are worthy of more than you can imagine. Just take the first step to be free. Love yourself. Don't look back because your future is shining. The angels are always behind us."

---

[56] *See* SUSAN SCHECHTER, WOMEN AND MALE VIOLENCE, 34 (1982). For instance, the founders of the first domestic violence shelter in Boston, Transition House, were survivors of domestic violence. *Id.* at 65.

2

Fearless/Less Fear: The History, Infrastructure, Orientation, and Trauma of Child Welfare

In front of a live audience, then child welfare Director of the Baltimore City Department of Social Services, Molly McGrath Tierney opened her TED Talk with the following, "Among the gifts that Albert Einstein left us is a definition of insanity—Doing the same thing over and over again and expecting a different result."[1] At times she folded her hands, and at other times she crossed them at her heart, changing the meaning of the tattooed words of "Fear" and "Less" across her fingers. She continued, "My work is an interesting example. Child Welfare. The government business of protecting children. The primary intervention is to take kids from their parents and put them in foster care. There is a prevailing belief that this is the responsible thing to do for children who are abused or neglected. Now there are fifty child welfare agencies in the country, and the funds to underwrite

[1] Molly McGrath Tierney, *Rethinking Foster Care*, TED Talk at TEDxBaltimore 2014 (Feb. 2014), https://www.youtube.com/watch?v=c15hy8dXSps&t=72s.

them are in the billions. But there is not one among them that is reputed to be working well."[2]

Flashing with her hands alternating messages of "Fearless" and "Less Fear" as she spoke about family and home, "Just to be clear, it is not an address, it's a state of mind. It is knowing that someone loves you, knowing that you belong. It is the glue that gives you a chance at a successful life. . . . we [don't] give kids what they need. This is the infrastructure of modern child welfare. Despite an overwhelming lack of evidence that it is working, we persist."[3] Gesturing her hands as an offer of "Fearless" or "Less Fear" depending upon her or the audience's vantage, she concluded, "Einstein gave us a definition of insanity. Perhaps we should review."[4]

Heeding Einstein's adage, Molly's journey to becoming the director of one of the most challenged child welfare agencies in the country was a process of trading fear for fearlessness in responding to injustice by approaching and practicing child welfare differently, aiming to avoid the insanity of repetitious futility. When Molly assumed the directorship, the Baltimore City Department of Social Services (DSS) was in a state of disrepair, but within ten years, it was lauded as "worst to first." Molly was commended as an effective director to emulate. As Molly revealed at the end of her TED Talk, by the conclusion of her directorship, the success she found was not enough, the system was still falling short for families. Making the existing child welfare system function more efficiently requires a transformative shift that would result in a system that gives families what they need in their time of struggle, a profound pivot for child welfare that is critical to the effectiveness of child welfare interventions involving domestic violence.

Molly came to her directorship with the following philosophy that had evolved throughout her childhood, education, and career. To Molly, the current function of the child welfare system is unjust, *and* families deserve just interventions. Injustice occurs when punitive and policing responses are targeted to "fix" problems caused by social conditions. This injustice becomes a form of oppression—the socially supported, systematic mistreatment of a group—when misguided and misplaced

---

2 *Id.*
3 *Id.*
4 *Id.*

interventions are launched that neither ameliorate the conditions leading to the problem nor elevate the well-being of those targeted. To rectify this injustice and turn oppressive interventions into opportunities for growth, the issue of child maltreatment must be viewed as a social problem with societal causes rather than a problem with individual people and families; a strikingly identical truth about domestic violence underscoring the importance of this approach at the intersection of child welfare and domestic violence. In child welfare, the "personal" is also "political" such that individual experiences exist in the larger societal context. By stripping away the moral construction around those involved in the child welfare system, the system will then look to societal solutions that provide families with what they need to find enhanced safety, stability, well-being, and healing, rather than punish families for their struggles in ways that further rob them of their potential and dismantle communities. Such child welfare policy and practice exist on the other side of fear, and that is where Molly located her fearlessness on behalf of families involved in the child welfare system.

• • •

Molly grew up on a little island off North Carolina and lived by the tyrannical moods of her father's alcoholism. Molly's father piled unpredictable autocracy and pain atop the familial and communal scorn of Molly's sexual identity. Molly lived each day among the injustice that occurs when needs are ignored and repudiated, a void deepened by derision and pugnacity. Molly's own fear, born through oppression, compelled her to the experiences of injustice of others. Throughout her teenage years, Molly participated in service projects in Appalachia, working alongside people oppressed by the industries they fueled despite their indispensability, solidifying in her mind that opportunity is not doled out equitably. As a teenager, Molly readily perceived that like her, the coal workers were not the cause of their own oppression, their poverty, or their struggles.

Molly entered college academically equipped yet equally reticent. In the early months of Molly's freshman year, she was present during a brutal break-in during which the intruders raped her sister. Throughout college, Molly witnessed acts of violence and degradation on campus alongside activism and intellectual prowess. Not knowing what to do about the injustice of others became the embattled drive of her young adulthood, a fear-filled calling that Molly did not wish to escape. Searching for the key to undoing injustice, Molly traveled the county by car for a year following graduation, seeking an understanding of America by traversing its folds. Amidst the low parts of the low country she knew, experienced, and witnessed, Molly now saw beauty in the country's corners, like the hot springs she explored by following a map a biker drew for her, and promise in its existence, like the bridge she stood on in Juarez as she watched migrants crossing the border seeking a better life in the country she called her own. The co-existence of pain and beauty, challenge and possibility inculcated within Molly. Molly now carried with her a commitment to service based upon promise and strength amidst struggle. Molly ended her expedition by moving to Chicago where professional opportunities enabled her to practice the essence of her sense of justice; her fear of not knowing how now subsided.

Molly's service to others entailed identifying their needs by asking and listening and then delivering on those needs. Molly recognized that the political will to meet the needs of others was connected to the perceived blamelessness, and thereby deemed worthiness, of those in need. People in the programs she developed—young children with developmental delays, individuals displaced by government housing plans, families evacuated by a natural disaster exacerbated by human error—were not to blame for their status as help-seekers. Yet, in other contexts, like the child welfare system, Molly observed that individuals and families with similar needs were not viewed or treated with the same empathetic and deferential regard nor viewed as a resource in navigating their struggles.

Molly would soon grapple with the profound contradiction that child welfare interventions resist affording families, especially parents and often their children caught in their net, the same understanding of their problems and approach to creating pathways toward safety, stability, well-being, and healing.[5] The origins, history, and orienta-

[5] Dorothy Roberts, Shattered Bonds: The Color of Child Welfare (2002). Law professor and scholar Professor Dorothy Roberts articulates the "profound contradiction" that "American child welfare policy reject[s] the view of child maltreatment as a social problem that had to be addressed with societal remedies . . . [and] allows child welfare agencies to claim that children's problems are caused mostly by parental deficits."

tion of the child welfare system, the resistance to recognizing trauma, the late and nonbinding judicial parameters of government intrusion for half a century and beyond; and legislation that imbued the state with strong intervention powers contribute to explaining why modern-day child welfare practice is a contradiction that does not meet the needs of families.

The Origins, History, and Orientation of the Child Welfare System

The origins of the child welfare system bear in part three original sins. First, the child welfare system was conceived in response to physical harm to a child yet applied the resulting response of family separation to inform and justify intervention into the lives of families who were morally constructed by those with power. Second, the child welfare system engrained itself in an intervention based upon separation that might serve the minority of cases in which physical harm has occurred to children (abuse), while the vast majority of cases involve similar family struggles as today: poverty, substance abuse, mental health issues, and domestic violence (neglect). Third, the child welfare system ignored the reality of the sources of family's struggles, thereby punitively assigning blame to parents and resisting supporting families, rather than recognizing the societal conditions in which these struggles develop and marinate. These historical, political, and socially sourced deficits have resulted in a system that often harms families and children and fails to meet their needs in ways that would enable them to experience enhanced safety, stability, well-being, and healing.

The history of the child welfare system reveals the conception and impact of these original sins. In 1874, private societies to protect children formed following a photograph published in the newspaper of a ten-year-old girl with bruises and cuts who had been removed from her home where she had been hurt. Harnessing this photograph to spur the importance of "saving" children from their homes, those who laid the foundation for child welfare practice felt called to "rescue" children like the girl in the photo and those from poor, immigrant, unassimilated families. Using the same intervention of removal for all, the "child savers," as they affectionately, righteously, and tellingly called themselves, tore countless children from their families in the name of a better life elsewhere, somewhere, maybe, just not with their families. The very notion that families in need should be separated rather than helped together was born within the privatized child welfare system's inception. As such, these early days set the course for the system's current orientation that permits and endorses the dismantling of families to be the norm rather than the exception, missing opportunities to really help families. The child welfare system operated unfettered for its first fifty years during which it honed its adeptness at responding to the struggles of families by removing their children, debasing and obfuscating the harder work of determining how to strengthen families and communities amidst challenging societal conditions.

A possible influence to steer the budding child welfare earlier on could have occurred when Dr. Sigmund Freud discovered the causes of trauma as an explanation for the struggles many people, especially women, faced. The opportunity, however, to be a counterpoint to the destructive child welfare practices was lost in part by Freud himself. Society was not ready to accept the rampant reality of violence that Freud discovered was causing the trauma. Freud recanted his findings, relegating the influence of trauma—the context of many families' struggles (and the effect of taking children from their families)—to the forgotten. At the same time, the newly professionalized social workers began recognizing similar sources of trauma such as violence in the home but blamed mothers for the problems they identified in families.

Checks and balances on the child welfare system did not arrive until after five decades of mechanized operation. Although the first juvenile court was started in 1899, the U.S. Supreme Court did not toil with the relationship between parents, their children, and the state until it heard its first case regarding the fundamental constitutional rights of parents in 1923. These cases did not involve the child welfare system because the child welfare system was privatized. By then, the progeny of three cases in two decades did little to constrain or redirect the system in practice; the nongovernmental child welfare system was outside of the Court's influence.

Following a reinvigorated public outcry about the physical abuse of children in the 1960s, the resulting series of federal legislation indoctrinated, codified, and bolstered the practices that had been in operation for a century by infusing the *parens patriae* power of the state with the power of the purse. By the time the battered women's movement of the 1970s made public the violent experiences of women within their homes, the child welfare system was far afield from being the trauma-informed, strength-based, family-centered, and equity-focused intervention that is required to accept the reality of people's lives, respond with respect and not impunity, and foster the will to partner with people in the struggle to meet their needs.

When Molly took the helm in Baltimore City, she inherited this history. Molly had to constantly contend with the underlying original sins of the child welfare system and laboriously overcome these historic, political, and social conditions in order to craft a child welfare system in Baltimore City that was instead oriented toward viewing child maltreatment as a social problem that had to be addressed with societal means that involved meeting the needs of children within their families and communities.

The Photograph

After orphan trains had already displaced 150,000 poor children from their families to live on farms in the West, the child welfare system, as it is known today, began with a ten-year-old girl in ways that foreshadowed the rest of its history. In 1874, a neighbor heard the sounds of a child screaming and crying. Concerned, the neighbor approached the only organization that existed outside of the reluctant police, the American Society for the Prevention of Cruelty to Animals (ASPCA). The founder of the ASPCA was moved to act as he envisioned the child to be like the horses he routinely saved from violent stable owners, a vulnerable member of the animal kingdom needing protection.[6] An ASPCA officer tricked his way into the apartment and found ten-year-old Mary Ellen Wilson with a wound across her face, and bruises, scrapes, and scars traversing her legs and arms. After being removed from the home, Mary Ellen Wilson was photographed, solemnly, in a tattered dress, shoeless, and with the gashes covering her body prominently visible. Recognizing the value of public opinion and awareness in furthering the cause of the "humane"

[6] Howard Markel, *Case Shined First Light on Abuse of Children,* The New York Times D5 (Dec. 15, 2009).

movement—whether for animals or children—the founder of the ASPCA contacted a newspaper who ran the story and the photograph, providing the public with its first impression of the need for child protection.

In the wake of this photograph, the birth of child protection occurred in 1875 when the founder of the ASPCA started the New York Society for the Prevention of Cruelty to Children, believed to be the first child protection agency in the world. Within a decade of its founding, thirty-four similar societies formed in the United States and fifteen formed elsewhere. The child savers of the societies were both upper-class Protestants hoping to subordinate the new immigrant poor and conservative, feminist reformers hoping to impose their vision of domesticity and gentle childrearing.[7] And they acted quickly.[8] By the end of 1881, after only three and a half years of work, the society in Boston had handled 2,017 cases involving 3,600 children.[9]

Now that child abuse had been discovered, child cruelty became visible everywhere. The photo of Mary Ellen with injuries and threadbare clothes comported with the child cruelty that the child savers were observing on streets of cities such as New York, Boston, and Baltimore. Seeing poor, immigrant children languishing on the street begging, working, and not in school left a pugnacious taste for those who took up the cause as child savers. They deemed the conditions Mary Ellen experienced morally wrong for children and saw the same ills imposed on children who would never be molded into good citizens if left to the devices of their unassimilated, predatory, or inept parents.[10] In imposing a "campaign to control social order," Historian Linda Gordon describes that the child savers

> . . . saw cruelty to children as a vice of inferior classes and cultures which needed correction and "raising up" to an "American" standard. Their emphasis on cruelty made children's mistreatment seem willful rather than structural.[11]

---

[7] LINDA GORDON, HEROES OF THEIR OWN LIVES: THE POLITICS AND HISTORY OF FAMILY VIOLENCE, (1998).

[8] *Id.* at 27.

[9] *Id.* at 37.

[10] *Id.* at 29.

[11] *Id.* at 28.

Cruelty was a moralistic notion of the depraved and migrant parent versus the virtuous and vulnerable child; good versus evil; them versus us; the rescuers and the rescued; the saviors and those saved. The combined moral construction of poverty and violence, therefore, originated in the earliest days of what would become the child welfare system. As a result, the child savers responded to physical harm and struggles related to poverty in the same way—by dismantling families, rather than supporting children with their families and in their communities.

With these footings, the societies grew in number and reach from 1875 to 1910, earning the name "Cruelty" by families fearful of their grip. Many societies lacked the legal authority to remove children,[12] so they instilled fear and terror to coerce parents to agree, or at least not object with the little power they had, to the placement of their children.[13] The first laws that allowed these societies to remove children without a judge's permission were passed in the early 1880s, creating a shadow foster care system that would persist through today, engulfing more families than would ever see a juvenile court judge.

Yet, the movement of the societies sparked by a photograph was rooted in an incomplete truth. Indeed, Mary Ellen's untold story started years before her photograph was taken—when she was a baby, when her father died fighting for freedom from slavery in the Civil War, when her mother tried desperately hard to care for her but was not able to support her daughter on $2 per week, when Mary Ellen was placed in an orphanage, when a wife and husband falsely claiming he was Mary Ellen's illegitimate father adopted her, and when the wife physically abused Mary Ellen leading the ASPCA to remove her—resulting in the photograph. Physical maltreatment became the lens that framed what would become the child welfare system, enduringly losing the message that Mary Ellen was given to the woman who hurt her after her own mother could not care for her because of *poverty*.

The true story of the case that started the child welfare system over a century ago resembles countless cases Molly could have pulled from the DSS casefiles—a child living with a single parent in abject poverty

---

12 *Id.* at 51.
13 *Id.* at 52.

is removed and harmed in placement. How would history have differed if the public outcry to Mary Ellen's photograph led to headlines that read "State Unwilling to Help or Support Mother Widowed by Veteran Unable to Afford Raising her Daughter" instead of "More of the Little Neglected Waif, It's Brief and Sad Life History"?[14] What if the "humane movement" had focused on helping parents like Mary Ellen's mother to be able to meet the needs of her child rather than on centering the privatized intervention on removing children and controlling families? How would Molly's DSS function differently now if the system that Mary Ellen's case fomented focused not on child protection, but on child welfare? The answer to this question does not invite the punitive, regulatory, and destructive system the societies created to respond to families because of poverty or other struggles; rather, had a more holistic view of families occurred, the very system responding to families in need would have looked very different by disposing of removals as the primary method of intervention in place of support. The media, the public, the private state child protection agencies that responded to Mary Ellen's photograph missed a critical lesson that could have changed the tide of history—supporting her mother years before could have kept Mary Ellen safe.

This message may not have been lost on the societies because it was unclear or unknown. Rather, it was likely lost because they did not want to see supporting families as the solution. In channeling the public outcry that commenced a movement based upon an instance of physical abuse, the original child savers' own set of values, motivations, and objectives led them to transpose their concerns about physical abuse to the ills they saw on the urban streets that they deplored.[15] Deeming *these* families the causes of both violence

---

[14] *The Courts, The Child Cruelty Case, Further Examination of Witnesses, More of the Little Waif, It's Brief and Sad Life History, as Told by Various Witnesses,* New York Herald (April 11, 1874).

[15] Like today, predominate coverage of the sensational cases, the ones in the most dire circumstances like the abuse Mary Ellen endured, capture public attention but skew the public's view. Mary Ellen's foray into the limelight incorrectly implied that physical abuse spurred the majority of cases when in fact most cases in the child welfare system—then and now—were more ambiguous, more related to neglect. Indeed, the majority of cases that have come to the attention of the child savers and the child welfare system for over a century involve neglect, not abuse.

and poverty, they universally applied their tool of intervention to families that looked very much like Mary Ellen's mother who was trying to care for her daughter, those experiencing poverty and other struggles.

Even before she was abused in her adopted home, the child savers would have likely concluded that Mary Ellen was better off anywhere else but with a poor mother whose instability was contributing to the deterioration of their society. Importing this view of widespread deficiency and otherness spurred the notion that families in need should be separated rather than helped together. The work of the societies ignored the societal factors impacting the reality of these struggles, the value of each and every family, and the source of strength in families as part of the solution. Supporting families could not be the solution because doing so would require reforming the very societal structures that gave the child savers station and power. The refusal to provide families with what they need, like Mary Ellen and her mother, become red flags of intentioned social control; otherwise known as, in Molly's own words, oppression.

At the same time, the realities underlying people's struggles were elsewhere being ignored, missing a critical opportunity to alleviate decades of suffering to come as well as to influence systemic interventions that were becoming professionalized arms of regulation and intrusion into the lives of families.

An Episode of Amnesia

While honing its adeptness at responding to the struggles of families by removing children and debasing and obfuscating the harder work of determining how to strengthen families and communities, a possible influence to re-steer the budding societies could have occurred in 1896, but the opportunity was drastically lost.

As the societies were gaining force, Dr. Sigmund Freud was in Paris at the Salpêtrière Hospital investigating a problem that seemed unsolvable—the cause of hysteria in women. Hysteria was so common that it was undefined but was used to "describe a disease with incoherent and incomprehensible symptoms"[16] that reared themselves at unexpected times (an etiology similar to what would later

---

[16] JUDITH HERMAN, TRAUMA AND RECOVERY at 35 (1992, 1997).

become known as post-traumatic stress disorder).[17] By listening and building trust with his patients (the genesis of psychotherapy), Freud discovered that physical and sexual abuse in childhood caused trauma that could explain the symptoms that many of his patients, especially women, were experiencing. Freud exuberantly published his findings in a report entitled the *Aetiology of Hysteria*, revealing the widespread trauma-inducing violence that occurred in his patients' lives. Rather than acknowledging the crucial discovery that Freud described as the *caput Nili*—the source of the Nile, the fertile truth—his report was met with incredulity and rejection.[18] Society was not ready to accept the rampant reality of violence that Freud discovered was causing the trauma. Attempting to salvage his professional reputation, Freud recanted his findings, relegating the influence of trauma—the context of many families' struggles as well as the extrapolated effect of removing children from their families—to the forgotten, to the outright overlooked and ignored.

The odyssey of trauma's relegation into oblivion only one year after its discovery revealed that the realities uncovered lacked the "social context . . . created by political movements to give voice to the disempowered."[19] Instead, those voices were disregarded, then silenced, and then outright rejected, causing devastating effects to both individuals and the ability to respond to peoples' experiences of violence in ways that could meet their needs.[20] Avoiding the "episodic amnesia of trauma," as Dr. Judith Herman coined, could have had far-reaching repercussions.[21] Millions of people could have found a remedy to their suffering. The prevalence and universality of violence in homes would have lifted a veil of shame seventy-five years earlier than when its silence was broken. Freud's revocation and the anathema of trauma that followed validated the rescuing practices of the child savers and denied the next generation of professionalized social workers critical knowledge and understanding to better respond to

---

17 *Id.*

18 *Id.* at 44.

19 *Id.* at 32.

20 Bertha Pappenheim, known Anna O., was hospitalized and ill for several years after Freud's colleague, Joseph Breuer, stopped his sessions with hysteria patients following Freud's recantation. *Id.* At 55, 56.

21 Herman, *supra* note 16 at 25.

families like Mary Ellen's, cementing a course that rejected supporting children and families together.

Progressively Blaming Mothers

By the turn of the century, the field of social work had been expanding globally. Jane Addams founded the Hull House in Chicago in 1889, three years after Freud published and recanted the *Aetiology of Hysteria*. Without a guidepost that could have come from a recognition of trauma and its nondiscriminatory, yet life-altering impact on its blameless targets, the influence of social work penetrated the societies across the United States. By 1910, the workforce was shifting from religious and charitable volunteers to specifically educated paid professionals, best described now as child-saving Progressives.[22] The newly developed casework method expanded notions of child protection such that the role of the caseworker was to address more than only protection. Collecting information about a family led to an uncovering and acknowledgment of the family's struggles—poverty, alcohol use, violence between parents, and more. Without a lens of trauma, the Progressives viewed these struggles as symptoms of the decline of families. Rather than consider societal causes for their perceived weakening of families, the Progressives pointed their fingers at mothers. The now professionalized child savers ascribed the increase of female autonomy and single motherhood at the turn of the century as the causes of the growing number of problems families and their children experienced.

Specifically, when the social workers uncovered violence between parents (that would now be understood as domestic violence), they blamed mothers for their shortcomings in motherhood and wifehood. Hence, from the early 1900s through the present, child welfare interventions have viewed battered mothers as neglectful. Rather than measuring neglectfulness by remaining in an abusive relationship like today, the child-saving social workers resented mothers who left abusive partners. Leaving broke up the family, causing greater poverty and contributing to the epidemic of single motherhood. The Progressives thereby "den[ied] abused mothers sympathy, let alone

---

[22] Gordon, *supra* note 7 at 61.

help."[23] Providing abused mothers with economic aid to survive independently or a place to live in temporarily or permanently, which is what many in fact needed, was deemed to contribute to the abhorrent problem of single motherhood that further weaken the threads of society.[24] When the efforts of the child-saving social workers to reform men did not work, "in search of any ways to influence troubled families, social workers not unnaturally focused on those most open to influence"—the mother, a practice inherited into today.[25] As such, mothers were expected to conjure ways to preserve peace in the home. If their female virtue failed to fulfill such burdensome expectations, abused mothers were deemed responsible for neglecting their children by failing to maintain the appropriately peaceful environment for their children, while also jeopardizing the stability of society with the newly minted middle class to which the social workers clung.[26] The biased focus on mothers as both the cause and solution, the problem and the only cure, the curse and the spell to undo the affliction, have been imported into contemporary child welfare practice.[27]

Born to a poor and soon-to-be widowed mother, Mary Ellen's fate in being removed from her mother would have likely been sealed in the Progressive Era, too.[28] The Progressives sloganeered prevention but ignored conditions surrounding families beyond their control. They spoke of help but aimed to obstruct undeserving recipients from accessing assistance. They identified as social workers but acted with superiority and distance from those with whom they worked. They focused on neglect in families but fomented clouds of fault. Many single mothers who resembled Mary Ellen's mother lost their children to societies because they could not support them.[29]

---

23 *Id.* at 253.

24 *Id.* at 257.

25 *Id.* at 282.

26 *Id.* at 252.

27 Like the yesterdays of child welfare practice, today non-offending parents who steadfastly commit to keeping or reunifying with their children are often the sole amenable focus of child welfare intervention.

28 Gordon, *supra* note 7 at 166.

29 *Id.* at 96.

The operation of child protection remained the unconstrained work of nongovernment actors, resulting in interventions of removal that were unencumbered. The societies and the Progressives, therefore, were left unchecked by an overseeing and examining branch of government, the federal judiciary. And when the U.S. Supreme Court did send its initial messages, its holdings reinforced the approach of the Progressives—only families that do not threaten societal standards and conform to parental expectations deserve to be free from intrusion, and deference to the family is based in a respect for privacy rather than the value of family connection.

Too Little, Too Late

Toward the end of the Progressive Era, the U.S. Supreme Court heard a progeny of three cases that grappled with the relationship between the parent, the child, and the state, the triad of actors also involved in child protection. These cases neither contended with the practice nor controlled the private actors who operated the existing child protection system. The holdings established a framework that grounded the alignment of parents and children not in their shared needs, but in privacy interests, an easily penetrable source of connection.

In *Meyer v. Nebraska* (1923),[30] *Pierce v. Society Sisters* (1925),[31] and *Prince v. Commonwealth of Massachusetts* (1943),[32] the Court wrestled with two competing doctrines. The parental authority doctrine holds that parents have a fundamental constitutional right to raise and control the upbringing of their children without intrusion. The *parens patriae* doctrine gives states the power and imposes the responsibility to protect children as part of the state's police powers. In *Meyer* and *Pierce*, the Court held that the state could not intrude upon the parents' decisions respectively to allow their children to learn a language other than English in school and to send their children to private school—two parental decisions that did not compromise social norms at the time. The Court held that the parents

---

30 Meyer v. Nebraska, 262 U.S. 390 (1923).

31 Pierce v. Society of the Sisters of the Holy Names of Jesus and Mary, 268 U.S. 510 (1925).

32 Pierce v. Commonwealth of Massachusetts, 321 U.S. 158 (1944).

had a constitutionally protected privacy interest in doing so that the state could not penetrate. The parental authority doctrine, therefore, trumped *parens patriae*. In *Prince,* however, the Court found that *this* family's privacy interest in religious observance as a Jehovah's Witness, a religious minority, did not justify the potential harm to a nine-year-old girl who distributed religious pamphlets on the street. Here, *parens patriae* trumped the parental authority doctrine. While the families and circumstances in *Meyer*, *Pierce*, and *Prince* would not concern the child-saving social workers of the time, the Court left space that interference with parental decisions was tolerated, justified, and encouraged for certain families in ways that privacy interests could not buffer.

The Court's entrée into excavating the bounds of these two doctrines has forever stood for the elevation of parental authority above the state's *parens patriae* power and the limited circumstances of justifiable state intrusion. In practicality, the Court's rulings fit squarely within the historical, political, and social conditions that fueled the societies' approach to child protection—only some families deserve the protection and deference to their privacy. In other words, the family is easily penetrable when is not perceived as deserving enough to warrant privacy. The alignment of children with their parents based upon privacy leaves children and parents vulnerable to misguided intrusions and misses the opportunity to more meaningfully and fundamentally connect the interests of parents and children together. Privacy becomes an easy and one-sided tradeoff when children's perceived safety is at stake, an exchange often at the expense of children's well-being, stability, and healing as well as connection with the source of many of their needs, their families.

Families are fundamentally important not because they deserve privacy but because they are what children need. (This is the ultimate distinction between liberals and conservatives who become unlikely bedfellows in the support of the rights of families.) Even when families are struggling or when children experience harm within their family that warrant state (or society) intervention, inherent value in that family exists. Had the Supreme Court asserted this early on or at all, the inherent value in all families would have pervaded interventions in ways that could have shifted child welfare practice. Without this legal orientation, opposing state intervention has found counter in the more feeble arguments that such actions are an intrusion into the family's privacy, privacy which may have contributed to the abuse or neglect of a member of the family in the first place. This is not to say that privacy is not important, that individual privacy should not be respected, or that certain people with certain struggles are not entitled to privacy, but privacy arguments have nudged out more fundamental arguments about the importance of family, a concept that has greater staying power to guide the balance between the child, the parent, and the state and guide answers to the "hard questions" that child welfare raises.

Judge Leonard Edwards, a retired judge who served on the juvenile court bench for over twenty years in California (introduced in chapter 7), sagely expressed, "The touchstone of our response to children must be the family. The same family which was in part responsible for the plight of the child often contains within it the solutions for that child's best chance."[33] Sourcing solutions in the family requires support, rather than blame. If all families were seen as the source of children's needs even amidst struggle, the orientation of the societies, Progressive social workers, and state-run child welfare agencies to come may have been more inclined to center their practice around the preservation of those connections and supporting conditions that enhance those relationships. Family rights rooted in privacy did not and have not protected the value in families of all races, classes, ethnicities, nationalities, and neighborhood geographies, especially as images of physical child abuse once again fomented and framed the creation of governmental child welfare agencies and demands for children's rights grew.

Abuse-Inspired State Intervention

Just as the solitary and detached image of Mary Ellen sparked the child savers, a report about physical child abuse from the medical field impelled the formation of the state-run child welfare systems of today. In 1962, Dr. C. Henry Kempe and his colleagues published an article in the *Journal of the American Medical Association* entitled

---

[33] John Hubner & Jill Wolfson, Somebody Else's Children: The Courts, The Kids, and the Struggle to Save American's Troubled Families (1996).

"The Battered-Child Syndrome."[34] The article identified the prevalence of physical child abuse they observed in their patients. The article accurately universalized child abuse, yet in doing so, once again, the minority of cases (those involving such abuse), would shape the response to the majority of cases (those involving family struggles), and the bounds of neglect remain defined by those in power.

The worst-case scenarios that both the image of Mary Ellen and Dr. Kempe offered into public discourse mobilized risk-averse practices that became an arm of the state adroit at undoing families by engulfing those experiencing conditions that were designated as abusive or neglectful.

Dr. Kempe's report created a severance between children and their parents that was reinforced by a burgeoning dialogue about children's rights. The children's rights movement found its birth in the 1960s and was conceived from an era of activism—the fight for civil and women's rights and an anti-war movement—an age of individual protectionism against forces greater than oneself, a time of tumult, upheaval, and distrust. The movement ordained children as individuals and not solely as part of a family. The Progressives were seen as "regressives" who wanted to control the lives of children rather than improve them. Children were viewed as oppressed who needed to be freed, freed from outside intruders *and* even their own families. Proponents of children's rights were focused on creating autonomous freedoms for children.

The U.S. Supreme Court reinforced the orientation of this movement in the case of *In re Gault.*[35]

For the first time, the Court held that children were considered "persons" under the Bill of Rights and extended Fourteenth Amendment safeguards to children in delinquency proceedings. A series of additional cases followed that imbued children with additional non-severable specific rights, thereby proffering children as distinct subjects who needed legal protection from both the state and their parents.[36]

---

34 C. Henry Kempe, et. al., *The Battered-Child Syndrome,* 181 J. OF THE AM. MEDICAL ASS. 17 (July 7. 1962).

35 *In re* Gault, 387 U.S. 1 (1967).

36 Tinker v. Des Moines Independent Community School District, 393 U.S. 503 (1969) (students have First Amendment rights in school to wear armbands in

Yet, legal scholar and professor Martin Guggenheim cautioned against decisions that promote an orientation around children's rights.[37] Because children indeed are not independent or autonomous individuals, they depend upon others to have their needs met. They exist in their environments because they need what those environments can provide to survive and thrive. Enumerated rights independent of where those rights can be filled will lead to empty actions, rendering children lone right-filled beings yet sustenancely depleted, an evergreen tree in a desert, a boat without oars or water. To give children's rights any meaning and heft, the rights of children should be located in what they need. This is not to deny children what they need specifically as unique from their parents, siblings, family unit, extended relatives, and community. But it is instead to preserve exactly what they need—their family as the source of those needs whose cradle of satisfaction and fulfillment cannot be fully replicated elsewhere. The foundation that family is the indispensable source of children's needs remains true even when a family may be struggling to meet some of the children's needs; as such, struggles to meet some needs should not move families from the center as the inherent source of their children's needs. As could have been predicted, a children's rights framework that infiltrated the relationship between children and their parents may have had contextual benefits, but significantly, the denigration of this relationship that looked outside the family for solutions for children rendered certain families susceptible to easy dissection later by the state, especially when the federal government accepted Dr. Kempe's call-to-action.

Public Child Welfare

The federal government eventually accepted the call-to-action in Dr. Kempe's report to respond to abused children and their parents. What Mary Ellen's case sparked in the charitable child savers is what Dr. Kempe's article did to contemporary child welfare practice. Again, worse case scenarios fomented and framed the response of

protest of the Vietnam War); Belotti v. Baird, 443 U.S. 6222 (1979) (pregnant minors have a constitutional right to seek an abortion by asking a court or parents for permission).

[37] Martin Guggenheim, What's Wrong with Children's Rights (2005).

the child welfare system. Dr. Kempe's article spurred the passage of federal laws that led to the creation of public, rather than private, government-run child welfare agencies. While aspects of child welfare have remained privatized, gone are days of the private societies as the primary operator of child welfare. (Here, the use of welfare in place of protection is aspirational, rather than an accurate reflection that the newly formed child welfare agencies actually met the needs of families.)

The federal legislature passed the first child welfare law in 1974, the Child Abuse Prevention and Treatment Act (CAPTA) that created incentives for states to develop the capacity to accept and respond to reports of child abuse and neglect.[38] CAPTA set a minimum definition of child abuse and neglect. CAPTA also required states to institute child abuse and neglect Hotlines if they were to receive federal funding as well as pass mandated reporter legislation that outlined who is required by law to report abuse and neglect. The resulting federal legislation indoctrinated and codified the practices that had been in operation for a century by infusing the *parens patriae* power of the state with the power of the purse. Exactly one hundred years after Mary Ellen's photograph catapulted the formation of the societies, every state or jurisdiction began creating statewide or local government-run child welfare agencies.

Newly formed public child welfare agencies along with juvenile courts continued to grapple with the hard questions. What if parents face struggles but are trying to do their best for their children who are suffering? What if parents hurt their children, but the children are attached to their parents? What if children have been away from their parents for a long time and in a stable foster home, should they return to their parents? What framework for decision-making can help guide answers to these questions about which reasonable minds can disagree? Even when harm may have occurred or risk might be present, decisions about the family can be made in ways that account for their shared interests, even if the shared interests are not absolute or complete.

In 1972, the Supreme Court provided a foundation for answering these hard questions by establishing procedural protection based

---

[38] Child Abuse Prevention and Treatment Act, 42 U.S.C.A.§ § 5106(g) (1974, 1996).

upon the notion that the existence of risk or harm does not automatically sever the shared interests of parents and children. In *Stanley v. Illinois,* the Court held that parents are entitled to a hearing on their fitness before the state's *parens patriae* power can intercept their fundamental constitutional parental rights.[39] Fitness is dependent upon the "minimum standard of parenting." Although the fitness standard did help protect the relationship between children and their families, mining and resourcing safety, stability, well-being, and healing within the family remained missing from both the rhetoric and practice of child welfare.

Subjectivity, perspective, and bias, therefore, continued to inform the answers to child welfare's hard questions and as a result, public child welfare agencies were generating similar criticism as the private societies had. Mounting evidence existed that children were removed from homes inappropriately, experienced multiple foster placements, languished in foster care for years, and received inadequate support. By the time the battered women's movement of the 1970s made public the violent experiences of women within their homes (discussed in chapter 3), the child welfare system was far afield from being the trauma-informed, strength-based, family-centered, and equity-focused intervention that is required to accept the reality of people's lives, respond with respect and not impunity, and foster the will to partner with children and parents in the shared struggle to meet their needs.

The federal legislation that ensued became both self-conflicted and a swinging pendulum. Following the passage of CAPTA, the Family Violence Prevention Services Act (FVPSA) of 1984 became the first source of federal funding for domestic violence shelters and programs.[40] Yet as CAPTA and FVPSA underwrote child welfare systems and domestic violence services respectively, a divide was established. As Kiersten Stewart imparts, "these two laws—CAPTA and FVPSA—remain the defining federal laws for addressing the overlap

[39] Stanley v. Illinois, 405 U.S. 645 (1972).

[40] Family Violence Prevention Services Act, 42 U.S.C.A.§ § 110 (1984, 2021). FVPSA is the only federal funding sources under the U.S. Department of Health and Human Services and over 1,500 domestic violence programs across the country rely upon FVPSA funding.

of domestic violence and child maltreatment but were initially built separately around competing visions of safety, different legal mandates, and a different view of who the victim is they are trying to protect."[41]

Continuing to toggle between moralistic construction and holistic partnership amidst struggle, federal policy proceeded to be a pendulum swinging between Kempian alarm-sounding protection and family support. After CAPTA, the Adoption Assistance and Child Welfare Act of 1980 responded in support of families. The law required state child welfare agencies to make "reasonable efforts" to keep families intact and to reunify children with their parents, develop service plans, place children in the "least restrictive environment" as close to home as possible, and set permanency goals. Criticism then focused on the length of time children were spending in foster care without finding permanency. In 1997, the Adoption and Safe Families Act (ASFA) tugged the pendulum in a turnabout away from families. On paper, ASFA passed with the expressed purpose of accelerating the path to permanency or shortening the time that children spent in foster care. In practice, ASFA became a destructive instrument that has made it more difficult for parents and their children to reunify.[42] ASFA effectively created a "permanency clock" that requires the filing of petitions to terminate parental rights if children have been in

---

[41] Kiersten Stewart, *Evolving Federal Policies and Their Implications for Greenbook Interventions,* 70 Juvenile and Family Court Journal. 4, 39 (2019). Stewart further explains, "Child welfare laws focus on protecting children from abusive parents . . . Mother who were victims of abuse were seen as at fault if they remained with their male partner (a decision understood by many child welfare system workers as a mother choosing her partner over her child), or because they had failed to stop the abuse. If she chose to stay with an abusive partner or could not stop the abuse, then she was seen as a perpetrator herself or was often accused of "failure to protect," meaning she did not do enough to protect her children from someone else's abuse . . . [Domestic violence agencies] viewed themselves as advocates for and protectors of women. Child welfare agencies were seen as controlling and disempowering to women, often no better than her abuser because they blamed women for their own victimization and used threats and coercion—namely the power to take a child away—to make her comply with their view of what would keep her child safe, even if that was impossible to achieve or was viewed by the abused mother as dangerous for her and her child." *Id.* at 39-40.

[42] Adoption and Safe Families Act, P.L. 105-89 (1997) (amendment to The Adoption Assistance and Child Welfare Act of 1980).

foster care for fifteen out of twenty-two months. In addition to establishing permanency reviews every six months, ASFA also outlines circumstances that do not require states to make reasonable efforts to prevent removal or reunify children with their parents, expands criteria for terminating parental rights, and encourages adoption through financial incentives. ASFA reinforces a draconian approach to the struggles of families, expecting enduring challenges like domestic violence or substance abuse to ameliorate within stringent time periods. ASFA has been responsible for the permanent disconnection and severance of children from parents who may have been struggling but who were dedicated to parenting and reunification until the end when their rights were terminated (discussed in chapter 7).[43] ASFA's tangible orientation of the child welfare system away from the alignment of children and their parents led to another pendulum swing.

After over two decades of ASFA's impact that has hampered reunification and left thousands of legal orphans in its wake, the pendulum has swung once more, now toward supporting families. In 2018, the Family First Prevention Services Act was passed to fund specific services to prevent children from entering, remaining in, or returning to foster care (discussed in chapter 11).[44] For the first time in history, state child welfare agencies are able to receive federal (partial) reimbursement in supporting families in need without first removing children from their families. Family First is a significant attempt to meet the needs of children within their families whose impact remains to be written.

This history of child welfare continues to be scribed by and lived through families like Isabel Rodriguez's and leaders such as Molly McGrath Tierney. Yet, the child welfare system cannot escape its past and the realities of its present. Denying the origins of the child welfare system greatly risks the repetition of the same mistakes despite the insights gained. Domestic violence and child abuse and neglect are social problems that must be addressed with social remedies, and

---

[43] Patricia E. Allard & Lynn D. Lu, *Rebuilding Families, Reclaiming Lives,* Brennan Center for Justice at NYU School of Law, (Sept. 7, 2006), https://www.brennancenter.org/our-work/analysis-opinion/national-study-faults-federal-adoption-safe-families-act-consigning.

[44] Family First Prevention Services Act, Bipartisan Budget Act, H.R. 1892 (2018).

children need the parent who experienced domestic violence in order to recover from any harm the domestic violence caused. However, the origins of the child welfare system, the amnesia around trauma, and judicially and statutorily permissive state intrusions reveal layered historical patterns of paternalistically and willfully imposing blame on families especially mothers, operating with distrust, and refusing to acknowledge the actual cause of harm to children and families. These fatal flaws are magnified at the intersection of domestic violence and child welfare, where overlapping social issues are responded to as individualized deficits.

The north star of child welfare interventions, therefore, must be guided by the needs of children and thereby their families. This need-focused lens will help navigate through the ubiquitous competing considerations underlying the hard questions. At each step of the child welfare process, asking, what does the child need, will capture the multifaceted decisions that child welfare interventions face. For instance, when a child welfare investigator goes to a home in which a child has been living amidst domestic violence, asking, what does the child have a right to, does not provide direction like asking, what does the child need. The child needs safety, which is inextricably linked to the safety of his mother, the adult survivor of domestic violence (discussed in chapters 4 and 5). The child needs to see his father in a safe way because he is also attached to his father. The mother also needs supportive services, such as assistance with housing, transportation, and childcare in order to provide stability for her child. The mother and her child have the need to heal together (discussed in chapter 10). The person who uses violence and coercive control also needs to find an avenue of healing through accountability (discussed in chapter 4).

Amidst these hard questions, Dr. Jill Duerr Berrick, professor of social work, researcher, and scholar, instructs the child welfare system faces "the impossible imperative."[45] As she describes, child welfare workers, "wield the enormous power of the state with the authority to recommend the ultimate devastation to a parent: the removal of a child from a parent's home. But child welfare workers

---

[45] Jill Duerr Berrick, The Impossible Imperative—Navigating the Competing Principles of Child Protection (2018).

rarely feel like powerful actors . . . child welfare workers carry out difficult work."[46] In doing this difficult work, an orientation that values keeping children in their families and recognizes the realities of and reasons behind their struggles becomes the clarifying and driving force to provide children and their families what they need through support and partnership in order to find enhanced safety, stability, well-being, and healing. Constricting and misplaced interventions have resulted in individuals and families harmed and unserved rather than stronger and helped, leaving a legacy on the current infrastructure of child welfare that responds to families with punitive, policing, and destructive approaches—the original sins that Molly fearlessly intended to absolve.

• • •

Based on her work in Chicago in administering crisis and long-term social services to meet the needs of families, Molly was accepted as an Annie E. Casey Fellow, a prestigious fellowship for leaders in child welfare. Throughout her fellowship, Molly developed a concept of children's rights as needs that informed her mantra about the importance of families—within the family lies the solution. The fellowship became a turning point for Molly, a platform to buck the history of the child welfare system, trauma, denials, and rescue-oriented interventions in favor of approaches to families that help and work. Fearlessly, Molly contemplated: what is needed to radically alter the century-old child welfare practice of treating certain families as incompatible with and separate from their children immediately upon an allegation of harm or risk, thereby denying children with the full panoply of what they need?

Molly's opportunity to put her commitment to all families into practice came when she was hired first as the Chief Operating Officer and soon thereafter as the Director of the Baltimore City DSS. As Molly described in her TED Talk, in 2007 the Baltimore City DSS was, "the worst organization of its kind."[47] DSS itself was a liability and risk to children. Children were missing, others were dying in foster care, policies were scant, fraud was rampant, families

---

[46] *Id.*

[47] Tierney, *supra* note 1.

were not assigned caseworkers and those who were could not reach them because they were not answering their phones that often did not work. Offices lacked pencils and toilet paper, as well as methods and reasons for existing. Joining DSS with eyes wide open, Molly promised, albeit more like warned, the governor that she would fix the system but to be ready and brace for change. A decade later, Molly realized that even successful system reform falls short of really helping people if progress exists in a fundamentally broken system, a system whose very existence is orientated on breaking families apart.

As the director of DSS, Molly's first step was to familiarize and assess the infrastructure of Baltimore and DSS. Baltimore is both a city and a county, bigger than most in Maryland and smaller than some. Crime and poverty in Baltimore were widespread, manifesting into reality the proverbial broken window theory. Blocks of abandoned and condemned houses with broken windows became a metaphor for the disorder within neighborhoods. In Baltimore City, half of young African Americans were involved in the criminal justice system,[48] 40 percent of calls to the child abuse and neglect Hotline hailed from one zip code, nearly every person in Baltimore City knew someone in foster care, and one-third of the city was on public aid. In a city with such trials and tribulations, families mirrored the struggles around them, and child welfare workers replicated the struggles around them, struggling to give families what they themselves did not have.

In Baltimore City, public benefits and child welfare were administered in the same department. Both public benefits and child welfare were state-wide programs administered at the county level. All calls reporting alleged child maltreatment were centralized through a county-run hotline. DSS employed 2,500 people among seventeen offices in every hospital and in three satellite offices. DSS faced many of the same challenges as other child welfare agencies of translating behemoth bureaucracies into helping hands amongst infrastructures that vary among systems across the country.

• • •

[48] Roberts, *supra* note 5 at 526.

The Infrastructure of Child Welfare Systems

There is no federal child welfare system. Each state is endowed with the *parens patriae* duty to protect the safety and well-being of its children resulting in wide variation in child welfare form and substance across the country. The main functions of most child welfare agencies are to receive reports of abuse and neglect; maintain a registry of findings of abuse or neglect; provide services to at-risk families; remove children if they are at imminent risk of harm; and manage and administer foster care and reunification services to families who have a juvenile court case.

Despite these common elements, the infrastructure of child welfare agencies varies significantly across the country. The majority of child welfare agencies are statewide,[49] nine states are county-administered,[50] and three are hybrid states.[51] Child welfare agencies can be independent state agencies or a division within a state agency.[52]

---

49 Colleen Garlington, Kirkland & Ellis LLP Cover Memorandum of Nationwide Survey on Domestic Violence in Child Abuse and Neglect Investigations, to Sara Block, Domestic Violence Project Attorney, The Family Defense Center (April 2017) (on file with the author). States identified with centralized administrative system are Alabama, Alaska, Arizona, Arkansas, Connecticut, Delaware, District of Columbia, Florida, Georgia, Hawaii, Idaho, Illinois, Indiana, Iowa, Kansas, Kentucky, Louisiana, Maine, Massachusetts, Michigan, Mississippi, Missouri, Montana, Nebraska, New Hampshire, New Jersey, New Mexico, Oklahoma, Oregon, Rhode Island, South Carolina, South Dakota, Texas, Tennessee, Utah, Vermont, Washington, West Virginia, and Wyoming.

50 *Id.* States identified as county administered are California, Colorado, Minnesota, New York, North Carolina, North Dakota, Ohio, Pennsylvania, and Virginia.

51 *Id.* "Hybrid" states are Maryland, Nevada, and Wisconsin.

52 *Id.* States identified with independent departments on children/family services or child safety are Arizona, Connecticut, District of Columbia, Florida, Illinois, Indiana, Kansas, Louisiana, Massachusetts, Mississippi, New Mexico, Rhode Island, Tennessee, Texas, Utah, Vermont, Wisconsin, and Wyoming. States that have a departmental division or office responsible for children/family services or child safety are Alabama, Alaska, Arkansas, California, Colorado, Delaware, Georgia, Hawaii, Idaho, Iowa, Kentucky, Maine, Maryland, Michigan, Minnesota, Missouri, Montana, Nebraska, Nevada, New Hampshire, New Jersey, New York, North Carolina, North Dakota, Ohio, Oklahoma, Oregon, Pennsylvania, South Carolina, South Dakota, Virginia, Washington, and West Virginia. Child Welfare Information Gateway, *State vs. County Administration of Child Welfare Services*, U.S. Dep't of Health and Human Services, Children's Bureau, 1 (2012), https://www.childwelfare.gov/pubPDFs/services.pdf.

Under CAPTA's requirement,[53] every state has a child abuse and neglect reporting mechanism, the majority of which are statewide Hotlines while others are regional.[54,55] All states have statutes identifying specific persons who are required to report suspected child maltreatment to the child welfare agency.[56] Anyone is allowed to call the Hotline but mandated reporters must call upon the suspicion of child abuse or neglect. Although the statutory lists of mandated reporters differ state by state, mandated reporters typically have frequent contact with children in their professional capacity.[57] In some states, domestic violence advocates are statutorily designated as mandated reporters.[58] Around eighteen states have universal reporting which requires any person, except a lawyer, who suspects child abuse or neglect to report it.[59] Every child welfare agency has a unit responsible for investigating child abuse and neglect. Closed to the public but accessible by certain employers, nearly every state has a central registry that maintains a record of people who have been found to have abused or neglected children.[60] The infrastructure of child welfare agencies is the foundation for the approach to and impact on families and children.

---

53 CAPTA, *supra* note 16.

54 Garlington, *supra* note 20. States with statewide Hotlines include Arizona, Arkansas, Colorado, Connecticut, District of Columbia, Florida, Georgia, Hawaii, Idaho, Illinois, Indiana, Kansas, Louisiana, Maine, Maryland, Massachusetts, Michigan, Missouri, Montana, Nebraska, Nevada, New Hampshire, New Jersey, New Mexico, New York, Oregon, Oklahoma, Pennsylvania, Rhode Island, South Dakota, Utah, Vermont, Virginia, Washington, and West Virginia.

55 *Id.* States that have separate Hotlines for different regions are Alaska, California, Minnesota, North Carolina, Ohio, South Carolina, Wisconsin, and Wyoming.

56 Child Information Gateway, *Mandatory Reporters of Abuse and Neglect* (2015), https://www.childwelfare.gov/pubPDFs/manda.pdf.

57 *Id.* at 2.

58 *Id.* Domestic violence workers are mandated reporters in states such as Alaska, Arizona, Arkansas, Connecticut, Maine, South Dakota, and Illinois. Humane officers are mandated reporters in California, Colorado, Maine, Ohio, Virginia, and West Virginia.

59 *Id.* The following states have "universal" reporting: Delaware, Florida, Idaho, Indiana, Kentucky, Maryland, Mississippi, Nebraska, New Hampshire, New Mexico, North Carolina, Oklahoma, Rhode Island, Tennessee, Texas, and Utah.

60 Child Welfare Information Gateway, *Review and Expunction of Central Registries and Reporting Records*, U.S. Dep't of Health and Human Services, Children's Bureau (2014), https://www.childwelfare.gov/pubPDFs/registry.pdf.

• • •

Within the infrastructure of Baltimore City's DSS, Molly commendably and impressively improved the way child welfare functioned by connecting operations and missions. Molly began (and concluded) her decade-long directorship with the sanctified refrain that children belong in families. She used language that connected, rather than severed, children and families and placed families first, by repeating the phrase, "families and their children." To practice this mission, Molly committed child welfare interventions to give families what they need in order for children to experience safety, stability, well-being, and healing therein whenever possible. Molly's child welfare leadership style, approach, and implementation strategies were steadfastly aimed at this goal.

First and foremost, Molly adhered to the reality that staff could not give families what they needed if the staff themselves lacked the belief, support, and means to do so. Through an intentional approach of parallel process, Molly practiced the ministry of presence. She demonstrated to her staff that she cared about them as people, not just employees, and ensured that their work environment was a reasonable place to carry out their responsibilities while noting the difficulty of their jobs. When Molly entered the many DSS offices, she greeted people with gratitude for the work they did and then made sure there was printer paper in the copy room and toilet paper in the bathrooms. If the staff felt cared about, they would be more likely to care about and support their families. Feeling supported and capable of doing their jobs, staff would be less mired by judgment and moralistic constructions of the causes of families' problems. Without projecting system inadequacies onto families to explain their deficiencies, staff would more naturally view the value in every family. How Molly treated her staff could translate into how her staff treated families.

Molly gave her staff what they needed to succeed so that the staff could in turn provide the families with what they needed to succeed. When Molly became the Director of DSS, the system was fatigued. If sleep is the remedy for tiredness, movement is the antidote to fatigue. The system needed to move, and specifically move in the direction of the articulated mission that was "repeated like a broken record, kids ought to be in families."[61] Molly then "used data to drive our work so we could see all the time globally what was happening in the system and know very specifically which kid needed what thing from us right now to get home . . . [and] embraced the practice of accomplishing tasks, one after another."[62] Molly developed leadership in senior management within DSS so the system could start moving. Those tasks could include finding housing and obtaining public benefits for a mother so that her children could live with her while providing counseling for the children who had experienced domestic violence in the home. The resulting model for child welfare operations defined positive outcomes only in terms of individual children. If the system had forward momentum by completing tasks along the way, families could do the same.

Molly preached acceptance of mistakes and emphasized the learning that comes from them. She coined "fail fast, fix fast" in order to impart that working to avoid getting in trouble was not consistent with their mantra or goals. Although mistakes in child welfare could be fatal, Molly committed to her staff that so long as they followed procedure and acted in accordance with their supervisors, DSS would stand behind them. Molly stood with them in their grief when tragedy did occur. Her staff, therefore, could feel unhampered by the fear of deviating from the most publicly perceived conservative intervention (i.e., removing children) and rather could make holistic determinations about the most effective ways to support families by mitigating risk and enhancing protective factors in their lives. Molly gave her staff the luxury of not being held to an unattainable standard of perfection so that her staff could do the same for the families with whom they worked. Her tattoo inked along her fingers, Molly had broken fear in herself and aimed to break fear within DSS too.

Through this mission-driven approach, Molly's leadership was extolled as a success. For those children who could not live at or return home, relatives were the first placement priority and then foster parents within the children's zip code. Children under eight years old were ineligible for group homes and must be placed in foster families. Anyone in substitute care at age fourteen was automatically

---

61 Tierney, *supra* note 1.

62 *Id.*

eligible for extended services and support until age twenty-one. Caseworkers had a caseload of no more than fifteen children, and DSS paid its bills on time.[63] Throughout her ten-year tenure, Molly reduced the number of children in foster care by 72 percent, reduced the number of children living in group homes by 89 percent, and by the time she was done, 70 percent of the children who had come into foster care went home to their own parents within the first twelve months without returning to child protection.

Molly was praised for achieving the unforeseeable—making a child welfare agency, especially one that was previously so fatigued and splintered, run efficiently with noteworthy outcomes. At the same time, Molly personally experienced the unimaginable—the love of becoming a mother. At the same time, Molly and her wife adopted a young girl who was in foster care and whom the system had already made a legal orphan. Yet, the love for her daughter felt incompatible with the accolades. Molly somberly reflected on and questioned her work at DSS to the TED Talk audience, "I run a well-oiled machine that does an excellent job of taking other people's children . . . the error is the intervention, but we keep doing it."[64]

The error of the intervention is the very premise of the child welfare system—that the primary solution to families who are struggling is to remove their children from them and place their children in foster care. Although family struggles exist without demographic boundaries, only *certain* families, those of color and living in poverty, have typically been subject to child removals,[65] historically and presently fueled by a morally constructed belief in "otherness" and self-untouchability that conciliated the actions of the child-saving societies and mollifies child welfare practice today. To Molly, family separation of any family should be perceived as repelling, incompatible, and irreconcilable to any notions of morality, equity, and service; the last resort in the face of actual harm rather than the default in the face of struggles; the only viable option required by the children's most pressing need among competing needs. Like the images

---

[63] Tierney, *supra* note 1.
[64] *Id.*
[65] Robert, *supra* note 5.

of orphan trains[66] from the 1850s do now, the dereliction of family—the removal of a family's children—should shock the conscious each and every time it happens. But every year, it happens at least 250,000 times.[67]

As Molly observed, the reoccurring practice of child removal is not questioned in the public space. It is only noticed by the caseworker who carried out the separation, the children who endured it and continue to suffer from the trauma of both the separation and the attendant harms of foster care, the parents who are devastated, the siblings who cannot see each other, the bereft extended family, the community who has lost its children, and the judges who approved it. The fight against separation happens in individual courtrooms across the country by parents who may not have an attorney to represent them when their most fundamental liberty interest has been invaded, when their most precious connections have been torn. Many parents express that they would prefer any other response befall them, even incarceration, rather than have their children placed in foster care.

The risk-benefit balance skews away from removal and separation. Yet stories of children being harmed in their homes when the child welfare agency has previously been called is a consumed and vehemently criticized news story while the experiences of foster youth experiencing physical, sexual, and emotional trauma each day as a result of state intervention is rarely presented, devoured, or met with the warranted vitriol. Despite the prevalence of harm in foster care, a rallying cry for its slaying as the default practice is never heard in the mainstream. Why, as a society, are we willing to accept the known risks and actual harms that are more likely to befall children in foster care than in the homes from which children are being taken? Why are we fearful and not courageous (and rational) enough to give child

---

[66] Between 1854 and 1929, more than 100,000 children were sent via orphan trains to new homes in rural America. These children were predominately white children of poor immigrant families living in large cities. *See* THE ORPHAN TRAINS (EDWARD GRAY FILMS, INC. 1995).

[67] Vivek Sankaran, Christopher Church & Monique Mitchell, Article, *A Cure Worse Than the Disease? The Impact of Removal on Children and Their Families*, 102 MARQ. L. REV. 1163, 1165 (2019). (based on author's access to and analysis of National Data Archive on Child Abuse and Neglect (NDACAN) from fiscal years 2009-2017).

welfare systems the leeway, grace, and resources to support families without removal, with the humility to acknowledge the reality that sometimes, much less often than in foster care, children might experience harm there too under the watchful eye of child welfare? Molly answers that question with two words—money and history. Dismantling families is a lucrative endeavor for those involved, a cottage industry founded upon unnecessary separations. Dismantling the approach that dismantles families, as Molly did in DSS, contends with the everlasting way child welfare has operated since the child-saving societies, a history that necessitates, but does not itself request, a new chapter. Molly's principled approach to child welfare that centers on the needs of the children rooted in their family must interrogate and disrupt the fuel of the child welfare system—foster care, the defining deviation from the alignment of children, parents, and families—as the solution to families who are struggling. The original sin of the intervention of removal is that it breeds trauma at every level.

Trauma of the Intervention

The lens through which to view family separation is the lens of trauma. In espousing how removals to foster care can be a "cure worse than the disease," Vivek Sankaran, a clinical law professor at the University of Michigan writes, "trauma is often explored through the lens of what has happened to a child before or after he/she enters foster care; however, it is critical to consider how children may experience trauma due to entering foster care."[68] Just as the political will did not support Freud's discovery of the causes of trauma, the historical, political, and social context now cannot ignore the trauma that results from children being removed, separated from their families, taken into foster care, and kept apart. The consequences of ignoring these realities will mirror the catastrophic consequences of closeting trauma moments after discovery—children and parents will be silenced, their experience scorned and shamed, harm will result, healing will be illusory, and opportunities for support will be lost. If trauma from removal, separation, and foster care are denied, the

[68] *Id.* at 1166.

error of the intervention will reoccur in perpetuity with preventable collateral damage in its wake, a fate that could have befallen Isabel Rodriguez and her son, Nathan.

Following the knock by the child welfare investigator, Nathan was at risk of being removed from his mother. Nathan was fortunately not removed from Isabel, which now feels like a life-saving gift. Had Nathan been removed, however, the harm from the removal, the impact of the separation, and the short- and long-term risks of foster care would have been more detrimental than the reason for Nathan's removal—his exposure to and experience of domestic violence—and Nathan would have been denied what he needed—to live with his mother in safety and stability.

The Trauma of the Removal

The apprehension transaction, or the act of removing children from their home and the successive transfer into foster care, is traumatic for any child,[69] even for children who are removed from parents who have hurt them."[70] The act itself, the removal, is often unexpected, without warning, scary, emotional, uncertain, unrehearsed, and often chaotic, as Nathan and Isabel would have traumatically experienced had the following occurred. The decision to remove children is often deemed to be an emergency situation, where the totality of circumstances surrounding the family's strengths and vulnerabilities are unclear.[71] Compounding gender bias atop racial and class inequities and the assessment of Isabel as an unmarried, teenage mother increased the likelihood that Nathan would be separated from her, a removal that could have transpired as follows.

When Isabel awoke that morning, her fear was that she would not be able to execute her plan to leave Jason, but now, the fear of losing Nathan was unimaginable. The investigator would have told Isabel that he is removing Nathan because domestic violence posed

---

69 *Id.* at 1168.

70 Rosalind D. Folman, *"I Was Tooken": How Children Experience Removal from Their Parents Preliminary to Placement in Foster Care*, 2 ADOPTION Q. 2, 10-11 (1998); Michael Wald, *State Intervention on Behalf of Neglected Children: A Search for Realistic Standards*, 27 STAN. L. REV. 985, 993-94 (1975).

71 Andrea Charlow, *Race, Poverty, and Neglect*, 28 WM. MITCHELL L. REV. 763, 783 (2001). (noting the correlation between poverty and foster care placement).

an imminent risk of harm to him. Isabel would have protested, trying desperately to explain that she has kept her son safe. The investigator would repeat that Isabel kept her son in a home filled with violence. The investigator would see Isabel's weakness, not her strength; he would see risk, and not her protection. Later Isabel might not even remember what she put in her son's bag, her brain's way of protecting her from the memory of her son's imminent departure too difficult to later recall. Maybe Isabel would cry or maybe she would be stone-cold stoic. When the investigator would scoop Nathan up, juggling his bag and the resisting toddler, Nathan would begin to sob. Nathan would reach his arms toward his mother, aching to be rescued back by Isabel, who can barely hold herself back from grabbing her son out of the investigator's grip. "Nathan, my love, you will be okay. Mommy will see you soon," Isabel would muster, hoping to bring some comfort to her son in her life's worst moment—worse than the fear of being apprehended when she crossed the border from Mexico into the United States, worse than when she was bullied in school, raped, dragged into a dog kennel filled with urine, and when she learned that Nathan's father murdered their dog. Losing her son at that moment would be the worst. Isabel would watch until she could no longer see the car transporting her son away from her to an unknown place, his ongoing screams ringing phantomly in her head. The apprehension transaction complete.

If Nathan were older, the apprehension transaction would have additional dimensions. Questions would race through an older Nathan's mind: why can't I stay; did I do something wrong;[72] why is my mom being punished; why I am being punished; how long will I be gone; where am I going; will I go to school tomorrow; how will my friends know where to find me; when will I see my mom next; how do I decide what to pack; why does my mom get to stay here and I have to leave; shouldn't my dad be the one to leave; should I pack my winter coat even though it is only fall; is my dad is going to jail; will they let me see him; and will my mom

---

[72] Michael S. Wald, *State Intervention on Behalf of Neglected Children: Standards for Removal of Children from Their Homes, Monitoring the Status of Children in Foster Care, and Termination of Parental Rights*, 28 Stan. L. Rev. 623, 648 (1976).

be safe without me. Nathan might resist; he might threaten to run; he might acquiesce. His mother would help him pack his belongings as tears streamed down her face. He had seen his mother cry before, but she never would have looked this sad. This would feel worse than anything else he has seen or heard at home. As Nathan is driven away from his home, he would see his mother wave, an incessant wave like she never would want to stop, one lingering connection between a son and his mother even as the physical distance would grow by the speed of the car. Nathan would crane his neck to look out the back window. When she thinks he is too far away to see, Nathan would watch his mother crumble to her knees and begin to sob, a sob that would shake her entire being. Nathan would then begin to tremble.

For Nathan, being removed from his mother would not be a quick, isolated, onetime event. It would be a significant turning point, one that he would relive over and over in his mind.[73] As the car continued taking him further from his mother, he would feel abandoned, rejected, worthless, guilty, and helpless. Nathan would not know where he was going,[74] causing him to feel frustrated and anxious.[75] As the distance between his mother and him grew, and he would no longer recognized the streets of his neighborhood, he would be overcome by feelings of loss—the loss of everything he knew, the loss of what he loved, the loss of part of himself that was left behind. The removal from his mother would also remove Nathan from the Spanish language, traditional Mexican cooking, and other influences of his culture and community.[76] Feeling stigmatized and isolated, Nathan's sense of self would begin to fracture.[77]

The Trauma of the Separation

Children, even newborn babies, are impacted by separation from their parents. For young children, their connection to their parents

---

[73] Shanta Trivedi, *The Harm of Child Removal*, 43 N.Y.U. Rev. L. & Soc. Change 523, 531(2019).

[74] *Id.*

[75] *Id.*

[76] *Id.* at 540.

[77] *Id.* at 541.

is based upon physical proximity and their parent's attunement to their needs.[78] These conditions create an attachment between children and parents that is an essential foundation for social development, cognitive abilities, and security to explore the world and profit from eventual independence.[79] Attachment theory suggests that emotional distress and later problems such as aggression and depression can be attributed to early childhood disruption of the parent-child bonding process.[80] Because children can be attached to parents who are struggling and/or cause harm to their children, interventions that disrupt the parent-child relationship can be extremely damaging to children.[81]

Nathan's attachment to his primary caregiver, who never harmed him, would be disrupted and the impact worsened by being thrust into a foreign place with strangers—foster care.[82] Nathan might struggle with social and emotional functioning, adaptive coping, self-regulation, decision making, and healthy relationships.[83] Nathan could experience difficulty sleeping and eating, developmental regression, and health issues.[84] The trauma could cause

---

78 *Id.* at 529.

79 Wald, *supra* note 67 at 671.

80 Trivedi, *supra* note 68 at 528.

81 Wald, *supra* note 67 at 639–40.

82 Vivek S. Sankaran & Christopher Church, *Easy Come, Easy Go: The Plight of Children Who Spend Less Than Thirty Days in Foster Care*, 19 U. Pa. J. L. & Soc. Change 207, 211 (2017).

83 *Id.* at 212.

84 Sara Goydarzi, *Separating Families May Cause Lifelong Health Damage*, ScientificAmerican (June 2018), https://www.scientificamerican.com/article/separating-familiesmay-cause-lifelong-health-damage/; Allison Eck, *Psychological Damage Inflicted by Parent-Child Separation is Deep, Long-Lasting*, NOVA Next (June 20, 2018), http://www.pbs.org/wgbh/nova/next/body/psychological-damage-inflicted-by-parentchild-separation-is-deep-longlasting/?utm_source=FBPAGE&utm_medium=social&utm_term=20180620&utm_content=1603761016&linkId=53285432&utm_source=FBPAGE&utm_medium=social&utm_term=20180623&utm_content=1608267756&linkId=53391996; Stephanie Carnes, *The Trauma of Family Separation Will Haunt Children for Decades*, Huffington Post (June 22, 2018), https://www.huffingtonpost.com/entry/opinioncarnes-family-separation-trauma_us_5b2bf535e4b00295f15a96b2.; Martin H. Teicher, *Childhood Trauma and the Enduring Consequences of Forcibly Separating Children From Parents at the United States Border*, BMC Medicine (August 22, 2018), https://bmcmedicine.biomedcentral.com/articles/10.1186/s12916-018-1147-y.

permanent architectural changes in his brain, including a lower intellectual quotient.[85] Nathan would experience ambiguous loss.[86] He would miss his mother and, based upon his development and age, would grieve her loss although she was not dead. Knowing she was out there, somewhere in the world, maybe nearby or maybe far away, the nondeath loss could provoke further anxiety, confusion, despair, and hypervigilance as he would wait for his life to return.[87]

Above all, separation would deny Nathan what he needed to heal—his mother. The risk the domestic violence may have posed to Nathan does not sever his needs from his mother. In fact, Nathan's safety and well-being are inextricably linked to the safety and well-being of his mother. Any harms that may have befallen Nathan, at any age, from living in a home with domestic violence would be significantly and efficiently mitigated by remaining with Isabel in safety and stability. Separating Nathan from Isabel would worsen the impact, if any, of his exposure to and experience with domestic violence. And now Nathan would worry about his mother's safety, using his imagination to fill in the unknown. In order to enhance Nathan's safety, stability, well-being, and healing, he would need to remain with his mother. For Isabel and Nathan, removal would be unequivocally counter-indicated to their shared needs.

---

[85] William Wan, *What Separation from Parents Does to Children: 'The Effect is Catastrophic'*, Washington Post (June 18, 2018), https://www.washingtonpost.com/national/health-science/what-separation-from-parentsdoes-to-children-the-effect-is-catastrophic/2018/06/18/c00c30ec-732c-11e8-805c4b67019fcfe4_story.html?noredirect=on&utm_term=.cf5ca597dc72.

[86] Sankaran, *supra* note 62 at 1165-66. "Ambiguity inundates the removal process: children are faced with unpredictability, unfamiliarity, and a lack of clarity about: (1) why they are in foster care (i.e., placement reason ambiguity); (2) the meaning of foster care (i.e., structural ambiguity); (3) how long they will be in foster care (i.e., temporal ambiguity); (4) where they will be living (i.e., placement context ambiguity); (5) the people with whom they will be living (i.e., relationship ambiguity), and (6) their roles in familial environments (i.e., role ambiguity). When left unattended, ambiguity can and will traumatize children who have been removed from their parents."

[87] Theo Liebman, *What's Missing from Foster Care Reform? The Need for Comprehensive, Realistic, and Compassionate Removal Standards*, 28 Hamline J. Pub. L. & Pol'y 141, 17 (2006).

The Trauma of Foster Care

Compounded by the trauma of removal and separation, Nathan may also experience trauma in foster care. More than half of children placed in foster care are placed with people who are strangers to them, non-kinship caregivers, whom they have never met.[88] Loyalty conflicts and identity struggles may make it difficult for Nathan to make emotional commitments to his new foster parents, friends, and environment.[89] Uncertainty about his future could subvert Nathan's commitment to school and disrupt his studies.[90] Just as his mother could be taken from him, so too could these new circumstances.

Foster parents may not be equipped or willing to work with the struggles that children in their home are undergoing, exacerbated by the intervention itself. Children in foster care exhibit higher levels of behavioral issues than children who are not removed from their homes.[91] Nathan may struggle to cope with stress as a result of the attachment disruption to his mother. Foster youth have a three times greater risk for receiving an attention deficit hyperactivity disorder diagnosis, are twice as likely to have learning disabilities and developmental delays than children not in foster care,[92] and have higher rates of psychiatric problems than the general population.[93] All of these struggles make it more difficult to care for a child, and foster placements can disrupt foster care drift. Foster care drift occurs when foster children are moved from home to home. The longer children remain in foster care, the more likely they are to experience placement instability. Two-thirds of children who have been in out-of-home placement for more than two years, experience placement instability.[94] Foster care instability and changes in placement

---

[88] *Id.* at 145.

[89] Wald, *supra* note 67 at 645.

[90] *Id.*

[91] Kimberly Howard, Anne Martin, Lisa J. Berlin & Jeanne Brooks-Gunn, *Early Mother-Child Separation, Parenting, and Child Well-Being in Early Head Start Families*, 13 ATTACHMENT & HUM. DEV. 5, 6 (2011).

[92] Kate Lowenstein, *Shutting Down the Trauma to Prison Pipeline Early, Appropriate Care for Child-Welfare Involved Youth* 10 (2018), https://static1.squarespace.com/static/58ea378e414fb5fae5ba06c7/t/5b47615e6d2a73314 1a2d965/153140464 2856/FINAL+TraumaToPrisonReport.pdf.

[93] Trivedi, *supra* note 68 at 549.

[94] Lowenstein, *supra* note 87 at 7.

would reinforce the stigma associated with being a foster child, in turn causing Nathan to internalize the message of inferiority and feel that something is wrong with him because he is unwanted or is too difficult to deserve care.

The homes in which children are taken are often safer than the foster placements they endure. Indeed, foster children may experience neglect or abuse in foster homes that is equivalent to or worse than they experienced in their homes. Although foster homes are licensed, Nathan could be placed in a home with unsafe and unsanitary conditions, with poorly trained foster parents, and without crucial mental health, medical, and education services.[95] In a survey of foster children, 22 percent reported that they were not getting enough food and 26 percent revealed that they did not have appropriate seasonal clothing.[96] As Attorney Shanta Trivedi opined, "Ironically, similar conditions could have provided the impetus for a child's initial removal from their family, begging the question of whether many of these children could have been spared the trauma of removal by simply being provided with better resources in their own homes."[97] Foster homes can also be unsafe places. The rates of physical and sexual abuse in foster care are two to four times greater than outside of foster care.[98] Foster parents are more likely to be reported for abuse and neglect than families in the general community.[99] Many children would be safer if they were kept with their parents rather than placed in foster care. Like an ambulance that crashes on the way to the hospital, a lifeboat that sinks, or an antibiotic that causes a near-fatal allergic reaction, harm may befall Nathan in the place that is supposed to provide refuge, thereby questioning the need for refuge at all or in this form.

---

95 Liebman, *supra* note 82 at 141–42.

96 Trivedi, *supra* note 68 at 543.

97 *Id.*

98 *See,* "One study in Baltimore found the substantiated rates of sexual abuse in foster homes to be more than four times that of the general population. A similar study in Indiana found "three times more physical abuse and twice the rate of sexual abuse in foster homes than in the general population." Trivedi, *supra* note 68, 542–43.

99 M. Benedict, S. Zuravin, D. Brandt, H. Abbey, *Types and Frequency of Child Maltreatment by Family Foster Care Providers in an Urban Population,* 18 CHILD ABUSE AND NEGLECT 577, 582 (1994).

A Traumatic Future

The trauma underlying the intervention of removal, separation, and foster care foments a prognosis toward a trauma-filled future. Foster care can become a war zone of survival in which foster youth are stripped of the protective gear of their families, connections, and attachments and set to navigate the minefields alone. In an important study of former youth-in-care, 25 percent of those who had been in foster care were found to experience post-traumatic stress disorder, a rate which is nearly twice as high as the rate documented by U.S. war veterans.[100] While each child and youth is unique, with their own strengths and promise, the following identifies the lifetime risk factors attendant to both having been in foster care and from aging out of foster care. Had two-year-old Nathan entered foster care that evening when the investigator knocked on the door, he would have faced the following odds to overcome in comparison to people who never experienced foster care:

- Twice as likely to have learning disabilities and developmental delays;[101]
- Six times more likely to have behavioral problems;[102]
- Higher rates of mental illness;[103]
- Earlier and riskier sexual behavior;[104]
- Higher rates of teenage pregnancy;[105]
- Higher likelihood of abuse and neglect allegations as a teenage parent;[106]

---

[100] Sankaran, *supra* note 62 at 1168–69.

[101] Lowenstein, *supra* note 87.

[102] *Id.*

[103] Trivedi, *supra* note 68 at 549. ("In one study, 54.4 percent of a population of 659 foster care alumni were diagnosed with mental health disorders including depression, social phobia, post-traumatic stress disorder ("PTSD"), and drug dependence, and about one in five of the same population had three or more mental health problems.")

[104] *Id.* at 548.

[105] *Id.* (teen girls in foster care are two and a half times more likely to become pregnant before their nineteenth birthdays than teens that are not in foster care).

[106] Rebecca Bonagura, *Redefining the Baseline: Reasonable Efforts, Family Preservation, and Parenting Foster Children in New York*, 18 COLUM. J. GENDER & L. 175, 176 (2008).

- Greater frequency of losing children to the state as a parenting foster child or teen parent;[107]
- Use and abuse of illicit drugs;[108]
- Less likely to graduate high school;[109]
- Long term health problems caused by trauma and inadequate medical care while in foster care;[110]
- Lower employment rates;[111]
- More likely to live in poverty;[112]
- More likely to be dependent upon public benefits;[113]
- Higher rates of homelessness (e.g., one in five foster youth experience homelessness after leaving foster care);[114,115] and
- More likely to be arrested, involved in the juvenile justice system, commit a serious or violent offense as an adolescent, criminally charged, and incarcerated.[116]

---

[107] *Id.*

[108] Trivedi, *supra* note 68 at 548 ("One study found that almost half of the foster children studied had used illicit drugs at some point and more than a third of them met the criteria for a substance use disorder. Another study found that children whose foster care stay was a year or more had over seven times the rate of drug dependence and almost twice the rate of alcohol dependence as the general population").

[109] Joseph J. Doyle, Jr., *Child Protection and Child Outcomes: Measuring the Effects of Foster Care*, 97 Am. Econ. Rev. 1583, 1583 (2007); Bonagura, *supra* note 101 at 197. ("In New York and other locations, foster care alumni were less likely to complete high school. Only fifty percent of those who aged out of the foster care system had finished high school or earned a GED two to four years later, and only nine percent entered college. Only fifty percent maintained consistent employment two to four years after leaving foster care, and one-third ended up on public assistance within fifteen months of aging out. One quarter had experienced at least one night of homelessness, and several studies showed high levels of incarceration, lack of medical care and medical insurance, and extremely high occurrences of depression or psychological distress.")

[110] Trivedi, *supra* note 68 at 548.

[111] Liebman, *supra* note 82 at 143.

[112] Peter J. Pecora, et al. *Improving Family Foster Care: Findings From the Northwest Foster Care Alumni Study* 2 (2005), https://caseyfamilypro-wpengine.netdna-ssl.com/media/AlumniStudies_NW_Report_FR.pdf.

[113] Doyle, *supra* note 104 at 1583.

[114] Liebman, *supra* note 82 at 143.

[115] Peter J. Pecora et al., *Improving Family Foster Care: Findings from the Northwest Foster Care Alumni Study 1,* 2 Casey Family Programs (2005).

[116] Lowenstein, *supra* note 87 at 8, 11; Doyle, *supra* note 81 at 761.

Children need continuous, safe, and stable relationships with their primary attachments in order to evolve into autonomous, contributing adults. Removal, separation, and foster care often deny children what they need and create additional barriers to overcome. Short- and long-term trauma is endemic to the experience of foster care. Sending children to foster care is boarding them on a lifeboat with a hole when the buoyancy of their family is reckonable.

Half of the children removed from their parents are returned home. Some are only in foster care for a short time, yet the removals and episodes of separation for even only days cause deleterious effects.[117] Had Nathan been removed and returned to Isabel, the experience of being removed and separated would linger, forever changing their dynamics, their security together. Others are in foster care for years, as the system attempts to "fix" each part of a family separately to maybe bring the pieces together again. Yet the pieces that once fit together may now have inconstant edges, joiners that no longer connect, indefinitely missing the last piece of the puzzle, a family forever changed. For those families on the margins where the hard questions persist, Joseph Doyle, an MIT economist, found that "children who remained at home had better long-term well-being outcomes than children who were removed and placed in foster care."[118]

What then has the child welfare system done to families, like Isabel and Nathan, for more than a century? Like Freud's discovery of the source of trauma, the reality is unpalatable but cannot be ignored. The child welfare system must depart from its regressive history that targets certain families in order to rescue children from the very people and places they need and that denies the realities of people's lives in order to take the ineffective approach of ignoring and replacing. The error of the intervention must be corrected by supporting families. When Molly asks the question, "is foster care what this child needs," the answer is almost always in the negative. The forcible separation of children from their families and communities must be omitted as the primary solution. Yet what Nathan and most children need, the child welfare system is not designed to do, has not been funded to do, and may not imagine is in its ability to provide.

---

117 Sankaran and Church, *supra* note 77 at 216.

118 Doyle, *supra* note 104.

• • •

Having left DSS, Molly thinks about Veronica Williams often. Veronica was a mother of two children whose father physically and emotionally abused her.[119] Veronica and her children were in hiding. Veronica was pursuing criminal charges against Cleaven Williams, yet the police refused to arrest him in accordance with the warrant because he was a community organizer and a friend to many law enforcement officers in Baltimore. Veronica left the safety of her place of hiding to attend court for the protective order that she had filed against Cleaven. As the respondent on the protective order, Cleaven received notice of the date and time of the court date. Although he should have been previously arrested, Cleaven now had a rare opportunity to know where Veronica would be. As she left the courthouse on November 17, 2008, with a protective order in hand, Cleaven attacked her, stabbing her repeatedly, in broad daylight, hundreds of feet from the courtroom. Now, Cleaven was arrested and was ultimately convicted of murder. On the day of Veronica's death, DSS was called because the children had lost both parents. Molly and her staff filed a dependency petition, and the children were placed with their mother's sister. Molly followed the children's journey through child welfare until they were adopted by their aunt.

In reflection, this injustice brings Molly back to the days of serving families in Appalachia. There is no them and us—Veronica and her children were just like herself and her daughter, all worthy of finding freedom from fear. In recognizing the blameless needs of others, keeping fear at bay requires the understanding to know how to help others. Therefore, what did Cleaven need years before he killed the mother of his children that he did not receive? What did Veronica and her children need to stay safe? What if Veronica also harmed her children by action or omission? What do their children now need to heal? What role do systems have in meeting the needs of the Cleavens', the Veronicas', the Isabels', and their children?

Despite the paternalistic and destructive legacy of child welfare—the practice of denying that which we do not want or are not ready

---

[119] Kevin Koeninger, *Family Accuses Baltimore Police of Complicity in Woman's Murder*, Court house News, (Nov. 18, 2011).

to accept especially around trauma; judicial opinions that come too little, too late, and without the clout to undo what was started; a concept of children's rights disconnected from the source of children's needs; federal legislation that lacks the undercurrent of valuing all families; sources of harms to children and families levied by removal, separation, and foster care; the perpetuation of moralistic constructions of people and their struggles—injustice by denying families and their children what they need does not need to persist.

At the intersection of child welfare and domestic violence, the personal is political. Individual and familial experiences that transpire must be understood and responded to within their broader societal causes and context for solutions, an antidote to the moral construction marked onto them, the misidentification of the original sin. Then mothers like Isabel will hear and experience this effective message: "You are not alone. You are heard. I believe you. We will work together to find safety, stability, well-being, and healing for you and your son." Routine, punitive policing and destructive responses to social problems, especially those captured at the crossings of child welfare and domestic violence, deny families what they need. Child welfare interventions that repeat history's both entrenched and recent mistakes will incarnate Einstein's views on insanity, denigrating the indelible ink spelling "Fearless//Less Fear" across Molly's fingers.

3
The Radicalism of Transcendence: Conceptualizing Domestic Violence and its Crossings with Child Welfare through a Founding Mother and the Greenbook

For decades, public and private child welfare interventions interacted with families experiencing domestic violence, yet best practices were not developed until nearly the millennium. The guidepost for child welfare interventions into the lives of families experiencing domestic violence is commonly called the Greenbook. A book with a green cover principally authored by Susan Schechter and Jeffrey Edleson was published by the National Council of Juvenile and Family Court Judges in 1999.[1] The Greenbook represented a critical juncture, a concrete crossing, a culmination of sorts, in the journey toward uncovering the intersection of domestic violence and child welfare. The Greenbook aimed to help child welfare agencies, domestic violence service providers, and dependency courts work together to more effectively serve families experiencing domestic violence. The Greenbook has served as the foundation for practice, becoming a springboard for layering upon evolving theories and approaches to families experiencing domestic violence.

The Greenbook's legacy is its message that those intersecting with families experiencing domestic violence, including the child welfare system, courts, and domestic violence service providers, have an obligation to support families experiencing domestic violence in ways that enhance their safety, stability, and well-being, and that these outcomes are better accomplished together—through systemic partnerships and in partnership with the families themselves. But before this framework for practice could come to fruition, battered women had to become visible,[2] battering had to be understood, children of abused women had to be seen, and marrying practices with current social science research had to occur. The journey toward the creation of the Greenbook captures this essential history, without which the Greenbook remains disconnected from its rich evolution. The Greenbook is an outgrowth of the people who wrote it, their values, their histories, their professional work, the lived experiences of survivors of domestic violence with whom they worked, and their ability to guide practices consistent with the belief in the ability of all families to transcend adversity. The exploration of the Greenbook here is through the lens of one of its authors, Susan Schechter, who laid the groundwork for its creation, proliferation, and influence.

---

1 Susan Schechter & Jeffrey L. Edleson, Effective Interventions in Domestic Violence & Child Maltreatment Cases: Guidelines for Policy and Practice, (1999) (hereinafter the Greenbook).

2 This chapter uses the language of "battered woman" and "battery" to capture the language that was used during the time period being described.

A Founding Mother and the Emergence of Understanding Domestic Violence

On February 3, 2004, Susan Schechter, a founding mother of the battered women's movement,[3] died of endometrial cancer at the age of fifty-seven, leaving behind her loving husband and son, and a legacy of transcending victimization—her own and others'—through a steadfast belief in equality and humanism, and a resolute commitment to partnering with those who struggle in order to find the roots of strength in all. Through this lens, Susan was one of the first to identify the overlap of child abuse and neglect and domestic violence as well as construct the policy and practice at this intersection, an influence that continues reverberating throughout child welfare systems and in the lives of families today.[4]

Dichotomies predominated Susan's self and life, as she straddled the world in which she experienced and the world for which she toiled to create for herself and others. Susan was born in 1947 in St. Louis, Missouri to parents who were the anomalies of her extended family in their tight-knit, Jewish community. Throughout her life, Susan was quiet and pensive, often cautious until sure then steely, and fiercely intelligent, ingenious, persuasive, and courageous.[5] Susan's presenting strength and warmth resulted from her intentional rejection of being crippled by feelings of inadequacy stemming from a childhood with parents who were incapable of meeting the needs of their children. [6] Plagued by the deficiencies of her parents as though they were her

3 This chapter uses historically accurate terms, and a shift in terms in the chapter is consistent with the chronological shift in terms that occurred historically. The terms, "battered women's movement," "battered women," and "domestic battery" were used from the 1970s through the 1990s.

4 As Susan's husband, Allen Steinberg, shared, "While Susan may not have been the first or only person to recognize the connection between battered women and their children, she was the first do to something about it." In person interview with Allen Schechter (Nov. 26, 2018).

5 Susan's professional and personal papers are catalogued and held at the Arthur and Elizabeth Schlesinger Library on the History of Women in America is a research library at the Radcliffe Institute for Advanced Study, Harvard University. Permissive review access is granted by Allen Steinberg.

6 Susan is eulogized as, "The smartest and loveliest person on earth." *Greenbook Coauthor Dies,* The Greenbook Initiative (Feb 2004), http://thegreenbook.info/schechter.htm.

own in ways that unwaveringly filled Susan with a lifelong struggle against fear, Susan developed an undergirding personal and professional philosophy that would culminate in guiding how child welfare agencies should respond to families experiencing domestic violence. *The antidote to strife is support, and therein lies the transcendence of overcoming.* The iterative co-existence of struggle and connection ensures that adversity does not predestine individuals and families but that rather overcoming is everyone's potential and promise. Like Molly McGrath Tierney, the fear Susan felt in her personal existence provided her fodder for connecting with the gravity so many women she would come to work with faced, likewise traversing to the other side of fear armed with her impactful antidote.

Susan's guiding principle egalitarian and constructive support can transcend victimization was born out of parallel experiences as a young adult in Chicago in the 1970s, as a member of a consciousness-raising group, as an advocate in a rape crisis center, and her involvement in the Women's Liberation movement and later the battered women's movement. After graduating college, Susan joined a radical, Jewish, feminist, socialist collective that was part of the New Left and that ran a political newspaper called *Chutzpah*.[7] Through the safety of consciousness-raising groups and collectives like *Chutzpah*, women began revealing their truths about childhood and adult violence they had endured, creating an environment in which people could both speak out about and come to understand violence.[8] The women of the consciousness- raising groups resurrected and cemented the truth about trauma that Freud had relegated into denial for the past seventy years. These shared stories and common experiences moved Susan and sisterhoods of women toward a collective view of violence—people who experienced violence were not alone. At the premise of the Women's Liberation movement, "the private and the social were no longer separable categories"[9] and when the individual

---

7 Joyce Antler, Jewish Radical Feminism: Voices from the Women's Liberation Movement (2018). The New Left was a response to the inequality that women and other minorities faced in the leftist anti-Vietnam War movement.

8 *Id.* at 33; The Chutzpah Collective, *Introduction* in Chutzpah: A Jewish Liberation Anthology 3 (Steven Lubet, Jeffrey (Shaye) Mallow, Adar Rossman, Susan Schechter, Robbie (Sholem) Skeist, Miriam Socoloff eds., 1993).

9 Antler, *supra* note 7 at 31.

is linked integrally with the collective, the "personal is political" and "sisterhood is powerful."[10] Susan's time at *Chutzpah* solidified her belief that finding commonality amidst peoples' experiences of both adversity and promise leads to the ability to overcome and then invaluably to grow. The feminists of the Women's Liberation movement also began exploring the causes of collective violence against women by identifying the unequal gender division of labor and women's lack of control over their bodies, sexuality, and lives.[11] Susan began understanding that violence against women by individual men carried the message of a society based on unequal power between men and women. As part of women's liberation, Susan committed herself to social action aimed at reorienting and rebuilding society in order to eradicate marginalization and preserve human dignity and respect for all.

While in social work graduate school in Chicago, Susan began working as a rape crisis counselor at the Loop YWCA. Combining truth with action, the anti-rape movement was the first movement to stem from the Women's Liberation movement and would later birth the battered women's movement. Rape crisis centers were the first organized response to the realities of violence that the Women's Liberation movement revealed. At *Chutzpah* meetings, Susan shared reflections about her work at the rape crisis center, imparting that many of the rapes women were experiencing were part of a larger context of violence against women, including those that occurred behind closed doors at the hands of husbands or boyfriends. It was becoming clear that women were being raped (and otherwise attacked, brutalized, and violated) at home, and they could not be safe so long as they had nowhere to go. Many of the women, therefore, who were being raped were also being battered, and extricating

---

[10] *Id.* at 23. For early writings on these themes, *see* Carol Hanisch, *The Personal Is Political*, NOTES FROM THE SECOND YEAR: WOMEN'S LIBERATION (1970), accessed September 27, 2017, http://www.carolhanisch.org/; Susan Brownmiller, Sisterhood Is Powerful, NEW YORK TIMES, March 15, 1970; and ROBIN MORGAN, ED., SISTERHOOD IS POWERFUL: AN ANTHOLOGY OF WRITINGS FROM THE WOMEN'S LIBERATION MOVEMENT (1970). The Redstockings, a consciousness-raising group from Boston coined the slogan "the personal is political," which "proved to be a powerful change agent throughout the world." Antler, *supra* note 4 at 91.

[11] SUSAN SCHECHTER, WOMEN AND MALE VIOLENCE: THE VISIONS AND STRUGGLES OF THE BATTERED WOMEN'S MOVEMENT (1982).

themselves from those relationships was even more complicated. As the needs of battered women were exceeding the capacity of incident-focused rape-crisis centers, shelters for battered women started forming. The Loop YWCA met the need, and Susan helped open the first battered women's shelter in Chicago.

When the first Chicago battered women's agency opened in 1976, Susan began working as a social worker at the newly formed Chicago Abused Women's Coalition (CAWC). Susan wrote about her early experiences as an advocate for battered women at CAWC:

> All I can remember are phone calls, constant, never-ending calls from battered women with no place to go and with endless stories of institutional indifference. I can remember just wanting to cry and cry. There were moments I dreaded talking to another battered woman. Working with battered women and not being able to help them find what they concretely need creates a panic, a stream of adrenaline that continues until help is found. Where would she go for now; what would she do if the local shelters for homeless people were filled; would she be safe; where would the kids be; what would her husband do if he found her; were there weapons involved; did she have money to buy food; did she have carfare to get to the Salvation Army; where were the birth certificates and medical records for the welfare office or hospital. The details are endless, but they must not be forgotten. We had to assess safety, give her support and information, and help her weigh alternatives.[12]

Susan felt angst and turmoil alongside the uncertain and dangerous challenges the women faced, yet Susan also appreciated the vital importance of the burgeoning battered women's movement. Susan's warm demeanor and ability to listen so someone felt heard made her an effective advocate in this new field.

From those early days at the first battered women's shelter in Chicago, Susan identified that shelters were places in which gender, race, ethnicity, class, religion, and language came together. Rather than ignoring the places in which these intersecting elements of identity

---

[12] *Id.* at 70.

caused schisms in a newly mounting and unifying movement, Susan vocalized the importance of keeping issues surrounding race and culture visible and central to an expansive view of how the battered women's movement was meeting—or failing to meet—the unique needs of each woman. Susan was talking about race, culture, identity, and poverty when few others were willing to do so, and Susan's views were often unpopular. Susan was criticized for identifying the strains of feminism at the time—the potential places of current or future divide in the young movement. Susan felt unsettled by pushing the boundaries and the limits of a movement in its infancy yet was steadfast that being honest about the places of challenge and opportunity would ultimately strengthen, rather than undermine, the movement and its ability to meet the needs of the women. Amidst these fractures, Susan believed that every woman deserved liberation from oppression in the version of freedom that met her needs, and together, supporting her would enhance her strength, potential, and her promise to overcome.

Through friends in *Chutzpah*, Susan met Allen Steinberg, who would later become her husband, and with him, Susan moved to New York City where she continued to work within the evolution of the growing battered women's movement. Susan became a court advocate at the Henry Street Settlement House helping women in family court obtain the newly created protective orders against the people abusing them. Shortly thereafter, Susan worked for the Park Slope Safe Homes Project, a network of individual homes that provided safety to women and children in crisis, and in doing so expanded the reach of one-building shelters, engaged the community in playing a role in the safety of its members, and avoided some of the disincentives that women identified in moving into the communal living of a shelter.

Susan, an activist social worker, and Allen, a historian, together explored the causes of inequality, oppression, and violence. The first paper Susan wrote, she wrote with Allen for the journal *Radical America* that Linda Gordon edited.[13] In that paper, Susan and Allen

[13] Linda Gordon was an active participant in the Women's Liberation movement, and is a historian, professor, and author of many books on feminism and gender, including *Heroes of Their Own Lives: The History and Politics of Family Violence*

explored the cause of battering, which they concluded was rooted in a system of power—not hatred of women—called patriarchy. They described patriarchy as a system of authority that is nonegalitarian and that violence inflicted upon others is a source of the nonegalitarian authority. Battering was not inherent to maleness nor was there something essential about men that made them harm others; rather larger structures of power placed authority in the hands of some (men) and not others (women). Eliminating and delegitimizing patriarchy would result from empowering those with less power. Equality would occur from rising up, rather than tearing down. As a socialist feminist, Susan also ascribed to the need to address poverty at the same time as patriarchy. From this paper, Susan pursued a deeper exploration of the battered women's movement's response to such violence and wrote the groundbreaking book, *Women and Male Violence: The Visions and Struggles of the Battered Women's Movement*. As Allen described, "Susan wanted to tell the story of something coming from nothing, so that it would not be forgotten."[14]

In the book, Susan documented the formative years of a movement that was still in the process of making its own history of which she was a central part. A history book written in the present tense, *Women and Male Violence* achieves as living history and evolving theory of various strains of the battered women's movement. Susan poignantly and irradicably moved battery from an isolated event to its overarching context. Susan presented that unequivocally "battering is a way to maintain control"[15] and that "violence is more than a physical assault; it is an attack on women's dignity and freedom."[16] Susan entered into prevailing discourse that violence against women is socially constructed.[17] As Susan wrote, "women's vulnerability to violence was a result of not only male domination in the family but also of the social system that sanctioned male violence, and privatized the family, exploited women at home and work, and left them few viable

(1988), which is a historical study of the response to child abuse and spousal abuse.

14 Schechter, *supra* note 4.

15 Schechter, *supra* note 11 at 219.

16 *Id.* at 317.

17 *Id.* at 238.

alternatives to escape from violence."[18] Susan's enduring contribution to the understanding of violence against women centered on describing the nature of this violence on the indelible published page and identifying the social causes of the collective experience of violence. She succeeded in describing how the young, battered women's movement met the needs of women through respect, self-determination, understanding, sisterhood, empowerment, and harnessing resources, and how direct services that captured the complexity and strength of battered women were leading to systemic changes.[19] For Susan, the cornerstone of the nascent battered women's movement reaffirmed that transcendence away from struggle requires support and opportunity, promise existing amongst risk.

The year 1982 welcomed two significant contributions to the understanding of battering as a form of violence against women with both the publication of *Women and Male Violence* by Susan and the creation of the Power and Control Wheel by the Domestic Abuse Intervention Project in Duluth, Minnesota.[20] In what would become the most widely-used graphic depiction of domestic violence, Ellen Pence and her colleagues relied upon the experiences of abuse that battered women shared with them, and devised an image of a wheel to capture the dynamics they endured. Each spoke of the wheel represented a tactic that made up the larger system of abuse: physical and sexual violence, coercion and threats, intimidation, emotional abuse, isolation, minimizing/denying/blaming, using children, economic abuse, and male privilege. The visual of the wheel captures the reality that battering is not an incident that begins and ends but rather a cyclical pattern of behavior that repeats over and over. Like

---

[18] This is a feminist analysis of battering. Yet ascribing feminism universally to the battered women's movement is not accurate. As Susan described, "If feminism is broadly defined, then the battered women's movement is a feminist movement . . . However, women who do not consider themselves feminists have played a significant role in the battered women's movement . . . Most important, battered women themselves are, obviously, not always feminists." *Id.* at 47, 49.

[19] *Id.* at 252.

[20] Duluth Domestic Violence Intervention Programs, Power and control wheel, (Sept. 18, 2019), https://www.theduluthmodel.org/wheels/. The Power and Control Wheel has been translated into over forty languages and has been culturally modified to capture the tactics of abuse that can stem from different cultures.

a wheel gaining speed as it accelerates down a hill, the pattern of abuse escalates as it repeats, becoming more severe and dangerous over time. The moments of peace and apology do not signify that the violence and coercive control have come and gone, but rather these reprieves are part of the pattern, creating greater confusion, glimmers of hope, reminders of the good, compelling minimization of the bad, and motivation for survival the next time the abuse occurs, which it inevitably does. The description of the lived experience captured in Power and Control became part of the vernacular of the battered women's movement and still informs the current understanding of the dynamics of domestic violence.[21]

As the understanding of battering increased, so did the understanding of the needs of battered women as well as the need for additional services and supports. And as services grew, the number of people in the movement grew as well as the variety of perspectives they brought to the movement. For instance, most women who were abused were also mothers and perspectives differed about whether their children should be included in the battered women's movement's base. Two-thirds of the shelter residents were children who were there with their battered mothers.[22] A movement that originated to serve the needs of women now had to confront the role of battered women as mothers and determine if and how to attend to the needs of their children. In response, many shelters began developing programs for children, such as group therapy, yet doctrinally serving battered women remained the mission and political orientation of the movement. As the movement expanded, so did the complexities and politics of the battered women's movement that was no longer only a network of shelters but also a vehicle of systemic change which ushered in multifaceted considerations.

The battered women's movement was presented with the opportunity to merge the issues of women and child abuse yet decided to keep the constituents separate. When Ronald Reagan became president, he

---

[21] To describe the behaviors that are the opposite to those in battering relationships, Ellen and her colleagues created the Equality Wheel to characterize intimate relationships based upon equality, the antithesis of relationships based upon unequal power.

[22] Schechter, *supra* note 11 at 88.

closed President Carter's recently formed Office on Domestic Violence and moved its few staff members to the National Center on Child Abuse and Neglect (NCCAN). Those from different fields now together at NCCAN saw the overlap between abuse to women and children by the same person and made arguments that correlated child abuse and spouse abuse. The April 1981 National Conference on Child Abuse and Neglect, sponsored by NCCAN, opened with five-minute debates on major issues facing the field which focused on whether the fields of child abuse and domestic violence should unite under the umbrella of family violence. The following proposal was debated in front of 2,000 participants:

> With data indicating a considerable correlation of spouse abuse with child abuse and neglect, it would be both cost-effective and treatment effective to combine funding and programs for child protection and spouse abuse in a new framework of family violence.[23]

The battered women's movement opposed the proposal, and Susan wrote a statement that she read at the conference entitled "Against Consolidation with Child Abuse Services."[24] She cited that the "majority of men who beat their wives do not beat their children."[25] In reflection, Susan described that the battered women's movement opposed the merger because "everyone knows that merging child abuse and wife abuse services will mean that battered women will be treated like children."[26] In her statement, Susan drew the distinction between vulnerable and dependent children and "women who are competent to control their own lives."[27] She distinguished that "child protection services were organized because children are dependent. Battered women's service provision fundamentally challenges women's dependence, asserting the necessity of independence in order to be free from violence."[28] Her fellow battered women activists also

---

23 *Id.* at 195.
24 *Id.* at 323.
25 *Id.* at 323.
26 *Id.* at 195.
27 *Id.* at 324.
28 *Id.* at 324.

viewed that a merger with the child abuse camp would denigrate the spirit and uniqueness of their movement's self-help response to abuse.[29] As Susan commented, "the autonomy of women's organizations is essential; the women's movement is too young and sexism too old for women to give up their own base of support. Defining mutual goals and strategies, not merging, seems a necessary first step among groups, some of whom are highly suspicious of each other."[30] Viewing themselves as the only reliable stalwart for battered women, the battered women's movement refused to incorporate child abuse and neglect into their mission, a decision that led to insular responses that would ultimately take two decades for the battered women's movement to redirect. Because the activists of the battered women's movement declined to insert themselves into the issue of how to systemically meet the needs of children who lived in homes where domestic battery occurred, others, namely the medical and child welfare fields, did. Dr. Kemp had made child abuse visible a decade earlier, and the Kempian approach to child welfare resulted in responses that conflicted with the values and approach of the battered women's movement.

By retreating from influencing the response to child abuse, the activism and advocacy aimed at conveying the urgency and seriousness of domestic battery backfired in the response to the children of battered women. To underscore the severity of violence and to create a public demand that does not tolerate such abuse, battered women advocates argued for the recognition that witnessing maternal abuse was harmful to children. This position invited the child welfare system to view domestic battery as grounds for intervening with families. Rather than marshaling support around the battered mother and her children together like the battered women's movement did, the

29 As Beverly Birns would later opine, "Women's shelters came from women's desire to help other women. The model was neither the medical nor the social service model, but rather that of the self-help movement. The goal is to help women to gain control of their lives; to stop abuse and; to make wife abuse punishable as any other form of violence perpetrated by one individual against another. Whereas many shelters now seek public financial support, there are problems about "social control" which conflict with the basic philosophy of the shelter movement." Beverly Birns, Ph.D., Wife Abuse and Child Abuse: The Same or Different?

30 Schechter, *supra* note 11 at 302.

child welfare response held battered mothers, rather than battering fathers, responsible for the abuse and removed children from their battered mothers. This response was consistent with the historically judgmental and blaming approach of the child welfare system to abused mothers that did not understand the trap that battering created for mothers and their children. Distancing the movement from the issue of child maltreatment created a vacuum in which child welfare responses operated and deepened the divide between the fields of child welfare and domestic violence, which both provided a greater opportunity for punitive child welfare responses for battered mothers to endure. As researchers and activists Dr. Evan Stark and Dr. Anne Flitcraft concluded, because the battered women's movement did not adopt the issue of child abuse, the "child abuse establishment [came to] assign responsibility for abuse to mothers regardless of who assaulted the child, and respond punitively to women, withholding vital resources and often removing the child to foster care, if women are battered or otherwise fail to meet expectations of 'good mothering.'"[31] Even by the late 1980s, feminists would have had little impact on how child abuse was understood or managed.[32] Susan's life work would later reclaim the intersection of domestic violence and child welfare.

Awakening

By 1985, Susan, Allen, and their new son had settled in Boston where Susan began working as a social worker at a clinic for children who had been physically abused. Considering her initial and published resistance to connecting the battered women's movement with the systemic response to abused and neglected children, her work with families in the clinic became her primary introduction into the child welfare system. The families with whom Susan worked began revealing to her the co-occurrence of child abuse and domestic violence. In the clinic, many of the mothers revealed that they had been or were being battered. Susan concluded that although the majority of children of battered women are themselves not abused, the *majority*

---

[31] Evan Stark & Anne H. Flitcraft, *Women and Children at Risk: A Feminist Perspective on Child Abuse*, 18 Int'l J. Health Serv. 97 (1988).
[32] *Id.*

of mothers of abused children are battered. Despite the prevalence of seeing both abused women and children, most clinic and child welfare staff lacked training and understanding about domestic battery, leading to their frustration with and bias against mothers. Staff felt that they must choose between caring for the child or helping the mother, a house divided. When clinic cases evolved into child welfare cases, Susan observed that the needs of both the children and their mothers were not being met. As she reflected on these challenges in her handwritten notes:

> Many families have mother victims, who then through the inability to protect themselves and/or their children, lose these children to the foster care system. Further, while we advocate well for the children, these women are lost in our system. We end up blaming and punishing them, albeit indirectly, for their victimization. While we try to give them the phone numbers of shelters in their neighborhoods, it is generally apparent that, by the time we are through, they will not use these numbers. Often, our evaluations end, and these women disappear. We know that they continue to be battered, even while we rest uneasily knowing that their children may be slightly better off in a foster home or victimized in foster care.[33]

To Susan, the child welfare response to the "victim mothers" and the "failure to protect" accusations that ensued were contrary to the values and orientation of the battered women's movement that responded instead by offering opportunities for refuge from the violence, building supportive relationships based upon trust, and finding ways for women to exercise self-determination over their lives and control over decisions impacting themselves and their children. The battered women's movement was predicated on fighting violence with its opposite—empowerment—yet the response to battered women who were mothers of abused children was not only disempowering but missed opportunities to meet the needs of each person who was being victimized. Strong advocacy with tangible support

---

[33] Susan Schechter's handwritten notes are on file at the Schlesinger Library and with the author.

for battered mothers was needed to meet the needs of both them and their children.

Susan also began realizing that many of the women who had children referred to the Family Development Clinic had never accessed services from a battered women's agency or shelter. To Susan, this meant that, despite the rapid growth of the shelter movement, there were thousands of women whom the movement was not reaching. Battered women's agencies wait for women to walk through their shelter or counseling doors, but now Susan realized that there were intervention points that could proactively reach battered women who may not otherwise walk through their open doors or who may do so much later.

After witnessing the harm that a siloed approach was rendering and committed to constant self-reflection, Susan reconsidered the efficacy of serving abused women and children in conjunction with each other.[34] Susan began formulating an innovative program for joint advocacy, a model rooted in the commitment to serving the needs of women who are battered while simultaneously responding to the needs of their children. Ultimately, Susan and her colleague Lisa Gary founded a program called Advocates for Women and Kids in Emergencies (AWAKE) at Children's Hospital in Boston. AWAKE began in 1986, consolidating the goals of avoiding punishment of battered women and protecting children. In her notes, Susan ascribed the following as AWAKE's objectives: "prevent further abuse; keep children out of unnecessary foster placement; refer mother and child to resources where they can receive help together and where services are offered on a voluntary basis, providing women choices at a time when they feel they have few; support and empower women rather than coerce and intimidate; move women out of isolation through advocacy; and intervene with battered women who have not otherwise been identified, as such women seeking help for their children can now receive the care and support they desperately need." Two former battered women were hired as the first AWAKE advocates for battered mothers of abused children.

---

[34] Susan Schechter and Sue Doucette, *Summary of AWAKE/Lessons Learned*, Violence Against Women and Children: The Awake Model of Intervention.

AWAKE not only aimed to proactively reach battered women outside of the shelter system's now 1,200 organizations but also aspired to transpose the shelter movement's approach to assisting women into other systems to better serve mothers and their children. Integrating the self-help model into hospital-based advocacy, the advocates would ask, listen, and strategize with the mothers about ways to enable them and their children to live more safely and heal. The advocates documented the strength, coping strategies, protective efforts, and methods the mothers used to stem the abuse. The advocates worked collaboratively with hospital staff and the mother to both develop safety plans to keep themselves and their children safer and access services such as legal, law enforcement, housing, public benefits, childcare, and transportation. The advocates also provided much-needed training to the hospital staff.

AWAKE proved its effectiveness within its first year. From October 1986 to September 1987, AWAKE worked with 194 clients, seventy-three women and 121 children. The data collected confirmed AWAKE's discovery, corroborated by several studies, that in 30 to 60 percent of child abuse cases, there was also a battered woman. The data further suggested that the father or adult male in the family was the one abusing the child and the mother, and the mothers in the caseload were, for the most part, not abusive to their children nor were they passive in their efforts to protect their children. By mobilizing advocacy services on behalf of the mother, the program was effective in keeping children with their mothers. Within the first year, only two of the 121 children served by AWAKE had been placed in foster care. These outcomes challenged assumptions that battered women would not discuss the violence in their families, chose their partner instead of their child, and failed to protect their children. Battered women who worked with AWAKE were open about their abuse when they felt supported and described how they had acted to protect themselves and their children. Following the advocacy from AWAKE, most of the mothers were now living free from violence and rebuilding lives with their children. Imbuing battered women's advocacy into settings that had contact with battered women proved to both reach additional women and improve the host system's response.

Investigating Child Welfare

AWAKE operated as an effective child welfare diversion program of sorts, but to more comprehensively meet the needs of battered mothers and their children within the child welfare system, Susan now needed to better understand the policies underlying child welfare practice. As the project coordinator at AWAKE, Susan wrote a letter to a child welfare administrator at the Boston office of the Department of Social Services (DSS). In that letter with her delicate yet impactful balance of information seeking, investigation, and advocacy, Susan inquired about whether the law specifies that it is the responsibility of the battered mother to protect her children against the violence of their father, whether battered women are held responsible for controlling the batterer's violence, and whether the phrase failure to protect exists in the law or practice.

Shortly thereafter, Susan met with a DSS child welfare worker who answered many of these questions. The worker shared that she had not been trained to assess for the nonviolent parent but rather she was trained to find the guilty parent and protect the child. In her notes, Susan circled and asterisked the worker's statement that "the nonviolent parent is assumed inadequate, and the child's injury proves her inadequacy. If there is any doubt about safety, foster care is the solution." The worker stated that working with the mother was not her job and that supporting the child's mother was not the solution to the child's problem. The worker expressed that many mothers needed coercive intervention, like their children being removed from them, in order to get away from the batterer. Albeit just one voice from child welfare, Susan's work at AWAKE had proven the contrary—an understanding of domestic battery informed an understanding of child abuse, most abused parents strived to be protective, and supporting the battered mother translated into support for the abused child.

From this correspondence, Susan concluded that both bias, misunderstanding, and misdirection inhibited child welfare responses to families experiencing adult and child violence. Susan pondered in her notebook, "How do child welfare workers reframe so that mothers are seen as protective resources that their children need?" As AWAKE demonstrated, cross-discipline models of practice were capable of such reframing, and children were better served by collaborative advocacy in nontraditional settings. Susan saw the applicability of the AWAKE model in any system that locates and connects with battered women in order to both reach women that the shelter system often did not and to shift systemic practice to better meet the needs of abused women and their children. Despite prior missed opportunities, the feminist-based empowerment approach began to reach additional women and specifically influence the child welfare system when the AWAKE model was applied in the Massachusetts Department of Social Services. As the first outgrowth of AWAKE, DSS created the Domestic Violence Unit in which Domestic Violence Specialists worked alongside child welfare workers to build the systemic capacity for more effective responses and to support families (discussed in chapter 8). Shortly after the Domestic Violence Unit began in 1990, Susan and her family moved to Iowa for Allen's professorship.

As Susan worked in the shelter network in Iowa City, she carried with her a story that had made national headlines a few years before. In 1987, Hedda Nussbaum was charged with murder after her husband killed their daughter. When the police arrived, Hedda had been holding her daughter in her arms for twelve hours, paralyzed from calling 911. Hedda was covered in bruises, and a vicious history of domestic violence surfaced.[35] Overnight, Hedda became the most famous face of a battered woman, but more definingly, the most recognized image of an inadequate mother.[36] Amidst public outrage that stripped Hedda of her humanity, Susan could not shake the reality that Hedda had never accessed battered women's services, a shortcoming of the movement rather than the fault of Hedda herself.

In an impassioned letter, Susan wrote to Ellen Pence, one of the co-creators of the Power and Control Wheel, who was now also a friend, to express her distress that the majority of battered women were becoming entangled in systems or experiencing tragedy before ever utilizing the services that the battered women's movement had created. Susan further decried that "none of us were in these places,

---

[35] Francine Russo, *The Faces of Hedda Nussbaum*, THE NEW YORK TIMES MAGAZINE, March 30, 1992, at 26.

[36] *Id.*

and many of the women's encounters with them were negative or unhelpful." Susan proposed in the letter that "we need to take our advocacy efforts into institutions, borrowing from models like . . . AWAKE in healthcare." Susan further articulated that reaching women and improving systemic responses would be based upon the following principles: (1) the institution must unequivocally reject violence and see itself as responsible for helping to stop it; (2) the victim must be protected and supported in a way that does not compromise her self-determination; (3) the perpetrator and community agencies must be held accountable for ending the abuse; and (4) the model of help to institutionalize would be advocacy. The notion of working outside of the traditional battered women services in order to connect with women was controversial within the battered women's movement,[37] yet Susan remained committed to the duality of reaching women within their realities and improving the systemic response to their realities.

Susan began formulating the concept of a triad that surrounded families experiencing domestic violence and allegations of child maltreatment. Domestic violence agencies, the child welfare agency, and the courts composed the three components of the triad. After attending a training, Susan reflected about the shortcomings of each member of the triad. In her notes, Susan described that the child welfare agency inconsistently screened for domestic violence, unpredictably responded (often under or overreacting), issued case plans that were not realistic, and the workers' own values and history drove the analysis of the battered mother's alleged failure to protect. The courts were removing children to their detriment and many parents were left without resources to fully participate in the court case. The domestic violence community typically engaged with women for a short period of time, knew how to advocate well for women but not as well for

[37] As Susan's friend and colleague Mary Haviland Esq. explained, expanding to large systems outside of battered women's services led to concerns that the outside institutions might not take a stand against abuse, could co-opt the feminist underpinning the work, and that safety could be compromised when handled by institutions with less experience working with battered women. Interview with Mary Haviland (Jan. 2019). Mary is the former Executive Director of the New York City Alliance Against Sexual Assault and co-founder and Co-Executive Director of CONNECT, NYC.

children, became angry with mothers who did not protect or parent sufficiently, broke trust with clients when calling the child abuse and neglect Hotline, and felt intimidated by the power of the child welfare agency and the courts. And no one was engaging effectively with the person who battered nor cultivating circumstances that would foster offender accountability. Grappling with how this triad could better respond, Susan attended a conference in Minneapolis.

A Translational Partnership

With a focus on the impact of domestic battery on children, the 1992 conference brought together researchers, activists, advocates, and policymakers. Dr. Jeffrey Edleson sat toward the middle of the auditorium listening to the keynote address by Peter Jaffe.[38,39] In the third row, sat friends Susan and Ellen Pence. Following the keynote, Jeff turned to greet Ellen, and Ellen introduced Susan and Jeff to one another, thereby sparking an impactful professional collaboration.

Jeff came of age in a Jewish home that valued *tikkun olam*—the responsibility of each person to help heal the world—and was on the edge of the anti-war movement. Like Susan, Jeff attended graduate social work school during the second wave of feminism. Focusing his dissertation on children with social skills deficits, Jeff ran groups with elementary-aged boys, some of whom were outwardly misbehaving in school, bullying, using violence, and struggling to have

---

[38] At the time of this book's publishing, Dr. Edleson is a professor of the Graduate School and Harry & Riva Specht Chair Emeritus in Publicly Supported Social Services in the School of Social Welfare at the University of California, Berkeley. He served as Dean of Berkeley Social Welfare from 2012 to 2019. He is also Professor Emeritus at the University of Minnesota School of Social Work and was the founding director of the Minnesota Center Against Violence and Abuse.

[39] Dr. Peter Jaffe was the keynote speaker at the 1992 Minneapolis conference and is a psychologist and professor in the Faculty of Education at Western University and the Academic Director of the Centre for Research and Education on Violence Against Women & Children. He is the Director Emeritus for the London Family Court Clinic, a children's mental health center specializing in issues that bring children and families into the justice system in London, Ontario, and is an expert on the impact of domestic violence on children. Following the conference, Jeff, Dr. Jaffe, and Dr. Einat Peled co-authored a book called *Ending the Cycle of Violence: Community Responses to Children of Battered Women* published in 1995.

healthy peer relationships. After obtaining his doctorate, Jeff was introduced to an evolving area in the field of social work—working with men who batter—and volunteered to co-facilitate a counseling group for men who used violence with Dr. Daniel Saunders, who had established one of the early programs for men who batter at Madison Family Services.[40] These men resembled the boys in Jeff's social skills groups, just all grown up. After returning from his post-doctoral year in Israel, Jeff had moved to Albany for a professorship when two directors of battered women's shelters called a meeting to address their observation of serial batterers who were perpetrating domestic violence against multiple women. The directors were looking for men to partner with to start a program for the men battering their clients. Jeff, along with two local ministers and a graduate student, accepted this call to action, and they formed the Men's Coalition Against Battering. Placing an answering machine in the closet of a church to field calls in 1991, began Jeff's devotion to the field of domestic violence prevention by working with men who batter.[41]

At the Minneapolis conference, both Susan and Jeff digested the nascent social science research on the impact of domestic violence on children. The current research had determined that exposure to domestic violence impacts children differently.[42] Unable to predict children's experiences just based on the existence of domestic violence in the home, Dr. Jaffe imparted that the effect of domestic violence on children is impacted in part by the severity of the violence, the children's individual coping abilities, the passage of time, and most determinatively by the ability of nonviolent parents to be resources for their children.[43] This last finding—that the nonviolent parent matters—resonated with Susan's values and her professional experience, and became the social science truth upon which to build

---

40 Dr. Saunders is now a Professor Emeritus at the University of Michigan School of Social Work.

41 Two years later, Jeff became the founding director of the Minnesota Center Against Violence and Abuse, established by the Minnesota State Legislature to "improve the quality of higher education related to violence" and would serve as the director until 2012.

42 Child Abuse and Family Violence as Determinants of Child Psychopathology (1991) David A. Wolfe & Peter Jaffe, *Child Abuse and Family Violence as Determinants of Child Psychopathology*, 23 CAN. J. BEHAV. SCI. 282 (1991).

43 *Id.* at 291–92.

responses to violent realities. In that finding, the battered women's movement and the child welfare system could come together.

Susan and Jeff remained in contact following the conference. When Susan was awarded a grant to host a conference to specifically explore the overlap of domestic violence and child maltreatment and the responses of child welfare systems, she asked Jeff to work with her to plan the meeting, as their skills, expertise, and experiences were complimentary. While Jeff came to work in the field of domestic violence by working with children and then men, Susan came to the field by working with adult survivors and then children. Susan was a great thinker, policy maker, and connector. Jeff was a robust researcher, scholar, and practitioner. Both valued the importance of using research to impact policy and practice, the approach of translational research. Susan and Jeff knew that spotlighting the impact of domestic violence on children was only one piece of the knowledge needed to inform systemic policies—there was more to this reality that should impact the response. They shared the belief that the visibility of children living in homes with domestic violence and raising the plight of battered mothers was leading to punitive child welfare responses that were harmful to families. The conference was called Domestic Violence and Child Welfare: Integrating Policy and Practice for Families and took place at the Wingspread retreat in Racine, Wisconsin designed by Frank Lloyd Wright.

Susan and Jeff co-wrote a position paper to form the foundation for the conference discussion entitled "In the Best Interest of Women and Children: A Call for Collaboration Between Child Welfare and Domestic Violence Constituencies."[44] The paper highlighted the overlap between child welfare and domestic violence, placing the impact of domestic violence on children and the role of battered mothers in context and together. The paper announced that "some of the most difficult cases both child welfare and battered women's programs confront are ones they confront in common."[45] To underscore this intersection, the paper conveyed that domestic violence and child abuse

---

[44] Susan Schechter & Jeffrey L. Edleson, *In the Best Interest of Women and Children: A Call for Collaboration Between Child Welfare and Domestic Violence Constituencies,* 11 Projecting Children 6 (1995).

[45] *Id.* at 7.

frequently occur in the same family, children who witness domestic violence may be at risk for developing a variety of problems, and those perpetrating some of the most dangerous abuse against children are also assaulting their partners. Susan and Jeff summarized the risk that witnessing violence may pose to children and emphasized the resilience—the strength from within that can be further fostered from the outside—of children. "In spite of tensions between child welfare and battered women's programs," Susan and Jeff imparted that the commonalities are far more transformative.[46] In concert, concern for children's safety and well-being is often the driver of decision making for both the child welfare system and battered mothers. As Susan and Jeff explained, "the decision to stay or leave often hinges on the mother's assessment of what will be in the best interests of her children. A sympathetic understanding of her reasoning and the many forces that shape her decision is of critical importance to ensuring safety for her and her children."[47] Of particular relevance, the support or backlash mothers anticipate receiving from abusive partners and systems in response to their decisions is one of the forces that impact their determinations of what is in their children's best interest. Positioning women and children's best interest in tandem, rather than severed from each other, Susan and Jeff aimed to steer interventions toward a concept of the children's best interest that encompassed the research-grounded means to ensuring the child's safety, stability, and well-being through supported connection between children and their mothers. As such, the paper contended with the historical predisposition of the child welfare system in severing the interests of children from their families, reinforced Molly McGrath Tierney's orientation to the inherent value of families involved in the child welfare system, and supported the sound social science research about what children need to recover from any harm they may have experienced—connection with the abused parent.

The Wingspread paper was a mutual call to action—a summons to the domestic violence community to come forward and an invitation to the child welfare agency to let them in so that together they could meet the needs of families. In direct evolution away from

[46] *Id.* at 9.

[47] *Id.*

Susan's opposition statement at the NCCAN conference in 1981, the paper asserted that "the time is right to link and expand the constituency of advocates for women and children,"[48] and this expansion should pertain to child welfare agencies as well as domestic violence providers. Susan's observations, investigations, and analysis over the past couple of years found a constructive place in this paper. Providing cursory direction to best meet the needs of these families, Susan and Jeff proposed that child welfare agencies and battered women's advocates should work together to support the mother-child unit,[49] such that enhancing the safety of their mother provides protection to the children.[50] Citing the impact of child and woman advocates working side by side at AWAKE, the paper further laid the groundwork for effective interventions that strengthen the "active protective steps"—the countless courageous and creative actions that the vast majority of abused mothers take every day to try to protect their children, revealing their inherent strengths and promise,[51] and accurately understand and work with the perpetrator to promote accountability in order to increase the safety of the adult and child survivors.[52]

While those in attendance in 1994 debated the specifics of translational research to inform practice, a family was living out the reality of their discussions that would prove illustrative of the Wingspread conclusions. As seen through the eyes of a daughter whose mother was the target of domestic violence, the experiences described below of Casey, her siblings, and their mother underscore the position of the Wingspread conference that the nonabusive parent is central to a child's experience of safety and recovery from domestic violence. As the Wingspread Conference concluded and as the experience of Casey's family demonstrates, common ground between domestic violence and child welfare should center "on the need for supporting the remaining family unit—mother and children—in the aftermath of violence."[53] Although the child welfare system did not intervene in Casey's family, the power of Casey's relationship with her mother

---

[48] *Id.* at 6.
[49] *Id.* at 9.
[50] *Id.* at 8.
[51] *Id.* at 9.
[52] *Id.* at 8.
[53] *Id.* at 10.

proved transcendent, not as a panacea but as essential and critical above all else. Upon that reality, within that orientation, dedicated to that premise, child welfare systems must be guided to respond.

• • •

Love, Casey

May 26, 1993 (13 years old)
Dear Diary,

> It is 3:20 in the morning. I don't know if I'll ever be able to get to sleep knowing that Roger knows. About an hour ago, Roger was laughing outside of the study window—on the front porch. Mom was just hanging up the phone from a conversation with Nana when she looked out the window and saw him. He laughed his evil laugh and then ran away, disappearing into the night. Will he come again to do something more damaging? Will he kill Mom or take Will? Who knows what to expect? All I know is that I'm deathly afraid. The police have done all that they can do. They're checking out Roger's apartment and have checked around our house. Still, they haven't found him or any evidence of him being here except for Mom's testimony. I hope everything will turn out okay. If I have to pray a million times to make it go away, that's what I'll do. I don't think Mom should suffer so much, and I despise and loathe Roger for doing this to our family. Why now? Why when we think we've finally got ourselves together, must everything fall apart within seconds? I wish something would start to make sense. I'm going to try to get some sleep now, even though I've been up for half of the night. Thanks for being an ear.

Love, Casey

Following their parent's amicable divorce, Casey and her sister, Liz, four years her junior, lived with their mother. Kathlene, who preferred to be called Kathe, held a master's degree and became a teacher of history and religion at a boarding high school for girls in Amish country. The three lived together in a cozy apartment in the teachers' quarters.

Then, Kathe met Roger. Roger was not like Casey's father. Roger raised his voice at Kathe. Quite suddenly, Roger would begin yelling. The times between break-ups and make-ups seemed shorter each time.

August 1, 1988 (9 years old)
Dear Diary,

Mom and Roger just got back together again. I made it to level 5 in swimming lessons.

Love, Casey

Despite feeling that they had not known Roger for long enough, his role in their lives solidified, hardening all that followed.

August 3, 1988 (9 years old)
Dear Diary,

Mom and Roger just got engaged.

Love, Casey

While Casey and Liz were spending the weekend with their father, Kathe and Roger eloped and were married. That night, behind the closed doors of their hotel room, Roger hit Kathe for the first time.

January 19, 1989 (9 years old)
Dear Diary,

Tonight, Roger and Mom are fighting. I AM SAD! (P.S. Mom and Roger were married in Las Vegas on New Year's Eve.)

Love, Casey

The three moved into a house with Roger, and Casey and Liz shared a bedroom. The sisters often awoke in the middle of the night to the sounds of their mother screaming. Many nights, Roger would call Casey into the bedroom to interrogate her with questions that would require Casey to side with him or her mother. There was never a right answer.

Kathe became pregnant and William was born when Casey was in fourth grade. Roger insisted on calling his son Will. Roger doled out new names for the others, too. He called his wife Kate, a name that had never been nor ever felt like her own. More overtly insipid, Roger's nickname for Casey was DB, short for dumb butt.

To punctuate the darkness with contrast, Kathe created intentional moments of joy and normalcy for her children. During periods of peace, Kathe would wake up her girls at 9:00 pm, and jump in the car to get ice cream in their jammies. Other times, Kathe would take her children on long car rides, turn the music up blaringly loud, and everyone would sing at the top of their lungs. It was not lost on Casey that her mother was doing all this despite the level of violence she suffered; Casey saw her mother as remarkable.

As the periods of tepid calm became shorter, a reoccurring nightmare fastened to Casey as she slept. She dreamt that a bad man chained her to a wall in the garage and sliced her body with razor blades. In an effort to make their bedroom feel safe, Casey and Liz created rituals in their bedroom. Even though they could not change what was happening outside of their door, they could control the environment within these walls. Each and every night, they ceremoniously flicked the light switches and looked in all four corners of the room before going to bed, superstitiously believing that if they sacramentally practiced their ritual, that the night—for their mom, for themselves—could be better.

Kathe was becoming Kate—the woman Roger demanded. Forbidden to work, Kate put on weight and focused on preparing elaborate weeknight dinners that Roger came to expect. As they sat around the table one evening, Casey and Liz put their napkins on their laps, kept their elbows off the table, and crossed their legs at their ankles, desperately believing there was something they could do to avoid Roger's rage. As they ate, Casey could feel the tension, subtle at first and then nearly bubbling. One evening, Casey focused on the peas on her plate, devising how she could get the small round vegetables from her plate to her mouth. She discretely used her finger to nudge the peas onto her fork. Roger exploded. He threw his plate against the wall, and screamed at Kate, "Your girls have disgusting eating habits, just like their cunt mother." "Take your baby brother and sister to your room, Casey," Kate urgently instructed. Casey grabbed Will from his highchair and the three children went quickly and quietly to their bedroom, shutting the door. Flicking the light and checking the corners, Casey turned on the radio, so the only sound the three children could hear was the sound of music and not the screams, bangs, and crashes coming from the kitchen. A while later, and without Roger, Kate came to the room, as she always did after an incident like that, to comfort her children. She tenderly yet with conviction said, "Casey, I am so proud of you for closing the door and turning the music on.

None of this is your fault." Casey was proud of herself for being able to help—a soldier for her brave and strong mother. And Casey felt empowered by being a part of the team with her mom to help keep herself and her siblings safe. The next day, Roger came home from work, this time with flowers for Kate and an apology as temporary as the longevity of the out-of-season cut flowers in the vase.

Weekend visits with their father were a sporadic reprieve from the fear permeating their home, but Casey always worried about leaving her mom and brother alone with Roger. Casey coveted being at her mother's side whenever she could and as often as possible when Roger was not around. Countless mornings, Casey would sit in her mother's bathroom as she got ready for the day. Casey bore witness to her mother's broken bones, black eyes, and bruises in different stages of healing all over her body. Casey sat on the bed watching her mother put on her make-up, covering up evidence of the violence and terror. The mask the make-up created to disguise their reality sent the message to Casey that this violence, this terror, was not to be talked about in the world from which they are hiding it.

Casey knew that their survival rested in her mother's hands, hands she deeply trusted. Roger taunted Kate to reach out for help, and whenever she did, the responses buttressed Roger's violence. Kate devised a code in which she would turn the porch light on if she needed her neighbor to call the police. After doing so and after the police would leave, Roger would return from his walk-around-the-block; the cooling-off that was supposed to have occurred turned into more heated violence. When Kate went to the hospital for a cut that bled for longer than it should or for an x-ray of a possibly broken wrist, the medical personnel believed Kate's unlikely explanations for her repeated injuries. Roger knew that Kate's worse fear was not his violence but losing her children, so he threatened to call the child welfare agency for "allowing this to happen around her kids." The risk of sharing the truth was too great for all of them.

As Will approached his first birthday, Casey felt that Roger was capable of killing her mother. She forced herself to feel the feelings now—the sadness, the despair, the love—all so she would be prepared when it happened. She would need to be strong and would not have time to cry. She would have to keep the three siblings together because that is what her mom would have wanted. Previewing her mother's death at Roger's hands often shifted to plotting Roger's death at Casey's own hands. Casey thought countless times about killing Roger and setting her family, especially her mom, free. When she would hear the sounds of her mom suffering, Casey fantasized about bursting into the room to save her and kill Roger, but she was held back by the rational consideration of her own strength and size in contrast to his, the practicality of what she could actually do once in the room, and the reality that he had a gun, and she did not. The thought of anyone, including herself, using a gun terrified Casey.[54]

At 5:00 in the morning one day, Kate woke up Casey and Liz from a sound sleep and put their grandma on the phone, who said to Casey, "You are a good girl; your mom needs your help. Help pack bags. You are going to a safe place called a shelter." Casey did not know that her fears about her mother's death had almost come true the night before when Roger broke her mother's ribs and strangled her with a phone card. With the cord around her neck, Kate realized that Roger could and would in fact kill her. Her most real and actual fear of what would happen to her children if she died permeated her thoughts just before she lost consciousness from being strangled. When she awoke, Roger had already left for work. Kate called her mother.

The shelter was at an undisclosed, downtown location, a world away from their suburban home. A woman with a kind smile opened the door and asked their names. "I am Kathlene, but you can call me," she paused, "Kathlene." Turning to her three children, "My oldest daughter is Casey. This is Liz, and the baby is Will."

Both Casey and Kathlene began rebuilding together and individually from the inside out. Kathlene worked with the shelter staff and an attorney at the local legal services program to get a protective order against Roger and eventually filed for divorce and custody of Will. Kathlene engaged in individual and group counseling with her

---

[54] Ten children in the United States are murdered by gunfire every day, nearly one every 2 1/2 hours, and the risk of Kathlene's murder increased eightfold by the presence of guns in the home as the majority of domestic violence homicides include a gun. Betsy McAlister Groves, Children Who See Too Much: Lessons from the Child Witness to Violence Project 21 (2002); Rachel Louise Snyder, No Visible Bruises: What We Don't Know About Domestic Violence Can Kill Us 175 (2019).

advocate. Casey found respite in the basement of the shelter, listening to music on an old record player and writing in her diary. Knowing how important school was to Casey, Kathlene made arrangements so Casey could receive her schoolwork at the shelter. Slowly, the foursome started feeling the calm of safety, the lull of peace, but these feelings would dissipate outside the walls of the shelter. They envisioned Roger scouring the city for their whereabouts and were direly scared that he would find them.

On a trip back from court one day, Kathlene spotted a walled cemetery near the shelter. Despite the mortal calamity of possibly being discovered, Kathlene wanted her children to be able to go outside, to breathe fresh air, to put a stake in their childhood. Kathlene gathered her children and they scurried down the block, a basket in hand. Kathlene opened the gate to the cemetery, shooed her children in, and scanned the street before entering the cemetery where her children were waiting. Among the headstones, Kathlene laid down a blanket and set up a make-shift picnic of food from the shelter. Casey and Liz skipped around the plots and made gravestone rubbings with paper and crayons that Kathlene had brought. The outing felt like another late-night trip to enjoy ice cream, an exclamation point punctuating happiness despite the reality that they were in hiding. At that moment, surrounded by those who had passed, slowly their past was starting to be laid to rest. Among the dead, slowly they were reclaiming their lives.

July 15, 1992 (13 years old)
Dear Diary,

Mom found a house for us. Excitement shone in her eyes as she drove on the windy back roads of Lancaster County to show me. When we got to Beaver Valley Pike, we craned our necks with anticipation. As we came to the top of a hill, we began to see a large, white, beautiful farmhouse. We pulled into the driveway and jumped out of the car without even closing the doors. I ran into Mom's arms, and we jumped and hugged and laughed out loud. Then, we ran around the house dancing in delight. For such a low rent, we couldn't believe that this house could be ours! Then we went to the windows and looked in. It was incredibly filthy. The floors were covered with about an inch of dirt. It was literally falling apart inside. But Mom was convinced that she could make it beautiful for us! She went there every day and worked on it while Liz and I were in school. At night she went to her job waiting tables. After about a month we were ready to move in. Mom had cleaned and fixed every nook and cranny. There were hardwood floors that Mom painted and stenciled. She had made the house into a glorious home in which to begin again.

Love, Casey

Surrounded by land farmed by others, the big white farmhouse became their new home. Casey loved spending time in one of the barns, immersed in the pungently sweet smell of fresh tobacco. She would get lost in the cornfields and roller skate on a slab of concrete that was the former foundation of a silo. Casey and Liz attended school and Casey made dinner for her sister and brother while their mom worked. Among the cadence of their new routines, Roger continued to reach into their lives. Although Roger no longer had visitation with Will after trying to kidnap him from a supervised visit, the phone would often ring with the caller cackling, "I found you." Many nights Kathlene slept in the kitchen with a pot of hot oil burning on the stove. That night in May 1993 when Roger did come to the farmhouse, Kathlene screamed, and Casey came running down. Kathlene stood at the window, the phone in her hand, talking with the police as Roger's silhouette faded into the dark night. It was hard to compare the terror of living with Roger to the terror of leaving him.

From a restaurant to the mayor's office, Kathlene then began working at a domestic violence agency, similar to the one that had sheltered her and her children. Throughout her 20-year career, Kathlene went on to direct a shelter, start a new one from the building up, establish a transitional housing program, begin a supervised visitation center, and create a summer camp for children who have experienced domestic violence, all the while deepening her own healing as she helped other women and children journey through fear and crisis. Each year on the anniversary of their shelter stay, Kathlene brings roses to the shelter as a token of her gratitude.

As time went on, Casey's sense of safety felt less temporal. She continued to be a stellar student, succeeding in her advanced placement classes, yet at night she was smoking, sneaking out, and dating boys who were disrespectful and hurt her. Battling an eating disorder, self-harming behaviors, and several abusive relationships, she felt an inner resentment that she did not have a childhood like other children. Yet, her mother remained her compass. Identifying as a feminist from early on, Casey completed her domestic violence advocate certification and would often volunteer by spending nights at the shelter her mother ran, giving back to a movement that had given them the first days of their new life. Like her mother, Casey has since dedicated her career to the field of domestic violence, with a focus on policy and prevention.[55] Casey and Kathlene have spoken together at conferences, as a mother and daughter who survived domestic violence together. Casey eventually met her husband and together began a family; Casey's role model for being a mother is her own.

To this day, Casey struggles to imagine what her fate would have been if she had lost—either by murder or separation—the wellspring of love and support, the source of her growing identity, the anchor of her sense of security, her mother. Because in her mother, Casey found a sense of safety amid violence. In her mother, Casey found a reason to hope. In her mother and as time passed, Casey found the security to be angry, struggle, and explore. Casey and her mother both carry the imprint of Roger's violence and control with them, but they bear those scars in tandem, together.

• • •

Casey's family captures the understanding and reality of the intersection of domestic violence and child welfare that the Wingspread conference nurtured. The dynamics of the violence in Casey's family were consistent with the interpretations of battering that Susan posited in *Women and Male Violence* and that Ellen Pence captured in the Power and Control Wheel. Roger's reign of terror was patterned, the violence littered the pervasive tenor of fear he fomented through intimidation, isolation, and the use of the children as pawns. Amidst the abuse escalating over time, becoming nearly lethal, Kathlene's primary concern was her children. Casey was impacted by seeing and hearing the violence and witnessing its aftermath, and each of

---

[55] Casey is the Director of Programs and Prevention at the National Resource Center on Domestic Violence.

her siblings was affected differently. Casey was fearful as a child, had nightmares, and carried the burden of wanting to rescue her family. The emotional violence targeted at her denigrated her sense of self-esteem. Casey also lived with an omnipresent fear that her mother and siblings could be taken from her if Roger would follow through on his threat to call the child welfare agency. Had the child welfare agency become involved, Kathlene would likely have been accused of failing to protect her children from the domestic violence—deeming her a neglectful mother—and Casey and her siblings would have likely been removed from her and quite possibly each other. Separated, Casey's worry for her mother's well-being would have consumed her growing mind. Without her mother, Casey's ability to process and recover from the trauma of the domestic violence would have been thwarted, exacerbated by the risk of further victimization in foster care and separation from her siblings. Centralizing Casey's experience on her relationship with Kathlene does not place undue responsibility on her mother to prevent that which she cannot control, but it does locate the most basic yet transcendent source of support—the quality of the relationship with the parent surviving domestic violence.

The Wingspread Conference represented a call to action: take what is known from the lived experiences of Casey's family and understood from social science research and transform child welfare practice into a different reality—into interventions that work together with the battered women's movement. In doing so, prioritize the combined interests of the nonoffending parent and their children because that connection is what children *need* to find enhanced safety, stability, well-being, and healing.

The majority of child welfare systems and battered women's services did not heed the call, but the notable few who did greatly benefited families. The Domestic Violence Unit of the Massachusetts DSS, that began when Susan was still in Boston, had grown to eleven Domestic Violence Specialists (discussed in chapter 8).[56] In Michigan, the Families First family preservation program placed eighteen workers to formulate plans with battered women as they left domestic

[56] Jeffrey L. Edleson, *The Overlap Between Child Maltreatment and Woman Battering*, 2 VIOLENCE AGAINST WOMEN 134, 151 (1999).

violence shelters.[57] The Miami-Dade County Juvenile Court hired battered women's advocates to work with abused mothers of children who came to their court.[58] Children's programs at domestic violence agencies were growing. For the rest of the countless child welfare and domestic violence agencies, expanding their constituency to include mothers and children respectively remained stymied.

Yet, rifts persisted. The inherent obstacles existing between the worlds of domestic violence and child welfare professionals dominated over shared interests. Domestic violence advocates continued to claim that "child welfare agencies blame women for the violence that men perpetrate," that they "hold men and women to different, gender-based standards of care for children,"[59] and become "more angry at abused women than they are at the men who batter them."[60] Child welfare agencies continued to infer that if a woman is unable to protect herself, she cannot keep her child safe and surmised that domestic violence agencies ignore the needs of children.[61] Their respective mandates—protect children and empower women—were portrayed as mutually exclusive goals.

Amidst these persistent schisms, families experiencing domestic violence had become significant parts of child welfare caseloads. Similar to the statistics that AWAKE revealed, multiple studies revealed that 30 to 60 percent of families within child welfare agencies were experiencing domestic violence.[62] Despite this prevalence, interventions were still generally punitive, blaming, and misdirected. Child welfare agencies were holding mothers solely accountable for their child's safety because they were the most amenable partners even though they were the least able to prevent further abuse. Fathers were at the periphery and often unseen at all. As child welfare systems became increasingly aware of domestic violence in their families, Susan and Jeff observed that the following deficits persisted even within and among well-intentioned systems and professionals:

---

57 *Id.*

58 *Id.*

59 Schechter and Edleson, *supra* note 43 at 8.

60 *Id.* at 7.

61 *Id.* at 8.

62 Edleson, *supra* note 60, at 136.

- Lacking understanding about the dynamics of domestic violence, as evidenced through language such as, "the parents engaged in domestic violence;"
- Misidentifying the appropriate designation of roles of the abuser and the nonoffending parent, especially if the nonoffending parent used resistance violence or acted in self-defense;
- Measuring the nonoffending parent's worth as a parent based upon whether the parent stayed or left the abusive relationship;
- Removing children from the nonoffending parent and placing children in foster care or with the abuser's family;
- Forcing the nonoffending parent to get a civil protective order or participate in a criminal prosecution despite the danger such steps may pose;
- Making inappropriate service referrals, such as referring the abuser to anger management classes rather than a batterer's intervention program and encouraging marriage counseling;
- Failing to hold the abuser accountable or holding the nonoffending parent accountable based upon notions of failure to protect or the misnomer that the nonoffending parent "allowed" the domestic violence to occur; and
- Allowing judgment, bias, stereotypes, racism or classism, and lack of cultural competency to interfere with professional conduct.

To overcome these divisions, and ineffective and often harmful interventions, Susan and Jeff's Wingspread call to action required additional instructions, stimulus, and influence.

The Greenbook

The National Council of Juvenile and Family Court Judges (hereinafter "the National Council") recognized this need for guidance, too.[63] In the late 1990s, Merry Hofford, of the Family Violence Department

---

[63] Established in 1937, the National Council is a membership organization of professionals involved in juvenile, family, or domestic violence court systems in order to improve the lives of families and children seeking justice. *See* National Council of Juvenile and Family Court Judges, *Family Violence: Emerging Programs for Battered Mothers and Their Children* (1998).

of the National Council, identified the opportunity to provide concrete guidance to child welfare agencies, the domestic violence community, and courts to better serve families experiencing domestic violence consistent with the Wingspread message.[64] With Susan's advocacy lens and Jeff's clear sense of the implications of social science research to guide practice, the National Council selected them as the primary authors of a more extensive roadmap, a best practice guide. Recognizing that the project would require perspectives from different social and legal systems, the National Council named an advisory committee of diverse professionals from the courts (including judges), child welfare and domestic violence services, federal agencies, and the academic community.[65]

---

[64] Merry envisioned a publication with recommendations for practice and enlisted others to assist. Maureen "Mo" Sheeran worked at the National Council with Merry. Mo was connected to the domestic violence community and had edited a publication in the late 1990s that centered on the emerging responses to battered mothers and their children. At the same time, Susan was working with Janet Carter at the Family Violence Prevention Fund (now Futures Without Violence) to form the Children & Youth Program. Merry approached Janet and Susan about creating a publication that expanded upon the theories and approaches discussed at the conference at Wingspread. Embracing the invitation, Merry, Maureen, Janet, and Susan began formulating the vision of an expansive framework for practice at the intersection of domestic violence and child welfare. The National Council and the Family Violence Prevention Fund, along with Susan until her death, would continue to champion this endeavor together.

There appeared to be momentum in the federal government to support and fund such an endeavor. The momentous Violence Against Women Act had just passed the year before. In 1994, for the first time, domestic violence organizations received $20 million; by 1998, $87 million was appropriated. In 1995, Susan was appointed along with forty others to the Department of Justice Advisory Council on Violence Against Women under Bonni Campbell. Merry had attended a conference and heard a presentation on the co-occurrence of domestic violence and child abuse. The speaker was Olga Trujillo and Olga was the Chief Legal Counsel at the Department of Justice's Office for Victims of Crime.

Merry approached Olga seeking funding for developing a publication to guide interventions around domestic violence and child maltreatment. Through interagency government support and a combination of public and private dollars, the Office for Victims of Crime, the U.S. Department of Justice, the Office on Child Abuse and Neglect, the Children's Bureau, the U.S. Department of Health and Human Services, as well as the David and Lucile Packard Foundation and the Johnson Foundation, awarded grants to the National Council to develop The Greenbook.

[65] Greenbook, *supra* note 1 at 4. Judge Leonard Edwards of the Santa Clara County, California Juvenile Court and Dr. Carol Spigner of the Administration

Susan and Jeff were tasked with drafting and editing recommendations that were developed by the Advisory Committee. Susan took the lead, and Jeff provided feedback and commentary before sharing the evolving recommendations with the Advisory Committee. Spanning a period of eighteen months, the Advisory Committee met to discuss and often debate the recommendations that Susan and Jeff had drafted,[66] delving deeply to touch on the core places of friction where the recommendations would resonate most. After many months of continuous consultation with the Advisory Committee and Susan and Jeff's authorship, the National Council published *Effective Interventions in Domestic Violence & Child Maltreatment Cases: Guidelines for Policy and Practice*. The resulting Greenbook, a shorthand title derived from the forest color of the cover, consisted of five chapters with sixteen principles and sixty-seven recommendations supplemented by commentary intended to guide the collaborative practice of domestic violence providers, child welfare systems, and juvenile courts—the triad that Susan had scribed in her notes years before.

Reading the Greenbook is advisable for any professional who works with families, or any part of a family, who has experienced or perpetrated domestic violence. As long-standing juvenile court at the time Judge Leonard Edwards (introduced in chapter 7) wrote in the introduction to the Greenbook, the Greenbook is a "context-setting tool to develop public policy aimed at keeping families safe and stable."[67] The task of the Greenbook's user-friendly presentation of distinct principles and recommendations offers a comprehensive set of responses to address the enormous risks that individual adult survivors, advocates, caseworkers, and judges must take on behalf of families.[68] As such, the Greenbook is a framework—a starting point—for developing interventions and measuring progress upon

on Children, Youth and Families and the U.S. Department of Health and Human Services, co-chaired the Greenbook National Advisory Committee.

66 The Advisory Committee also formed task forces to develop recommendations on the topics of culturally competent practice, batterers who abuse their children, batterer accountability, battered immigrant women, supervised visitation, and the Indian Child Welfare Act.

67 Greenbook, *supra* note 1 at 5.

68 *Id.* at 12.

which each entity can develop public policy and practices based upon following core Greenbook principles.[69]

- Interventions of the triad should aim to create safety, enhance well-being, provide stability for children and families, and provide concrete, respectful, and culturally competent support.[70]
- The safety, stability, and well-being of children is inextricably linked with their nonoffending parents,[71] such that enhancing the safety and stability of their mothers makes children safer and more stable.[72]
- Children should be kept in the care of their nonoffending parent whenever possible.[73]
- Witnessing domestic violence is not a per se form of child abuse or neglect[74] and nonoffending parents are not neglectful so long as they took steps to protect their children.[75]
- Interventions should assess each family's unique risks, strengths, and protective factors,[76] and the specific impact of domestic violence on each child.[77]
- Perpetrators of domestic violence, not nonoffending parents, should be held responsible through a variety of legal, social service, and community-based avenues.[78]
- Collaboration and cross-training between the triad is necessary to effectively meet the needs of families.[79]

At the core of the Greenbook are the truths established in *Chutzpah*, the battered women's movement, and AWAKE—strength and promise amidst struggle, support and connection over isolation—a reflection of Susan's approach to her own life's journey. An

69 *Id.* at 12.
70 *Id.* at 12, 13.
71 *Id.* at 19.
72 *Id.* at 19.
73 *Id.* at 13.
74 *Id.* at 20.
75 *Id.* at 109.
76 *Id.* at 21.
77 *Id.* at 51.
78 *Id.* at 13.
79 *Id.* at 24, 25, 70.

understanding of domestic violence that the Greenbook promotes is not incident-focused but rather conveyed as an omnipresent context in which choices are limited and risks are many and often weighted. Within this context replete with fear and constriction, safety is broader than physical protection. Safety, stability, well-being, and *healing* are reachable aspirations for abused women and their children if they receive the necessary resources. The Greenbook outlines the duties of each member of the triad to advocate for and access these resources needed by families experiencing violence, thereby embodying the organized and constructive compassion characteristic of Susan's philosophy and practice.

As the Greenbook was released, Jeff published two comprehensive literature reviews that served respectively as substantiation for the Greenbook and reiterated caution about the intersection of domestic violence and child welfare. Translationally, Jeff comprehensively summarized the social science research about the impact of domestic violence on children and that which they need to recover from the harms of domestic violence—to live in safety and stability with the adult survivor, evidence-based conclusions that substantiated the recommendations in the Greenbook.[80] To those persuaded by the visibility of children impacted by domestic violence, Jeff also warned against the mistake of defining domestic violence as child maltreatment.[81]

Heeding Jeff's validation and caution, an ensuing child welfare intervention that incorporated the tenets of the Greenbook would not have been such a threatening proposition to Kathlene and her children. Carrying out his threat, Roger may have called the child abuse and neglect hotline in retaliation against Kathlene for leaving him, alleging that she kidnapped the children or had harmed them. The child welfare investigator would then likely meet Kathlene and the children at the domestic violence shelter. Even though there would likely have been allegations against Kathlene in the Hotline report, the investigator would ground herself in the orientation that Kathlene cared about the well-being of her children and that amidst her current struggles, strength exists. The investigator would share her intention to

[80] Edleson, *supra* note 60 at 151.

[81] Jeffrey L. Edleson, *Children's Witnessing of Adult Domestic Violence,* 14 J. OF INTERPERSONAL VIOLENCE. 839, 865 (1999).

partner with Kathlene to enhance her safety, stability, and well-being, and thereby her children's. In speaking with Kathlene, the investigator would ask questions and listen to Kathlene's responses about the ways she tried to keep her children safe, the impact of domestic violence on her children, the support in their lives, and the ongoing risk that persists. The investigator would ask Kathlene what she wanted for her herself and her family and the supportive resources needed to reach these goals. The investigator would speak with Casey and Liz and observe Will. With Kathlene's consent, the child welfare investigator and Kathlene's advocate could work together to connect and provide Kathlene with legal referrals, employment assistance, housing advocacy, transportation help to and from court and school, and links to public benefits. The domestic violence advocate would also connect Kathlene's children with services and supports. The whereabouts of Kathlene and her children would be kept confidential. At the conclusion of the investigation, no findings of neglect would be issued against Kathlene and child welfare support would not be contingent upon deeming Kathlene neglectful. Kathlene would feel that she was respected, treated with dignity, and that the intervention enhanced, rather than detracted, the safety, stability, and well-being of herself and her children. As a result, the harm that her children experienced from witnessing domestic violence would be significantly mitigated by remaining with Kathlene in safety and stability.

Had Roger called the Hotline as a method of further terrorizing and exerting his control over Kathlene while Kathlene was still living at home, a different version of events guided by the Greenbook could have transpired. The investigator would likely meet Kathlene and her children at their home or in the children's school. The investigator would interview both Kathlene and Roger separately and would navigate any false allegations Roger conjured. The investigator would express to Kathlene that she is worried about the safety of Kathlene and her children and inquire whether Kathlene feels that she and her children are safe. The investigator would recognize that Kathlene may be hesitant to disclose or be forthcoming about the abuse because she may never have told anyone before, or she may be worried about the systemic or retaliatory consequences of doing so. Kathlene may also fear that the intervention may not be able to keep her and her children safe or could increase the risk to her and her children. With Kathlene's consent, the investigator would suggest involving a domestic violence advocate at a local program to help explore options for safety for Kathlene and her children. Together with Kathlene, they could consider sending the children to stay with a relative or friend, seeking a civil protection order that requires Roger to leave the house, finding a shelter or other housing, or creating a domestic violence safety plan that accounts for the likelihood of Roger's continued abuse. Kathlene would be invited to share the risks and benefits she ascribes to each option.

Kathlene may also fear that any form of separation or change to the status quo would put her and her children in grave danger because no assurance exists that the support would ameliorate the risks Roger poses. The investigator may conclude that the children are at imminent risk of harm, compelling protective custody and removal of Casey, Liz, and Will from Kathlene, thereby prompting a petition for dependency to initiate a court case. In dependency court, the judge would insist upon understanding both the risk that the domestic violence posed as well as the steps that Kathlene took to protect her children. The judge would require the child welfare agency to make reasonable efforts to keep the children with Kathlene, which may include finding a hotel for them to stay in temporarily, locating a shelter, accessing housing vouchers, or entering an order at the court's directive prohibiting Roger from being near Kathlene and the children. Because Roger has control over his choice to abuse Kathlene, the separation imposed by the court may lessen Roger's violence, or it may exacerbate it like kerosene added to a fire. The dependency case would progress by adjudicating whether the exposure to domestic violence rendered the children abused or neglected under the law. If so, the court would determine Kathlene's fitness as a parent not based on whether she endured domestic violence, but based on the innumerable, creative, and brave steps she took to protect her children and meet their needs. The child welfare agency would provide services to Kathlene and her children and facilitate as much contact as possible between Kathlene and them, as they progressed toward being allowed to reunify together.

In any of these scenarios, Greenbook-centered interventions would not ignore Roger. The investigator would attempt to engage with Roger in order to locate sources of motivation to change. To foster accountability, he would recommend services such as a batterer intervention program as well as issue investigative findings consistent with the harm and risk Roger caused. In a dependency case, Roger would receive a service plan, and supervised or therapeutic visits between Roger and Will may occur. A supervised visitation center may be utilized in order to keep Kathlene and the children safe during transitions. If Roger demonstrated a willingness and ability to stop abusing his family, the court could increase Roger's contact with his son if consistent with his best interest inclusive of his safety, stability, well-being, and healing.

From Paper to Practice through the Greenbook Initiative

In order to mirror the hypothetical interventions into Casey's family, the next task became translating the Greenbook into actual practice. As an initial step, the National Council hosted a summit on the Greenbook in 2000 with the goal of determining how to materialize its impact into action.[82] There Susan and Jill Davies, lawyer and author, contextualized the options that adult survivors confronted by proffering to the attendees that enhancing safety, stability, well-being, and healing for nonoffending parents and their children together requires addressing both batterer-generated risks and life-generated risks.[83] Addressing both sets of risks in partnership rather than as an adversary to the nonoffending parent is the responsibility of each member of the triad. The expectation that the nonoffending parent

[82] Attendees included judges, child welfare administrators, the domestic violence community, and representatives from the federal government. In addition to Susan and Jeff, faculty for the conference included David Berns (discussed in chapters 4 and 11), Lonna Davis (as Clinical manager at DSS, discussed in chapter 8), Jill Davies, Judge Leonard P. Edwards, Betsy McAlister Groves (discussed in chapters 5 and 10), Barbara Hart, Judge Richard J. FitzGerald, Loretta Frederick (discussed in chapter 11), Peter Jaffe, Fernando Mederos, Linda Spears, Olga Trujillo (Director, Special Projects Division, U.S. Department of Justice, Office for Victims of Crime, discussed in chapters 4 and 10), Pamela Whitney (discussed in chapter 8), Ruby White (discussed in chapter 4), Isa Woldeguiorguis (Domestic Violence Coordinator, DSS, discussed in chapter 8).

[83] Jill Davies & Welfare and Domestic Violence Technical Assistance Initiative, *Building Opportunities for Battered Women's Safety and Self-Sufficiency* (Nat'l Resource Ctr. on Domestic Violence, Working Paper No. 1, 1998).

should or can leave as the measure of safety is a fallacy and absolves those in the triad and in the wider community of responsibility for more broadly thinking about reducing risk as a way of increasing safety, stability, and well-being for women and children. The conference participants also focused on the ways in which each member of the triad could collaboratively work together on behalf of families.

Then, following the conference and before Susan was diagnosed with cancer, the National Council sought and received significant federal dollars to fund six demonstration sites to implement the Greenbook into actual practice.[84,85] Over the five-year Greenbook Initiative, the demonstration sites established collaborations among domestic violence, child welfare, and court systems in accordance with the Greenbook principles and recommendations with the intention of fostering systems change to improve the safety, well-being, and stability of families at the intersection of domestic violence and child welfare. The evaluation of the demonstration sites revealed the potential of the Greenbook to foster collaboration and systems

[84] The National Council approached the Office of Victims of Crime again and asked Olga Trujillo (discussed in chapters 4 and 10) if the federal office would fund pilot sites focused on implementing the principles and recommendations of the Greenbook to translate the words of the Greenbook into practice. Olga had participated in the Greenbook Advisory Committee meetings and was invested both personally and professionally in the intersection of domestic violence and child welfare. Now as the Director of Special Projects at OVC, Olga committed to using OVC funding sources to partially fund the pilots and approached other federal agencies to supplement funding that OVC could not cover. In the spirit of collaboration, eight offices among two federal agencies unprecedentedly pooled money to fund six Greenbook demonstration sites as part of the Greenbook Initiative. The Greenbook Initiative was funded through a memorandum of understanding among four offices in the U.S. Department of Justice (DOJ) and four agencies in the U.S. Department of Health and Human Services (HHS). In the DOJ, the Office on Violence Against Women, the Office for Victims of Crime, the Office of Juvenile Justice and Delinquency Programs, and the National Institute of Justice participated in funding the Greenbook Initiative. HHS agencies included the Children's Bureau and the Family Violence Program in the Administration for Children and Families, the National Center for Injury Prevention and Control (part of the Centers for Disease Control) and the Assistant Secretary for Planning and Evaluation. Because of this unique arrangement, each department pooled funding from various discretionary grant programs.

[85] The six Greenbook demonstration sites included Grafton County, New Hampshire; St. Louis County, Missouri; El Paso County, Colorado; Lane County, Oregon; Santa Clara County, California; and San Francisco, California.

change, yet the Greenbook's full impact remained both unmeasured and ever-evolving.[86]

In the demonstration sites, the Greenbook most significantly created a demand for collaboration among the triad and showed that collaboration between previously siloed systems is possible. The Greenbook's message of collaboration between child welfare agencies, domestic violence providers, and dependency courts was seized and came to define both the efforts and achievements in the sites. Each of the six sites undertook major collaborative efforts which were unique to the location, time, history, and relationships of those involved.[87] The collaborations were thoroughly planned, taking nearly half of the years of the five-year Greenbook Initiative. Each site created a structure to their collaborative and cross-system teams that consisted of representatives from each member of the triad as well as other community partners. Each site also "created or refined specialized positions and continued to support, expand or modify

---

[86] Three evaluation reports were completed at various phases of the Greenbook Initiative: 1) The Greenbook Demonstration Initiative: Process Evaluation Report: Phase 1, described the planning and goal setting phase in the sites; 2) The Greenbook Demonstration Initiative: Interim Evaluation Report, summarizing the planning to implementation phase midpoint; and 3) The Greenbook Demonstration Initiative: Final Evaluation Report, assessed the extent to which the Greenbook implementation activities facilitated cross-system and within system change and practice in child welfare agencies, dependency courts and domestic service providers. The Journal of Interpersonal Violence published a series of articles following the evaluation of the Greenbook Demonstration Initiative. *See* Jeffrey L. Edleson & Neena M. Malik, *Collaborating for Family Safety: Results from the Greenbook Multisite Evaluation,* 23 J. of Interpersonal Violence 7, 871 (2008); Duren Banks, et al., *Collaborative Efforts to Improve System Response to Families Who Are Experiencing Child Maltreatment and Domestic Violence,* 23 J. of Interpersonal Violence 7, 876 (2008); Duren Banks, et al., *Changing Policy and Practice in the Child Welfare System Through Collaborative Efforts to Identify and Respond Effectively To Family Violence,* 23 J. of Interpersonal Violence 7, 903 (2008); Neena M. Malik, et al., *Coordinated Community Response to Family Violence, The Role of Domestic Violence Service Organizations,* 23 J. of Interpersonal Violence 7, 933 (2008); Neena M. Malik, et al,, *Domestic Violence and Dependency Courts, The Greenbook Demonstration Experience,* 23 J. of Interpersonal Violence 7, 956 (2008); Colleen Janczewski, et al., *Crafting the Greenbook, Framers Reflect on the Vision, Process, and Lessons Learned,* 23 J. of Interpersonal Violence 7, 981 (2008).

[87] The Greenbook National Evaluation Team, *The Greenbook Initiative Final Evaluation Report* 66 (Feb. 2008).

these positions over the course of the initiative."[88] These specialized positions included "domestic violence advocates co-located in child welfare offices, court staff responsible for holding batterers accountable, and systems analysts who regularly reviewed potential gaps and improvements in the way the systems responded to families."[89] Most of these positions were located within child welfare systems or the courts and they helped facilitate cross-system information sharing within the bounds of confidentiality protections, ensure more appropriate handling of cases involving child maltreatment and domestic violence, engage frontline workers in the collaboration, form a bridge of institutional empathy across systems, and provide resources to respond to family violence in a more collaborative and comprehensive manner.[90] As the evaluators found, these specialized positions put the collaborative framework into practice and were the conduit to bringing the Greenbook principles into the triad.[91]

Most significantly, relationships developed among the primary partners of the triad, particularly between the child welfare agencies and their domestic violence organizations.[92] They learned about each other, the other systems, and developed trust that had not previously existed.[93] Planning the collaboration and forming these relationships took time and patience, and often required revisiting issues previously addressed until all of the partners felt heard and comfortable.[94] Each site was devoted to the collaboration, and the collaboration developed and changed over time.[95] For instance, at the start, survivors of domestic violence and domestic violence agency partners were at the collaborative tables, but over the course of the five years, batter intervention programs became more involved.[96] Each of the triads reflected on needing to more thoroughly engage other community partners, seek more widespread input, and mobilize those

---

88 *Id.* at 12.
89 *Id.*
90 *Id.* at 21.
91 *Id.* at 59.
92 *Id.* at 19.
93 *Id.* at v.
94 *Id.* at v.
95 *Id.* at 61.
96 *Id.* at iv, 14.

outside of the triad around the intersection of domestic violence and child welfare.[97]

Despite the achievement of collaborative structures and improved relationships, challenges to collaboration still existed. High turnover and limited resources handicapped participants in the triad from dedicating the time and resources needed to foster collaboration. Power differentials endemic in most collaborations were present in the demonstration sites too. In the triad, judges were endowed with the greatest authority, child welfare agencies had power that domestic violence agencies did not, and domestic violence agencies struggled to maintain their influence as independent grassroots organizations rather than members of a unified system. With power not inherently equalized, collaborators needed to learn how to leverage their power and give space to those with less power. Yet even those with apparent power did not have the unleashed leeway to act. Judges, for instance, were limited by statute and case law precedent, and child welfare agencies had legal mandates of child protection. Frustration often arose when those with seemingly the most power were restricted from acting.

While improved relationships between the members of the triad were lauded as collaborative achievement, relationships that become too intertwined sacrificed the integrity of the professional orientations of the partners. Working together, partnering, and crossing systems requires each to maintain their individuality while remaining open to learning from the others. For instance, a co-located domestic violence advocate was less effective at bringing together the expertise of the two disciplines of child welfare and domestic violence in the better service of families if she adopted the traditional beliefs about domestic violence from her child welfare hosts. (Many of these lessons are further explored in chapter 8.) The existence of collaborative structures did not guarantee that collaborative practice, needs-based service delivery with many points of entry, or individualized responses to families necessarily followed.

Systems change grounded in the Greenbook also occurred in the triads of each demonstration site. The courts implemented judicial training and cross-training opportunities that increased judges'

[97] *Id.* at iv, 17.

knowledge about domestic violence.[98] Domestic violence agencies increased their knowledge about child welfare and abuse and neglect.[99] Child welfare agencies, however, experienced the most significant systems change. Each child welfare agency in the demonstration sites created or enhanced domestic violence screening and identification tools,[100] and underwent trainings that aimed to increase worker knowledge about domestic violence, what families need, and how to deliver on those needs.[101]

While the evaluation revealed significant structural improvements, the evaluation fell short of establishing Greenbook's most important aspiration—improved outcomes for families. Evaluating whether collaboration and systems changes could be linked to enhanced safety, stability, and well-being for families was outside the scope of the evaluation.[102] As such, many principles of the Greenbook were left unmeasured, such as whether fewer nonoffending parents were accused of failure to protect, fewer children were placed in foster care, more children remained with the nonoffending parent, more nonoffending parents received the resources they need to mitigate the risks they faced, and more offending parents were held accountable. Collaboration and system changes, rather than the outcomes, were documented and extolled as the successes of the Greenbook Initiative.[103] As a result, collaboration and systems change became viewed as ends in themselves, when in fact, collaboration and systems change must exist for a reason—as a means of achieving improved outcomes for families. Susan's vision that the approach of the battered women's movement to mothers and children would find its place within systems did reach thousands of women and move the compass of the triad, even though her life's mission of improving the lives of women, children and families remained quantitatively unanswered yet full of promise.

Susan was diagnosed with endometrial cancer in the summer of 2003, becoming a challenge, for the first time, she could not overcome.

---

98 *Id.* at vi.

99 *Id.* at vii.

100 The sites produced many documents that could serve as useful resources for other jurisdictions.

101 *Id.* at 37.

102 *Id.* at 8.

103 *Id.* at 62.

Susan's death months later predated the evaluative conclusions of the Greenbook Initiative and the constructive critique that followed. For instance, Susan was not able to share her reflections about the criticism that the triad was too limited and should have also included law enforcement, social service preventions agencies, and the community. She also did not have the time to bring her insights and wisdom to reflect on the lessons learned from the demonstration sites nor could she foster or witness the next horizon of the Greenbook, yet others carried her torch when she no longer could. In Susan's spirit of being one of the first advocates of the battered women's movement to recognize and write about race, culture, and identity, the *Activist Dialogues* became a compendium of sorts to the Greenbook in order to imbue a lens of diversity into the dialogue and practice at the intersection of domestic violence and child welfare.[104] Just as Susan would have sought and elevated the voices of those impacted, the *Activist Dialogues* captured both the experiences and recommendations of women of color who experienced both domestic violence and child welfare.

The *Activist Dialogues* created additional recommendations similarly "anchored in the passionate conviction to strengthen families and communities,"[105] but also "recognize[d] the necessity for forming partnerships with a dynamic circle of people concerned with ending violence."[106] As a sequel to the Greenbook that expands upon the triadic responses, the dialogues with survivors revealed the importance of cultivating and leaning on the leadership of women of color, supporting the capacity of culturally-specific organizations, and holistically investing in communities as drivers of the social change

[104] Chic Dabby &Angela Autry, *Activist Dialogues: How Domestic Violence and Child Welfare Systems Impact Women of Color and Their Communities*, Family Violence Prevention Fund (April 2005), https://www.futureswithoutviolence.org/userfiles/file/Children_and_Families/Activist.pdf. Becky Masaki, who was on the Greenbook Advisory Committee, approached Lonna Davis at the Family Violence Prevention Fund (now Futures Without Violence) to partner on the project and together they received funding from the Packard Foundation. As the project director, Lonna oversaw the production of what became called the *Activist Dialogues* in partnership with six organizations that serve women of color experiencing domestic violence.

[105] *Id.* at 13.

[106] *Id.* at 6.

necessary to meet the needs of families of color at the intersection of domestic violence and child welfare, as well as stem the intergenerational perpetuation of abuse.[107] Originating from the voices of those once impacted by and now impacting this intersection, Susan's endorsement of the *Activist Dialogues* as a companion to the Greenbook, had she had the chance, would be consistent with both her history and hope for the future.

Susan's legacy lives within the Greenbook and beyond. The Greenbook remains *the* best practice guide for interventions into the lives of families experiencing domestic violence and child welfare. Its principles and recommendations are sound and have been further substantiated by research, lived experience, advocacy, and activism. Posthumously, the tenets of the Greenbook have been the source of statutory changes in states like Illinois (discussed in chapter 9), the inspiration for domestic violence/child welfare co-location programs in places like Iowa, Ohio, and Pennsylvania (discussed in chapter 8), and previewed equity as the prism through which to evaluate the basic functioning and fairness of systems. Susan's work laid the foundation for the demand for trauma-informed, strength-based, family-centered, and equity-focused child welfare practice that enhances, rather than impedes, a family's ability to find greater safety, stability, well-being, and healing (discussed in chapter 4). Like Susan who was didactic but not proscriptive, the Greenbook left itself room to evolve while remaining true to itself.

In 2019, fifteen years after Susan's death, the National Council of Juvenile and Family Court Judges published a special issue of the *Juvenile and Family Court Journal* entitled "Twenty Years of the Greenbook." The journal was dedicated to Susan's memory. Jeffrey Edleson co-edited the series, and in the introduction wrote, "The articles in this special issue reflect on some of the remarkable work that has been done since the publication of the Greenbook and show how far we have come in the past twenty years. The articles offer ideas for new directions that build on the past work and that address current gaps in research, services, programs, and policies."[108] Captured in the

[107] *Id.* at 12–13.

[108] Lucy Salcido Carter & Jeffrey L. Edleson, *Twenty Years of the Greenbook, Introduction,* 70 Juvenile and Family Court J. 4, 7 (2019).

words of those carrying her torch in spirit and following Greenbook's vicennial, the need remains for greater translational interventions based upon deepened research, assessment, training,[109] codification of Greenbook principles into federal policy supported by adequate funding,[110] multidisciplinary responses and judicial leadership at the intersection of domestic violence and child welfare,[111] integration of Greenbook principles with issues that often co-occur with domestic violence such as substance abuse and struggles with mental health,[112] systemic capacity building that is sustainable beyond individual relationships,[113] alignment of Greenbook principles with the priority to reduce the overrepresentation of families of color in the child welfare system,[114] shifts from mother-blaming to acknowledging how fathers' choices affect the safety and well-being of the family,[115] and new approaches for engaging with fathers to reduce their use of violence and coercive control.[116] As Judge Leonard Edwards (chapter 7) co-wrote as an epilogue to the Greenbook's impact from theory to transformation, "Greenbook was only the beginning—the foundation of what was to come."[117] Susan's legacy continues to be written through this constructive reflection and demand for continued growth, just as she would do if she could do so herself.

---

[109] Megan R. Holmes, et al., *Research Foundations of Greenbook Interventions to Address the Co-Occurrence of Child Maltreatment and Adult Domestic Violence,* 70 Juvenile and Family Court J. 4, 11 (2019).

[110] Kiersten Stewart, *Evolving Federal Policies and Their Implications for Greenbook Interventions,* 70 Juvenile and Family Court J. 4, 37 (2019).

[111] Judge Leonard Edwards (Ret.) & Judge Katherine Lucero, *The Santa Clara County Greenbook Story: From Theory to Transformation,* 70 Juvenile and Family Court J. 4, 49 (2019).

[112] Lucy Salcido Carter, *Advocacy Perspectives on the Greenbook: Interviews with Domestic Violence Advocates from Three Federally Funded Greenbook Sites,* 70 Juvenile and Family Court J. 4, 100 (2019).

[113] *Id.*

[114] Judge Karen Aileen Howze (Ret.) & Associate Justice Anne K. McKeig, *The Greenbook and the Overrepresentation of African American, Hispanic and Native American Families in the Child Welfare System,* 70 Juvenile and Family Court J. 4, 103 (2019).

[115] David Mandel & Claire Wright, *Building on the Greenbook: A Perpetrator Pattern-Based Approach to Improve Child Welfare's Response to Domestic Violence,* 70 Juvenile and Family Court J. 4, 122 (2019).

[116] *Id.*

[117] Judge Leonard Edwards (Ret.), *supra* note 109 at 71.

Susan's legacy is also ingrained as a woman, mother, wife, friend, social worker, founding mother, policy maker, activist, reformer, and radical, who lived life diligently, intentionally, and with grace, constantly striving to better herself and the world around her. Throughout her life, Susan transcended her own fate in order to do the same for others. She was a bridge-builder between the world as it was and the world that could be, between what is needed and what is delivered, between historical flaws and progress that is possible, between adversity and promise, between isolation and the transcendent centrality of connection that Susan used to guide her life's work. Susan shaped movements, shifted systems, and impacted families by embodying and indoctrinating the spirit of transcendence captured in Casey's words to her mother:

May 10, 1998, Mother's Day (18 years old)

> I feel no shame about my experience. I just remain ever grateful that I was born to a woman of such bravery. Her loyalty to her children kept her alive and her love for us allowed her to prove her inner strength. When I look at my mother, I see a tower of beauty; I see a pillar of love; I see a reason to enjoy the freedom and happiness with which she has provided me. I love Mom with everything in me. She is what I aspire to be.

Love, Casey

4
Infuse with Gold: Trauma-Informed, Strength-Based, Family-Centered and Equity-Focused Child Welfare Interventions

For hundreds of years, the Japanese have mended broken pottery with gold. Dissatisfied with the traditional method of repair that rendered broken pottery more damaged, a Japanese shogun in the late 1350s challenged craftsmen to find an alternative, a method that did not denigrate the broken piece but rather enhanced its beauty and strength. Rather than discarding that which was broken, Kintsugi became the centuries-old tradition of repairing broken ceramics with precious metal, rendering the fault lines of something as simple and ordinary as a cup or plate worthy of the art of golden joinery. Kinstugi celebrates strength and grace in the places once fractured. In the process of repair, there is *hope* of creating something more unique, beautiful, resilient, and strong.

To hope is to believe that a broken piece of pottery has a meaningful and fulfilling future, that something can be stronger now than it was, that someone can find greater happiness tomorrow than today, that healing is possible with a chosen injection of epoxied gold. As Casey Gwinn, an advocate for identifying, teaching, and measuring hope describes, "Hope is the belief that your future can be better than your past and that you play a role in making it so."[1] To hope involves setting goals, finding the motivation to reach those goals, and creating pathways toward reaching those goals; willpower and way power (the pathway) must accompany the vision for a better tomorrow. Hope can be learned, hope can rise, and hope can be measured.[2] Hope is a significant predictor of well-being.[3] Hope is one of the twenty-four universal character strengths that is morally valued across cultures and contributes to the capacity of human beings to flourish.[4] Hope can buffer the effects of adversity and stress. Hope forecasts adaptive thoughts and behaviors.[5] Hope is an important coping resource for both children and adults.[6] Rising hope in parents leads to rising hope in their children.[7] Gwinn notes that rising hope is a protective factor for survivors of domestic violence[8] and reduces the impact of trauma because rising hope helps heal trauma.[9] Dr. Chan Hellman, a hope researcher, describes that hope is the mindset that drives resilient behavior. Hope enables a person to grow beyond the last, worst incident that happened to them. Individuals can have hope, and groups, communities, and systems can be hopeful, too. Collective hope is the shared belief in, the will for, and the way toward futures founded upon strength in the once fragile cracks. Gwinn and Hellman have called for hope-centered organizations in all disciplines.

The child welfare system must orientate itself to be collectively hopeful and should be accountable for increasing hope within the

---

1 Telephone Interview with Casey Gwinn (March 19, 2019).

2 Casey Gwinn & Dr. Chan Hellman, Hope Rising: How the Science of Hope Can Change Your Life 38, 48 (2019). Hope Scales exist for children and adults and indicate the level of an individual's hope, or his/her belief in and ability to change his/her future. *Id.* at 47–49.

3 *Id.* at 18.

4 *Id.* at 18.

5 *Id.* at 18.

6 *Id.* at 18.

7 *Id.* at 109.

8 *Id.* at 114.

9 *Id.* at 29.

families subject to its interventions. Systems cannot give or expect what they do not have. Systems that are hopeful will foster hope in the families with whom they work. The child welfare system must be the shogun who believes that the families who are struggling, those that come to the system's attention experiencing domestic violence, deserve responses of gold-constructed kindheartedness instead of punitive paternalism. Each family has value warranting such response no matter the fissures. The system must believe that families can move from struggling to stronger and view themselves as a partner in that journey. Susan Schechter manifested this hope-filled demand in her approach to women, children, and families and strove to create systemic hope at the intersection of domestic violence and child welfare. The brokenness of Kintsugi pottery does not signify that families experiencing domestic violence are themselves broken; rather the cracks in the pottery are analogous to the trauma and adversity the family is experiencing, instead of who the families are. Just as a broken vessel can become an object of enriched and enduring fortitude, so too can families experiencing domestic violence and the child welfare system become stronger by addressing the tenuous clefts that were endured and supporting strengths amidst adversity. This must be the child welfare system's will—the needed belief in hope. Then, the *pathway* toward hope is the gold resin. To infuse with gold in the child welfare context means to engage in *trauma-informed, strength-based, family-centered, and equity-focused interventions* that partner with families in ways that meet their needs for enhanced safety, stability, well-being, healing, and hope. Only then can families remain together unbroken following child welfare interventions.

Trauma-informed, strength-based, family-centered, and equity-focused interventions are grounded in and layered upon the best practice tenets outlined in the Greenbook; this too is Susan's legacy. As the gold-infused lacquer, trauma-informed, strength-based, family-centered, and equity-focused interventions become the mechanism for realizing the collaborative, multilayered responses of the Greenbook that locate the mitigation of harm in the child's connection with his family, link together the safety and well-being of adult and child survivors of domestic violence, and prioritize accountability for those who use coercive control and violence, ultimately enabling each member of the family to find a way toward healing. Just as there are various ways to repair with gold, so too must trauma-informed, strength-based, family-centered, and equity-focused approaches respond to the unique needs of each family and individual as the Greenbook guides.

The experiences of Isabel Rodriquez, Ruby White Starr, and Darrell Jackson will demonstrate each aspect of these approaches to families. Trauma-informed, strength-based, family-centered, and equity-focused child welfare interventions are the pathways to hope, the gold-inflected glue leading to greater safety, stability, well-being, and healing. When child welfare system interventions exit the lives of families experiencing domestic violence, the remaining vessel should be stronger at the places where struggle existed.

The First Ingredient of the Golden Joinery: Trauma-Informed Practice

Enduring years of trauma, each insult, punch, and rape were part of an ongoing terror-inducing barrage, robbing Isabel of hope and attacking her safety and the core of her being. Moments of shadowed reprieve were tarnished by the pervasive certainty that the end of one assault would usher in another, the thread of fright sewing her existence. Isabel held the trauma in every part of herself—her brain registered risk everywhere, her gut felt like it was at war, her body reacted as though she were constantly under siege, and she felt disconnected from her own sense of self. She struggled to feel fully alive and present. Yet, Isabel had a goal and a plan (a pathway) and retained a belief in herself that the trauma had not completely stolen. Isabel decided to leave Jason, for her safety and for the well-being of her son. But when the child welfare investigator knocked on the door, Isabel walked out of her abusive boyfriend's home and into a system that felt hauntingly similar. Toxin rather than gold was used to enjoin Isabel to greater instability and pain. The child welfare intervention should instead have been a golden foil to Isabel's trauma.

The Evolution toward Trauma-Informed Practice

As Isabel experienced, trauma researcher and practitioner Dr. Bessel van der Kolk, describes that trauma is ". . . not just an event that took place sometime in the past; it is also the imprint left by that experience on the mind, brain, and body."[10] In 2001, Maxine Harris and Roger Fallot underscored the importance of identifying the imprint of trauma in order to address the underlying trauma itself. In a paper that both disinherited Freud's recantation of the impact of trauma and created a paradigm shift, Harris and Fallot alerted mental health and substance abuse providers that the presenting problems of the majority of people seeking services had roots in traumatic experiences.[11] Harris and Fallot coined the term "trauma-informed" to crystalize the importance of avoiding re-traumatization and re-victimization to enhance healing for countless help seekers.[12]

In order to meet the needs of trauma survivors, trauma-informed child welfare practice must understand trauma in order to provide support and a connection that fosters a less obstructed pathway to enhanced safety, stability, well-being, and healing. In doing so, growth after trauma is not stunted. Post-traumatic growth "highlights the human capacity for transformation in even the most ominous circumstances. Transformation is a change . . . that involves being strengthened, rather than destroyed, by trauma."[13] Both trauma and strength are aspects of the overall experience of responding to adversity, surviving it, and growing beyond it.[14] Child welfare interventions devoid of this orientation not only hinder healing but also cause additional trauma, compounding trauma upon trauma, thereby contributing to the poly-victimization of trauma in people's lives, as Isabel experienced.[15] Trauma-informed interventions understand the pervasiveness and impact of trauma and commit to developing the necessary knowledge and skills to minimize re-traumatization, support healing and resiliency, and address the root causes of violence.

---

10 Bessel A. van der Kolk, The Body Keeps the Score: Brain, Mind, and Body in the Healing of Trauma (2014).

11 Maxine Harris & Roger D. Fallot, *Envisioning a Trauma-Informed Service: A Vital Paradigm Shift,* New Directions for Mental Health Services Volume. 89 (March 2001).

12 *Id.* at 1.

13 Kim M. Anderson, Fran S. Danis, Kristen Havig, *Adult Daughters of Battered Women: Recovery and Posttraumatic Growth Following Childhood Adversity,* 92 Families in Society: The J. of Contemporary Social Srvs. 2, 154 (2011).

14 *Id.*

15 Harris and Fallot, *supra* note 13 at 9.

The Pervasiveness of Trauma

The longitudinal Adverse Childhood Experiences study, known as the ACEs study, established the pervasiveness of childhood trauma as well as the long-term impact of early traumatic experiences. The study correlated ten types of childhood trauma with disease, quality of life, and mortality in adulthood.[16] The study originated from information that Dr. Vincent Felitti learned from the patients he was treating for obesity. Like Freud had heard a century earlier from women struggling with hysteria, the patients struggling with obesity had experienced trauma in their childhood. The prevalence of childhood trauma and health struggles in adulthood prompted the Centers for Disease Control and Prevention and Kaiser Permanente to conduct a multi-faceted longitudinal study. Published in the *American Journal of Preventive Medicine* in 1998, the ACEs study revealed three important discoveries: adverse childhood experiences are more common than not, these traumatic experiences are interrelated, and adverse childhood experiences can impact a person's health and well-being throughout their lives.[17] The majority of people experience trauma in childhood as two-thirds of the respondents reported at least one adverse childhood experience.[18] Specifically, the ACEs study revealed that nearly a quarter of respondents were physically abused as children, over one-quarter of women and over 15 percent of men were sexually abused as children, and more than 12 percent lived in a home where their mother was physically abused.[19] Adversity does not often occur alone. Of the two-thirds of respondents with an ACEs score of one, 87 percent had at least one more trauma marker.[20] Each additional adverse experience compounds the toll of trauma. Higher ACEs scores correlate to a greater likelihood of health, well-being, and mortality risks such as depression, substance abuse, heart disease, cancer, suicide, and traumatic experiences in

---

16 Dr. Vincent J. Felitti, et al, *Relationship of Childhood Abuse and Household Dysfunction to Many of the Leading Causes of Death in Adults, The Adverse Childhood Experience (ACE) Study,* 14 Am. J. of Preventive Medicine 4, 245 (1998).

17 van der Kolk, *supra* note 12 at 427.

18 *Id.* at 427.

19 *Id.* at 428–29.

20 Gwinn, *supra* note 2 at 74.

adulthood.[21] As such, the "impact of these adverse childhood experiences on adult health status is strong and cumulative."[22] Understanding how trauma transforms the mind and body to cause such long-term impact is an important element of being trauma-informed.

The Impact of Trauma

As Isabel embodied, Dr. van der Kolk's explanation of the physioneurosis of trauma describes how trauma is held in a person's entire being, impacting both mind and body, causing the health detriments that the ACEs study revealed.[23] Trauma's imprint has ongoing consequences for how the human organism manages to survive in the presence of trauma and its aftermath. When a traumatic event occurs, basic human survival ushers in the fight, flight, or freeze responses, which occur in the most primitive, emotional part of the brain. The part of the brain that integrates information from the senses deactivates because the full perception of the overwhelming feelings and sensations of the traumatic incident is too overbearing to be ingested in their entirety. The sensory information thereby passes on as "fragments of sounds, smells, sights, and touches," so most traumatic memories are not recalled as a story or a narrative with a beginning, middle, and end but rather as "isolated sensory imprints accompanied by intense emotions of terror and vulnerability" or not remembered at all.[24] People experiencing trauma often lose access to rational thought, their sense of time and even the ability to speak about the event because the prefrontal cortex is unplugged.[25]

Reoccurring and ongoing trauma, like the domestic violence Isabel experienced, further results in the "fundamental reorganization of the way the mind and body respond to the outside world."[26] The neuroplasticity of the brain creates a default position that anticipates that threats will occur, and the brain is primed for the next assault. Those who experience reoccurring trauma progress through

---

[21] van der Kolk, *supra* note 12 at 430. Provides a thorough summary of the ACE study findings.

[22] Felitti, *supra* note 20.

[23] van der Kolk, *supra* note 12.

[24] *Id.* at 215–16.

[25] *Id.* at 213.

[26] *Id.* at 84–85.

varying degrees of psychological responses from social engagement, to fight or flight, to freeze to dissociation. Each proceeding psychological state is a response to the lack of safety necessary to ensure the effectiveness of the prior survival mechanism. Dissociation—the separation of awareness from experience—occurs on a continuum. Nearly every survivor of reoccurring trauma experiences some form of dissociation in the way that the overwhelming experiences are split off and stored in sometimes inaccessible fragments of sounds, sights, smells, and touches to protect against the full extent of the pain and horror. As such, the direst state of survival causes the mind to disconnect from the body.[27]

The omnipresent threat of future and inevitable trauma and the impact of triggers and flashbacks keep trauma survivors in the space of their emotional brains and in the physical manifestations of the constant fight, flight, or freeze mode, thereby living as though the traumatic incidents are always occurring. The world is filled with triggers for those who endure repeated trauma, anything "might be perceived as a harbinger of catastrophe."[28] Flashbacks pull the traumatized person into the past to re-experience the traumatic event as though it were happening all over again.[29] Trying to protect against future attacks, triggers, and flashbacks that quite circularly causes trauma survivors to be "not being fully alive in the present" thereby "keeping them more firmly imprisoned in the past" or held hostage by the impending future.[30,31]

When regions of the brain responsible for regulating breathing, heartbeats, digestion, hormone secretion, and immunity are consumed with defending against real or perceived threats, regulation is disrupted and health conditions can ensue.[32] Somatic symptoms such as pain, headaches, and digestive issues may develop.[33] Because minds and bodies' of trauma survivors are always primed for an attack,

---

27 *Id.* at 276; *See,* Olga Trujillo, The Sum of My Parts: A Survivor's Story of Dissociative Identity Disorder (2011).

28 *Id.* at 320.

29 *Id.* at 35.

30 *Id.* at loc. 205–06.

31 *Id.* at 205-07.

32 *Id.* at 283.

33 *Id.* at 294.

their immune system follows accordingly, often attacking their bodies' own cells.[34] To deal with actual or imagined threats the body continues secreting adrenaline to activate the fight or flight response of the sympathetic nervous system. Because trauma survivors may never feel fully safe, the body does not signal the release of cortisol, causing many trauma survivors to struggle to maintain a state of calm and balance, resulting in agitation and hypervigilance.[35] The physical manifestation of trauma and the eventual loss of self mark the experience of many traumatized people.[36]

Dr. van der Kolk's explanation of the physioneurosis of trauma is a compass rather than a map. Just as the trauma itself is unique so too is the trauma survivor. Some survivors want to talk about what has happened to them while others remain quiet or share in snippets not because they are recalcitrant, but because they cannot remember, cannot find the words, or do not feel safe and comfortable.[37] Some have trouble connecting and trusting other people while others cling to strangers for friendship, support, or intimacy.[38] Some appear angry, agitated, visibly emotional, or frantic while others are withdrawn, frozen, and shutdown, carrying blank expressions on their faces.[39] Some are dogged by shame and struggle to make eye contact while others appear eager to reveal their continued experiences of trauma. Some engage in self-harming or risky behaviors while others remain connected to the present by identifying a powerful source of motivation.[40] Shackled to the past, some lose a sense of purpose and direction in the present while others are quickly driven to overcome that which haunts them and search for avenues of healing. Many do not understand how their lives have landed them in a state in which they feel dysregulated and crushed, like they do not deserve each breath and step forward, yet most find the courage and resolve to keep breathing and walking despite the treachery they face inside and out. For many, safety exists on a continuum connected to the risk of

---

[34] *Id.* at 375–75.
[35] *Id.* at 111, 157, 468.
[36] *Id.* at 200.
[37] *Id.* at 149.
[38] *Id.* at 60, 256.
[39] *Id.* at 81.
[40] *Id.* at 149.

the present, the influence of the past, and the threats of the future. Seemingly opposing manifestations of trauma can occur simultaneously, in succession, or iteratively. Neither one reaction nor another is more credible or believable. Current symptoms, effects, behaviors, or decision-making skills are the "sequelae"[41] of past or ongoing trauma, and the reminder of it.

Child welfare interventions often become part of the sequelae of ongoing trauma by transferring organizational trauma onto the trauma survivor and by replicating similar experiences of trauma in the intervention itself. The child welfare system itself is traumatized, as Dr. Sandra Bloom explains,[42]

> The resulting organizational trauma both mirrors and magnifies the trauma-related problems their clients seek relief from. Just as the lives of people exposed to chronic trauma and abuse become organized around the traumatic experience, so too have our social service systems become organized around the recurrent stress of trying to do more under greater pressure: they become crisis-oriented, authoritarian, disempowered, and demoralized, often living in the present moment, haunted by the past, and unable to plan for the future.[43]

Because of the high levels of past and present trauma in the social service workforce,[44] the history of distrusting the families coming to the attention of the system, the demanding charges to child welfare, and the inherent power imbalances between child welfare workers and their families, the child welfare system and its actors may struggle to overcome their own organizational and individual trauma and embody the necessary qualities to meet the needs of families. If

---

41 *Id.* at 5.

42 Dr. Sandra Bloom developed "The Sanctuary Model," which provides s a blueprint for clinical and organizational change which, at its core, promotes safety and recovery from adversity through the active creation of a trauma-informed community" and focuses "not only on the people who seek treatment, but equally on the people and systems who provide that treatment." Dr. Sandra Bloom, *The Sanctuary Model,* (May 30, 2019), http://sanctuaryweb.com/TheSanctuaryModel.aspx.

43 *Id.*

44 *Id.*

families need to move out of the fight or flight response by feeling safe and reorganizing their perception of danger,[45] child welfare systems often feel unpredictable, fear surfaces from the threat of separation, and danger may befall children in out-of-home placements. If families need the reciprocity of seeing and being seen, hearing and being heard, families often feel worthless, invisible, and isolated when a child welfare worker identifies flaws within their walls and looks to outside sources for rescue.[46] If children need their parents to heal, that resource is often taken from them. If families need to gain control over the residues of past trauma, coercive and belittling interactions often reinforce familiar trauma-invoked feelings of rage and helplessness.[47] If families need to locate their own agency and restore their autonomy, the power of child welfare workers often strip decision-making and control from those whose lives are affected.[48] Importantly, traumatized systems are capable of post-traumatic growth just as individuals are.

Equipped with an understanding of the widespread travesty of trauma and its devastating impact, Dr. van der Kolk cautions against a backlash that relegates traumatized children as indelibly damaged or dismisses parents as unworthy of parenting.[49] Even though trauma is not a "single discrete event but rather a defining and organizing experience,"[50] trauma survivors are more than the trauma they have experienced.

• • •

The Child welfare intervention became another trauma that took years of Isabel's young life to heal. Isabel's experience with the system replicated the dynamics of terror, victimization, blame, and constriction that she had endured. It did not build upon the resources

---

45 *Id.* at 1013.

46 *Id.* at 1017.

47 *Id.* at 38.

48 *Id.* at 135.

49 Dr. van der Kolk states, "Recognizing the profound effects of trauma and deprivation on child development need not lead to blaming parents. We can assume that parents do the best they can, that all parents try to help nurture their kids." *Id.* at 495.

50 Harris and Fallot, *supra* note 13 at 10.

she possessed that enabled her to survive near-fatal trauma, and it ignored the causes of her trauma, thereby missing the opportunity to provide her and her son what they needed to find enhanced safety, stability, well-being, and healing. As Casey Gwinn explains, the system itself stole Isabel's hope about her future.

The investigator did not seek to understand the transformative trauma that surrounded Isabel or the teenage mother who was steadfast in her commitment to her son and his well-being. The barrage of his questions brought Isabel back to the abuse through flashbacks and triggers. Drilling Isabel for explanations about what had happened in Jason's home, he interpreted Isabel's lack of details and inconsistent sequences as signs that she was not forthcoming or that she had played a role in the violence she endured, rather than that the memories of the trauma were so severe and overpowering that her mind was protecting her. The investigator never asked Isabel about how she had cared for her son, but if he had, he would have realized that Isabel remembered everything that pertained to her son. Her rational brain retained what the pediatrician last said, when Nathan's next immunization was, how well he was napping in the school daycare, how to make him laugh from the depth of his belly, how many diapers she needed to bring each day from home, which snacks she made sure she always had in her purse, and every time she placed Nathan in a room with his grandmother so he would not see his father abuse his mother. The investigator never sought to understand that Isabel's strength was sourced and embodied in her role as a mother, as she was driven to survive the trauma to continue caring for her son so that her son would not be motherless.

The investigation felt like an extension of the abuse as someone else's power stripped Isabel of her own. That evening when the investigator brought Isabel to her parent's home, he turned away from Isabel and spoke only to Isabel's mother and father, revealing information that Isabel was ashamed he shared. His blaming words to Isabel messaged, "Look what you did," and, "What's wrong with you?" rather than, "What have you endured?" and, "Are you okay?" Fear swarmed Isabel as it had with Jason. Still fearing that Jason would find and kill her now that she left, Isabel now also feared losing her son to the system. Like so many of Jason's threats, this fear came true when the investigator prohibited Isabel from being alone with her son. Still constricted by outside forces, Isabel asked that she be allowed to take her son to and from daycare. Without being able to take Nathan to daycare, Isabel would have had to drop out of school months before graduation, jeopardizing the goal that enabled Isabel to wade through the trauma and see to the other side of its grip on her. The investigator's proposed intervention nearly caused Isabel to lose her lifeline to her future.

The investigator conflated his insufficient understanding of the source of trauma—the domestic violence—with a condemnation of Isabel's motherhood, thereby devaluing the only remaining source of Isabel's self-worth. Although Isabel lost much of herself throughout her five-year relationship with Jason, she never lost her confidence that she was a good mother to Nathan. Jason's torture did not strip Isabel of this assurance, but the child welfare intervention did. When she was not allowed to be alone with Nathan and when she later held the letter notifying her that the investigative finding deemed her to be a neglectful mother, for the first time she thought that she must indeed be what Jason told her she was—worthless.

Yet even then, had the investigator asked Isabel what made her the proudest, he would have heard Isabel say, "My son."

Trauma-Informed Child Welfare Practice: Counter and Aspire Higher

In order to manifest the bullion of trauma-informed practice, Roger Fallot and Maxine Harris recommend welfare systems adopt a "universal assumption of inclusion" that treats all people entering the child welfare system as trauma survivors.[51] Consistent with the reality that the majority of the people have had adverse experiences in childhood, viewing everyone in the child welfare system as trauma-survivors decreases exceptionalism, emphasizes commonality, removes stigma, increases respect while reducing bias, and prioritizes the promise that clearing a path for healing is integral to the system's hope of enhancing the safety and well-being of families. Even though child welfare professionals are not delivering direct trauma services like Dr. van de Kolk, at the heart of trauma-informed child welfare practice is the recognition, intention, and dedication that every interaction be an

[51] Harris and Fallot, *supra* note 13 at 9.

opportunity to counter the person's experience of trauma and then to aspire higher. As such, the purpose of understanding the source and impact of trauma is to be able contribute to a present that is antithetical to the person's past. In aspiring higher, it is within the purview of everyone who interacts with trauma survivors to strive to give that person what they need—even if only a small piece—on their journey toward enhanced safety, stability, well-being, and healing. Intrinsic in "counter and aspire higher" practice is the commitment to not being a detriment to the healing process. Trauma-informed child welfare practice at best will provide the support that creates conditions for healing and, at a minimum, will avoid creating additional trauma.

Elemental to being a counterpoint to trauma, child welfare interventions need to support the trauma survivor. Support constitutes the single most powerful protection against being traumatized and the most significant ingredient in finding enhanced safety, stability, well-being, and healing.[52] Support involves making the trauma survivor feel safe, which requires being validated and heard.[53] Then, fostering connection based upon understanding, reciprocity, respect, compassionate honesty, trust, and shared humanity can serve as counterweights to trauma that was isolating, chaotic, and shame-filled. Like the physiological balances necessary in the mind and body, systemic responses must both confront the negative and foster the positive.[54] The willingness to understand a person's experience with trauma and its impact must be accompanied by an exploration of the incredible strengths that they have harnessed throughout their battle with trauma. As Susan Schechter adhered, within struggles, strength exists.[55] It is this strength that must be revived or bolstered in order to find greater safety, stability, well-being, and healing. Rising hope counteracts the power of trauma's impact.[56] Every ACEs score should be followed by a Hope score.[57] Child welfare systems should measure a person's level of hope at the beginning and end of

---

52 van der Kolk, *supra* note 12 at 605.
53 *Id.* at 879.
54 *Id.* at 405.
55 *Id.* at 135.
56 Gwinn and Hellman, *supra* note 2 at 71.
57 Hope scores can rise. *Id.* at 38.

their interventions as a way of taking responsibility for being a conduit of rising hope.

Systems that aim to respond with this balance will mirror externally what those who have experienced trauma need internally. Trauma-informed child welfare interventions strive beyond the important yet limited goals of crisis intervention, risk minimization and stabilization, and aim to return a sense of control and autonomy to the trauma survivor while promoting growth through open collaboration with the trauma survivor.[58] Conscious of the trauma in others and the trauma that systemic involvement can perpetuate, those working within the child welfare system must be cognizant of their own trauma, of secondary or vicarious trauma, and compassion fatigue. Self-care must also be integral to a trauma-informed system. The golden hue of a trauma-informed child welfare intervention would have been a pathway, rather than a barricade, to Isabel and Nathan's enhanced safety, stability, well-being, and healing.

• • •

After receiving the report that a teenager and her son were at risk due to domestic violence, the investigator would have grounded himself in the orientation that the young mother and child he was about to meet had both experienced trauma and were so much more than the trauma they had experienced. Before knocking on that door behind where Isabel stood, the investigator would check himself for his own biases and burdens of past experiences that he might bring to the interactions.

When Isabel opens the door, the investigator would introduce himself and suggest that they find an appropriate place to talk. At Isabel's direction, he would take Isabel to her parents' house. He would ask Isabel privately if she wants to speak with him in the presence of her parents or alone. The structure and the content of their conversation would aim to reduce her fears, foster connection, provide a degree of predictability, and share control. He would ask Isabel where she prefers to sit and whether she needs food or water. He would remain calm and breathe deeply, hoping to set a tone that Isabel could emulate. He would use open body language and make eye contact with

[58] *Id.* at 16–17.

Isabel. He would further explain his role, the role of the child welfare agency, the purpose of a child welfare investigation, the possible actions that might occur during the intervention, and overview the information he would like to learn from Isabel and why. He would be forthcoming that some of his questions might be difficult to answer and that outwardly expressing emotions and not remembering are understandable. He would explain why he is taking notes, offer to read back his notes to Isabel, and provide Isabel with paper and a pen to take notes if she would like. He would actively listen, often summarizing what she says so she would know she has been heard. He would offer Isabel breaks and would alternate his questions between those that could be triggering and those that would restore calm.[59] The investigator would ask open and nonjudgmental questions like the following:

> Tell me what you love about your son.
> What concerns do you have for him or about him?
> Do you feel safe? Why or why not?
> Do you think your son is safe? Why or why not?
> Who do you feel safe around? Who is there to support you? Who can you count on?
> Share with me how you have kept or tried to keep your son safe. What strategies have been effective?
> How has domestic violence impacted you? How has it impacted your son?
> What risks to your safety and well-being do you and your son still face?
> What are your personal goals, hopes, and aspirations?
> What barriers do you face in realizing these aspirations?
> What are some practical steps you can take toward each goal you have?
> What do you think are your greatest strengths?
> What ideas do you have for trying to make sure you and your son stay safe and well?

---

[59] Laurie Leitch, *Action Steps using ACEs and Trauma-Informed Care: A Resilience Model,* HEALTH JUSTICE (2017).

What can I do to help you? What do you think you and your son need?
What makes you the proudest?

Through the empathetic cadence of the questions, Isabel and the investigator would develop a broader understanding of each other and their shared humanity in each of their roles. Through his questions, the investigator would create the opportunity to know Isabel as a caring mother who has faced enormous danger, has prioritized her son's safety and well-being, and who needs further support to provide continued safety and stability for her son. Requiring Isabel to be supervised with her son would be unnecessary for a mother who protected and cared for her son. The investigator may still express ongoing concerns about Isabel and Nathan's safety, yet he would seek Isabel's input about ways to reduce the risk that Jason posed and build upon Isabel and Nathan's strengths. The investigator would explore pathways in which he could support Isabel's goal of graduating high school on time, such as by helping Isabel find a tutor to catch up on her studies. Despite ongoing concerns that her child might be taken, Isabel would view the investigator not as an adversary but as someone who has a mandate to keep children safe *and* has the potential to help her and her son. They could reach these objectives together. Through connection and access to supports, Isabel and Nathan could embark upon their healing journey together.

When the time would come to enter the findings of abuse or neglect, the information gathered would lead the investigator to determine that Isabel is not a neglectful mother (discussed in chapter 6). Yet, if he concluded that a neglect finding was legally required, he would prepare Isabel and explain his reasoning so that when Isabel opens the letter notifying her of the results of the investigation, she would not be filled with a sense of shock and shame that was reminiscent of the abuse she had endured. While the means and ends are both important to Isabel, the means of a trauma-informed intervention that endeavored to counteract the trauma and aspire higher would have avoided or, at least, mitigated the effect of an unwelcomed end.

Isabel's journey toward rebuilding her life was made more difficult by being a survivor of both domestic violence and the child welfare system, yet Isabel has experienced both trauma's transformation and growth in its aftermath.

Each year, the domestic violence agency that helped Isabel construct her hope-filled pathway to healing asks Isabel to speak at their yearly gathering. Balancing empathy with empowerment, the ying of devastation with the yang of growth, the precious equilibrium of mind and body, Isabel spoke:

> *Trauma is not* you. *Domestic violence is not* you. *Yes, we went through times that almost became our demise. But we need to remind ourselves of how we got through it, how brave we are, and how much we have done. Look at how much you have accomplished. You deserve happiness. You are more than anybody says. You are like* gold.

Trauma-informed child welfare interventions mine, rather than bury, Isabel's golden message.

The Second Ingredient of the Aurelian Adhesive: Strength-Based Practice

> You are Wise, Interdependent and your Natural Rights
> are not wrong.
> I know you have Grace, and that your spirit is Strong.
> So I offer you this Feather with Hope that it brings,
> The sky all that closer as you spread your WINGS.
> I know I can fly, fly high or fly low.
> I know I can fly because I was told so.
>
> -Excerpted from *I Can Fly* by Ruby White Starr

A child welfare system that is hopeful about the future of families after the trauma endured from domestic violence will utilize strength-based interventions along the path toward greater safety, stability, well-being, and healing, thereby contributing to the resilience of individuals and families.

Strength-based interventions ultimately aim to foster resilience. Resilience is a belief in the promise of all people's capacity for health and well-being, for optimal outcomes and positive behaviors.[60] Resilience can also be understood as the actions of "accessing internal and external resources during trauma"[61] or a "pattern of successful adaptation despite challenging or threatening circumstances."[62] As resilience researcher Ann Masten found, "Resilience does not come from rare or special qualities, but from everyday magic of ordinary, normative human resources in minds, brains, and bodies of children, in their family and relationships, and in their communities."[63] Both attributional and contextual, resilience is broader than locating a birthright to survival, rather resilience grows in individuals, families, communities, organizations, systems, and culture.[64] As such, resilience is sourced in internal strengths and external protective factors. Therefore, a strength-based intervention both identifies strengths as well as builds protective factors that cultivate resilience.

Strength-based child welfare intervention shifts the paradigm from viewing children and families as at-risk to at-promise. To move from risk to promise, children, families, and communities need both roots to thrive where they grow and to receive feathers as opportunities to experience transformative change. A strength-based child welfare intervention can serve as the golden glue by holding the families' experience with trauma and adversity alongside the families' inner resources of strength, ingenuity, resourcefulness, perseverance, love, and effort and provide support to families in becoming safer and more stable along their journey toward healing and a greater well-being.

A story of resilience, Ruby White Starr grew up in a home surrounded by both severe domestic violence as well as internal and external sources of resilience—strengths and protective factors—that enabled her to survive, find meaning, and grow beyond her trauma.

---

60 Z. Ruby White, *Tapping Innate Resilience in Children*, 7 NCJFCJ Synergy 2 (2003).

61 Anderson, *supra* note 13 at 155.

62 Janice C. Humphreys, *Turnings and Adaptations in Resilient Daughters of Battered Women*, J. of Nursing Scholarship 245 (2001).

63 Ann Masten, *Ordinary Magic: Resilience Process in Development,* 56 Am. Psychol 227 (2001).

64 "Resilience is an inside-out process—an existential process of every child and youth "being and becoming." White, *supra* note 61.

A reflective child who used writing to make sense of her experiences, Ruby has since dedicated her professional career to working with families who have experienced domestic violence. She was a leader in the Greenbook Initiative, has guided projects and systems grounded in the importance of equity, and has launched a federally-funded, national resource center on domestic violence and child welfare to promote, as Ruby describes, "truth-telling as the new innovation."[65] As a young adult, Ruby conceptualized an analogy for understanding sources of her resilience. In her life, she received feathers that became her WINGS—each letter signifying a different feather, an acronym of protective factors. In her professional life through her writings and presentations,[66] Ruby has offered WINGS as both an interpretation of her own experiences and a guide for understanding strength-based interventions in the context of families who have experienced violence, control, or abuse as well as joy, happiness, dedication, and love. The various feathers that contributed to Ruby's wings provide examples of the innumerable sources of protective factors upon which interventions should look and enhance. Some of the storytelling and lessons here are synopsized from Ruby's own words.

---

65 Ruby is the architect and founder of the National Center to Advance Peace for Children, Youth and Families (National Center) that in 2021 became the national resource center focused on improving outcomes for families experiencing domestic violence in the child welfare system. The National Center is a project of Latinos United for Peace and Equity (the national arm of Caminar Latino), the nonprofit that Ruby co-founded and currently serves as its co-CEO. The National Center is part of the Domestic Violence Resource Network that is funded by the U.S. Department of Health and Human Services, Administration for Children and Families, Family and Youth Services Bureau. Through this multimillion dollar federal investment, the National Center will ensure that cases involving children and youth are handled in a manner that recognizes the complex legal, cultural, and psychological dynamics of domestic violence and provides access to the best possible sources of information and tangible assistance to those working in the field of child welfare and custody in the context of domestic violence. The National Center will work in partnership with black and indigenous communities with partners that include Ujima National Center on Domestic Violence in the African American Community, National Indigenous Women's Resource Center, and the Alaska Native Women Resource Center.

66 Ruby White Starr, *Children and Domestic Violence: Moving from "At-Risk" to Resilience,*" Presentation at the Laredo County 19th Annual Domestic Violence Coalition Annual Domestic Violence Task Force (October 1, 2015).

Feathers for WINGS

As a little girl, Ruby believed she was a small bird trapped in a box. Sometimes she felt safe, sheltered, and protected. Other times she felt caged and full of fear.

Ruby, her parents, and her siblings lived in a home in a town bordering Mexico. In that home, Ruby and her siblings repeatedly saw their father cause their mother to scream and bleed, run through the house, fall from pushes and punches, lay unconscious on the floor, turn blue in the face, and return from the hospital. Sometimes the children would try to intervene like when five-year-old Ruben climbed on his father's back as he was strangling their mother, and sometimes upon their mother's instruction, they would seek refuge behind their closed bedroom doors.

One particular afternoon, Ruby's father was watching television when Ruby interrupted him to report that her siblings called her "caca." Her father called all of his children into the living room, took off his belt, and whipped each one. He calmly put the belt back on and resumed watching his show. The cause of her sibling's pain, Ruby learned that using her voice had dangerous consequences. Within this power of silence, her father began sexually molesting her, which continued throughout her childhood and into her early adulthood, regularly at times and sporadically at others.

Ruby was resolute to free herself from her parents' home as soon as she could. Infused with her mother's tenacity, work ethic, and drive, Ruby entered and won beauty pageants and used that money to pay for college. While Ruby was in college, her brother, Ruben, at age fourteen was labeled incorrigible, made a ward of the court, and sent to a juvenile detention facility due to marijuana and petty theft offenses. After two years in the juvenile delinquency system, Ruben was released. Something had changed; something was missing; Ruben had faded. Ruben turned to drugs, and days before entering a drug rehabilitation program, Ruby's beloved brother was murdered over a twenty-dollar drug debt.

At twenty-one years old, Ruby reflected on how her path and her brother's fate were so divergent. Most overtly, Ruben experienced significant systems involvement while Ruby's was minimal. More subtly, Ruby reflected on the parts of her life that had given her hope, bolstered her strength, and enabled her to soar out of the box like the quetzal bird that, according to her cultural tradition, would die if held captive. Ruby recognized the multiple providers of feathers in her own life that helped her construct her wings. Despite a high ACEs score, the feathers that she collected had told her that she was not broken and de-venomized the hardships she experienced. The feathers showed Ruby that she was not defined by the trauma she endured but was capable of overcoming and achieving her goals. All along the way from a home filled with violence to a life committed to peace, Ruby believed she could fly because she collected messages on feathers that told her she was *wise and interdependent and had natural rights, grace, and strength, giving Ruby her* WINGS.

Ruben gave Ruby the feather of *wisdom* through the letters he wrote while in juvenile detention. By experiencing the opposite there, Ruben wisely imparted that resilience can be found in one's roots—both who one is and from where one comes, including home, family, and culture. Feathers should reinforce the value of these roots, but for Ruben, the messages he received told him that there was something wrong with both him and from where he came. Keeping him away unnecessarily to "fix" something unidentifiable decimated the importance of his connections and belief in his own potential and robbed Ruby's brother of sources of feathers in his own community and culture. The fatal consequences of denying Ruben his roots demonstrated the wisdom of identifying strength and value in each person's sense of self and connections.

Social supports gave Ruby the feather of *interdependence*. A friend in school always pointed out that which Ruby had to offer. Ruby's friend cared about her, listened to her, and believed her, thereby moderating the impact of the violence Ruby experienced at home. When she read an essay that Ruby had written, she encouraged Ruby to write for the high school newspaper. Her friend declared, "Ruby, one day you will grow up to do great things," and Ruby believed her. Through these words, Ruby developed pride in herself and saw her strength in connection to others.

A teacher gave Ruby the feather of *grace* by seeing promise rather than risk and illuminating the pathway to reaching potential. Her teacher demonstrated grace by seeing beyond the defiant, insolent, apathetic student with red, bloodshot eyes who rarely attended her class. Recognizing Ruby's gift for storytelling, her teacher enticed

Ruby to join the speech team. Ruby went on to win awards and was motivated to go to college to pursue this talent that she had not before perceived in herself. Grace became the touch of truth that enabled Ruby to see the world differently and believe in her ability to change it. The lens of grace looks beyond the surface, questions assumptions, and posits creative and compassionate alternatives.

Ruby received the feather that confirmed her *natural right* to live free from violence. Ruby dated a man who was abusive. No one knew of the abuse until her boyfriend's roommate and his girlfriend returned to the apartment while Ruby's boyfriend was hitting and yelling at her. Without hesitating, the friend shuffled the boyfriend out of the room, removing him rather than making Ruby leave, and the girlfriend remained with Ruby. Their words and actions showed Ruby that she had a right to be free from abuse with no explanation required, that what happened to her was not her fault, and that change was her boyfriend's responsibility to make. Ruby began believing in her *natural right* to safety, respect, support, nonjudgment, dignity, love, and happiness—the humanity that she unequivocally deserved.

Ruby received the feather of *strength* when she spoke her truth to her father. Five years after her father stopped sexually abusing her, Ruby found the strength to confront her father about the instances of abuse in her memory. Even if her father was not ready to be wholly accountable to her in that conversation, Ruby recognized the power of her truth and committed to never surrendering her voice again. Her voice became the catalyst for her future work. Over time, her father has taken responsibility for the violence and trauma he created in their family and now encourages Ruby to share their story. With strength and a sense of purpose, Ruby not only survived but transformed and transcended adversity. Ruby's strength has strengthened others, as her father now carries a feather of being forgiven and her own children do not go to sleep to the lullaby of screams—a cycle of abuse interrupted.

Feathers in the Child Welfare System

To ascribe to the promise of strength-based practice, the child welfare system must adhere to the premise that the strength and the capacity for resilience exist in every person, regardless of circumstances or degree of risk and without predetermining who is resilient and who is not.[67] A system focused on only risk and safety without attempting to build hope and resilience will continue to fall short of meeting the needs of families. The feathers Ruby received are replicable in and accessible protective factors that child welfare interventions can foster.

Practice that responds to risk through a lens of potential, rather than deficit, can foster protective factors, especially by, again, treating every interaction as an intervention. First, by expecting to find strengths, interventions send messages about potential, like the *interdependence* Ruby received from her friend. Second, by preserving and supporting caring and supportive relationships, interventions can value and preserve roots of family and community connection, like the *wisdom* Ruby gained from Ruben's letters and the message about *natural rights* shared by her abusive boyfriend's friends. Third, by providing meaningful opportunities for partnership and participation, interventions can find and provide the support that becomes pathways to reaching goals, like the *grace* given to Ruby by her teacher and the *strength* Ruby found within.[68] Instead of traumatizing the traumatized, hurting the hurt, and disempowering the disempowered, child welfare interventions infused with gold will both respond to risk and develop resources within individuals, families, and communities by being and locating feathers.[69] It is the responsibility of the child welfare system to foster these protective factors rather than merely (yet importantly) identify strengths.

Feathers come from countless places, resonate differently in each person, and are culturally nuanced. Feathers exist in strong schools with committed teachers and extracurricular activities; in physicians who treat the whole person; in available mental health clinics and substance abuse treatment; in law enforcement officers who partner with civilians; in low-barrier safe and affordable housing; in a culture that does not tolerate racism, xenophobia, or homophobia; in viable employment opportunities; in access to healthy food, transportation, and child care; in religious institutions that unite its members in peace

---

[67] Kathy M. Marshall, Resilience Research and Practice, Educational Resiliency: Student, Teacher and School Perspectives (2004).

[68] *Id.* at 69.

[69] *Id.* at 66.

and acceptance; in the presence of nature, parks, and playgrounds; in social service agencies that provide a range of supportive services and recognize those who they are not reaching; in multiple access points and pathways for those who use coercive control and violence to develop accountability; and in coordinated systems that are oriented and primed to build upon the strengths of those within its reach. The child welfare system has an obligation to work collaboratively to create community conditions that produce feathers, creatively access feathers where they exist, and contribute to the wings of those they grasp, thereby leading to transformative change that families and communities deserve and need—the essence of the golden joinery.

The Third Ingredient Along the Kintsugi Pathway of Restoration and Growth: Family-Centered Practice

Molly McGrath Tierney's mantra that all families matter is at the heart of family-centered child welfare interventions. Translating words into actions sources strength within families and locates the least intrusive ways to meet the needs of the family. To do this, a family-centered approach must commit to engaging with all members of the family in order to meet the needs of the individual and the collective. When families experiencing domestic violence come to the attention of the child welfare system, child welfare workers often struggle to engage effectively or at all with each member of the family—the adult survivor, the child survivor, and particularly the person who uses coercive control and violence. If the child welfare system traditionally struggles to center a child with his mother who was abused herself, like Nathan and Isabel, the system struggles even harder to center children with a parent who uses violence and coercive control. Yet, family-centered practice cannot ignore any member of the family. Central to the goal of engaging with the person who causes harm as elemental to family-centered practice is the goal of fostering accountability that will enhance the family's safety, stability, well-being, and healing, consistent with the key tenets of The Greenbook. Because each member makes up the vessel—the family—receiving the gold-inflected glue, the challenging work of engaging with people who use coercive control and violence must be an integral aspect of child welfare interventions.

Pupae in a Chrysalis

In a converted house up a crooked staircase is a room filled with men of all ages, races, motivations, and persuasions sitting in a circle surrounded by walls covered in reminders and guidance.

> It is easier to build strong children than to repair broken men.
>
> —*Frederick Douglass*

> Responsibility without choice is torment. . . .Choice without responsibility is greed.
>
> —*Leland Beaumont*[70]

> We delight in the beauty of the butterfly, but rarely admit the changes it has gone through to achieve that beauty.
>
> -*Maya Angelou*

Darrell Jackson finds his seat, a place with which he is quite familiar. He removes his heavy coat; his work boots steady on the floor grounding him in his space. Tonight, his eyes again settle on the quotations on the wall, words he has read many times before. With the wisdom around him resonating, Darrell feels both responsible and tormented. Darrell's son, Elias, has been in foster care since he was two months old. Nearly four years have passed, and Darrell is participating in a batterer intervention program for the second time as part of his child welfare service plan, the roadmap of services he must complete for his son to return home. Darrell's visits are still supervised with his son who is in a pre-adoptive placement with a foster father who is committed to keeping Elias. Darrell is beleaguered by the possibility that he will lose his parental rights to his son despite the changes and growth he is committed to maintaining. Darrell now understands how unhealed trauma and shame brought him here and

[70] Leland Beaumont, *Responsibility: My Role,* Emotional Competency (March 31, 2019), http://www.emotionalcompetency.com/responsibility.htm.

envisions how healing and new learnings can carry his son and him forward together.

Darrell was born shortly after his parents moved north from Tennessee seeking job opportunities and safety that did not exist in the segregated south for an African American family. Darrell's father came home from the Vietnam War as a man who grabbed that which he desired, leaving a stain of betrayal on Darrell's mother and an impression of unchecked manhood on his son. Bobby Trap, a twenty-eight-year-old man, also left his stain on Darrell when he was only six years old. Playing outside with other children on their street, Darrell found a hiding spot by the window of the neighboring house. Bobby saw Darrell crouched down with no other children around and offered him chocolate-covered raisins if he came in through the window. Enticed by the candy, Darrell climbed through the window and found himself alone in Bobby's bedroom. Bobby undid his pants, put his hands on stunned Darrell's buttocks, and tried to penetrate Darrell's mouth. On two other occasions, Bobby tried to grab Darrell, who got away each time. As a six-year-old, Darrell knew that what Bobby tried to do was wrong and it made him feel wrong too for whatever part he had in the wrongness. Over the years, the sense of wrongness maintained the secret, morphed into self-disgrace, and then shame that festered into frustration, resentment, anger, and abuse.

Filled with shame and its progeny, Darrell entered high school armed with the shared legacy of these two influential examples that men are entitled to do as they please without regard for the bounds of morality or law. Due to convictions from stealing candy to burglarizing a police officer's house to selling stolen luxury goods, Darrell would spend thirty years in and out of prison six times. During one of his incarcerations, Darrell wrote a letter to Bobby Trap. In the letter, Darrell wrote, "What you did to me has haunted me my entire life. I have always felt dirty and ashamed. Why did you hurt a child?" Bobby replied in a letter, "I did that to you because it was done to me."

Between times in prison, Darrell would father eight children, three of whom were born the same year. Darrell left prison for the last time when he was nearly fifty years old. When Darrell's ninth child, Dominic, was born something in Darrell changed. He recognized his son's birth as a reason to change course in order to remain an uninterrupted part of his son's childhood. Darrell and Dominic's mother married. Disagreements about the African food his wife cooked or the clothes she left on the floor now ended with pushes, shoves, and hair-pulling until the police were called. They divorced with an Order of Protection against Darrell in place.

While looking for work at a job center, Darrell met Leticia, thirty years his junior who was living at a women's shelter nearby. Leticia moved in with Darrell and became pregnant. As his father had, Darrell felt entitled to call Leticia names, lock her out of the house if she stayed out late, and forbid her from wearing clothes he bought her outside of his presence. When their son Elias was born, they went to the county public aid department which was housed in the same building as the child welfare office to apply for Women, Infants, and Children (WIC) benefits. As the caseworker processed Leticia's application, she discovered that Leticia's name was flagged because her two older children were in foster care. As Elias was screened and weighed, a child welfare investigator was called. The child welfare investigator told Darrell and Leticia that she deemed Elias to be at "imminent risk of harm" due to Leticia's open child welfare cases and the past history of domestic violence evidenced by the Order of Protection against Darrell. Darrell became enraged and yelled, "My baby ain't going anywhere." The investigator called the police and Elias was removed from his parents.

In court, Darrell and Leticia were appointed separate attorneys and a *guardian ad litem* was appointed to represent Elias. The juvenile court case progressed past the temporary custody hearing and both parents stipulated to the grounds for adjudicating Elias abused or neglected in order to move the case along more quickly. At the disposition hearing, Darrell was deemed to be "unfit, unwilling, or unable" to parent, and Elias was made a ward of the court. The judge set the permanency goal of reunification. In order to establish his fitness as a parent, Darrell was required to participate and make progress in his services, including parenting classes, parenting assessment, a psychological evaluation, random drug and alcohol tests, and a batterer intervention program. Darrell was committed to regaining custody of his son and steadfastly completed the services required in his service plan. The progress the system required of him was predicated on becoming accountable for the choices he had made in his relationships and as a father.

The Reparative Framework of Accountability

The response to people like Darrell has often been filled with anger and fear that mirrors the historical construction of ignoring (e.g., Freud) or demonizing (e.g., the child savers) causes of violence and struggle. Knowing instead that empathy supports growth, activist and author who went by the pen name of bell hooks, captures the family-centered task of child welfare interventions in a question she posed to writer and poet Maya Angelou, "How do we hold people accountable for wrongdoing and yet at the same time remain in touch with their humanity enough to believe in their capacity to be transformed?"[71] Like the opposing biological responses that need to find their balance following trauma and the necessary paradigm shift from at-risk to at-promise, family-centered child welfare practice cultivates conditions for change, providing a pupae in a chrysalis[72] that which is needed to emerge transformed. In infusing with gold, the child welfare system must aim to cultivate restorative accountability in order to provide men and fathers like Darrell the pathway toward transformation—the healing of themselves, their relationships, and their communities.

By working with men like Darrell for over three decades, Juan Carlos Areán has dedicated his career to developing the practice in answer to bell hook's question. In order to define how the chrysalis could be transformative, Juan Carlos first had to understand the experiences and needs of the pupae. In the men's groups that he led for years, Juan Carlos listened as men disclosed, often for the first time, past trauma they had experienced. These disclosures, that occurred for the first time in adulthood, revealed the long-lasting impact of trauma along with the shame that swells from secreting one's own truth. Many of the men in Juan Carlos' groups were further united in their experience of past undisclosed trauma that was unhealed. As

---

71 Melvin McLeod, *"There's No Place to Go But Up"—bell hooks and Maya Angelou in conversation,* LION'S ROAR,: BUDDHIST WISDOM FOR OUR TIME (Jan. 1, 1998), https://www.lionsroar.com/theres-no-place-to-go-but-up.

72 *Id.*

Juan Carlos observed, replicating pain onto others often originates from a place of unhealed trauma.[73]

Likewise, Bobby's admission of past trauma and Darrell's experience of trauma are not unique among those who harm others.[74] The majority of people who harm others were abused or witnessed abuse as children.[75] Significantly though, only 30 percent of children who were abused or witnessed abuse will abuse others, leaving 70 percent of children who will not grow up to harm others.[76] The divergence of these two paths, Juan Carlos determined, is caused by healed or unhealed trauma and unlearning socialized and harmful behaviors. Unhealed trauma generates the shame that is a precondition for violence. Men are socialized to be entitled to violence and control and are taught how to treat others by how they are both treated and by how others are treated in their presence. Juan Carlos concluded that healing and education are necessary to stem the perpetuation of harm.[77]

Juan Carlos then composed a pathway of accountability for men who misused their power and caused harm through violence and coercive control. Accountability is an inward and outward process of change that involves stopping or reducing violence and coercion and adopting healthy behaviors. Accountability, like the goal-setting in the science of hope, cannot be imposed from outside but rather is developed from within along with pathways that the outside interveners and supporters can help provide. Accountability involves self-examination, taking responsibility for violence in all its forms, acknowledging the impact of harmful conduct, accepting the

---

[73] *Id.*

[74] Repeated studies reveal a 60 to 70% correlation between men who abuse their partners and their past experiences of domestic violence as a child, and that one in five boys who are sexually abused will sexually abuse other children as adults. Lori L. Heise, *Violence Against Women, An Integrated, Ecological Framework*, 4 Violence Against Women 262, 268 (1998).

[75] Lori L. Heise, *Violence Against Women, An Integrated, Ecological Framework*, 4 Violence Against Women 262, 267-68 (1998); *See, The Increased Importance of the Violence Against Women Act in A Time of Economic Crisis: Hearing Before the Comm. On the Senate Judiciary,* 111th Cong. 2 (May 5, 2010) (statement of Sen. Al Franken and Dr. Richard Gelles).

[76] *Id.* at 267–8.

[77] *Id.* at 150.

consequences of violence and coercive control, and making significant changes in belief systems and behaviors based upon nonviolence and respect for all.[78] Accountability does not require punishment, and punishment often falls short of producing genuine and sustainable accountability. Instead, Juan Carlos and his colleagues developed the Reparative Framework as a philosophy and framework for people who use violence and coercive control to cultivate accountability.[79] The Reparative Framework is grounded in the following observations of working with people who cause harm: many of the men hold unhealed trauma; men must be treated with respect, dignity, and humanity if they are going to learn to treat others accordingly; and the safety of survivors must drive the path toward accountability. Based upon these truths, the Reparative Framework balances the principles of acceptance and growth, support and consequences, boundaries and connection, and healing and repair.[80] The Reparative Framework involves the three R's—renunciation, responsibility, and reparation. Intrinsic to the Reparative Framework is healing from past trauma and education about how to change harmful behaviors and choices.

By providing opportunities for healing as well as education, batterer intervention programs have become a channel for cultivating the possibility of change. Many batterer intervention programs began in partnership with battered women's advocates and organizations in the 1970s and have continued to grow in response to court-mandated services for men who use violence.[81] Expanding

---

78 Brenda Hill, *Domestic Violence Awareness: Action for Social Change, An Open-Ended Discussion of Some Terms Used,* Domestic Violence Awareness Project, National Resource Center on Domestic Violence, Pennsylvania Coalition Against Domestic Violence (2005), https://vawnet.org/sites/default/files/materials/files/2016-07/ActionForSocialChange.pdf.

79 Juan Carlos Areán developed the Reparative Framework in partnership with Future Without Violence. Interview with Juan Carlos Areán (Jan. 4 2019).

80 The Reparative Framework stirred controversy among those who believed punishment was the only path toward accountability, rather than recognizing the efficacy of healing and repair. *Id.*

81 Bernard Auchter & Juan Carlos Areán, *Batterer Intervention: Doing the Work and Measuring the Progress, A Report on the December 2009 Experts Roundtable,* National Institute on Justice, Family Violence Prevention Fund (2010), 2, https://www.futureswithoutviolence.org/batterer-intervention-doing-the

upon its consciousness-raising and then criminal justice origins, between 1,500 and 2,500 programs, like Juan Carlos has led, exist around the world.[82] Most programs are small group, psycho-education treatment approaches, ranging in length from twenty-four to fifty-two weeks.[83] Regardless of whether men are mandated to attend or participate voluntarily, people who cause harm need to find an incentive to change. Like Darrell, fatherhood is often an effective motivation for developing accountability. Many participants see themselves as good fathers or want to be good fathers and are more likely to renounce violence because of its impact on their children, rather than out of empathy for their partners. Batterer intervention programs and fatherhood after-care programs demonstrate that meaningful engagement with men who cause harm and are involved in the child welfare system can begin around their roles as fathers.[84]

-work-and-measuring-the-progress-a-report-on-the-december-2009-experts-roundtable/.

[82] *Id.* at 5.

[83] Jeffrey L. Edleson, *Groupwork with Men Who Batter: What the Research Literature Indicates,* VAWNET NATIONAL ONLINE RESOURCE CENTER ON VIOLENCE AGAINST WOMEN, (2012), https://vawnet.org/material/groupwork-men-who-batter-what-research-literature-indicates.

[84] "Fathering After Violence" is an initiative to help end violence against women by motivating men to renounce their abuse and become better fathers (or father figures) and more supportive parenting partners using fatherhood as the leading approach. Juan Carlos Areán, *Fathering After Violence: Working with Abusive Fathers in Supervised Visitation,* FAMILY VIOLENCE PREVENTION FUND (2007), https://www.futureswithoutviolence.org/userfiles/file/Children_and_Families/fathering_after_violence.pdf. "Caring Dads" is a program developed by the University of Toronto Ontario Institute for Studies in Education, for men in a fathering role who have physically abused, emotionally abused, or neglected their children, or exposed their children to domestic violence or who are deemed to be at high-risk for these behaviors. Scott Research Lab, *Caring Dads*, UNIV. OF TORONTO ONTARIO INST. FOR STUDIES IN EDUC. https://wordpress.oise.utoronto.ca/scottlab/caring-dads-2/ (last visited Dec. 9, 2018). "Strong Fathers," developed by the North Carolina State University, was designed with the goal to enhance safety and well-being for victims and survivors of domestic violence and their children. Joan Pennell, *Strong Fathers Evaluative Findings,* NC State University, Center for Family and Community Engagement 1 (June 2013),https://cdn.chass.ncsu.edu/sites/cfface.chass.ncsu.edu/documents/Strong_Fathers_Evaluation_Findings.June_2013_w_format.pdf.

The impact of batterer intervention programs has been extensively researched, and although not a panacea,[85] the programs have been established as an effective method for fostering accountability in ways that enhance the safety and well-being of adult and child survivors of domestic violence.[86] A review of over forty studies revealed that 40 to 80 percent of former or current female partners report that program completers were nonviolent at the end of a six month to one year period.[87] Another study found that following completion, the majority of men reached sustained nonviolence, and around two-thirds of partners reported that their quality of life improved and 85 percent felt safer.[88] About 20 percent of participants continued re-assaulting.[89] Expanding the measure of effectiveness to capture violence and coercive control as well as safety and well-being indicators that partners identified as important to them, a study found that women used the words more thoughtful, supportive, respectful, and calm to describe the changes in their partner after completing the program.[90] Women expressed being able to enter the house without being scared, make a mistake without fear, enjoy less restricted freedom of movement, experience increased socialization with friends and family, feel less tension, and endure decreased harassment—all of which contributed to an increased feeling of safety and enhanced well-being.[91] A follow up study established that 71 percent of adult survivors felt little to no safety when their partner started the program but at the twelve-month marker, 81 percent of the partners felt

---

85 The self-described process of change that occurs can be understood as "as a series of sparks, different for each man," a nonlinear progression that takes time. Liz Kelly & Nicole Westmarland, *Domestic Violence Perpetrator Programmes, Steps Towards Change, Project Mirabal Final Report,* Durham University (Jan. 2015), http://repository.londonmet.ac.uk/1458/1/ProjectMirabalfinalreport.pdf (hereinafter Mirabel Study) (hereinafter "Mirabel").

86 Auchter and Areán, *supra* note 82, at 2.

87 Edward W. Gondolf, *Evaluating Batterer Counseling Programs: A Difficult Task Showing Some Effects and Implications,* 9 Aggression and Violence Behavior. 605, 606 (2004).

88 *Id.* at 605, 617.

89 *Id.*

90 Nicole Westmarland, et al., *Domestic Violence Perpetrator Programmes, What Counts As Success?,* Durham University (Aug. 2010), http://dro.dur.ac.uk/11515/1/11515.pdf?DDD34+dss4ae.

91 *Id.* at 4–6.

somewhat safe or very safe.[92] Also important to them, many of the adult survivors reported that the following occurred:[93]

1. An improved relationship underpinned by respect and effective communication;[94]
2. Expanded "space for action" for women that restored their voice and ability to make choices;[95]
3. More safety and freedom from violence and abuse for women and children;[96]
4. Safer, positive, and shared parenting;[97]
5. Enhanced understanding of the impact of domestic violence on their partner and children;[98] and
6. Safer and healthier childhoods in which children feel cared about and heard.[99]

The findings confirm that ending violence is often not enough for some women and children to feel at ease and restoring the freedom that living with coercive control steals requires more.[100] Interventions, therefore, should focus on acknowledging harm and accepting responsibility for using violence, while simultaneously focusing on the reality that men who use violence have choices even in the presence of stress, unhealed past or present trauma, and exacerbating circumstances. Yet, as Jeffrey Edleson cautioned, "Many question efforts to treat a society-level problem only through individual-level responses."[101] Rather than operating in a vacuum, the effectiveness

---

92 *Mirabel,* supra note 86.

93 Westmarland, *supra* note 91, at 5.

94 *Id.* at 11.

95 *Id.* at 15.

96 *Id.* at 18, 19. Physical and sexual violence significantly decreased. For instance, from the baseline surveys to the surveys twelve months later, 61% had been injured, down 2%, 87% had been slapped or pushed, down to 7%, 94% had partners who punched or kicked walks, or smashed property, down to 23%, and no one was made to do something sexual against her will or was victimized with a weapon. *Id.* at 18, 19. Emotional abuse declined by 40 to 50%. *Id.* at 19.

97 *Id.* at 23.

98 *Id.* at 25, 26.

99 *Id.* at 7, 30.

100 *Id.* at 46.

101 Edleson, *supra n*ote 84, at 8.

of batterer intervention programs increase if programs exist in connection with community and systems, including the child welfare system, that reinforce the importance of both connection and accountability,[102] thereby strengthening the pathways for behavior change and healing—the chrysalis around the pupae.[103]

• • •

Darrell has been attending a batterer intervention program that is grounded in the Reparative Framework. The Intervention Program of Domestic Abuse and Violence (IPDAV) is part of a domestic violence agency that also serves the needs of victims of domestic violence and their children. The IPDAV is a state-certified twenty-six-week program for men; a separate battering intervention program runs for women. The goals of IPDAV are to help participants understand unhealthy (controlling, abusive, and violent) behaviors that are used in relationships, to assist participants in replacing these unhealthy behaviors with new healthy, learned behaviors, and to foster healing from past traumas to create a new future. As such, the outcomes of the program aim to reduce violence and abuse and increase safety and other markers of well-being for participants, their families, relationships, and communities.

To achieve these goals, the program utilizes a circular curriculum with threads of education, skill-building, and healing woven throughout the lessons. Regardless of whether volition or mandate initiates participant attendance, the IPDAV staff determines if the person is eligible for the program based upon a psychosocial evaluation to determine whether other issues, such as mental illness or substances abuse, are co-occurring, and considers the level of violence and control they perpetrate. If such co-occurrence is present, the staff will make referrals for those services prior to being able to enroll in

[102] As a Blue Shield Foundation study significantly found, "Evidence alarmingly suggests that this punitive approach may actually do more harm than good for some victims." *Breaking the Cycle: A Life Course Framework for Preventing Domestic Violence,* Blue Shield of California Foundation 25 (Feb. 2019), https://blueshieldcafoundation.org/sites/default/files/publications/downloadable/BreakingtheCycleLifeCourseFramework.pdf.

[103] McLeod, *supra* note 72.

the IPDAV; changing beliefs and behavior cannot sustainably occur under the grip of mental illness or the cloud of substance abuse.

Within the circular curriculum, veteran participants act as mentors to newcomers, and newcomers are able to benefit from the growth of the more seasoned participants. Every session begins with an accountability statement and a check-in about the past week. During a newcomer's first week, a likely accountability statement is, "I am here because my caseworker told me I have to attend." As the men learn from each other, the lessons and the IPDAV counselors, accountability statements often become, "I am here because I have used violence and control in ways that have hurt the ones I love."

Darrell has participated in nearly two years of the IPDAV, including after-care sessions with his counselor. When Darrell first started, he attended, not because he wanted to, but because he was required to do so. He viewed his participation in the program as a means to the end of demonstrating compliance. His motivation to attend was to get one step closer to reunifying with his son. Slowly, Darrell developed a rapport with the program counselors and the other men, and gradually he became receptive to the content and spirit of the program. His motivation to engage was now rooted in his desire to be an active and strong father to his son. He listened. He heard the message that everyone has value, deserves to be respected, and treated with dignity, including those sitting around this circle. He learned. Darrell became educated about domestic violence. He can describe the domestic violence Power and Control Wheel. He understands that abuse is not limited to physical violence but rather words, threats, and controlling actions constitute the unjustifiable treatment of others and also qualify as domestic violence.

During the weekly meetings, Darrell heard from others about their experiences of trauma, and he began to feel safe to share his truth. For the first time, he revealed that he was molested as a child. By constructing the narrative of this trauma, Darrell began to understand how this experience influenced the choices he has made. He now recognizes how his shame caused pain to beget pain. The molestation robbed Darrell of self-respect. He could not give what he did not have. Without self-respect, he could not respect others. Soon the shame began to lift as he sat with other men. As the shame dissipated, Darrell realized that he could meaningfully connect with others despite his experiences and that the trauma did not define him nor should it control his existence.

Darrell has committed to his changed behavior. Darrell *renounces* the use of violence and control over others. Darrell now identifies that the core values and beliefs upon which he placed importance—respect, family—did not align with his actions. He has developed a deeper commitment to the importance of consent in all intimate relationships in all aspects. His worldview has shifted from believing in a man's entitlement to plunder to believing that no man or woman should control the other. He developed a personal philosophy that the way a person responds to obstacles is the measure of the quality of the person. Recognizing that he was acting incongruently with this value, Darrell acknowledged that his choices harmed his children and those around him. Darrell's counselor and the other men helped Darrell accept *responsibility* for the harm he caused while encouraging Darrell to believe in his ability to translate his renunciation of violence and coercion into action by replacing aggression and control with other behaviors he learned and skills he now has. After healing himself, Darrell focused on *repairing* his relationships. He is dedicated to being a good father and fatherhood continues to be the spring of his motivation. To Darrell, a good father smiles at his children, demonstrates affection, loves them, openly communicates, fosters trust, feels gratitude, and offers support. Fathers and sons should laugh and cry together. Nothing brings Darrell greater joy than the rare afternoons when Elias can join a supervised visit with his father and half-brother, Dominic. Darrell believes that people can change, and he believes in his own change. Darrell identifies as an accountable man; the schisms that once were are now filled with the universal Golden Rule of doing unto others as they would have done unto themselves.

Yet, the Leland Beaumont quote continues to capture Darrell's attention. He has met his responsibility to be a sound father, but he is not being given the opportunity to fulfill his responsibility to parent his son.

Darrell's house is ready for Elias' return. When the caseworker pulls up to Darrell's house for a visit, Elias shouts, "That's my daddy's house." When Darrell opens the door, Elias hugs him and exclaims, "That's my daddy." Darrell has expressed his willingness to allow the foster father to maintain a relationship with Elias after he is returned home. Darrell told him, "I would not deny you, so please do not deny me my son."

Every time Darrell comes close to crossing the finish line of reunifying with Elias, the race is extended, and the finish line is quickly moved. After graduating from the first batterer intervention program, he was required to do it again. Despite the indicators of progress detailed in his counselor's court reports that demonstrate his accountability, Darrell sensed that the court wanted his counselor to offer her professional opinion that Darrell will not be abusive again, a guarantee that is well beyond the bounds of her professional responsibility. Increased day visits were delayed, inevitably prolonging the sequential start of unsupervised visits, which is one of the required milestones before reunification. Despite maintaining his job managing apartments, visiting with Elias, attending the IPDAV, and preserving his spotless house, the caseworker ordered a lengthy parenting capacity assessment to determine if Darrell's age would interfere with his parenting abilities. The longer Elias is in a stable foster care placement, the harder it will be to establish that it is in his best interest to return to his father. But time here has been two-faced—time favors maintaining the status quo yet time has also demonstrated that Darrell's accountability is sustainable.

In a letter Darrell wrote to the judge, his emotionally laden words, read,

> I have completed every service . . . My accomplishments, me being compliant with the court, and how well I interact with my son should be the only concerns the court has. So I ask the court, if your child was taken and kept from you because of prejudice and bias, would you be happy or hurt? I have no reason to smile or rejoice until my son is returned to my home.

Nearly four years after entering foster care, the child welfare agency began transitioning Elias to his father's home. Darrell has centered himself on being accountable internally and externally, and now the child welfare system is finally being accountable to Darrell and Elias by centering Darrell as his son's family. As Elias' primary caregiver for the first time, the challenges that Darrell may face should not be viewed as detriments or a poor prognosis of permanence. Rather, challenges should be expected, and supports should be in place to help Darrell face the daily joys and struggles that a parent faces. While the end of the intervention moves toward reinstating a family, family-centered child welfare interventions should question whether there were less destructive means of engaging with Darrel and his family to provide them the support needed to find the enhanced safety, stability, well-being, and healing that ultimately occurred.

The Fourth Ingredient Lacing the Golden Seams: Equity-Focused Practice

Inequitable child welfare interventions, like those that Isabel and Darrell experienced, not only obstruct safety, stability, well-being, and healing but also continue the legacy of child welfare systems as arms of state-sanctioned oppression. The child welfare interventions that Isabel and Darrell experienced were inequitable because they did not meet the needs of their families and existed within a system in which statuses of race, gender, and class both implicitly and structurally influenced the response to children and parents.

Equity colloquially encompasses notions of fairness and justice. Yet because "the notions and norms of what 'just is' isn't always justice,"[104] equity focuses on providing unique support based upon the specific needs of individuals, families, or communities. Equity acknowledges the unequal starting places of individuals and families, often caused by marginalization, discrimination, and oppression.[105] Equity meets individuals where they are rather than delivering the same interventions to everyone.[106] Trauma-informed, strength-based,

---

[104] Amanda Gorman, *The Hill We Climb,* Performance at the U.S. Inauguration of President Joseph Biden and Vice-President Kamala Harris (January 20, 2021).

[105] Shadi Houshyar, Alexandra Citrin, Senior Policy Fellows, Center for the Study of Social Policy, Equity and Disproportionality Training to the Management and Implementation Teams of the Illinois Research and Capacity Building Project of the Quality Improvement Center on Domestic Violence in Child Welfare (March 16, 2021).

[106] Equity and equality are different. For instance, if everyone has a need to ride a bike, equality provides the same bike to everyone regardless of a person's height and ability to ride; some bikes will be too big, and some will be too small so some people will not be able to ride. Equity provides a unique bike to each person so that they can actually ride; some bikes will be bigger, some smaller, and others will

and family-centered interventions are necessary, although not sufficient, elements of equitable interventions that meet the needs of enhanced safety, stability, well-being, and healing for families experiencing domestic violence. An equitable child welfare intervention concretely supports the whole family and meets the shared and individual needs of children and parents.

Yet more is needed for child welfare systems to be equitable. Especially when domestic violence is present, equity must also have a lens of race, gender, and class. Separating Darrell from his son should not be predetermined because they are Black. Indicating Isabel for neglect should not be influenced by her status as an undocumented teenage mother. Neither family should be dismantled because they are poor. The preceding three statements likely appear self-evident, but history and practice reveal that structural discrimination, fueled by white privilege and implicit and explicit bias and entrenched in the child welfare,[107] has normalized and legitimized cumulative and chronic adverse outcomes for families of color, women, and people living in poverty.[108]

In dedicating her career to the field of violence against women, Ruby White Starr has worked across the country to address and improve equity in social services, government agencies, and systems. In addressing equity directly, Ruby instructively guides:

---

be adaptive. In the child welfare system, an equality-driven intervention would provide a parenting class to every parent. Equitable interventions instead would ask the parents what their families need and accordingly would provide concrete supports such as transportation to work and day care assistance to one family, and to another family, access rent subsidy, make referrals to domestic violence counseling, and facilitate a connection with the local Boys and Girls Club chapter. Equitable interventions often require support and resources beyond the child welfare system itself.

[107] *See* examples, White Supremacy Iceberg, https://www.wearebeloved.org/blog/2020/5/29/white-supremacy-amp-anti-blackness-a-covert-amp-overt-beast and https://uucsj.org/study-guide/legacies-of-systemic-injustice/white-supremacy/.

[108] *See,* Keith Lawrence, Terry Keleher, *Chronic Disparity: Strong and Pervasive Evidence of Racial Inequalities, Poverty Outcomes, Structural Racism,* Race and Public Policy Conference (2004), http://www.intergroupresources.com/rc/Definitions%20of%20Racism.pdf; Alan Dettlaff, Reiko Boyd, *Racial Disproportionality and Disparities in the Child Welfare System: Why Do They Exist, and What Can Be Done to Address Them,* 692 Annals of the American Academy of Pol. and Soc. Science 253 (2020), https://journals.sagepub.com/doi/pdf/10.1177/0002716220980329.

> To understand structural racism, researchers, policymakers, and providers need to recognize it, analyze how each issue we work on is shaped by it, admit how what we design is influenced by it, and acknowledge how each of us, our work, and our organizations is shaped by it. To resist structural racism, researchers, policymakers and providers need to acknowledge our complicity in perpetuating it, cease amassing power, and instead engage in collective problem-solving and decision-making, equitable partnerships, and meaningful collaboration.[109]

Ruby addresses structural racism, yet her guidance applies to all forms of structural discrimination, including those based upon race, gender, class, and any other morally constructed source. Central to Ruby's wisdom is the need to share power in order to counteract inequity. Hope-filled child welfare systems and individuals will believe in their duty and ability to undo overwhelming wrongs as well as identify that the pathway for doing so is to share power with families through supportive and collaborative partnerships that are trauma-informed, strength-based, family-centered, and ultimately equitable.

• • •

The ancient Japanese tradition of Kintsugi has left an enduring lesson. The method of repair that is a counterpoint to the source of the struggle leads to transformation. Responding with the opposite finds the balance that is necessary to the Kintsugi art form, to our body's response to trauma, to locating strength amidst adversity, to valuing all families, and to meeting their needs. As the experiences of Isabel, Ruby, and Darrell reveal, the child welfare system must similarly respond to families experiencing the trauma and adversity of domestic violence with gold. Interventions that are trauma-informed, strength-based, family-centered, and equity-focused are counterweights to the families' experiences of domestic violence. Domestic violence is shrouded in secret, confusion, and shame. Trauma-informed child welfare interventions understand the experience of domestic violence and its impact and aim to create new maps of the trauma survivors'

---

[109] Ruby White Starr, *Moving from the Mainstream to the Margins: Lessons In Culture and Power,* 33 J. of Fam. Violence 551, 553 (2018).

world. Domestic violence strips control from those it dominates and infuses adult and child survivors with a sense of weakness, powerlessness, and fear. Strength-based child welfare interventions locate and build upon sources of resilience. Domestic violence creates cracks in families through the co-occurrence of love and pain. Family-centered child welfare interventions engage with all members of the family and facilitate the pathways toward healing and growth for each. Domestic violence denigrates the natural right of respect, safety, and connection. Equity-focused child welfare interventions give families what they need and share power. By achieving balance through these opposing forces, trauma-centered, strength-based, family-centered, and equity-focused child welfare interventions are the golden pathway that can enable the child welfare system to fulfill its hope of partnering with families to find greater safety, stability, well-being, and healing.

5
Therapeutic Justice: The Path and Impact of the *Nicholson* Class Action Lawsuit

Child welfare responses that are trauma-informed, strength-based, family-centered, and equity-focused should lead to interventions in which individuals and families are better off exiting the system than when they entered because the partnered intervention provided them with what they needed. Therapeutic justice captures this notion that system interventions have the potential to and should aspire to impact a person's overall safety, stability, well-being, and healing. Typically centered in the criminal justice context, courts that can be described as therapeutically just utilize a relational and interdisciplinary approach to ensure that the system is meeting the needs of those in front of it, even when those individuals have allegedly broken the law in some way. At their core, courts that are therapeutically just are trauma-informed, strength-based, family-centered, and equity-focused as the means to the end of meeting the families' needs.

Although seldom applied as a framework or aspiration outside of criminal courts, the most defining case and judicial opinion on domestic violence and child welfare is an exemplar of therapeutic justice. In examining the questions of whether exposure to domestic violence constitutes child neglect and whether victims of domestic violence are neglectful parents, the courts in the *Nicholson v. Williams* class action lawsuit and related cases made findings and issued holdings that are consistent with trauma-informed, strength-based, family-centered, and equity-focused notions.[1] As such, the series of class action *Nicholson* cases demonstrate the effectiveness when courts vet policies and practices against the standard of whether such actions enhance or impede the path toward giving individuals and families what they need. Significantly, such an approach that is consistent with the notions of therapeutic justice has Constitutional support.

In hearing the case of *Nicholson v. Williams* in 2002, the written decision of Federal District Judge Jack Weinstein can be oriented in therapeutic justice. To understand and determine what children and families ultimately need to heal from domestic violence, Judge Weinstein was receptive to and relied upon the interdisciplinary social science knowledge, clinical approaches, and best practice presented to him during the trial to assess the constitutionality of New York City's child welfare interventions into the lives of families experiencing domestic violence. Through adroit attorney strategy, the voices of three women, among many others, surfaced in the *Nicholson* litigation. Sharwline Nicholson, Betsy McAlister Groves, and Liz Roberts brought to life the experience of a mother and her children, that which children and families need to heal, and the challenges with which child welfare systems struggle. The *Nicholson* class action lawsuit demonstrates the positive impact on families when courts embody the notion of therapeutic justice—that systems and courts can be change agents, or at least not be impediments, in working with individuals and families to find greater safety, stability, well-being, and healing together.

The Named Plaintiff

By the time Sharwline Nicholson was two years old, her mother had moved from Jamaica to the United States, leaving her as a young

1 *In re* Sharwline Nicholson, 181 F.Supp.2d (E.D.N.Y 2002); Nicholson v. Williams, 203 F.Supp.2d 153 (E.D.N.Y. 2002); Nicholson v. Scoppetta, 344 F.3d 154 (C.A.2 (N.Y.) 2003); Nicholson v. Scoppetta, 3 N.Y.3d 357, 820 N.E.2d 840 (N.Y. 2004).

girl with her father on the island. Sharwline was her father's only child, received her father's love and devotion, and grew up among her cousins, aunties, and grandparents. When Sharwline graduated high school, her mother sent her a dress to wear from America. Sharwline's father wished to send her to college in Jamaica, but the American dream visited Sharwline each night as she slept.

Seeking opportunities that were not in Jamaica, Sharwline immigrated to the United States when she was twenty years old. She moved into her mother's apartment in New Jersey, just outside of New York City; the two barely knew each other, and Sharwline wondered if her mother's life in America was worth the cost of missing the entirety of her daughter's childhood. Sharwline obtained a job as a home health aide, like all of her cousins and aunties in New Jersey. Living with her mother for the first time was challenging, and as soon as Sharwline had saved enough money, she moved to her own apartment with a friend. Sharwline became pregnant and gave birth to a baby boy she named Kendell. The slow-paced life in New Jersey dragged, so Sharwline moved to Brooklyn with her son. Kendell had some developmental delays that qualified him for government assistance, and these resources helped Sharwline to support the two of them in their new apartment.

Just as Kendell was starting to walk and talk, Sharwline met Claude Christopher Barnett. Claude was also from the Caribbean and her friends knew his. Claude acted like a gentleman, a man who seemed responsible and caring like her father. They soon had a baby together. Shortly after Destinee was born, Claude decided to move to South Carolina. Seeing herself in her daughter, Sharwline could not comprehend how he could move away from his daughter. Sharwline did not consider leaving Brooklyn because Kendell was receiving occupational and speech therapy in school. Claude made regular trips back to Brooklyn for a couple of years. One of these visits would usher the child welfare system into the lives of Sharwline and her children, an intervention that would eternally shape their lives and the topography of the intersection of domestic violence and child welfare.

As Sharwline's life with her children in New Jersey was unfolding, the professional work of two other women would soon become relevant to their lives.

Through the Lens of Children

Filling an existing gap in 1992, Betsy McAlister Groves founded the Child Witness to Violence Project (CWVP) in the Department of Pediatrics at Boston Medical Center to provide mental health services to children from birth through eight years of age and their parents who were exposed to domestic or community violence. It became readily apparent that the children entering the clinic were more likely to be exposed to violence within their homes than outside in their community, a reality that would soon become the experience of Sharwline's children.[2] Within the first year, CWVP found that 85 percent of children seen at the clinic were living in homes where domestic violence was occurring.

Although an understanding of the neurobiology of childhood trauma was nascent, CWVP focused on understanding the cause and impact of trauma in order to foster healing for the children. The practice of CWVP confirmed that the very young children were vulnerable to trauma and that this exposure caused a range of unique emotional and developmental consequences. Working with families affected by domestic violence was sometimes difficult for Betsy and her fellow clinicians. Betsy experienced complicated feelings toward parents, even parents who had been abused themselves. Some women could not or did not leave their violent relationships because of a lack of resources or denial about the impact of domestic violence on their children. Some mothers' own trauma made them numb to the distress of their children.[3] Betsy and her colleagues also saw the heroic and resourceful efforts of parents each day to try to prevent harm from befalling their children. Were their decisions putting their children in danger? Were these parents doing enough to help their children despite their own trauma?

Betsy and the CWVP clinicians worked through these judgments by focusing on the clinical needs of children and supporting the child-parent relationship. They recognized that parents were the first and most important resource for children.[4] Children endured stress

---

2 Betsy McAlister Groves, Children Who See Too Much: Lessons from the Child Witness to Violence Project (2003).

3 *Id.* at 63.

4 *Id.* at 80.

better when they were near rather than separated from their parents.[5] Attachment and maintaining those attachment relationships was critical in good times and bad. Strengthening the parent-child relationship was ultimately CWVP's most potent and valuable intervention for the child trauma survivors.[6] Clinicians reinforced with parents that "even though there was little they could have done to prevent their child's exposure to trauma, there is a lot they can do to help their child regain a sense of equilibrium following exposure to violence."[7] Blame and past deficiencies were significantly less important than building upon strengths in the present.

Betsy recognized that the work of the CWVP could also have a significant impact on social policy. Therefore, it was imperative for systems to respond in ways that supported the healing and recovery of children and families. Yet, Betsy and her colleagues witnessed disconnects between what families needed to recover and what systems delivered. They often felt conflicted because they were legally obligated to call the child welfare system hotline after hearing about significant violence in the home. These mandated reporting obligations often led to child welfare investigations that made the situation worse by holding mothers responsible for behavior they could not control, blaming mothers for inadequately protecting their child from exposure to domestic violence, and removing children from the source of their healing.

Elizabeth "Liz" Roberts joined CWVP after nearly a decade of working with children who had experienced domestic violence. In 1987, with Susan Schechter's advice and guidance from lessons learned at Advocate for Women and Kids in Emergencies (AWAKE) (discussed in chapter 3), Liz had created one of the first children's programs at a domestic violence organization. Revealing herself to be a skilled and empathetic clinician during her social work practicum, CWVP hired Liz in 1996, where she provided clinical services

---

5 *Id.* at 81.

6 Betsy McAlister Groves & Abigail Gewirtz, *Interventions and Promising Approaches for Children Exposed to Domestic Violence, in* CHILDREN EXPOSED TO VIOLENCE 113 (Margaret Feerick and Gerald Silverman, eds., 2006).

7 Betsy McAlister Groves & Barry Zuckerman, *Interventions with Parents and Caregivers of Children Who Are Exposed to Violence, in* CHILDREN IN A VIOLENT SOCIETY 188 (Joy Osofsky ed., 1997).

to children and parents who were exposed to domestic violence. Her ability to engage the adult victims (most often mothers) in a supportive relationship would ultimately become the cornerstone of their children's recovery and the family's healing.

As CWVP continued to provide trauma services to children and their families and while Sharwline settled into life as a single mother, the child welfare system in New York City embarked upon reform that would prove insufficient to effectively respond to families experiencing domestic violence and child welfare as Sharwline and her children would soon experience.

• • •

A series of child fatalities covered in the media led to the creation, in 1996, of a new child welfare agency in New York City, the Administration for Children's Services (ACS).[8] Nicholas Scoppetta, a lawyer with a distinguished public service career who had himself been in foster care for several years as a child, was chosen as ACS's first commissioner.[9] Commissioner Scoppetta created a plan for transformation to address the "fragmented"[10] and broken system, identifying that improving ACS's response to families experiencing domestic violence was a necessary area of reform.

ACS and the courts began various pilot projects to address domestic violence in its caseloads with promising outcomes. In the Zone A Domestic Violence Instant Response Pilot, the New York Police Department and ACS jointly investigated allegations of domestic violence with the involvement of a Domestic Violence Specialist.[11] Only 3 percent of cases resulted in removals.[12] In the Domestic Violence

---

[8] On November 22, 1995, six-year-old Elisa Izquierdo was beaten to death by her mother and repeatedly came to the attention of New York City's Child Welfare Administration before she died. Jo Craven McGinty, *State Keeps Death Files of Abused Children Secret*, N.Y. TIMES, Feb. 28, 2012, at REGION. In 1995 a class action suit was filed on behalf of a class represented by "Marisol," a child who had almost starved to death in a closet while the City of New York allegedly ignored evidence of her maltreatment. Marisol v. Giuliani, 929 F.Supp. 662 (S.D.N.Y.1996).

[9] Nicholson v. Williams, 203 F.Supp.2d at 197.

[10] *Id.* at 205.

[11] *Id.*

[12] *Id.* at 207.

and Child Maltreatment Project, all of the cases from the Bronx in which ACS had removed children from their homes because of or in part due to domestic violence were assigned to one family court judge with the goal of providing intensive and expedited services.[13] Within six months, the majority of the children in the forty cases were returned home to their mother.[14] At the same time, the concept of One Judge/One Family was tried in the new Bronx Integrated Domestic Violence Court, in which one judge would address the multiple legal issues—criminal, juvenile, family, civil—arising from a family's experiences with domestic violence.[15] A judiciary that was attempting to be responsive to the individual needs of each family, however, had to contend with contradictory state court decisions.

Amidst these innovative and promising programs, New York state law lacked clarity about whether exposure to domestic violence constituted per se neglect and whether the parent experiencing domestic violence was thereby conclusively neglectful. Some state court decisions established that domestic violence in the presence of children was insufficient, in and of itself, to support a finding of neglect against either or both parents.[16] Other state court decisions, however,

---

13 *Id.* at 215.

14 *Id.* at 215.

15 *In re* Sharwline Nicholson, 181 F.Supp.2d at 183.

16 Jill M. Zuccardy, New York State Child Protective Cases Involving Domestic Violence, SANCTUARY FOR FAMILIES' CENTER FOR BATTERED WOMEN LEGAL SERVICES (Dec.2002),http://docplayer.net/93472009-New-york-state-child-protective-cases-involving-domestic-violence-issues.html. Zuccardy lists the following cases examples: Matter of Anthony PP, 291 A.D.2d 687, 737 N.Y.S.2d 430 (3rd Dept. 2002) (proof that father lost his temper, hollered and screamed on prior occasions not sufficient for a finding of neglect based on domestic violence); Matter of Tali W., 2002 N.Y.App.Div. LEXIS 10675 (2nd Dept. 2002) (lower court erred in granting summary judgment against father based merely on criminal court conviction for domestic violence); Matter of Emily PP., 274 A.D.2d 681, 710 N.Y.S.2d 476 (3rd Dept. 2000) (domestic violence charges dismissed as against both parents); In Re Kayla B., 262 A.D.2d 137, 690 N.Y.S.2d 444 (1st Dept. 1999) (violent domestic incident insufficient to sustain neglect petition); In Re Uniqua M, 263 A.D.2d 359, 692 N.Y.S.2d 389 (1st Dept. 1999) (domestic violence charges dismissed as against both parents); Matter of Melissa U., 148 A.D.2d 862, 538 N.Y.S.2d 958 (3rd Dept. 1989) (mother was not neglectful for being victim of brutal assault in the presence of her children because she had terminated the relationship, although she was found neglectful for subsequently marrying abuser); Matter of R.F., N.Y.L.J. August 13, 1996 (Family Court, Bronx Co. 1996) (only father

established a strict liability standard in which domestic violence in the presence of children automatically deemed children neglected and both parents neglectful.[17] Amidst this discrepancy, ACS used *Lonnell J.* to claim that exposure to domestic violence constituted *per se* neglect by both parents warranting removal.[18] Although the court actually held that specific harm caused by the domestic violence must exist,[19] the court did hold both parents equally responsible for harm constituting neglect, justifying removal from the abused parent too.[20] By removing Lonnell J. from his mother, he lost the connection and relationship that he needed to recover from the harms he experienced. Despite the pilot programs and without sound policies on paper, ACS practice replicated the interventions of the *Lonnell J.* case; children were being separated from their abused mother at times when they needed her most.

The Child Welfare Committee of the New York City Inter-agency Task Force Against Domestic Violence formed a working group to document how ACS was responding to families experiencing domestic violence.[21] The task force's report detailed the experiences of advocates "assisting battered mothers who [were] losing their children to foster care and who [were] being charged with abuse or neglect for failing to protect their children from witnessing domestic violence."[22]

---

found neglectful for "engaging in" domestic violence); Matter of Michael M, 156 Misc.2d 98, 591 N.Y.S.2d 681 (Family Court, Kings Co. 1992) (only father found neglectful for perpetrating domestic violence).

17 Id. Zuccardy lists the following case examples: Matter of Nichole SS., 296 A.D.2d 618, 745 N.Y.S.2d 128 (3rd Dept. 2002); Matter of James MM, 294 A.D.2d 630, 740 N.Y.S.2d 730 (3rd Dept. 2002); Matter of Francis S., 296 A.D.2d 507, 745 N.Y.S.2d 486 (2nd Dept. 2002); In Re Athena M., 253 A.D.2d 497, 678 N.Y.S.2d 11 (1st Dept. 1998); Matter of Billy Jean II, 226 A.D.2d 767, 640 N.Y.S.2d 326 (3rd Dept. 1996) citing Matter of Tammie Z., 105 A.D.2d 463, 480 N.Y.S.2d 786 (3rd Dept. 1984); Matter of Tami G., 209 A.D.2d 869, 619 N.Y.S.2d 222 (3rd Dept. 1994); Matter of Antonio I., N.Y.L.J. p. 25, c. 5 (Family Court Suffolk Co. 2002).

18 David Lansner, *The Nicholson Decisions,* New York's Response to 'Failure to Protect' Allegations. 12 ABA Comm'n on Domestic Violence e-newsletter (Fall 2008).

19 In re Lonell J., 242 A.D.2d 58, 61 (1st Dept. 1998).

20 *Id.* at 63.

21 Nicholson v. Williams, 203 F.Supp.2d at 215.

22 *Id.* at 215–16.

The report concluded that ACS separated children from their mothers *because* the mothers had been abused. The report also documented the increase in the number of children who were placed in foster care as a result of domestic violence and of battered women who experienced an often coercive and punitive child welfare system.[23] As such, the prior localized reform efforts were not overcoming the biases, judgments, and abuses of power that were occurring at ACS.

• • •

When Destinee was nine-months-old and Kendell was five-years-old, Claude was visiting from the south. Sharwline arrived home after bringing Kendell to school, and Destinee was sleeping in her crib in another room. Claude began accusing Sharwline of having an affair. Despite her denials, Claude kicked and punched Sharwline. Sharwline ran out the front door, only to be hauled back into the apartment by Claude. Sharwline screamed and was hurt. Seeing the injuries he caused, Claude fled. Sharwline called the police. Sharwline was bleeding profusely from her head when the police and paramedics entered the apartment. Before attending to her own injuries, her first thought was of her children. Sharwline asked her neighbor who babysat to stay with Destinee and to pick Kendell up from the school bus stop. Before getting in the ambulance, Sharwline told the officers detailed information so they could locate Claude, although she was quite certain he was already on his way back to South Carolina.

In the hospital, Sharwline felt shocked and angry. This was the first time Claude had physically hurt her in any way, and she was in disbelief. He broke her arm, fractured her ribs, and caused head injuries resulting in a concussion. As Sharwline was recovering in her hospital bed, she was comforted knowing her children were in the care of their neighbor whom they knew well. That evening, three police officers visited her in the hospital. They told her that her children needed to be in the care of a relative, rather than a neighbor. Although no law made such a mandate, Sharwline called her cousin in New Jersey who agreed to go stay with the children. But as Sharwline slept that

---

23 *Id.* at 216. See also Supreme Court of the State of New York, Appellate Division, First Department, Lawyer's Manual on Domestic Violence: Representing the Victim 199 (Julie A. Domonkos & Jill Laurie Goodman eds., 3rd ed. 2000).

night, the police returned to the apartment, guns drawn, and took the children from the neighbor and placed them in an emergency shelter.

The next morning, a nurse informed Sharwline that she had a phone call. Sharwline took the phone and the voice on the other side said, "Miss Nicholson, this is the Administration for Children's Services (ACS). If you want to see your kids, you will have to report to court the following week and you are not allowed to go back to your apartment." The worker refused to tell Sharwline where her children were. Sharwline called her cousin who told her that when she arrived at the apartment as planned, the children were not there.

Sharwline insisted upon leaving the hospital against the doctor's orders to find her children. ACS waited five days before filing the case in juvenile court. For five days, Sharwline did not know where her children were. She did not know that her children were in a shelter overnight and then placed in a stranger's home. She did not know if they were healthy or sick, sad or happy, well cared for or hurt. The injuries Claude caused to her were far less painful than being separated from her children.

Sharwline's first juvenile court appearance was fast. She did not have a lawyer, and her children were placed in the temporary custody of ACS. Although everyone else in the courtroom knew, Sharwline still was not told where her own children were. She was instructed to return to court two days later. When she returned, a full week without information about her children, she met her attorney amidst a high stack of falling files. Sharwline read the dependency petition, which stated that she had "engaged in domestic violence" and thus had neglected her children. To Sharwline's relief, the judge ordered her children to be temporarily released to her, a transfer to be facilitated by ACS.

The following day, eight days since she had seen her children, Sharwline was given one supervised visit at the ACS office. When Sharwline entered the building, she followed the sound of her daughters' cries to find her children. Destinee was sitting in a chair all by herself, tears running down her cheeks. Her face was covered in a rash and scratches marked her nose while yellow pus dripped from it. Kendell had a swollen eye and he told Sharwline that his foster mother hit him across his face. She demanded to use a phone to call the police to make a report about her son's injury. When the ACS worker refused,

Sharwline said she needed to get formula for her daughter. Sharwline left the building and called the police from a payphone across the street, sacrificing the precious time she was allotted with her children to keep them safe. A new foster mother was sent to the ACS office. When the new foster mother approached her son, Kendell turned to her and said, "You are not going to hit me, are you?" Four days later, Kendell turned six years old, and he was not allowed to speak to or see his mother on his birthday.

In the weeks that followed, Sharwline tried to get a protective order against Claude but was denied one because he was not in New York. Finally, three weeks after being torn from each other, her children were brought to Sharwline at her cousin's apartment. As they were taken out of the car, Sharwline kneeled, embraced Kendell, and clasped Destinee to her. Kendell heard a police car drive by and started crying. Sharwline quickly realized that the separation, the unknown, the uncertainty, would now be etched into her son. Sharwline pressed her ACS caseworker to explain the delay in returning her children. Although the court paroled her children to Sharwline fourteen days earlier, the ACS worker assumed that the cousin's house would not have adequate bedding for the children. ACS did not make this reason clear during the prolonged delay nor did they provide new bedding or help Sharwline move the bedding from the apartment she was ordered not to enter. This alleged lack of linens caused two young children to be kept from their mother for three weeks.

The case remained open for supervision and the three were allowed to return to the apartment. Sharwline secured legal representation from the Sanctuary for Families' Center for Battered Women's Legal Services for the remainder of her open juvenile case. Sharwline found a job at the Home Depot, and even as a new employee, the store accommodated her need to attend her court dates and care for her children. Over seven months after Sharwline was brutally assaulted in a onetime incident of domestic violence, the judge dismissed the neglect petition against Sharwline. The State Central Register, nonetheless, still retained her name, along with Claude's, as a neglectful parent.

Sharwline remained deeply reflective. What makes a neglectful parent, she wondered? Surely not one who tends to her children, ensures they have food, clothes, and shelter. One who advocates for services when a child is struggling, who loves them, and who, with blood dripping down her head, calls a neighbor to take care of them after being attacked for the first time. What makes a system neglectful? Certainly, one that unnecessarily and wrongly separates children from their mothers only to be harmed in foster care. Sharwline felt that an injustice had occurred that was going to affect many more families, especially those with her accent, those with her color of skin, those living in her zip code, or those hailing from her culture.

Sharwline's lawyers at Sanctuary for Families referred her to the public interest law firm of Lansner & Kubitschek. Sharwline sought redress against ACS for the wrongs committed against her and to prevent other women and children from enduring additional harm during ACS interventions. Sharwline's legal team filed a civil rights case, and within nine months, Sharwline became the named plaintiff in a class action lawsuit against ACS and its employees.

• • •

In the years leading up to the class action lawsuit, Commissioner Scoppetta and his team sought to accelerate the reform effort, establishing for the first time a separate Office of Domestic Violence Policy and Planning and hiring Liz Roberts to direct it. In February 2001, ACS issued "Principles for Addressing Domestic Violence in Children's Services," declaring its policy to remove children only when "domestic violence creates an immediate danger of serious physical harm or serious emotional impairment to a child" and when "safety planning with the nonabusive parent and/or criminal justice intervention does not reasonably provide for children's safety."[24]

Together with her ACS colleagues, Liz spearheaded several ACS efforts to improve the response to families experiencing domestic violence. Consistent with the mantra that Liz had brought with her from CWVP, she wrote a domestic violence protocol that stated, "[t]he preferred way to enhance children's safety after the detection of domestic violence in their homes is to support and help the victim protect herself and her children, while engaging batterers in services

[24] Nicholson v. Scoppetta, 344 F.3d at 177. The dissent in the Second Circuit Court of Appeals case described this policy.

and holding them accountable for their actions."[25] Liz developed an interview tool to guide engagement with the person causing harm, launched a new training program on domestic violence based upon a curriculum that Susan Schechter created, and established a program to place specialists on domestic violence, substance abuse, and mental health in every field office in New York City.

Concurrently, lawyers filed Sharwline's case, and others like it, arguing that children were being removed from their mothers solely because they had been exposed to domestic violence, and their mothers were deemed neglectful for allegedly engaging in domestic violence or failing to protect their children.

Within months of taking the new position at ACS, Liz was now sitting on an acrimonious fault line. She felt part of multiple worlds—the worlds of domestic violence advocacy, child trauma services, and the child welfare system. At times, the divide seemed insurmountable. Domestic violence advocates saw mothers like Sharwline and children like Kendell and Destinee being harmed at the hands of both domestic violence offenders and ACS, expressing that for years they had been knocking at the gates of ACS calling for improved, nonpunitive, and supportive responses to abused mothers and their children. ACS responded that it had spent a decade investing in initiatives and policies to establish best practices and that domestic violence posed real and serious risks to children, requiring protective actions. In working with children who had experienced trauma, both Liz and her former colleagues at CWVP, like Betsy McAlister Groves, had seen that nearly always, the interest of survivors, like Sharwline, and their children were aligned. Soon Liz and Betsy would find themselves as expert witnesses on opposite sides of Sharwline's lawsuit.

The *Nicholson* Journey toward Therapeutic Justice

The path of Sharwline Nicholson's lawsuit against ACS evolved into a class action that journeyed through federal and state courts over the course of three years. Along the way, the *Nicholson* class action

---

[25] *Id.*

rendered four judicial decisions, most notably Judge Jack Weinstein's written opinion that married the law with social science and clinical practice in order to ensure that child welfare system actions do not impede that which children and families need when they have experienced domestic violence. Each opinion of the *Nicholson* progeny solidified what Sharwline knew in her heart about herself and her children, that which Betsy learned through her work at the CWVP, and what Liz strived to implement at ACS—that the best way to help children exposed to domestic violence is to work with the survivor parent who is both the most important buffer and source of recovery for their children, and to support the adult and child survivors together as the path to enhanced safety, stability, well-being, and healing. Doing the opposite—blaming and deeming their mothers neglectful and removing children from them—harms children by denying opportunities to strengthen the very person who can best support their healing. Grounded in social science, clinical experience, and best practice, the four judicial opinions reached the conclusions that children's exposure to domestic violence is not per se neglect and that mothers whose children are exposed to domestic violence against them are not presumptively neglectful. Deeming mothers neglectful and removing children violates the Constitutional and statutory rights of both mothers and their children.

Class Certification

In April 2000 after Sharwline's juvenile court case closed, Sharwline's lawyers filed a complaint against officers and employees of ACS and the City of New York on behalf of Sharwline and her two children, Destinee and Kendell, thereby initiating the federal district lawsuit of *Nicholson v. Williams*.[26] Shortly thereafter, two other mothers with experiences like Sharwline found their way to Sharwline's lawyers, revealing that ACS's practices of defining exposure to domestic violence as per se neglect, removing children from battered mothers, and pursuing the mothers for child neglect were not aberrations.[27]

---

[26] Nicholson v. Williams, 203 F.Supp.2d at 165.

[27] David Lansner, *The Nicholson Decisions,* New York's Response to 'Failure to Protect' Allegations. 12 ABA Comm'n on Domestic Violence e-newsletter (Fall 2008).

The two mothers, as well as others, joined Sharwline's lawsuit. The case was assigned to Senior District Judge Jack Weinstein; his reputation as an activist judge made his courtroom a fortuitous home for the case.

Judge Weinstein certified two classes as part of the *Nicholson v. Williams* lawsuit against ACS. Through one of its named plaintiffs, Sharwline, Subclass A was certified on behalf of all battered mothers whose children were removed from them or in danger of being removed from them solely or primarily because the mothers were victims of domestic violence.[28] Subclass B consisted of the children of the mothers of Subclass A, those at risk of ACS's policy of being deemed neglected because of their exposure to domestic violence and/or being removed from their abused mother.[29] The plaintiff mothers alleged, in part, that ACS' policy violated their substantive and procedural due process rights under the Fourteenth Amendment and that plaintiff children were being removed without constitutionally adequate investigations, training, and supervision in violation of their Fourth Amendment Rights. The class members sought injunctive relief for ACS to stop deeming battered mothers neglectful and to cease removing children from battered mothers primarily because of domestic violence as well as declaratory relief to instruct ACS to change their policy. Any relief that the mothers and their children received would benefit others like them across the state of New York.

The Trial

After months of preparation, a trial in front of Judge Weinstein began on July 9, 2001. The main issue at the trial was whether the court would issue a preliminary injunction against ACS that would stop them from removing children from parents who had experienced domestic violence and deeming the adult survivor neglectful. Both sides addressed this issue by presenting social science research, clinical work, and best practices for Judge Weinstein's consideration in determining what state law and the nation's Constitution required.

---

28 *Supra* note 27, at 183–84.

29 *Id.*

The trial lasted for twenty-four trial days, forty-four witnesses testified, 212 documents were introduced, and extensive briefing and argument followed.[30] Sharwline was a centerpiece of the plaintiffs' case-in-chief. Sharwline was present in the courtroom for all twenty-four days of trial and testified in front of Judge Weinstein. Sharwline recalls how intently Judge Weinstein listened to each witness and asked questions of his own. Strategy for both plaintiff classes and the defense infused the trial with expert testimony.

Betsy McAlister Groves was a central plaintiff witness on behalf of the class of children who were removed or at risk of being removed from their homes and separated from their mothers because their mothers had been abused. Based upon her knowledge and experience at CWVP for two decades, Betsy was tendered and ultimately qualified as an expert on children's exposure to domestic violence, including how domestic violence impacts children and what they need to recover from exposure to domestic violence. Her expert report and testimony were evidence that helped establish that even in response to serious and risk-filled domestic violence, responses to children's exposure to domestic violence requires family-focused interventions.[31] Betsy's report and testimony substantiated domestic violence as one of the most toxic forms of violence exposure for children, yet established that responsive clinical interventions build upon the unique protective factors and vulnerabilities in each child and family in order to foster resilience and healing.[32] Connecting her clinical expertise to inform child welfare policy and practice, Betsy offered her expert opinion that:

> A mandatory policy that defines child exposure to domestic violence as child maltreatment or a blanket intervention . . . [does] not take into account the specifics of the child or the family. It assumes that all exposure to or experience with domestic violence is the same and has the same effects on children. Therefore, it cannot be tailored to take advantage of the strengths of the individual, the family, or the community.

---

30 *Id.* at 165.

31 Betsy McAlister Groves, Expert report at 2 (on file with the author).

32 *Id.* at 6.

> In the majority of cases, naming the mother as the neglectful party is wrong and becomes another way of blaming or punishing her for actions that are beyond her ability to control.[33]

Betsy offered as evidence to the court that when children are exposed to domestic violence and separated from parents, they experience significant trauma and lose their most immediate buffer of trauma and source of healing; therefore removal should be the last resort.[34] Betsy's testimony unequivocally concluded that the best way to protect children in situations of domestic violence is to provide safety and stability to the child and the nonabusive parent.[35] Betsy, along with other plaintiff experts like Jeffrey Edleson, provided Judge Weinstein with a road map for therapeutic justice, a strength-based, trauma-informed, family-centered, and equity-focused path for using the law to provide children and families with what they need to find enhanced safety, stability, well-being, and healing.

The defense also infused their case with experts and witnesses such as Liz Roberts. Liz's testimony was focused on describing the issue of children's exposure to domestic violence and its complexity, including the need for a nuanced approach, the importance of evaluating real and actual harm to children exposed to domestic violence, the value in an ACS response that was not punitive to adult survivors, and the need to partner with the nonoffending parent to plan for her family's safety and healing. At times Betsy could have sounded like an expert for ACS and at times Liz could have sounded like a witness for either the plaintiff mothers or children. Liz also explained ACS's current efforts around clinical consultation, guiding principles and training regarding domestic violence.

The terrorist attacks of September 11, 2001 punctuated the trial schedule, and as the nation faced collective trauma, Judge Weinstein grappled with how ACS should respond to mothers and children who had experienced trauma in their homes. The trial concluded at the end of December. Sharwline, mothers like her and their children prevailed.

---

33 *Id.* at 8.
34 *Id.* at 8.
35 *Id.* at 8.

In ruling for the plaintiff classes, Judge Weinstein issued a preliminary injunction on January 3, 2002.[36] The preliminary injunction explicitly required ACS, in part, to: (1) declare the report of abuse or neglect unfounded as to the mother where the sole basis of the report against the mother is that the mother has been a victim of domestic violence, or has failed to cooperate with domestic violence services;[37] (2) not remove a child from the mother without a court order when the sole basis is that the mother is the victim of domestic violence unless the child is imminent danger;[38] (3) make reasonable efforts to provide protection from the batterer by helping the mother and child together;[39] and (4) refrain from using the phrase "engaged" in domestic violence to describe the survivor of domestic violence.[40] Judge Weinstein acted to stop further harm to families like Sharwline.

Therapeutic Justice Incarnate

In a 108-page tour de force opinion, Judge Weinstein wrote one of the most comprehensive and passionate judicial opinions ever written on domestic violence. By substantiating the findings of fact and holdings that supported the issuance of the injunction against ACS to stop harming families like Sharwline's,[41] Judge Weinstein's sound legal analysis remained connected with the humanity of the people both impacting and impacted by the lawsuit. A reader of Judge Weinstein's *Nicholson* opinion receives an education on therapeutic justice, a schooling on the law's bounds of empathy and compassion.[42] Legally robust and constructively spirited, Judge Weinstein defined both the process and the outcomes that child welfare interventions must avoid in order to meet the needs of families experiencing domestic violence.

Judge Weinstein opened his opinion with the following pointed eloquence:

---

36 In re Sharwline Nicholson, 181 F.Supp.2d at 190.
37 *Id.*
38 *Id.*
39 *Id.*
40 *Id.* at 190-91.
41 Nicholson v. Williams, 203 F.Supp.2d at 166.
42 *Id.*

> The evidence reveals widespread and unnecessary cruelty by agencies of the City of New York towards mothers abused by their consorts through forced unnecessary separation of the mothers from their children on the excuse that this sundering is necessary to protect the children. The pitiless double abuse of these mothers is not malicious but is due to benign indifference, bureaucratic inefficiency, and outmoded institutional biases.[43,44]

After compassionately describing the experience of the plaintiff classes and the historical contexts of domestic violence and child welfare,[45] Judge Weinstein comprehensively summarized the evidence of the experts about the effect of domestic violence on children, the impact of the removals on children, and the important role of parents like Sharwline.[46] Directly referencing the expert testimony of Betsy McAlister Groves and Jeffery Edleson as well as defense experts, Judge Weinstein identified consensus among the experts that children are impacted by domestic violence in a wide range of ways and that a variety of factors affect this impact.[47] Judge Weinstein also recognized the cental role of the nonoffending parent by finding:

> Because ACS workers assume that the battered mother is weak and helpless, the caseworker is denied the single most important tool [that] a child protection service worker has when going into the home, [that is] the mother's strength [and] knowledge. . . ."[48]

Citing Jeffrey Edleson's testimony, Judge Weinstein identified translationally that defining witnessing domestic violence as conclusive maltreatment is a mistake, as he found:

> Automatically defining witnessing as maltreatment may also ignore battered mothers' efforts to develop safe environments

---

43 *Id.* at 163.
44 *Id.* at 167.
45 *Id.* at 168–198.
46 *Id.* at 197.
47 *Id.* at 187.
48 *Id.* at 217.

> for their children and themselves. A careful assessment of the risks and protective factors in every family is necessary before drawing conclusions about the risks and harm to children.[49]

The experts also persuaded Judge Weinstein that removing children from parents who have experienced domestic violence often results in medicine that is worse than the ailment.[50] Poignantly, Judge Weinstein found that "the total length of separations of mothers and children ACS has caused is measured in years. The suffering and trauma it has inflicted is so great it cannot be measured."[51]

Convinced that exposure to domestic violence does not automatically rise to the level of neglect and that removal is often harmful, Judge Weinstein then turned to the child welfare best practices involving families experiencing domestic violence. In an important caveat, Judge Weinstein cautioned that "failure to follow best practices is not unconstitutional. It does bear, however, on the justifications of ACS that its punitive attitude towards battered women is required by social service standards and that it serves children's best interests."[52] To substantiate how child welfare interventions can and should serve children's best interests, Judge Weinstein relied upon evidence presented by the Greenbook (discussed in chapter 3), lauding its credibility, and highlighting and substantiating its key recommendations. Guided by the tenets of the Greenbook, Judge Weinstein concluded that mothers should not be accused of neglect for being victims of domestic violence,[53] batterers should be held responsible,[54] children should be protected by offering battered mothers services and protection,[55] separation of battered mothers and children should be a last resort,[56] child welfare employees should be adequately trained to deal with domestic violence,[57] and agency policy

---

[49] *Id.* at 199.
[50] *Id.* at 199.
[51] *Id.* at 251.
[52] *Id.* at 200.
[53] *Id.* at 200.
[54] *Id.* at 201.
[55] *Id.* at 202.
[56] *Id.* at 203.
[57] *Id.* at 205.

should provide clear guidelines to caseworkers.[58] As Judge Weinstein emphasized from the Greenbook in accordance with Betsy's testimony, "trying to make mothers safe does make children safer and offers children their best hope for stability."[59] Judge Weinstein further referenced the Greenbook to support the inefficacy of victim-blaming and found that:

> [B]laming a battered mother for being abused, for not leaving the domestic violence perpetrator, or for not stopping his violence is simply counterproductive. The battered woman cannot change or stop the perpetrator's violence by herself. If she does not have adequate support, resources, and protection, leaving him may simply make it worse for the children.[60]

It desecrates fundamental precepts of justice to blame a crime on the victim.[61]

Significantly, both tangibly and symbolically, Judge Weinstein counteracted the moral construction of abused mothers by finding:

> Usually the mother is doing everything she believes is possible to protect herself and her children. The problem is that often her options are severely limited. Accusing battered mothers of neglect aggravates the problem because it blames the mother for failing to control a situation which is defined by the batterer's efforts to deprive her of control."[62] It also discourages mothers from seeking help.

---

58 *Id.* at 205.

59 *Id.* at 203. In quoting Betsy's testimony, Judge Weinstein wrote, "According to Ms. Groves children should be removed from mothers because of domestic violence only as a "last resort and . . . only in situations when there is a very real risk to the safety of the children." Because of the psychological and emotional injury incurred by the children and the battered parent as a result of removal, Ms. Groves believed that it is imperative that appropriate services be offered to parents and children before removal is considered. Preventing the offering of such essential services, she noted, are critical shortages in shelter space and counseling services." *Id.*

60 *Id.* at 200.

61 *Id.* at 252.

62 *Id.* at 201.

Policies and practices that deter help-seeking behaviors create unsound public policy.

Despite acknowledging and summarizing the past ACS efforts and future plans around domestic violence,[63] Judge Weinstein found current ACS policy and practice to be incongruent with established best practice. Attempting to explain the disconnect amidst well-intentioned administrators, Judge Weinstein opined that:

> Much of the actual policies as applied by ACS are driven by fear of an untoward incident of child abuse that will result in criticism of the agency and some of its employees. The concern over institutional self-protection, rather than children's best interests, explains a good deal of ACS's predisposition toward counterproductive separation of abused mothers and their children.[64]

Judge Weinstein concluded that "as a matter of policy and practice, ACS does not merely fail to advance the best interests of children—they also harm children."[65]

Judge Weinstein additionally found injurious inconsistencies between ACS's own policies and practice. Although the ACS Domestic Violence Protocol required "every effort to provide for safety without separating the nonabusive parent and child,[66] Judge Weinstein found an "agency-wide practice of removing children from their mother without evidence of a mother's neglect and without seeking prior judicial approval."[67] Based upon the evidence presented through expert and witness testimony, including that of Sharwline and Betsy, Judge Weinstein made findings of fact about ACS's current policy and practice such that:[68] ACS regularly alleges and indicates neglect

---

[63] *Id.* at 205, 206, 218.

[64] *Id.* at 206.

[65] *Id.* at 250–51.

[66] *Id.* at 220.

[67] *Id.* at 215.

[68] Judge Weinstein summarized the statistics that he used to establish that a policy and practice indeed existed at ACS for removing children because they were exposed to domestic violence and deeming their abused parent neglectful. *Id.* at 208.

against battered mothers,[69] ACS rarely holds abusers accountable,[70] ACS fails to offer adequate services to mothers before pursuing them for neglect or removing their children,[71] ACS regularly separates battered mothers and children unnecessarily,[72] ACS' written policies provide insufficient and inappropriate guidance to workers,[73] and that parents receive inadequate attorney representation in court.[74] In short, Judge Weinstein found that ACS did not follow its own guiding principles on domestic violence "in spirit or in letter."[75]

In applying the law to the findings of fact, Judge Weinstein found that ACS' policy and practice violated the U.S. Constitution. The Due Process Clause of the Fourteenth Amendment provides that no state shall "deprive any person of life, liberty, or property, without due process of law." The Fourteenth Amendment protects these liberty interests.[76] The subclasses of mothers and children have fundamental liberty interests in their right to family integrity and the mothers' right of parental authority to direct the upbringing of their children which separation denigrates.[77] Procedural due process requires the government to provide people with procedural safeguards before taking away their fundamental liberty interests.[78] Judge Weinstein held that without a court order, if an agency removes or unnecessarily delays the return of a child to a mother against whom it has no evidence of her abuse or neglect, on the grounds that the father is abusive to the mother, the mother's procedural due process rights have been infringed."[79] In order to afford parents their procedural due process rights, settled law requires children to be at "imminent risk of harm" before they can be removed from their parents without a judicial order, such that the nature of the emergency circumstances

[69] *Id.* at 207.
[70] *Id.* at 210.
[71] *Id.* at 211.
[72] *Id.* at 212.
[73] *Id.* at 218.
[74] *Id.* at 223.
[75] *Id.* at 220.
[76] *Id.* at 233.
[77] *Id.* at 233; 236, citing Wisconsin v. Yoder, 406 U.S. 205, 232 (1972).
[78] *Id.* at 236.
[79] *Id.* at 238.

justifies the ex parte removal.[80] Judge Weinstein also held that removing children due to domestic violence alone violates the children's Fourth Amendment right against unreasonable "seizures."[81] In addition, the opinion describes that ACS policies and practices violate the mothers' Ninth,[82] Thirteenth,[83] and Nineteenth[84] Amendment rights. While not imposing affirmative obligations on ACS, Judge Weinstein held that the Constitution restricts ACS from taking actions that are counterproductive to what social science, clinical approaches, and best practice have established that families need to recover from domestic violence and ultimately to heal from trauma.

Based upon these factual findings and holdings, Judge Weinstein issued and then stayed the preliminary injunction for six months in order to allow ACS to appeal his decision and to continue its efforts to "attempt remediation of the grave deprivations and threats of deprivations of plaintiffs' constitutional rights."[85] Practically, ACS needed to determine how it was going to address the names of abused mothers in the State Central Register, what ACS should do prior to removing a child, how ACS should draft and file petitions in court involving domestic violence, what ACS should do after removal has occurred, how prior petitions and active cases should be addressed, and what ACS training and administration improvements were needed.[86]

• • •

When Judge Weinstein issued his decision, Sharwline read every line. Judge Weinstein's words echoed in her head, ". . . the court finds as a matter of fact that the effect of the practice and policy of ACS is to punish both the faultless abused mother and her children by separating them from each other and by not providing them with adequate protection."[87] Judge Weinstein codified what she had known and felt and that which she had come to learn about the

---

[80] *Id.* at 237.
[81] *Id.* at 246.
[82] *Id.* at 247.
[83] *Id.* at 247.
[84] *Id.* at 248.
[85] *Id.* at 257.
[86] *Id.* at 258.
[87] *Id.* at 252.

other mothers through their new friendship born in the litigation. As mothers, they loved their children and tried to do right by them. When they faced struggles, they needed help and support, not punishment. When their children needed them the most and when they yearned to be there for them, they were prevented from doing so. They were not neglectful mothers. Their families' involvement with ACS left wounds as deep or even deeper than the abuse they had experienced.

But change had come because Sharwline and the others persisted. Judge Weinstein's words she read, re-read, and read again: "Just as the government has a responsibility to protect children from an abusive parent, so too does the government have a responsibility to protect a victim of domestic violence from her partner, a responsibility not met by punishing *her* through forcible separation from her children."[88] With Judge Weinstein's opinion in hand, Sharwline did not then realize the impact this decision would have but because she felt chosen for the cause, Sharwline would soon see. Sharwline attended the oral arguments in both the federal appeal and the state case, and she listened, just as Judge Weinstein had listened to her.

The Subsequent Nicholson Rulings

Following Judge Weinstein's decision, the case then proceeded to the Second Circuit Court of Appeals,[89] to the highest state court in New York,[90] back to federal court, and then settled. The Second Circuit Court of Appeals upheld Judge Weinstein's factual findings that ACS had a policy and practice of removing children from their battered mothers and erroneously deeming battered mothers neglectful.[91] The Court also upheld Judge Weinstein's holdings that these policies and practices violated the U.S. Constitution and sought guidance from New York's Court of Appeals by certifying three questions. The highest court of New York answered by holding that under New York state law, domestic violence victims are not per se neglectful parents, such that "when 'the sole allegation' is that the mother has been

88 *Id.* at 252.
89 Nicholson v. Scoppetta, 344 F.3d 154 (C.A.2 N.Y. 2003).
90 Nicholson v. Scoppetta, 3 N.Y.3d 357, 820 N.E.2d 840 (N.Y. 2004).
91 Nicholson v. Scoppetta, 344 F.3d at 165.

abused and the child has witnessed the abuse"[92] exposing a child to domestic violence is *not* presumptively neglectful;[93] the practice of removing children from battered mothers without a court order violates the law unless the child is in imminent danger without time to go to court, a stringent test;[94] and designating a parent as neglectful requires proof of the parent's failure to exercise a minimum degree of care.[95] In determining the course of action that constitutes a "minimum degree of care" for mothers like Sharwline, the court included considerations that echo Susan Schechter's messages of life and batterer-generated risk, including:

> . . . Risks attendant to leaving, if the batterer has threatened to kill her if she does; risks attendant to staying and suffering continued abuse; risks attendant to seeking assistance through government channels, potentially increasing the danger to herself and her children; risks attendant to criminal prosecution against the abuser; and risks attendant to relocation. Whether a particular mother in these circumstances has actually failed to exercise a minimum degree of care is necessarily dependent on facts such as the severity and frequency of the violence and the resources and options available to her.[96]

After capturing the lived experiences of the class of mothers and their children in confronting these risks, the New York Court of Appeals advanced the principle of balancing risks of the intervention by instructing that courts must "weigh the potential harm of staying in the home against the known harm of removal."[97]

The injunction restricting ACS was in place for over two years and was set to expire on December 31, 2004. After the New York Court of Appeals issued its opinion, *Nicholson* returned to the federal district court. On December 16, 2004, the plaintiff mothers and children entered a settlement agreement with the City of New York

[92] Nicholson v. Scoppetta, 3 N.Y.3d at 371.
[93] *Id.* at 375.
[94] *Id.* at 372.
[95] *Id.* at 370.
[96] *Id.* at 371.
[97] *Id.*

that acknowledged the applicable law and ACS's intention to comply and awarded fees for the plaintiff classes' attorneys.[98]

An archetype of therapeutic justice, the *Nicholson* cases defined the statutory and constitutional requirements of policy and practice in order to ensure that child welfare interventions do not impede that which families need.

The *Nicholson* Aftermath and Legacy

Nicholson represents a significant codification of expert testimony that married social science, best practices, and clinical approaches with child welfare policy and practice that the U.S. Constitution was deemed to support. In New York, *Nicholson* set a clear and useful standard for intervention: exposure to domestic violence does not mean that children are neglected, rather children must be specifically harmed or at risk, and abused parents are not neglectful when the sole issue is that children have been exposed to their parent's own abuse. Children can only be removed if there are urgent circumstances or conditions of imminent danger without time to go to court. The harms of removal must be weighed against the risks of remaining.

Once the litigation was over, Liz continued to work toward strengthening the practice and capacity of ACS. It became clear that sound child welfare practice with families experiencing domestic violence required other reforms as well. The potential success of domestic violence reforms was compromised by high caseloads, rapid burnout and turnover, and inadequate quality assurance measures. Liz became an assistant and then deputy commissioner with ACS focusing on prevention. She left the agency seven years after Judge Weinstein issued his opinion to return to the nonprofit sector as an administrator at a domestic violence service organization, Safe Horizon, where she is now the CEO. Just as Betsy continued the work of the CWVP after the lawsuit concluded, Liz remained committed to serving families exposed to abuse and trauma. *Nicholson's* influence continued.

---

98 *Id.*

Nicholson established law that must be followed in New York and an approach that is influential elsewhere. Outside of New York and the federal Second Circuit, on occasion *Nicholson* has been used as persuasive authority in states to support the findings that exposure to domestic violence does not inherently deem children as neglected and parents as neglectful. For instance, the Court of Appeals in Michigan used *Nicholson* as persuasive authority to establish that exposure to domestic violence alone was not sufficient to permanently sever children's relationships with their parents through termination of parental rights.[99] Courts in New Jersey have also cited *Nicholson* in support of the holding that harms resulting from exposure to domestic violence must rise to the level of neglect and cannot be presumed, and if such harm has been met, it is not attributed to the victimized parent.[100] Specifically, *Nicholson* influenced the New Jersey Superior Court to remove from the state's child abuse and neglect registry the name of a mother who was abused in front of her son.[101]

Within New York, *Nicholson* has shaped the way courts analyze cases involving domestic violence in the child welfare system. Although these cases demonstrate that children were still being removed from parents who are victimized by domestic violence and that such parents were still being deemed neglectful, *Nicholson* has had an influence on judicial review. For instance, in *In re David G.*, the New York Family Court found that children were wrongly removed from their mother following an incident of domestic violence.[102] Citing *Nicholson*, the court affirmed the stringent standard for emergency removal and found that "continued removal of children from their mother's care was unnecessary to avoid imminent risk to the children's lives or health[103] and that the abusive parent's violation of an Order of Protection does not establish imminent risk by a nonabusive parent."[104] New York Courts continued addressing these questions in

---

[99] *In re Seby*, No. 306370, 2012 WL 3321320 (Mich. Ct. App. Aug. 14, 2012).

[100] New Jersey Div. of Youth and Family Services v. S.S., 855 A.2d 8 (N.J. Super. Ct. App. Div. 2004). *See also* New Jersey Div. of Youth and Family Services v. R.G., 2009 WL 1287116 (N.J. Super. Ct. App. Div. May 11, 2009).

[101] New Jersey Div. of Youth and Family Services v. S.S., *supra* note 102 at 10.

[102] *In re* David G., 909 N.Y.S.2d 891 (N.Y. Fam. Ct. 2010).

[103] *Id.* at 897.

[104] *Id.* at 899.

Nicholson's aftermath. For instance, courts have reiterated that exposure to domestic violence is not per se neglect and that absent such a threshold,[105] neither parent would be deemed neglectful, yet practice has not consistently followed.[106] And although ACS has filed fewer neglect proceedings against victims of domestic violence, ACS still struggles at times to translate the holdings of the *Nicholson* ruling into reformed practice and families are still experiencing interventions like Sharwline and her children endured.[107] Nonetheless, the spirit and letter of the law of *Nicholson* remains a check on child welfare practice that, in Judge Weinstein's words, may curb "practices and policies in this field that harm children much more than they protect against harm."[108] The voice of *Nicholson* reverberated beyond courtrooms and its soul still does by constructively questioning interventions that deepen wounds without mending with gold.

• • •

Still driven to prevent other mothers and children from suffering like her and her children, Sharwline continued her advocacy following the conclusion of the class action lawsuit. Garnering attention in the legal, advocacy, and policy circles, Sharwline spoke at conferences with her lawyers, attended trainings, provided interviews, sat on advisory committees, and mentored other parents going through the child welfare system. Sharwline traveled the country speaking about

---

105 *Elizabeth B. v. New York State Office of Children and Family Services,* 47 N.Y.S.3d 515 (N.Y. App. Div. 2017); In re *Ilona H.*, 940 N.Y.S.2d 406 (N.Y. App. Div. 2012); Matter of Nevin H., 83 N.Y.S.3d 390 (N.Y. App. Div. 2018); In re *Dalia G.,* 10 N.Y.S.3d 113 (N.Y. App. Div. 2015); In re *Harper F.-L.,* 3 N.Y.S.3d 116 (N.Y. App. Div. 2015); In re *Kiana M.-M.,* 997 N.Y.S.2d 723 N.Y. App. Div. 2014); In re *Chaim R.*, 943 N.Y.S.2d 195 (N.Y. App. Div. 2012); In re *Imani B.,* 811 N.Y.S.2d 447 (N.Y. App. Div. 2006); In re *Ravern H.,* 789 N.Y.S.2d 563 (N.Y. App. Div. 2005); In re *Anthony S.*, 10 N.Y.S.3d 259 (N.Y. App. Div. 2015); In re *Gianna A.,* 18 N.Y.S.3d 658 (N.Y. App. Div. 2015); In re *Emily S.,* 44 N.Y.S.3d 743 (N.Y. App. Div. 2017); In re *Christy C.,* 903 N.Y.S.2d 365 (N.Y. App. Div. 2010); In re *Eryck N.*, 791 N.Y.S.2d 857 (N.Y. App. Div. 2005).

106 *In re M.S.*, 28 N.Y.S.3d 649 (N.Y. Fam. Ct. Oct. 1, 2015); Tysean P. v. Richard S., 971 N.Y.S.2d 75 (N.Y. Fam. Ct. May 21, 2013).

107 Lynn Beller, *When in Doubt, Take Them Out: Removal of Children from Victims of Domestic Violence Ten Years after Nicholson v. Williams,* 22 Duke J. of Gender & Pol. 205, 238 (2015).

108 Nicholson v. Williams, 203 F.Supp.2d at 253.

her experience and her case, hoping to influence child welfare agencies and other stakeholders to use her namesake lawsuit to inspire and guide improved practice around domestic violence.

Continuing *Nicholson's* legacy felt like Sharwline's calling and brought a sense of purpose to the pain she and her children suffered. Through this advocacy, Sharwline began to heal from the violence she experienced, from the trauma of being separated from her children, and the violations of her humanity she felt each step of the way. As the travels away began interfering with her time at home and work, Sharwline turned to concentrate on providing for herself and her children, Kendell and Destinee. At home and at work, the supportive spirit, constructive support, and empathetic strength of *Nicholson* lives.

Kendell lives at home and is a described introvert, whose mother understands, accepts, and buoys him through his special needs. Destinee is her mother's best friend, and Sharwline supports Destinee's dreams whether they take her to college or beauty school. As Sharwline enters her second half-century of life, she reflects on the days advocating for change following her eponymous case. With some longing, Sharwline reminds herself that the difference she is making in the lives of those around her—her children, her extended family, her colleagues—is now also part of her legacy, the legacy of a girl from Jamaica who rose from adversity on behalf of the dignity of all families and changed the world for the better.

6
It Fits on a Card: Child Welfare Investigations of Families Experiencing Domestic Violence

The front of a card reads:

> Believe in Yourself . . . We Do

We give this card to every mom or female caregiver connected to our agency.

Why? *Because whatever your story, whatever is happening with your children, you deserve help and support too.*

Our deepest hope is for safety for you and your children. The most important factor in children's healing from hard things is a strong and safe relationship with their mom. This card looks at the bigger picture of things that might be affecting you—studies show us when we invest in moms, we help kids. As a parent, you also have rights. And sharing what is happening to you might affect your case. Ask your lawyer for information about your rights and what can and can't be confidential.

The words on the back of the card continue:

Powerful Women.

If you get this card today, chances are you don't feel powerful; you may feel helpless.

Maybe your children were hurt, put in danger, or their needs weren't met.

We can't change the past, but we can change the future.

Let's change it right now. Learning how your childhood or your relationship can affect your parenting can help you be the mom you want to be.

We know some moms aren't fully understood. Maybe people don't understand what went on for you or what is happening to you right now. Being safer helps you be a better mom and gives you more power.

This card is not a card that would be given to a mother on her birthday or Mother's Day, or as part of domestic violence counseling. Rather, this "Moms Matter" card is intended to be handed to mothers who are subjects of child welfare investigations.[1]

A child welfare investigation is typically the first interaction families have with the child welfare system, like it was for Sharwline Nicholson. Unlike Sharwline, thousands of families experience child welfare investigations and related interventions without ever having a juvenile court case. Child welfare interventions outside of the court system often feel omnipotent, rogue, or amorphous to families but every state has laws, rules, procedures, policies, and/or practices that govern the operations of the child welfare system including investigations. Specifically, each state has statutes governing the child welfare agency and its investigations as well as administrative rules (that have the power of law), procedures, protocols, and/or policies that interpret the statutes and provide further guidance to child welfare workers, families, and practitioners

---

[1] Promising Futures, a division of Futures Without Violence, provides resources, tools, and trainings on best practices for serving children, youth, and parents experiencing domestic violence. Promising Futures developed the "Moms Matter" card and encourages child welfare agencies to use or modify this card and to provide it to all mothers. *In Child Welfare, We Believe Moms Matter Webinar PowerPoint,* Futures Without Violence, https://www.ncjfcj.org/sites/default/files/Child%20Welfare%20webinar%20%28rev%29.pdf.

about child welfare process and practice. Some child welfare agencies have specific policies or protocols that instruct child welfare investigators and workers on responding to domestic violence. Such rules and policies were at issue in the *Nicholson* class action lawsuit.

Amidst instructive policies or not, trauma-informed, strength-based, family-centered, and equity-focused principles and practices must guide any child welfare investigation. Such an orientation is transformative yet succinct enough to fit on a card like the "Moms Matter" card. The words of the card orientate child welfare workers toward, rather than away, from the sources of children's safety, stability, well-being, and healing. The messages internalized by the giver of the card and heard by the receiver convey: we care about your children, and we care about you; compassion drives us even when we are worried; we see you as the most important resource for your child; we can get the help you need and deserve here; we support and believe in you so you can support and believe in your children; and the greater we can work together here on the frontend, the less likely ongoing system involvement will be. Moving away from nonjudicial interventions that discount these messages and moving toward investigations that provide families with what they need can be found in expansive policies and procedures, but also in the individuals and norms that make up a system's culture toward families experiencing domestic violence as the divergent experiences of two mothers, Karen Johnson and Itan Nacuaa, reveal.

Moving Away From

Karen Johnson has always been moving—moving away from something of tangible distress—yet yearning to intentionally move toward something of promise. Karen moved throughout her childhood from state to state, school to school, from one source of trauma to another at the hands of school bullies, relatives, and boyfriends. As an adult, Karen moved between psychiatric hospitals, domestic violence shelters, homeless shelters, and transitional living facilities. Karen eventually moved to a psychiatric nursing home for six months, during which time she began to heal from the cumulative trauma surrounded by peace and safety. Karen then began working as a Certified Nursing Assistant (CNA) by day, attending community college in the evenings, and moving from couch to couch, hotel room to hotel room, homeless shelter to homeless shelter by night. In one of the homeless shelters, she met Jamal.

Karen moved in with a friend and discovered she was pregnant by Jamal. Jamal visited her and was violent for the first time. Karen went to a domestic violence shelter and refused Jamal's calls. When the time she was allowed at the shelter expired, Karen lived in a homeless shelter until she gave birth. With nowhere to go, Karen and her newborn daughter, Nia, moved in with Jamal into his mother's house.

Under his mother's roof, Jamal's abuse continued. He would grab Karen by her neck, push her into a corner, take Nia's car seat so Karen could not leave, and lock her out of the house. Repeatedly, Karen would take Nia into a bedroom and lock the door until Jamal calmed down. Karen chose not to call the police because she did not want to risk Jamal's mother losing her Section 8 voucher or getting evicted due to nuisance violations caused by police visits.[2] Karen felt that she was faced with an impossible choice—seek protection or preserve the roof over her daughter's head.[3]

---

2 Karen's concerns were well-founded, as many cities across the country have nuisance ordinances that cause survivors of domestic violence and other residents to face penalties and even evictions for calling the police. Sandra Park & Linda Morris, *A Disturbing Number of Missouri Towns Evict Residents for Calling the Police,* American Civil Liberties Union (Jan. 24, 2019), https://www.aclu.org/blog/womens-rights/violence-against-women/disturbing-number-missouri-towns-evict-residents-calling. A St. Louis study revealed that half of the women had been forced to move due to violations of nuisance ordinances, including many who were evicted for calling the police too many times. Many of these women called the police in response to an incident of domestic violence. Nuisance violations are more likely to impact properties in low-income neighborhoods with people of color. *Id.*

3 Unstable housing can be a factor causing children to be removed and stable housing is a prerequisite to returning children to their home, both of which are exacerbated in cities that penalize victims of crime for reaching out for protection. Unstable housing has a circular impact on a family's involvement in the child welfare system. A mother who is a victim of domestic violence is expected to call the police for protection, yet that protective step could cause her and her children to be evicted or ineligible for housing assistance. While children should not be removed due to homelessness, a lack of stable housing could, in part, deem her children at "imminent risk of harm," resulting in their removal from her. If the children are removed, she will be expected to secure stable housing in order for them to return, which will be difficult to find with an eviction on her record due to nuisance violations for calling the police because of domestic violence. But had

As a veteran, Jamal obtained a Housing and Urban Development (HUD) voucher. The three moved into a house and the abuse worsened. One morning Nia accidentally scratched Jamal's nose and Jamal hit his daughter on her thigh. Karen immediately locked herself and her daughter in another bedroom. When Jamal fell asleep that night, Karen packed their bags, took the car seat, and moved to a domestic violence shelter with Nia.

At the shelter, Karen disclosed that Jamal hit Nia, and the shelter staff informed Karen that they needed to make a call to the state's child abuse and neglect Hotline. Jamal was ultimately found to have abused Nia, resulting in an indicated finding of the investigation. With her domestic violence advocate, Karen set the goal of and identified the steps toward permanently leaving Jamal.

As that shelter stay expired, Karen was faced with another impossible choice. Without other options, she and Nia could live in Karen's car or they could return to Jamal's home. It was fall in the Midwest, and the weather was becoming cold. Had it been warm enough, Karen would have chosen her car as their refuge, but Karen could not afford the gas money to keep her car running all night long to keep them warm. Karen and Nia reluctantly moved back to the house they had left; this time, Karen was working toward her goal of leaving Jamal but needed time to ensure she would be able to provide for her daughter. Her path was clear—wait until she had a job and enough money.

As the new year approached, Karen was actively preparing to leave Jamal. She was hired as a CNA in a nursing home, and despite a one-hour commute each way, Karen accepted every shift she was given. She applied for public aid daycare assistance but was denied because Jamal was not working. Unable to afford daycare on her own, Jamal would often take Nia to his mother's house, which worried Karen because the house was heated by running the stove. Karen reenrolled in community college to obtain her associate degree. She remained on the two-year waitlist for low-income housing.

---

she not called the police in the first place, a child welfare investigator could conclude that she was not willing to protect her children and remove them due to the imminent risk of harm that the domestic violence posed to them and her alleged "failure to protect."

After working six days straight, Karen arrived home to an empty house. Snow was falling heavily, so the next morning Karen went to pick up her daughter from Jamal's mother's house. When she arrived, Karen collected her daughter's belongings. Jamal told Karen that Nia was not going anywhere. Every time Karen put an item in a bag, Jamal took it out. Karen put Nia in the stroller so she could focus on packing and keep her daughter secure. As Karen bent down to pack up the diaper bag, Jamal began shoving her. When she found a moment to free herself from his shoves, she stood up. Expecting that Jamal would continue pushing her or worse, she smacked him in the face, hoping to prevent what she was certain would ensue. She was right and Jamal hit Karen across her face with such force that her neck snapped back. Jamal's mother took Nia out of the stroller and brought her into the kitchen. Jamal grabbed Karen by her legs, dragged her into the bedroom, and barricaded the door so she could not leave. His mother screamed, "Stop it. I don't want the police here." Jamal backed down and went outside to smoke. Karen was unable to find her car keys, so as she had done many times before, Karen took Nia, diapers, and food and retreated to the bedroom. That night, Karen devised a plan, but yet again, she confronted an unbearable choice—in order to leave Jamal, she would have to leave Nia with him one last time.

The next morning because Jamal had confiscated her keys, Karen convinced him that she needed to leave to file the required paperwork to renew his housing voucher. Karen arrived home to pack up her and Nia's belongings. Karen moved to the domestic violence shelter she had stayed at before and sought guidance in getting her daughter back from Jamal. The crisis advocate thought that because of the prior abuse finding against Jamal, the child welfare agency would help return Nia to Karen. The advocate called the Hotline, and rather than assisting Karen, an investigation was started, this time against Karen.

• • •

In all states, after the child abuse and neglect Hotline is notified and the call passes the initial Hotline screening,[4] the first step of the child

[4] Typically, a case will pass the Hotline screening if there is credible evidence that abuse or neglect of a child has occurred, and if there is sufficient identifying information to locate the child.

welfare intervention is typically the investigation. While law enforcement investigations may occur simultaneously or not at all, child welfare investigations are distinct and separate from law enforcement investigations. Amidst varying qualifications across the country, child welfare investigators are supposed to be orientated in social work rather than in police work, yet their responsibilities and actions lead to roles that are a hybrid at best. During a child welfare investigation, dual objectives exist: (1) make investigative findings; and (2) evaluate safety. As such, child welfare investigators collect evidence of whether abuse or neglect occurred to make a finding at the end of the investigation and will continually evaluate the children's safety throughout the investigation. Most states mandate a short timeframe in which the child welfare professional must see the child, such as twelve or twenty-four hours following the investigation assignment. During the investigation, the child welfare investigator is supposed to gather information by interviewing the parents and children (when appropriate), observing the children, speaking to collateral contacts (e.g., teachers, doctors, law enforcement, friends or family with firsthand knowledge), and collecting documents (e.g., police reports, medical records, legal filings). Throughout these interactions, the investigator is also assessing the child's safety, determining if conditions need to be put in place for the child to remain safely at home or removing the child from the parents if there is an imminent risk of harm, in which a dependency case in juvenile court would then ensue. Investigations typically are time-limited typically to forty-five or sixty days.

At the end of the investigation, the parents will be notified as to whether the results of the allegations of abuse or neglect are substantiated/indicated or unsubstantiated/unfounded. Indicated findings will be entered in the state's registry of parents or caregivers who have abused or neglected children. With an indicated finding, parents in part can lose their jobs if they work with children, are barred from jobs that involve children, and cannot enter their children's school. In many states, parents are entitled to an administrative appeal of these investigative findings. This means that an administrative law judge, typically hired by the child welfare agency, will conduct an evidentiary hearing about whether the parent abused or neglected the child. Following the hearing, decisions can be appealed to the circuit court which sits as a reviewing court, and appeals can continue until all appeal options have been exhausted. The result of a successful appeal is that the parent's name is no longer held on the state's abuse and neglect database.

• • •

The child welfare agency refused to help Karen regain physical possession of her daughter. Karen then called the police for help but was told that law enforcement officers could not remove a child from a parent without a court order. When the courthouse opened the next day, Karen completed a Petition for an Emergency Order of Protection with the help of a domestic violence advocate at the courthouse. Karen was granted an Emergency Order of Protection that protected both her and Nia and gave Karen an enforceable order to use to get her daughter back from Jamal. Karen waited at a parking lot for eight hours until the police finally arrived with her daughter. As Karen and Nia made their way to the domestic violence shelter, Jamal was looking over the Order of Protection with which he had just been served. Jamal now knew where Karen and Nia were going. The courthouse advocate inadvertently listed the name and address of the shelter as their place of residence even though the law permitted and required this information to be kept confidential. Jamal called the shelter. Jamal's knowledge jeopardized the safety of Karen, Nia, and the other residents.

When Karen arrived back at the shelter with Nia, the shelter staff told Karen and Nia that they would have to move again. This time, Karen wanted to move somewhere inaccessible to Jamal. The shelter helped locate beds for Karen and Nia seventy-five miles away and unreachable by public transportation. With their belongings in garbage bags, Karen and Nia made the move that evening.

As Karen and Nia adjusted to the new town and shelter, a child welfare investigation began unfolding to determine whether Nia was currently safe and whether the incident at Jamal's mother's house caused Nia to be a neglected child and if so, by whom.

The Child Welfare Investigation

As Karen would soon experience, determining whether a child has been abused or neglected, and continually determining whether children are safe are the priorities of child welfare investigations.

Screening for domestic violence, understanding the child's exposure to domestic violence, determining the impact of domestic violence on children, and assessing for risk are critical investigative components that impact both investigative findings and safety determinations. Yet child welfare policies, procedures, and protocols often fall short of providing sufficient guidance and instruction to workers on how to make these important investigative decisions about families who are experiencing domestic violence. Even without policies or adequate protocols phrases like the following: We believe you, You matter, How can we support you, are words to anchor and guide investigations.

Screening

Sometimes the existence of domestic violence is known to the investigator as the presenting cause of the call to the Hotline, and other times domestic violence is not known such that it is underlying or co-occurring with the presenting cause for intervention. Screening aims to uncover the existence or extent of domestic violence. Concerns about ineffective or harmful interventions that follow disclosures of domestic violence hesitate against screening for domestic violence in all cases. It is argued, however, that routine, consistent, and sensitive screening for domestic violence is integral to effective responses. Screening for domestic violence occurs in contexts outside of child welfare such as in emergency departments,[5] other healthcare settings,[6] community pharmacies,[7] and mental health settings,[8] through a combination of direct screening and universal education.

---

5 John Krimm & Marjories M. Heinzer, *Domestic Violence Screening in the Emergency Room Department of An Urubn Hospital,* 94 J. Natl. Med. Assoc. 484 (2002). Screening for domestic violence was not routinely asked upon admissions.

6 Office of the Assistant Secretary for Planning and Evaluation, Office of Human Services Policy, U.S. Department of Health and Human Services, *Screening for Domestic Violence in Health Care Settings,* U.S. Department of the Health and Human Services (Aug. 2013), https://aspe.hhs.gov/system/files/pdf/76931/pb_screening Domestic.pdf.

7 Anyssa Garza, *Domestic Violence: The Power of Screening,* Pharmacy Times (June 14, 2017), https://www.pharmacytimes.com/publications/issue/2017/june2017 /domestic-violence.

8 *Information for Professionals—Mental Health—Screening for Domestic Violence in Mental Health Settings,* Office for the Prevention of Domestic Violence, New York

In the child welfare context, Minnesota,[9] Georgia,[10] Missouri,[11] and Illinois,[12] directly screen for domestic violence during investigations. In Illinois for instance, investigators use the Domestic Violence Screen to identify indicators of domestic violence, such as a criminal history of assault or damage to property, physical injuries to an adult, control over one partner by the other, damage to the home, involvement of police, and the existence of an Order of Protection. The screen also outlines questions that aim to expose the more nuanced dynamics of control, isolation, and threats.

Through screening that demands information, the child welfare investigator may be the first person ever asking the adult survivor about being abused and the investigator might be the first person to whom she discloses. The initial response to a disclosure of domestic violence greatly influences the adult survivor's belief that the systemic intervention can actually help her and her children; compassionate, nonjudgmental, creative, and resourceful responses of a child welfare investigation, therefore, are needed. Even if such rare responses occur, the power dynamics and the looming potential of losing one's children cause the demanded sharing to be less healing and more riddled with fear.

As an alternative method for grasping the existence and extent of domestic violence through a didactic screen, universal education is more consistent with a trauma-informed, strength-based, family-centered, and equity-focused approach by "creating environments and relationships that create an atmosphere of safety, connecting, and hope."[13] Universal education provides information to all parents

---

State (July 30, 2019), https://opdv.ny.gov/professionals/mental_health/screening/aboutdv.html.

9 *The Co-Occurrence of Domestic Violence and Child Abuse and Neglect, A Guide for Crisis Center Advocates,* The Greenbook Project (Aug. 2006), http://www.thegreenbook.info/documents/Final_Guide_for_Advocates.pdf.

10 *Children 1st,* Georgia Dep't of Public Health (Sept 2019), http://dph.georgia.gov/children-first.

11 Child Welfare Manual, Missouri Dep't. of Social Servs. (Sept. 2019), https://dssmanuals.mo.gov/child-welfare-manual/child-welfare-manual-2019-update/.

12 Domestic Violence Screen, SACWIS/CANTS 17A/DV, Procedures 300, Appendix J https://www2.illinois.gov/dcfs/aboutus/notices/Documents/Procedures_300_Appendix_C_to_L.pdf#search=CANTS%2017A%2FDV.

13 *Trauma-Informed Care for Mental Health Professionals: Athealth Interview with Carole Warshaw, M.D.,* He@lth (Oct. 2014), https://athealth.com/trauma-informed-care-for-mental-health-professionals/.

about domestic violence, trauma, and the connections to parenting. Universal education assumes that all mothers *may* have had trauma during childhood and/or experienced domestic violence and that all will benefit from knowledge, tools, and support. Disclosure is not rushed or forced, and parents retain and regain power by controlling the process of disclosure. This less demanding and more patient approach to information gathering provides general information and education that normalizes struggles so that an adult survivor may feel less isolated and judged, can connect the learnings with her own experiences, and can conclude that sharing her experience will be beneficial to her and her children. Universal education can improve child welfare screenings for domestic violence especially when the case was called into the Hotline for other presenting causes.

Universal education can begin with the "Moms Matter" card. Within the safety of a private conversation, the child welfare worker could impart:[14]

> I've started giving these cards to all moms because we know some struggles that can get in the way of being the mom you want to be and giving your children the childhood you want for them. I really think you deserve support and help just like your child does, and a lot of times people forget to think about how much you matter too. This card talks about everything from parenting strategies to ways being hurt by a partner or during your childhood can affect your health and parenting. In about half of my caseload, the mom is being hurt by her partner, and we know that supporting a mom is one of the best ways to support her child.
>
> Even if this doesn't apply to you, you might know someone who could benefit from this information. You could pass it along to a friend, a family member, a neighbor, or a co-worker. On the back are great resources, like the Domestic Violence Hotline.

---

[14] A similar dialogue was shared in a training offered by Futures Without Violence. *In Child Welfare, We Believe Moms Matter Webinar PowerPoint,* FUTURES WITHOUT VIOLENCE, https://www.ncjfcj.org/sites/default/files/Child%20Welfare%20webinar%20%28rev%29.pdf.

> Is any of this information something you need help with or is there anything you would like to talk more about? If not today, please know that you can reach out to me at any time.

If domestic violence is shared, rather than tasked with checking a box, the investigator can respond with genuine compassion expressed in the words, "I am so sorry to hear that's happening to you. I believe you. You are not alone. I want to help. What would be the most helpful for you and your children right now?" By listening to understand, the worker can avoid jumping into professional paperwork; stay present in the conversation; seek to understand the mother's perspective, her worries, the risks she is weighing, and the sacrifices she might have to give up to find physical safety; ask questions about sources of external and internal sources of resilience; explore her support system; grasp the children's relationship with the person using violence and coercive control; and engage the mother in safety planning for herself and her children. The personal and honest conversation will reveal the mother as more than a victim. Her humanity and strength will surface. The connection to her that is essential for her children will become readily apparent, and the risks that need to be addressed will be accurate and not the result of misunderstandings, presumptions, or withholding information. The worker can foster protective factors by treating every interaction as an intervention and can offer concrete supports based upon the needs the mother identifies. In the immediacy, this approach requires time, capacity, and the willingness to slow down in the face of perceived risk yet will be significantly more impactful over the course of the intervention. While the children's safety remains centered, the journey of the conversation has a wider lens that can later settle on the next steps.

Assessing for Children's Exposure, Impact, and Risk

If domestic violence is revealed as the presenting cause prompting the Hotline call, elicited through direct screening, or revealed through universal education, assessing for children's exposure to, impact from, and risk due to domestic violence should follow. To accurately determine what a family needs, child welfare investigators must understand the specifics of any exposure, impacted harm, and risk (past and future).[15] Importantly, the existence of exposure, harm, and risk do not in and of itself justify child welfare interventions. And most investigators ignore the specifics of children's exposure and conflate harm and risk leading to both overreactions and missed opportunities to respond to the nuanced needs of the children and their families. Tools do not currently exist to adequately address exposure, impact, and risk of domestic violence in the child welfare context, but two existing tools have important, albeit incomplete, applicability.

The Child Exposure to Domestic Violence Scale (CEDV), developed by Dr. Jeffrey Edleson (chapter 3), is a tool targeted to capture the extent of children's exposure to domestic violence.[16] CEDV is a self-report survey used to measure the degree of exposure to domestic violence reported by youth between the ages of ten and sixteen years of age. A youth responds to the CEDV's forty-two questions about violence, exposure to violence at home, exposure to violence in the community, involvement in the violence, risk factors, and other victimization. While this tool could be useful and a foundation for a more comprehensively useable tool, the application of the CEDV during a child welfare intervention is limited. The CEDV is not intended to be used by children, like Nia, under ten years old. In addition, while self-evaluation tools can be empowering and informative, child survivors, like adult survivors, may be resistant to didactically sharing information that is not confidential. Children may feel responsible, guilty, or deceived if their responses lead to child welfare interventions that are contrary to their wishes (e.g., the youth is removed but wants to remain home), harmful to their family (e.g., the family is separated and sources of healing are severed), or jeopardize their safety (e.g., investigator requires them to

---

[15] Harm and risk are distinct. A child could be at risk of being hurt but not yet harmed, such as when the mother obtains a protective order and now the father threatens to kidnap the child. Or a child could have been harmed but is not currently at risk, such that the child is struggling in school and has recurrent nightmares but is now living in a domestic violence shelter with his mother.

[16] Dr. Jeffrey L. Edleson, Katy K. Johnson, & Narae Shin, *Children's Exposure to Domestic Violence Scale User Manual,* MINNESOTA CENTER AGAINST DOMESTIC VIOLENCE (2007) 5, https://docs.wixstatic.com/ugd/1e71bb_56158f0c0caf4eb78191919bc1c7f817.pdf.

move to a domestic violence shelter but the mother's partner stalks them now at work and school). In the absence of a tool, however, information about the extent of the children's exposure to domestic violence can otherwise be gathered through discussions with parents, the child, and other collateral contacts. While the CEDV would need to be modified for child welfare investigations, it underscores the importance of determining the extent of a child or youth's exposure to domestic violence to inform an understanding of both harm and risk.

Determining the impact of domestic violence on children is also integral to an effective response and central to the basis and justification for child welfare intervention. As both social science and the *Nicholson* case have affirmed, exposure to domestic violence does not equate to automatic intervenable harm to children. Rather, children are uniquely impacted by the exposure to domestic violence. Domestic violence may impact children in the following ways: physical injury caused by intervening or being indirectly hurt, low self-esteem, depression, anger, fear, anxiety, hypervigilance, eating and sleeping disorders, bedwetting, vomiting, verbally and physically aggressive behaviors, guilt if the child believes he or she is the cause of the abuse, poor academic performance, problems thinking and reasoning, lack of compliance with authority, alcohol and drug abuse, and dating violence.[17] Determining the specific impact of domestic violence on each child is twice as important. First, the impact of domestic violence indicates what supports the child may need. Second, the impact determines if the child has been harmed by the domestic violence. The question then becomes whether the harm rises to the level of abuse or neglect to which the child welfare system has jurisdiction to respond. Without a model tool yet developed to determine both the impact and whether the impact constitutes intervenable harm, child welfare agencies should craft policies in partnership with social science researchers, clinicians, and lawyers in order to guide investigators in understanding the specific impact of domestic violence on children. Such policies must

---

[17] Jeffrey L. Edelson, *Brief: The Overlap Between Child Maltreatment and Child Abuse,* (1999). Judge Jack Weinstein adopted these findings in Nicholson v. Williams, 203 F.Supp.2d 153 (E.D.N.Y. 2002).

also consider protective factors, which include internal and external sources that buffer the harm children may have experienced. The most central protective factor that buffers the impact of domestic violence is the child's relationship with the nonoffending parent, like Karen.

Even if harm has not yet occurred, child welfare agencies are not constrained to wait but are permitted and (arguably) statutorily required to respond to children who have been or are at risk of harm that rises to the level of abuse or neglect. Assessing past or future risk is even more challenging than determining exposure and impact. Most child welfare agencies use general risk assessment tools that are not domestic violence specific.[18] Risk posed by domestic violence is very hard to predict and no domestic violence risk assessment tool currently exists for the child welfare context. A transferrable tool could be Dr. Jacquelyn Campbell's validated Danger Assessment. After years of reviewing domestic violence fatalities, police records, and court records, Dr. Campbell developed the Danger Assessment as a self-report tool, like the CEDV, aimed at capturing the "risk factors . . . associated with increased risk of homicide (murders) of women and men in violent relationships." With caution, the Danger Assessment could both be utilized with adult survivors involved in child welfare investigations and serve as a guide for developing risk assessments in the child welfare context that are particularized for domestic violence.[19] As Dr. Campbell has shared, using a validated

---

[18] Investigators in Illinois use a form called the Child Endangerment Risk Assessment Protocol (CERAP). The CERAP lists fifteen circumstances that could pose a risk to children, one of which states "the presence of domestic violence which affects caretaker's ability to care for or protect child from imminent, moderate to severe harm." After determining whether risk factors are present, the next step of the CERAP guides the investigator to describe the circumstances of the risk factor and the presence of family strengths and mitigating factors. The investigator then documents the conclusion of whether the children are "safe" or "unsafe." *Child Endangerment Risk Assessment Protocol, Safety Determination Form*, Illinois Department of Children and Family Services, https://www.illinois.gov/dcfs/aboutus/notices/Documents/cfs_1441_child_endangerment_risk_assessment_protocol_%28fillable%29.pdf

[19] The Danger Assessment is the most commonly used tool for assessing the risk of lethality to the adult survivor. *The Danger Assessment* (Aug 5, 2019), https://www.dangerassessment.org/.

risk assessment with good protocols will increase the effectiveness of systemic (and social service) interventions.[20]

Importing the Danger Assessment into the child welfare context would be important yet insufficient as a comprehensive risk assessment tool. While the Danger Assessment could be offered to adult survivors involved in a child welfare investigation to self-assesses the risk of lethality they may be facing the tool does not capture the extent of the risk that is relevant to child welfare. As a self-assessment tool about the risk of lethal domestic violence to the adult survivor, Dr. Campbell cautions that the Danger Assessment does not capture risk (1) to the adult survivor of further physical violence or other forms of coercive control, (2) to the children of neglect, abuse, kidnapping, familicide, or infanticide, or (3) of any family member's suicidality. The Danger Assessment also does not capture the factors that buffer against risk, which are the building blocks of trauma-informed, strength-based, family-centered, and equity-focused interventions. Needed in the child welfare field is guidance on how to utilize the Danger Assessment during a child welfare investigation for its intended purpose and to develop a domestic violence risk assessment tool that covers the panoply of risk within the purview of child welfare. Most importantly, filling either hole must be accompanied by good protocols to instruct on how to use any risk assessment tools in ways that are responsive to the family's needs, rather than reactive to the risk identified.

The good protocols that Dr. Campbell recommends would caution against drastic, sweeping, blaming, presumptive, and destructive fear-driven responses to the results revealed in the Danger Assessment or other risk assessment tools. Child welfare peddles in the realm of risk and any risk assessment cannot conclusively foretell the future. Assessing risk can be neither predictive nor protracted but rather must be limited to identifying a likelihood that may imminently occur. As Dr. Campbell guides, instead of dictating interventions, risk determinations should enable systems to to identify high-risk cases so that interventions can appropriately respond to the level of risk *and* protect the adult and child victims so they can live to be survivors who can heal. Accompanying protocols would also need to guide

---

20 Video Interview with Dr. Jacquelyn Campbell, New Directions in Fatality Review Conference, Phoenix (Aug 16-17, 2010), https://ndvfri.org/resources/videos/.

workers in how to mitigate the risk while also identifying the risk that the intervention itself poses. In response to even potentially fatal risk, forced separation of either the children from the adult survivors,[21] or the adult survivor from the person causing harm,[22] could increase risk to the children's safety, stability, well-being, and healing. As Dr. Campbell imparted, "We get very frustrated and impatient with mothers who do not leave or who return. But if intervention is predicated on separation, this could cause increased unsafety. A domestic violence risk assessment tool could be critical in turning anecdote into better, more creative practice."[23]

Promoting a thorough analysis of exposure, harm, and risk must fulfill Susan Schechter's expectation that such information will be used to support families rather than as ammunition for separation. As such, if the level of harm or risk of harm warrants intervention, policies should instruct child welfare investigators on how to craft interventions that partner with all members of the family to meet their individual and collective needs by addressing the identified struggles, building upon recognized strengths, supporting the adult survivor as the children's primary source of healing, facilitating connection to accessible and appropriate services, and engaging with the parent using violence and coercive control in order to generate pathways of accountability. Above all, such policies must move toward, rather than away from, the adult survivor of domestic violence as the centerpiece of her children's needs while building protective factors rooted in concrete supports so she is not left alone to "fix" a situation that, by definition, she cannot control.

Safety Determinations

Most fundamentally, child welfare investigators make determinations about the safety of children. Exposure to domestic violence,

---

21 Even in the face of grave risk, the well-being of children is inextricably linked to the well-being of their mother, and their mother is the greatest buffer against harm and resource in recovery from it.

22 Risk of homicide occurs during the first three months following separation, dips only slightly for the next nine months, then risk decreases a year after separation. Campbell, *supra* note 20; *see also,* Casey Gwinn & Dr. Chan Hellman, HOPE RISING, 2019.

23 Campbell, *supra* note 19.

the impact of domestic violence, and the risk domestic violence has and continues to pose are relevant to an assessment of children's current safety. Therefore, information that an investigator should gather about a child's exposure to domestic violence, the impact of domestic violence on the child that rises to the level of jurisdictional harm, and the risk of past or future harm to the child should inform determinations about the safety of the children.

The Illinois Domestic Violence Screen, for instance, provides an opportunity to bring these three considerations together in determining the safety of a child. After gathering information about indicators of domestic violence, the screen requires the investigator to assess harm, risk, and safety. Developed in consultation with Susan Schechter (chapter 2), the screen asks five questions:

> Was or is there physical danger posed to the child from the batterer?
> Does the physical, developmental, or emotional impact of the domestic violence on the children rise to the level of suspected child abuse or neglect?
> Are there strategies the adult victim has used in the past that can be supported or strengthened to protect the children?
> Has the batterer ever used or threatened to use weapons of *any* kind?
> In consultation with the supervisor, what if any action is required to address safety and/or risk?

Accurately responding to these central questions remains a significant challenge during child welfare investigations. Investigators regularly do not gather the information specific enough to answer these questions. Even when investigators do, they often do not receive sufficient guidance from training or protocols to transfer and interpret the information about domestic violence that they collected to make safety decisions. Subjectivity, therefore, rather than guided analysis, typically governs, often leading to presumptive conclusions that "exposure = harm + risk = unsafe."

Albeit thorough or cursory, safety determinations drive the direction of investigations. If the children are deemed safe (i.e., current risk does not exist) the investigation still proceeds. The investigator must still make investigative findings about whether the children have been abused or neglected based upon impacted harm or past risk, but because the children are deemed safe, changes for the family will likely not be recommended at that point. However, if circumstances change, this safety determination can change. For instance, when Karen and Nia were living at the domestic violence shelter, the investigator would deem Nia safe (which he did), but if they leave the shelter and return to the home with Jamal (which they did not), the investigator could then deem Nia unsafe. If children are determined to be unsafe, the child welfare investigator can do the following: (1) maintain the status quo, (2) remove the children from the parents by taking protective custody, or (3) recommend interventions without judicial involvement, such as a child welfare safety plan or services. Removal and interventions without judicial involvement occur regularly, and some parents never step foot in court or have their case heard before a juvenile court judge.

• • •

Shortly after Karen and Nia moved into the domestic violence shelter, Karen met with a child welfare investigator. Karen described in detail what had happened the morning after the snowstorm in Jamal's mother's house. Karen described the sequence of events imparting that she was trying to leave with the baby, that Jamal pushed her by the stroller where the baby was, and that she hit Jamal to protect herself because she anticipated that he would use more violence against her. Karen provided written consent for the investigator to communicate with her domestic violence case manager at the new shelter and vice versa. The investigator observed Karen and Nia together. He documented that Nia was dressed appropriately, was adequately supervised by Karen as she played and explored the toys, and did not show any fear of her mother. He completed the general risk assessment and deemed Nia safe without any signs of abuse or neglect.

The investigator collected other evidence about whether abuse or neglect had occurred by talking to witnesses and collateral contacts, as well as obtaining relevant documents. The investigator met with Jamal who alleged that Karen hit him first, denied harming her, and shared that he filed a police report against Karen but decided to not pursue the charges. The investigator interviewed Jamal's mother and her version of events corroborated her son's. The last collateral contact was a friend of Karen who shared Karen's history of moving, again and again, to be safe. With this information, the investigator decided whether or not Karen had neglected Nia—a decision that would also control whether Karen's name would be held on the state central register of neglectful and abusive parents.

Investigative Findings

At the conclusion of the investigation, the child welfare investigator determines, under the law, whether the children are abused or neglected, and if so, which parent(s) are responsible for the abuse or neglect. The investigator will then issue investigative findings against each parent accordingly.

Exposure to Domestic Violence as Neglect

Significant variations exist amongst the states regarding how their laws and administrative rules define the legal connection between the exposure to domestic violence and neglect—the very question that the *Nicholson* court grappled with in New York City.[24] Amidst those states that have an allegation system, only California (Los Angeles County), Florida, and Oklahoma have a maltreatment allegation specifically for domestic violence. Most states, however, encompass exposure to domestic violence in an umbrella allegation of abuse or neglect.[25] In addition to the definitions of abuse and neglect, thirty child welfare agencies have a domestic violence policy that aims to provide additional guidance.[26]

---

24 If a child has experienced direct child abuse, those circumstances will also be investigated.

25 The following states do not have a specific abuse or neglect allegation for domestic violence and domestic violence cases are encompassed in general abuse and neglect allegations: Alabama, Alaska, Connecticut, DC, Delaware, Hawaii, Idaho, Indiana, Kansas, Kentucky, Louisiana, Maine, Massachusetts, Michigan, Mississippi, Missouri, Montana, Nevada, New Mexico, New York, North Carolina, North Dakota, Ohio, Pennsylvania, South Carolina, North Dakota, Tennessee, Texas, Vermont, West Virginia, and Wisconsin. *Id.*

26 These states include: Alaska, California (Los Angeles County), Connecticut, District of Columbia, Delaware, Florida, Georgia, Idaho, Indiana, Maine, Michigan, Minnesota, Missouri, Montana, New Hampshire, New Jersey, New Mexico, New York, North Carolina, North Dakota, Ohio (Cuyahoga County), Oregon, Pennsylvania (Philadelphia County), Tennessee, Texas, Utah, Vermont, Virginia, West Virginia, and Wisconsin. *Id.*

Every state recognizes that exposure to domestic violence can cause a child to be abused or neglected, yet no state creates a per se rule that children who are exposed to domestic violence are abused or neglected. For instance, Washington's law states, "exposure to domestic violence . . . that is perpetrated against someone other than the child does not constitute negligent treatment or maltreatment in and of itself."[27] Likewise, Virginia law states, that a ". . . report in which the only allegation is domestic violence does not in itself meet the statutory definition for child abuse and neglect."[28]

Steering away from per se conclusions of neglect, the existence of harm, or the risk of harm to the child is required in order to conclude that the exposure to domestic violence renders a child abused or neglected under the law in most states. For instance, the child welfare procedures in the District of Columbia state that "acts of domestic violence do not, in and of themselves, constitute abuse or neglect, rather it is the impact of the domestic violence on the children."[29] Some states define harm or risk of harm more specifically. Washington goes on to specify that "domestic violence is considered child abuse and neglect when it causes harm or creates a clear and present danger of harm to the child's health, welfare, or safety."[30] Virginia also defines the threshold of whether exposure to domestic violence rises to the level of abuse or neglect by "consider[ing] a number of factors, such as instances of physical harm, or whether the child fears for his or her safety before concluding a child has been maltreated."[31] Illinois, too, provides further guidance by requiring that the domestic violence poses a "real, significant, and imminent risk of moderate to severe harm to the child's health, physical well-being, or welfare."[32] Texas' policy echoes this criterion by stating,

---

27 Washington, *Protecting the Abused & Neglected Child: A Guide for Recognizing & Reporting Child Abuse & Neglect*, 5, https://www.dshs.wa.gov/sites/default/files/SESA/publications/documents/22-163.pdf.

28 Virginia, *Child and Family Services Manual-Section C*, 21-22 (January 2016), http://www.dss.virginia.gov/files/division/dfs/cps/intro_page/manuals/07-2015/Section_02_Definitions_of_Abuse_and_Neglect_.pdf.

29 Washington, DC, *Investigations Procedural Operations Manual*, https://cfsa.dc.gov/sites/default/files/dc/sites/cfsa/publication/attachments/Investigations-POM_0.pdf.

30 *Id.* at 42.

31 Virginia, *supra* note 28.

32 Ill. Adm. Code 89 § 300, Appendix B.

> . . . child's exposure to domestic violence, in and of itself, does not constitute child abuse or neglect by the adult victim of domestic violence. Domestic violence that physically harms a child or puts the child at substantial risk of immediate harm, however, constitutes an allegation of child abuse or neglect.[33]

Based upon these rules and policies and consistent with The Greenbook's guidance and the holdings of *Nicholson,* an individualized assessment of the specific impact and risk of domestic violence on each child is required in order to translationally apply these legal requirements. Although laws, policies, and procedures establish lines that delineate when exposure to domestic violence constitutes child maltreatment, the standards remain arguably subjective and little practical guidance exists in determining when exposure constitutes harm that warrants legal intervention and systemically imposed consequences. As such, the very issue that ACS grappled with in *Nicholson* repeats itself all over the country.

If the child is not determined to be abused or neglected, the investigative finding will be deemed "unfounded" or "unsubstantiated." If it is determined that the exposure to domestic violence has risen to the level constituting child maltreatment, then the investigator must determine the responsibility of each parent.

Determining the Neglectfulness of the Nonoffending Parent

As the *Nicholson* court explored, child welfare investigators must determine whether being abused in a relationship makes a parent neglectful. Some states progressively take the position against indicating the nonoffending parent for neglect, as in the policy in Maine.[34] Like Maine, Montana's policy instructs that "the child protection specialists should identify the offending parent appropriately

---

[33] Texas, *Disposition Guidelines for Domestic Violence Resource Guide*, Texas Department of Family and Protective Services, (April 2016), https://www.dfps.state.tx.us/handbooks/CPS/Resource_Guides/Disposition_Guidelines_for_Domestic_Violence_Resource%20Guide.pdf.

[34] Maine, *Child Abuse and Neglect Findings*, State of Maine Child and Family Services, https://www1.maine.gov/dhhs/ocfs/cw/policy/iv__d1__child_abuse_and_negle.htm at 4.

and ensure that the nonoffending parent is not blamed for the abuse that occurred and its impact on the children."[35] Similarly, Florida's failure to protect allegation requires verification of the domestic violence victim's active participation in the abuse of the child and is not appropriate as an allegation simply because the victim is still with the perpetrator or the perpetrator is still in the home.[36]

Other states emphasize that the critical factor in determining whether nonoffending parents are considered neglectful under the law is the steps that they took to protect their children from the harm or the risk of harm that the domestic violence created. In Cuyahoga County, Ohio, the policy requires child welfare professionals to "validate the nonoffending parent's efforts to keep the children safe."[37] Further founded upon the lessons from the social science research and consistent with the Greenbook guidance, Illinois' administrative law states:

> . . . The adult victim of domestic violence, who is the nonoffending parent or caregiver, is presumed to not be neglectful or to not have created an environment injurious to the child so long as he or she has exercised precautionary measures to prevent or mitigate the real, significant, and imminent risk of moderate to severe harm to the child.[38]

Illinois' "presumption against neglect" for nonoffending parents is one of the most *Greenbook*-compliant rules in the country regarding the maltreatment status of the nonoffending parent. Although not yet further defined, examples of "precautionary measures," could include but are not limited to the following:

---

[35] Montana, *Domestic Violence Protocol Summary*, 3, https://dphhs.mt.gov/Portals/85/cfsd/documents/cfsdmanual/domesticviolence.pdf. (citing MT Code 41-3-102(23)(a)–(b) ("'Psychological abuse or neglect' . . . may not be construed to hold a victim responsible for failing to prevent the crime against the victim.")).

[36] Family Violence Threatens Child, Household Violence or Intimate Partner Violence, Sec. 39.01(30)(i) and (44) (2017).

[37] Cuyahoga County, *Policy Statement: Cases Involving Domestic Violence*, Division of Children and Family Services, http://cfs.cuyahogacounty.us/pdf_cfs/en-US/policies/2/20307.pdf.

[38] Ill. Adm. Code 89 § 300, Appendix B.

General Precautionary Measures:

- Attempts to stop the cause of the likelihood of harm;
- Takes steps to protect the child from the likelihood of harm;
- Responds to any harm the child has experienced;
- Reaches out to a support system;
- Utilizes social services to address needs in the family;
- Possesses and utilizes parenting skills;
- Maintains a healthy and loving relationship with the child;
- Attends to the child's emotional, psychological, physical, educational, and medical needs;
- Provides stability—emotional, educational, relational, financial—for the child;
- Cooperates with current efforts to address stressors or risk factors in the home; and
- Considers the child's best interest.

Domestic Violence Specific Precautionary Measures:

- Uses knowledge about the abuser and the situation;
- Uses safety strategies for herself and the child;
    - Takes preventative measures to keep the child safe when an incident of domestic violence occurs (e.g., keeping coats and shoes near the child's bed in case the nonoffending parent and child need to leave);
    - Attempts to keep the child safe from harm during an incident of domestic violence (e.g., moving to a room where the child is not, telling the child to leave the area where the domestic violence is occurring, instructing the child to seek outside help that the child can reasonably be expected to do, shielding the child from witnessing the domestic violence);
- Discusses with the child a plan to maintain safety during an incident of domestic violence (e.g., go to the neighbor's house);
- Develops a domestic violence safety plan individually or with the assistance of an advocate;
- Defends against the person using violence from harming herself or the child;

- Acknowledges the potential impact that domestic violence can have on the child;
- Attends individual therapy or domestic violence counseling;
- Seeks guidance from religious leadership;
- Calls the police;
- Seeks legal assistance;
- Obtains or attempts to obtain an Order of Protection, or initiates other legal proceedings;
- Ceases the relationship with the person causing harm; and
- Restricts the access of the person causing harm to herself and the child;

Like Illinois, Washington focuses on both the general care and protective steps that nonoffending parents have provided their children in determining whether an adult survivor is neglectful. Specifically, Washington's policy states:

> Child welfare professionals should consider a founded finding for negligent treatment on the adult victim if the following factors are present: domestic violence victim does not provide the necessities for the children, including but not limited to supervision, food, medical care, etc; and domestic violence victim does not act to protect the children from obvious physical harm by the domestic violence perpetrator.[39]

Importantly, precautionary measures should not have to be successful in preventing or mitigating the harm; rather, the adult survivor's neglectfulness should be measured by the efforts she made because she cannot control the actions of the person using violence and coercive control. The precautionary measures that the nonoffending parent took and fostered are also protective steps upon which strength-based interventions could support and build.

Investigative Findings and Responsibility

Holding the person using violence and coercive control solely responsible for the harm caused by domestic violence should be the goal of

[39] Washington, *supra* note 29.

the child welfare system.[40] North Carolina instructs that "domestic violence perpetrators, and not their victims, should be accountable for their actions and the impact on the well-being of the [nonoffending parent/adult victim] and child victims."[41] Consistent with the Greenbook principles and the *Nicholson* holdings, Vermont places sole responsibility on the abuser by affirming its commitment to adopting policies that "[r]emove blame for domestic violence from victims."[42]

Indicated findings against adult survivors of domestic violence often jeopardize the safety and stability for the child and adult survivors. With an indicated finding of abuse or neglect, adult survivors cannot work in a job or profession that interacts with children, such as in the fields of childcare, teaching, or nursing. Adult survivors, therefore, could lose their jobs or be barred from future employment, thereby destabilizing the financial support they can provide to their children and increasing their dependence on breadwinning abusers. Indicated findings could also deem adult survivors ineligible for immigration relief that requires proof of "good moral character," making it much harder to leave an abusive partner. Indicating adult survivors for neglect could additionally escalate the abuse because now a government agency is legally assigning blame to the recipient of the abuse, becoming kindling fueling the abusive partner's fire, a license to continue abusing. Branded with an indicated finding, the adult survivor more deeply internalizes the belief that she is a "bad mother," fortifying the message that the abusive partner has unceasingly drilled. Significantly, a freezing effect occurs when helping systems lead to harmful results, such that survivors of domestic violence who are indicated will be deterred from reaching out for help in the future. It contradicts public policy to pin an indicated finding on an

---

40 The word "responsible," rather than "accountable," is intentionally used here. Systems can impose responsibility on a person but cannot force someone to become accountable. Accountability is developed internally when a person heals, learns, and chooses to change their harmful behavior and repair the harm they have caused.

41 North Carolina, *Family Services Manual, Volume I: Children's Services, Chapter VIII—Child Protective Services, Domestic Violence*, Division of Social Services, https://www2.ncdhhs.gov/info/olm/manuals/dss/csm-60/man/cs1409.pdf.

42 *Id.* at 2.

adult survivor that makes it harder for her and her children to find safety and stability together, especially when the adult survivor is not a threat to children.

The majority of states with a child welfare domestic violence policy do support holding abusers responsible for the harm or risk of harm the domestic violence posed to the children. Vermont's policy, similar to Oklahoma's,[43] holds the "perpetrator responsible for the risk their abusive behavior poses to the child(ren)."[44] Investigative findings can be entered against parents who cause harm in an effort to hold them responsible and deter future harm. In order for indicated findings of abuse or neglect to also become possible avenues of accountability, meaningful engagement is needed between the investigator and the parent that focuses on safe partnering and parenting alongside connections to concrete supports and services such as batterer intervention programs. Consequences and punishment alone often fall short of excavating pathways toward accountability.

• • •

Karen received a letter in the mail informing her that she had been indicated for child neglect. No findings were made against Jamal. Karen received a copy of the investigative packet that documented the investigation, including the investigator's rationale for the investigative finding. With the packet in hand, Karen felt sad, confused, angry, and hopeless.

The investigative packet did not identify any harm to Nia but concluded she was at risk of harm in the stroller when Karen and Jamal "engaged in domestic violence" in Jamal's mother's house. Using language Judge Weinstein deemed impermissible in *Nicholson*, the investigator failed to accurately understand the dynamics of domestic violence as the unilateral control by one person over the other. The investigation further incorrectly identified Karen as the instigator of the incident described as a "fight," concluding that the "aggression"

---

43 Oklahoma, *Domestic Violence Manual for Child Welfare Professionals—A Desk Reference Guide*, Dep't of Human Services, Child Protective Services, http://okpsych.org/sites/okpsych/files/1613/8400/5667/DVdeskreference.pdf.

44 Vermont, *Family Services Policy Manual - Chapter 135*, Dep't of Children and Families, http://dcf.vermont.gov/sites/dcf/files/FSD/Policies/135.pdf.

did not start until Karen hit Jamal in response to being pushed and shoved to the ground; thereby severing the incident from its context of domestic violence. The investigator did not recognize Karen as a victim of domestic violence even though he knew that Karen and Nia were staying at a domestic violence shelter where only individuals who qualify as victims, not perpetrators, were allowed to stay, and the Order of Protection protecting them from Jamal was included in the investigative packet. Morally constructing a mother who used violence to prevent further violence against her, the investigator attributed the risk of harm to Nia solely to Karen. The investigative packet also disclosed the confidential location of the domestic violence shelter; yet again, Karen and Nia's whereabouts were made known to the person who threatened their safety. Despite meeting with Karen at a domestic violence shelter, Karen never did receive the message, in words or action, "We believe you. You matter. How can we support you?"

Post-Investigation Child Welfare Cases

As thousands of families across the county are impacted by nonjudicial child welfare interventions, in many states this "shadow" child welfare system impacts more families than those who have juvenile court cases.[45] In most states, child welfare investigators and caseworkers can recommend conditions and provide services without judicial involvement during or after child welfare investigations. Any recommendation or condition suggested outside of court is voluntary, such that parents are not required to comply. Although such recommendations and conditions do not have the force of law, many parents, especially nonoffending parents who may already feel powerless, perceive that they do not have an actual "choice" because of the power the child welfare system yields coupled with the fear of losing their children. Such conditions or recommendations often include:

[45] The "shadow" foster care system also describes interventions that occur *during* child welfare investigations through mechanisms such as "safety plans," later discussed.

- Limiting specific contact, such that the parent using violence and coercive control is not permitted to have unsupervised contact with the children or must pick-up the children for visits from a safe exchange location;
- Changing the living arrangement, such that the parent using violence and coercive control is no longer allowed in the home, the adult and child survivors go to a domestic violence shelter or temporarily move in with friends or family, or the children temporarily live elsewhere with family or friends;
- Utilizing or participating in other legal systems, such as criminal, civil protective orders, and/or domestic relations; and
- Accessing and participating in services, such as adult and child domestic violence counseling and batterer intervention services.

In some states, the worker will codify these recommendations or conditions into a written document. Some states have a formal post-investigation, nonjudicial program that monitors families and oversees their compliance with recommended services.

Ideally, child welfare workers would engage in trauma-informed, family-centered, strength-based, and equity-centered work with the family, rather than imposing conditions with a coercive undertone in form and substance. In doing so, both parents would share the steps they would be able and willing to take to enhance the safety, stability, well-being, and healing of their family, and the child welfare worker would brainstorm, problem-solve, and evaluate alongside them to provide assistance and support enabling the parents to realize these changes.

• • •

Following the conclusion of the investigation, the child welfare agency opened an "intact family services" case for Karen and Nia. While the post-investigation services were legally voluntary, Karen felt compelled to agree out of fear that Nia would be removed from her if she refused, and the services were presented to her in a manner that gave the impression of compulsory participation. Karen was willing to participate in services because she wanted to work toward her goals, provide a safe and stable life for Nia, and continue healing. Many of the services that the child welfare worker included in her service plan, however, were duplicative of the services she was engaged in at the domestic violence shelter. Raising this issue, the worker responded, "If you do not cooperate, I am taking your daughter," thereby exacerbating Karen's fear as well as the rift between a government agency with immense power and a trauma survivor who was slowly regaining a modicum of control over her own life. Following a misunderstanding about Karen's whereabouts, the intact family services worker almost took protective custody of Nia, but fortunately, Karen's domestic violence counselor advocated on her behalf and provided clarification. A week later, the intact family case unexpectedly closed.

Protective Custody and the Alternative of Safety Plans

Child welfare investigators have significant power because they, along with doctors and police officers, can remove children from their parents without judicial permission. This power can only be exercised in emergency situations, where there is not enough time to get an order from a judge. If the investigator believes that the children are at imminent risk of harm by staying with the parents and that "reasonable efforts could not prevent the removal," the investigator can remove the children from their parents by taking "protective custody." If protective custody is taken, every state entitles the family to be in front of a judge within a designated period of time, such as forty-eight or seventy-two hours. For the days between protective custody and the first court hearing, the children will likely be placed with relatives, in a temporary foster home, or in a shelter. Most states have an assigned state office that screens and initiates the dependency case, which is often the state's attorney, district attorney, or child welfare agency. If the case is not screened into court, the protective custody must end, and the children must be returned to their custodial parent. If the case is screened into court, the first court hearing will be in front of a judge who will determine if the case will proceed and where the children will be placed.

Taking protective custody of a child exposed to domestic violence should be a last resort. As the Greenbook informs and Judge Weinstein agreed, children function best if they can remain safely within their families, and research and practice have established that this is increasingly true for child survivors of domestic violence.[46] Practically, the safety of children exposed to domestic violence is inextricably linked to the safety of their nonoffending parent.[47] Accordingly, North Carolina's domestic violence policy provides appropriate direction by stating:

> Enhancing a nonoffending parent/adult victim's safety enhances his or her child's safety. Children should remain in the care of the nonoffending parent/adult victim whenever possible. When the risk of harm to the child outweighs the detriment of being separated from the nonoffending parent/adult victim, alternative placement should be considered."[48]

In accordance with this policy, child welfare investigators should ground themselves in keeping adult and child survivors of domestic violence together whenever possible.

Most states have an alternative to taking protective custody of children if they are deemed to be in "imminent danger." Child welfare safety plans are this alternative. Called by various names across the country, safety plans in essence are "voluntary," nonjudicial agreements between parents and child welfare investigators about conditions or changes that parents are willing to do in order to avoid the removal of their children. These conditions or changes ostensibly ameliorate the investigator's concerns necessitating the removal of the children. Common safety plan conditions involving domestic violence may include seeking a protective order, leaving the home with the children, preventing the person using coercive control and violence from entering the home (e.g., changing locks), allowing the children to stay with a friend or relative, or even placing the children with the family of the person perpetrating the domestic violence. Best

---

[46] Susan Schechter & Jeffrey L. Edleson, National Council of Juvenile and Family Court Judges: Effective Interventions in Domestic Violence & Child Maltreatment Cases: Guidelines for Policy and Practice (1999).

[47] *Id.*

[48] North Carolina, *Family Services Manual, Volume I: Children's Services, Chapter VIII—Child Protective Services, Domestic Violence*, Division of Social Services, https://www2.ncdhhs.gov/info/olm/manuals/dss/csm-60/man/cs1409.pdf.

practice and the law in some states dictate that the conditions of safety plans should be discussed together with both parents, that the plan should be short-term (e.g., five days), written, and regularly reviewed to be ended or renewed.[49] While a tool to thwart removal, safety plans have the potential to change the status quo for a family. When a safety plan ends, the child welfare worker may not have the power or the interest in helping the family return to their pre-safety plan status. Despite the spirit of safety plans as a more trauma-informed, family-centered, strength-based, and equity-focused approach to safety concerns, many parents do not feel that they are exercising free will when choosing between "the best of two evils."

• • •

Karen and Nia together moved on from the shelter to transitional housing, and after finally receiving a housing voucher, they moved into low-income housing in the same town. Karen enrolled in the local community college and resumed moving toward her goal of obtaining her nursing degree. Karen connected with a local nonprofit that provides her with subsidized childcare.

Karen now works at a long-term residential placement facility for children with significant disabilities—most cannot talk or walk. When Karen applied for the job, she was forthcoming about the indicated finding of neglect that had not yet reached its automatic expungement date of five years. (Karen appealed the indicated finding but was unsuccessful). The director of the program sought a waiver from the state licensing agency to allow Karen to work there, but the indicated finding nearly robbed Karen of an income and a meaningful job. Karen quickly proved herself to be a caring and responsible worker, and although she is registered as a neglectful parent, she is now caring for the state's most vulnerable children.

Karen knows that she has moved her family to higher ground, yet the pathway to the safer, more stable, and healing life she hopes for her and Nia remains a struggle. Nearly every moment of Karen's

---

[49] The legal basis for, use of, and parameters around safety plans has been litigated in Illinois. *2016 Safety Plan Settlements,* Ascend Justice (Jan. 5, 2021), https://www.ascendjustice.org/wp-content/uploads/2019/07/Ascend-Justice-2016-Safety-Plan-Settlements.pdf.

existence is focused on caring for Nia, going to school, and working. Yet, Karen's experience with the child welfare system has left her with a persistent feeling of powerlessness' that no matter what she does, it may never be enough. Even though she can barely afford the rent of their apartment despite working as many hours as she can, Karen is uninterested in child support from Jamal. Karen hopes that she and Nia will move again, not because Jamal has found them, but a final move to a house that Karen buys herself when she becomes a nurse. No longer moving away from, Karen and Nia will finally be able to stay.

Moving Toward

Fostering the change necessary to move child welfare investigations and nonjudicial interventions away from the experiences of Karen and toward trauma-informed, strength-based, family-centered, and equity-focused practice can occur through messages of the "Moms Matter" card, policies and protocols, *and* individuals who determine that something needs to change and are willing to be a part of finding and implementing solutions. One inspired, persistent, innovative, and resourceful person can move an agency toward interventions that understand what children need to recover from harm, do not turn away from locating the source of that healing in the very people who experience both risk and promise, and aim to cultivate strength and accountability that translates into resilience and recovery for everyone in the family. The child welfare intervention that Alessa Karadere led into the Nacuaa family did just that and improved nonjudicial child welfare practice along the way.

• • •

Alessa Karadere grew up in a traditional Mediterranean family that sowed within her the importance of meaningful, continuous relationships bonded through heritage and culture, giving her both roots and wings that carried her into the field of child welfare. Hailing as an investigator from a statewide child welfare agency whose mission and practice of preserving and strengthening families resulted in the lowest foster care rates in the country, Alessa became an emergency response supervisor in a different state-administered/county-based child welfare agency. In her new role, Alessa quickly observed a disconnect between the agency's mission and practice that often separated families without exhausting measures to keep them together and punished parents without providing support; challenges even more apparent in cases involving domestic violence.

Alessa and her manager discussed these challenges and set out to improve the practice. Alessa formed a task force on domestic violence that involved every department of the agency. Alessa guided workers to really speak with families and listen to understand to develop a clear, thorough, and nuanced understanding rather than making assumptions. For instance, a worker reported that a mother violated an Order of Protection by letting her husband back in the house. After clarifying that the person the order protects cannot legally violate the order, Alessa encouraged the worker to ask the mother why she allowed the father back into the house. The worker learned that the husband threatened to hurt the mother and the children if she did not open the door, so letting him in was actually the safer, more protective decision. To further use this nuanced information to drive more effective interventions, Alessa lobbied to enlist outside expertise.

Through Alessa's advocacy and persistence, the child welfare agency hired David Mandel to bring the Safe and Together Model to its workers and community partners. Used across the country and internationally, the Safe and Together Model builds upon the core tenets of the Greenbook as a trauma-informed, strength-based, family-centered, and equity-focused child welfare practice approach based upon the central concepts that children are best served when they are "safe and together" with their families and that partnering with adult survivors and parents who use violence and coercive control enhances the safety and well-being of children.[50,51] Even with a suite of tools, a common language, and an outline of the road toward improved practice following the Safe and Together training,[52] Alessa observed that effective domestic violence child welfare

---

[50] David Mandel, SAFE AND TOGETHER INSTITUTE (Feb. 28, 2019), https://safeandtogetherinstitute.com.

[51] *Id.*

[52] *Id.*

practice needs to occur within general child welfare practice invested in strengthening families together.

In order to provide support and services to families without the prerequisite of removing their children first, Alessa's child welfare agency began a family preservation program. Outside of the juvenile court system, the family preservation program would provide intensive services to families whose children were at imminent risk of out-of-home placement. Within the context of the influence of the Safe and Together Model and the expansion of the Family Preservation program, the Nacuaa family entered the county's child welfare system.

• • •

Sayu, Itan, and their seven children emigrated from Mexico as part of the migrant workforce moving north to harvest citrus and avocado groves. The Nacuaa family are Mixtec, the third-largest group of indigenous people from Mexico,[53] and speak one of the nearly fifty dialects of the Mixtec language.[54] Itan never attended school, and Sayu's formal education ended when he was ten years old. Traditionally patriarchal in family structure, Sayu, the father, was responsible for decision making and supporting the family,[55] and Itan, the mother, cared for the children and their home.

In both Mexico and the United States, Sayu was severely physically, sexually, emotionally, and financially abusive to Itan. The abuse persisted until one night when Sayu took Itan to a deserted alley. He beat her so brutally and relentlessly that he almost took her life. He said to her in their Mixtec language, "This is what I can do to you, and no one will know." Itan sought medical attention for her injuries, and the hospital staff called the county's abuse and neglect Hotline.

An emergency response worker on Alessa's team met with the Nacuaa children within hours of the Hotline call. She determined that the children had been exposed to and harmed by the domestic violence and were at risk of future harm. The children were more

---

53 *Mixtec.Org*, San Diego State University (March 1, 2019), https://mixtec.sdsu.edu.

54 *Id.*

55 *Id.*

than mere witnesses to the abuse—they saw it, heard it, and learned of it by seeing its aftermath, namely through the injuries their mother bore.[56] The children were afraid of their father and were simultaneously angry with their mother for enduring their father's abuse. After much effort, the worker located a translator so she could communicate with Itan in the hospital. Itan expressed her desire to leave Sayu but lacked the resources to provide for her seven children without her husband's support. She worried about what would happen to her children if Sayu indeed killed her, which she believed he could. The worker also spoke with Sayu through the translator who seemed to recognize the gravity of his actions.

Without instructive protocols, the worker faced the decision about how the child welfare agency would and should respond to the Nacuaa family. With information substantiating both risk and harm, the worker acknowledged that Itan tried to be protective, even if her children were still harmed. The worker also knew that foster care would generate risks to the children attendant from being separated from each other and their mother.[57] The worker consulted with

---

[56] Jane E.M. Callaghan, et. al., *Beyond 'Witnesses': Children's Experiences of Coercive Control in Domestic Violence and Abuse, 33* J. of Interpersonal Violence 1551, 1553 (2015).

[57] Siblings can be a powerful source of emotional support and comfort to each other both while living in homes where they are experiencing trauma and in the aftermath of separation from their parents. Sharon Connor, *Information Packet: Siblings in Out-Of-Home Care,* National Resource Center for Family-Centered Practice and Permanency Planning at Hunter College School of Social Work (March 2, 2019), http://www.hunter.cuny.edu/socwork/nrcfcpp/downloads/information_packets/siblings.pdf. Separating siblings who have been temporarily or permanently removed from their parents can significantly intensify grief and trauma. *Id.* Despite the importance of placing siblings together, estimates indicate that over half of children in foster care nationwide have one or more siblings also in care, but as many as 75% of these foster children are placed apart from these siblings. Rebecca L. Hegar, *Sibling Placement in Foster Care and Adoption: An Overview of International Research*, 27 Children and Youth Services Review 717, 718 (2005); Esther Wattenberg & Annette Semanchin, *Siblings in Foster Care: Maintaining the Ties that Bind*, Practice Notes University of Minnesota, Center for Advanced Studies in Child Welfare (March 2, 2019), https://cascw.umn.edu/portfolio-items/pn-09-siblings-fc/. It is difficult to find foster parents willing to take in sibling groups. Emily Kernan, *Keeping Siblings Together: Past, Present, and Future,* National Center for Youth and Law (March 2, 2019), https://youthlaw.org/publication/keeping-siblings-together-past-present-and-future/. Current and former foster youth have

Alessa about whether the children were at imminent risk of harm necessitating removal. After attending the Safe and Together training, the worker questioned, "If Itan is not safe, how can the children be safe?" Alessa then reframed the question, as "How can we support Itan to increase her safety, thereby increasing the safety of the children?" While neither removal nor maintaining the status quo met the needs of the family, Alessa advocated that the Nacuaa's be the first family experiencing domestic violence assigned to the family preservation program. A family preservation worker was then assigned to the family.

The family preservation worker first addressed safety. Finding a domestic violence shelter that could accommodate Itan and her seven children was not possible. The worker discussed whether Itan thought an Order of Protection would be protective and understood and deferred to Itan's conclusion that Sayu did not need a piece of paper telling him to stop hurting her. Instead, motivated by fear of authority, Sayu agreed to stay elsewhere, and Itan and the children remained at home, preserving the children's connection to their school, community, culture, and routine. The worker spoke with Itan and encouraged her to articulate the ways she had tried to protect herself and her children from Sayu's violence. She learned that Itan was proud that the oldest two children were doing well in school, that she loved her children, and that she was very disheartened that her children were living around so much violence. Itan was willing to engage in counseling and wanted her children to receive the help they needed too. The worker referred Itan and her children to domestic violence counseling at a domestic violence agency. Although Itan did not receive the "Moms Matter" card, the worker's words and actions manifested the card's spirit and effect. The worker also engaged with Sayu who agreed to participate in a fifty-two-week batterer's intervention program for which the child welfare agency would pay.

---

advocated for siblings' rights and as a result of these advocacy efforts, in addition to litigation, some states have enacted the "Sibling Bill of Rights." Oregon, Connecticut, Minnesota, Illinois, Massachusetts, and Nevada are examples of states that codified the importance of maintaining sibling connections and ties during child welfare system involvement. Yet no state has recognized a right of siblings to be placed together, although a few states (Connecticut, Kansas, Louisiana, Massachusetts, and Maryland) have established a "right" to sibling visitation. *Id.*

While the family was engaged with the family preservation program, the child welfare agency completed its investigation. The agency concluded that the domestic violence constituted emotional neglect as it endangered the children's emotional well-being and that Sayu, not Itan, was responsible for causing that harm. The findings were substantiated against Sayu and unfounded against Itan.

In a relatively short period of time of living with their mother in safety and stability, the symptoms of trauma the children had exhibited were dissipating. After working through the time of crisis, the worker helped Itan find a job so that she could financially support her children. Itan began believing that she was capable of parenting as a single mother. Sayu actively engaged in the batterer intervention program in Spanish, a language he understood. There, Sayu uncovered that he had experienced extensive trauma in his childhood that he had explained to himself as an expected part of his culture and his existence as a Mixteco boy. Sayu developed an understanding of, not a justification for, his actions, and he began to heal. The seed of Sayu's accountability was not isolated to the substantiated neglect finding but rather grounded in a commitment to change, grow, and repair. Although his empathy for Itan still waned, Sayu voluntarily sent money to Itan to help with the children because he valued the responsibilities that he associated with fatherhood.

The family preservation case remained open for nine months. Throughout, the family was viewed as at promise rather than at risk, treated as a source of strength and recovery, and the collective experience of trauma did not diminish the family's value. The interventions did not replicate the dynamics of abuse by stripping the adults and children of autonomy and self-worth but rather replaced deficit-oriented practice with a strength-based focus. The worker considered, engaged, and invested in all members of the family. The worker identified the internal strengths of both parents and the children and fostered protective factors that expanded the concrete supports for the family. Trust existed between the family and the worker, leading to better outcomes for the family than had the intervention not occurred. When the case closed, the children were safer, the family was more stable, each parent had grown in significant ways that would impact their parenting, and they were healing together and in relation to one another.

Alessa still contended with the embedded child welfare practice that is reliant on the fallacy that separation ends abuse or conclusively makes the family safer, yet including families experiencing domestic violence in the family preservation program became an important step toward more effective agency-wide interventions.

• • •

Child welfare interventions outside of the juvenile court system can meet the needs of families experiencing domestic violence. Drafting and implementing domestic violence protocols that translationally guide determinations of impact, harm, risk, and safety moving away from indicated findings of neglect against adult survivors of domestic violence moving toward keeping adult and child survivors together, assigning responsibility appropriately, and connecting families with community-based services and concrete supports are requisites of strength-based, family-centered, trauma-informed and equity-focused responses. Yet, even amidst scarce resources, historical resistance, bureaucratic hurdles, or nascent efforts, shepherding messages compact enough to fit on a mere card can be the inception of changed practice—messages emanating empowerment and support, a doctrinal commitment to the power of family, and the willingness to share the power the system yields with those whose lives are impacted by its interventions.

7
The Measure of Society: *In Re* the Needs of Children and Families in Juvenile Court Cases Involving Domestic Violence

It is often said that the measure of a society is how it treats its weakest or most vulnerable members. Yet this proposition is laden with the moral construction of what defines weakest or most vulnerable, supposing incorrectly that promise and strength are not co-existing. Rather, the adage should measure society based upon meeting the needs of its members.

For over twenty years, this is how Judge Leonard Edwards (retired) measured the impact of his courtroom for the families that were ushered through its doors.[1] From his days as a civil rights

1 Zoom Interview with Leonard Edwards, Retired Superior Court Juvenile Court Judge in Santa Clara County, CA, (January 9, 2022). While on the bench, Judge Edwards created the Family Violence Council, oversaw Santa Clara County as a Greenbook Demonstration Site, founded the Juvenile Court Judges of California

volunteer in Mississippi in 1964 to his time as a teacher in the Peace Corps in Malaysia to providing legal representation as a public defender, Judge Edwards has always valued and prioritized being in a position to help those in need. With this intention, Judge Edwards served as a juvenile court judge in the Superior Court of Santa Clara County, California from 1981 to 2006. Rather than perceiving the families before him as weak and vulnerable, Judge Edwards saw them as parents and children in need and with needs—needs that may warrant juvenile court jurisdiction and needs that do not, needs that have often failed to be met elsewhere only to be left caught within the net of the juvenile court system, or needs defined by and targeted by a net only intended to catch some families and not others. By grasping families in its net, Judge Edward's courtroom and the juvenile court system had both a moral and legal obligation to meet the needs of families.

The majority of families in Judge Edward's courtroom carried some allegation of neglect, yet their needs were not the same. Their needs were varied, unique, across a spectrum, and some more easily addressed than others. The traditional tools available to the child welfare system—removal and foster care—often exacerbated, rather than ameliorated, these needs. The juvenile court system in Judge Edwards' view was "a crude tool that did not have the resources needed to meet the needs of families." Judge Edwards knew that the very act of removing children through protective custody that is then affirmed by a judge conceives the beginning of separating the needs of children from their family that often leads families down an irreparable path of continued disintegration. Mandated services are often boilerplate and consume the family's time and limited resources, thereby failing to address the actual, ongoing, and potentially evolving needs of the family. As such, the needs in juvenile courts are not static. Unlike other court proceedings that reflect back on a happening that concluded in the past, the lives of families in juvenile

---

legislative advocacy association, and served many roles including President of the National Council of Juvenile and Family Court Judges. After retiring from the Superior Court of Santa Clara Count, Judge Edwards actively teaches, writes, consults, and plans conferences. Throughout his career, Judge Edwards has worked in nearly every state and over ten countries. The publication of the second edition of Judge Edward's book, *Reasonable Efforts, A Judicial Perspective,* is forthcoming.

court are transpiring and changing in real-time, each and every day and night, and in between court dates. And the passage of time in courtrooms—whether the court proceedings move too quickly or too slowly as governed by federal and state requirements as well as courtroom practice, capacity, and backlogs—alters the needs of the family over time and often change the responses that then become needed.

Within this context, the families in front of Judge Edwards often had complicated needs that were in turn more complex to address.[2] The needs then and now may have more to do with poverty than willful neglect and sometimes exist alongside direct abuse of children. When domestic violence was present in families coming before Judge Edwards, the violence was now more serious, extrication from the abusive relationship more unclear, the risks to leaving and staying more grave, the co-occurrence with mental health issues and substance abuse more common, the search for the "perfect victim" (the one who left soon enough, did not stay too long, fights back, does not fight back, prevents harm from befalling her children) who never existed perpetually in vain, and communities continually devoid of avenues of sustainable accountability for the parent causing harm. Judge Edwards challenged the perception that children's co-existing needs of safety, stability, well-being, and healing were mutually exclusive, as when their well-being and healing is slated to be sacrificed for their safety, which is often a greater statement about the system's shortcomings than a reflection of individual inadequacies.

Amidst these complexities, nearly every day Judge Edwards confronted what often felt like impossible tradeoffs in his courtroom when facing the hard questions involving families experiencing domestic violence. If a mother is not able to remain safe herself, how can she keep her children safe? But how can a child heal if he is placed in foster care, worried about his mother's safety and missing the most significant source of healing, his mother? And how can the pervasive and persistent perpetration of domestic violence stop if separation from his children does not motivate him to change?

---

[2] Judge Edwards tracked his own statistics about the types of circumstances present in the cases that came before him in juvenile court: more than 50% involved domestic violence, 50 to 70% involved mental health concerns, and 70% involved substance abuse.

What can the court do to meet the complex needs of each member of the family—the child, the nonoffending parent, and the person who uses violence and coercive control both before separating them and after separation has occurred? When the needs of individual family members appear to remain at odds rather than compatible with each other, this incongruence and fragmentation is often a product of the system's inability to find creative ways or to secure the resources needed to reconcile them. In that way, juvenile court cases often devolve into a tradeoff of needs.

The best interest standard that governs at each phase of abuse and neglect cases in every state did not offer Judge Edwards sufficient direction in preventing or brokering this tradeoff of needs and neither does the overarching goal to achieve permanency for children. Both best interest and permanency are amorphous concepts that become defined by circumstances rather than principled dogma. The Greenbook (discussed in chapter 3), however, provides concrete guidance that replaces tradeoffs with trauma-informed, strength-based, family-centered, and equity-focused judicial intervention. Judge Edwards was the co-chair of the Greenbook Advisory Committee and greatly contributed to the substance of the Greenbook. As the Greenbook instructs, the needs of children are intertwined with the needs of their nonoffending parents such that safety for the non-offending parent enhances safety for children. The Greenbook further orientates the child's best interest around remaining with the nonoffending parent whenever possible and that permanency includes ensuring the child's safety along with stability, well-being, and healing in connection to that relationship. In order to realize these principled best interest and permanency outcomes for children, the jurisdiction of the court must be based upon concrete, rather than protracted, harm or risk to the child—the presumption that the nonoffending parent is not neglectful, interventions grounded in family partnerships that buffer risk and build protective factors, accountability sourced in the person using violence and coercive control, and collaboration to meet the broad needs of the family.

To put these principles into practice, Judge Edward's juvenile court became a problem-solving court. As Judge Edwards said, "It is not true that all you have to do is intervene and that ends the domestic violence." Rather, caseworkers, attorneys, and judges had to understand the dynamics of domestic violence, know the resources available in the community, strategize ways for the child to remain safely with the mother, influence the abusive parent to stop harming his family, and advocate for the creation of necessary services if they did not exist. Just as a collaboration must be a means to an end, Judge Edward's courtroom problem-solved toward the aim of stable families. As Judge Edwards said, "Families are the unit in the country that hold that strength that will prevail over time." To Judge Edwards, "Success was stability." Judge Edwards' most meaningful work as a judge occurred when children and their families were able to live the lives they wanted to live after the juvenile court case closed, the manifestation of aspiring higher by responding with gold.

When juvenile courts deviate from the Greenbook tenets, the needs of parents and children become severed, tradeoffs become more likely, court interventions fall short of meeting the families' needs, and decisions compound harm upon harm. Juvenile court dockets that are plagued by tradeoffs demonstrate the need to support kinship care and alternatives to adoption, as well as develop innovative models of representation and support for parents involved in the juvenile court system. Jeopardizing one set of needs for another and struggling to comprehensively hold the needs of the entire family together, the juvenile court's involvement in James "Jimmy" Henderson's family diminished the measure of the system's effectiveness while Heather Cantamessa now pushes the system to meet the needs of parents like she once was.

A Mother-Stripped Child

When Carol Henderson was fourteen she became pregnant, seeking to create the loving family that she never had, and James was born. By the time he was two years old, Jimmy's father, an alcoholic who was occasionally violent, left Carol pregnant again and alone. With a toddler and infant to support, Carol met and married Andy. As a young boy, Jimmy revered his mother—her youth, her quietness, her commitment to work, church, and him. And as a young boy, the first time Andy hit his mom no longer stands out because the abuse that followed became commonplace. Andy's abuse torched their home, spilling outside, igniting a shame that made Jimmy know they were different but not different in a way that made them special.

At home, Jimmy was familiar with the rules that his mother instituted. Each room was to have a telephone. Even when the gas or water was turned off because they could not afford the bills, the phone company always was paid. If you call the police, do not let Andy see or hear. Spend as much time as possible out of the house. Church, of any sort, was also an acceptable escape. Jimmy, his mom, and his sisters went to church Sunday mornings and evenings and Wednesday evenings. Jimmy attended every bible school and camp in the area, no matter its orientation, solidifying a diverse spiritualism in Jimmy. These rules made Jimmy feel safer; he believed less in the rules' propensity to stop Andy and more in his mother's commitment and ability to protect him and his sisters.

When Jimmy was nine years old, his biological father passed away and his Aunt Mona instructed Jimmy that he was now the man of the house. At that moment, Jimmy committed to standing up to Andy to protect his mother.

Jimmy's chance to be his mother's hero came quickly. Andy was beating Carol, and Jimmy came into the room full of rage, trying to match Andy in presence and force. Jimmy ran toward Andy yelling, "You are not going to hurt my mom." Jimmy remembers that he indeed pushed Andy away from his mom, yet Jimmy ended up on the floor. Andy kicked him hard in the back. On the ground unable to breathe, Jimmy triumphantly watched Andy leave the house, the door slamming behind him. Jimmy had lost the wind in his chest but not the pride and satisfaction that he had indeed done it. He had stood up for his mom.

Carol took Jimmy to the emergency room with Jimmy feeling proud. Two police officers interviewed him, and Jimmy recounted the story as if he was narrating a movie about a superhero. When he was finished, one officer looked at him and said, "Jimmy, you did nothing wrong. You are a good kid. Usually, kids from homes like yours get in a lot of trouble." The words "homes like yours" rang through Jimmy's mind as those now familiar feelings of shame and embarrassment dulled Jimmy's euphoric feelings of heroism. Jimmy again felt different and not different in a way that made him special. The officer told Jimmy that he would be going home. To Jimmy, this was an obvious conclusion. A social worker then asked Jimmy a lot of questions, and afterward told Jimmy, "Your mom did nothing wrong, and you did nothing wrong." Again Jimmy felt as though she was stating the obvious.

Having fallen asleep in his hospital bed, Jimmy was awoken by a gray-haired man. Jimmy prepared to retell his story of gallantry, but the man's command stopped him.

"You are coming with me," he said to Jimmy.

"No," Jimmy insisted, "call the cops or the social worker. They said that my mom did nothing wrong, and I did nothing wrong and that I could go home." Jimmy was starting to panic.

The man replied, "The social worker is the one who called us."

A hero trapped by his own heroism, Jimmy pleaded, "Andy only wants to hurt my mom, not me. I placed myself in the middle of this." A hero captured, Jimmy was taken from the hospital with this stranger, placed in this stranger's car, only to arrive at another stranger's house. The child welfare agency had taken protective custody of Jimmy and his sisters.

Jimmy and his sisters were placed separately. Jimmy's first foster home was an emergency placement. The emergency foster parents were kind, but Jimmy felt overwhelmed by fear. He had lived for years scared of Andy, but Jimmy knew the rules of their house. He did not know the rules of this house. He was also confused because everyone told him that he and his mom did nothing wrong, but now he was forbidden to talk to his family. Even more than missing them, Jimmy was scared that his mother would not be safe without him. Despite being afraid he would get into trouble, Jimmy snuck in a phone call home. He dialed the number and he heard his mom's voice as she said, "Hello . . . hello? . . . hello?" Jimmy did not respond. He hung up, but at least he knew she was alive.

The odyssey through the juvenile court system was about to begin for Jimmy and his family.

The Stages of a Dependency Case

Most states have an assigned office that screens and initiates dependency cases, which is often the state's attorney, district attorney, or child welfare agency. If the case is not screened into juvenile court, the protective custody must end, and the children must be returned to their custodial parent.

Many people are involved in a dependency case, typically including the judge, court reporter, bailiff, court coordinator, the state's attorney or a district attorney, child welfare personnel, attorneys from the child welfare agency, attorneys for the parents, and representation for the children. It is best practice that parents have different lawyers, especially in cases of involving families where past or present domestic violence exists. In accordance with federal law,[3] children will also be given representation, yet the model of representation varies among states between an attorney, a guardian ad litem, and/or Court Appointed Special Advocate (CASA). A dependency case has the following main judicial hearings: (1) temporary custody/shelter care, (2) adjudication, (3) disposition, (4) permanency hearings, and (5) termination of parental rights if reunification does not occur.

State statutes define the legal elements at each phase of the juvenile court process and each state's case law determines how cases involving domestic violence are resolved, resulting in wide-ranging and often divergent judicial decisions in juvenile courts across the country. The majority of state statutes governing juvenile court proceedings do not specifically address domestic violence. Nonetheless, all states allow parents to be held responsible for the conduct of someone else who harms or poses a risk to their children in some way which is often used to hold adult survivors of domestic violence responsible for neglecting their children. The majority of states are silent about the intersection of domestic violence and child welfare, and therefore open the door for the application of the general, failure to protect allegations against adult survivors of domestic violence.[4] The statutory language in six states more directly applies this language in some way to survivors of domestic violence or concludes that exposure to domestic violence constitutes neglect without additional qualifiers.[5] Four state statutes mention domestic violence but

---

3 Child Abuse Prevention and Treatment Act, P.L. 93-247 (1974), CAPTA Reauthorization Act, P.L. 111-320 (2010).

4 Alabama, American Samoa, Arizona, Arkansas, Delaware, District of Columbia, Georgia, Guam, Hawaii, Illinois, Kansas, Kentucky, Louisiana, Maine, Maryland, Massachusetts, Michigan, Minnesota, Mississippi, Nebraska, New Jersey, New York, North Carolina, North Dakota, Ohio, Oregon, Pennsylvania, Rhode Island, South Dakota, Utah, Vermont, Virginia, Washington, Wisconsin, and Wyoming.

5 California, Indiana, New Mexico, South Carolina, Tennessee, and Texas.

do not provide instruction on when the exposure to domestic violence constitutes neglect, guidance on whether the adult survivor is neglectful, or language that prioritizes keeping the child survivor with the adult survivor.[6] Nine states have statutes that address domestic violence in an adult and child survivor-centered way, and they each do so differently.[7]

At every phase of the juvenile court process, the judge must make a finding of "reasonable efforts."[8] Specifically, as required by federal law and integrated into state statutes, child welfare agencies have the obligation to make reasonable efforts to prevent removal and later to reunify the family. As Judge Edwards describes, "reasonable efforts are the obligation of the judicial branch to oversee the actions of the executive branch. The reasonable efforts finding is the mechanism that judges have to hold child welfare agencies accountable." A judicial finding of "no reasonable efforts" means that the state cannot seek federal reimbursement for the costs associated with that family's juvenile court case. Judge Edwards has written extensively about the importance of reasonable efforts and the responsibility of judges to avoid rubber stamping the inaction of child welfare agencies.[9] To determine whether the child welfare agency made reasonable efforts

---

6 Connecticut, Idaho, Iowa, and Oklahoma.

7 Alaska, Colorado, Florida, Missouri, Montana, Nevada, New Hampshire, Puerto Rico, and West Virginia.

8 "Reasonable efforts" is a requirement of Title IVE of the U.S. Social Security Act. If a judge determines that the child welfare agency has not made "reasonable efforts" at any required stage of the juvenile court process, the agency will not receive federal reimbursement for the costs (i.e foster care subsidies, costs of services, concrete supports to the family) associated with that family's juvenile court case for the entirety of the case. *See* 45 CFR § 1356.21.

9 *See,* Judge Leonard Edwards, Reasonable Efforts, A Judicial Perspective (2014); *Overcoming Barriers to Making Meaningful Reasonable Efforts Findings*, Child Law Practice Today, ABA Center on Children and the Law (2019); *Ignoring Reasonable Efforts: How Courts Fail to Promote Prevention*, The Chronicle of Social Change (Dec 2018); *An Instructive Dependency Case Involving Reasonable Efforts*, The Bench, the official magazine of the California Judges Association (Summer 2018); *The Effective Use of the Reasonable Efforts Finding: Challenges Facing Attorneys*, 40 The Guardian 3, (May/June 2018); *Juvenile Court Corner, Reasonable Efforts to Prevent Removal: An Important New Case*, The Bench (Summer 2014), *Domestic Violence & Reasonable Efforts at the Detention Hearing*, The Bench (Winter 2013); *Reasonable Efforts*, The Bench, (Summer 2011).

in a case involving domestic violence, Judge Edwards would ask, in part, the following questions of child welfare workers:[10]

1. Did the petition allege specific facts about the domestic violence?
2. Have you asked the adult survivor what she wants and needs?
3. What steps did you take to remove the parent using violence and control from the home?
4. Did you give the adult survivor information about domestic violence shelters and services?
5. Did you assess the possibility of the adult and child survivors living with relatives?
6. What community-based or in-home services did you offer to support and protect the adult and child survivors?
7. Did you provide the adult survivor information about protection orders?
8. What concrete supports did the family say they need and what concrete supports did you offer?
9. What steps have you taken to obtain safe housing, transportation, or childcare for the adult survivor?
10. What engagement have you had with the parent using violence and coercive control?
11. Did this family receive a Family First prevention plan?
12. Is it safe to return the child to the adult survivor today, and if not, what would be necessary in order to make it safe for the child to return to the adult survivor?
13. Have you assisted the adult and child survivors in applying for victim-witness funding?

Throughout the proceedings, if child welfare workers could not provide evidence of affirmative actions in response to such questions, Judge Edwards would set short interim review dates to ensure that reasonable efforts were indeed, thereby contributing to the protective factors that would support the safety, stability, well-being, and healing of all members of the family.

---

[10] *Domestic Violence and Reasonable Efforts in Juvenile Dependency Court*, The Bench: The official magazine of the California Judges Association, Spring 2022.

Although Carol did not receive any offers of support or services from the child welfare agency, the dependency petition alleging that Jimmy and his sisters were abused and neglected based upon their mother's failure to protect was screened through and filed in court, which began the juvenile court process for their family.

Temporary Custody

The temporary custody or shelter care hearing is the first time a parent, like Carol, would be in front of the judge, and most children, like Jimmy and his sisters, would have likely already been removed. The judge must first determine whether there is probable cause that a child is abused or neglected.[11] Consistent with the Greenbook, it is unlikely that a state statute would create a per se rule that exposure to domestic violence constitutes abuse and neglect. Instead, the specific impact or risk rising to the level of intervenable harm to the child caused by domestic violence should be presented in evidence, but that specific information is not always available at this early judicial stage. In practice, the low threshold of probable cause errs on the side of identifying harm. If there is no probable cause that the child is abused or neglected, the petition is dismissed, and the child can go home. If probable cause is found, the judge must then determine whether "urgent and immediate necessity exists" for the children to be placed in substitute care and whether the child welfare agency made reasonable efforts to prevent the removal. A juvenile court judge in Illinois emphasized that the "urgency and necessity" of removal involves balancing the harms of removal against any identified risks and that reasonable efforts include supporting the adult survivor in finding enhanced safety with her children prior to a decision to remove.

If a judge grants temporary custody, the child welfare agency would then be appointed as the children's guardian, transferring many parental rights to the child welfare agency, such as the right to make decisions about the child's education or medical needs. A caseworker is then assigned to work with the family, a case plan with services is developed, and a visitation schedule is set. While it is possible, yet rare, for children to remain with their parents during the course

[11] 705 ILL. COMP. STAT 405/2-10.

of a dependency case, an initial separation resulting from protective custody sets a tone and force of severance that is hard to undo.

• • •

The testimony of the "gray-haired" child welfare investigator about Jimmy's injuries and the emergency room visit formed the basis of the judge's finding that probable cause of abuse and neglect existed. Although the child welfare agency did not make reasonable efforts to offer any support to Carol before taking protective custody of her children, the court took temporary custody of Jimmy and his sisters. Jimmy was moved to a long-term foster home. His mother—the one person Jimmy loved and needed the most—was taken from him. Who would help him now when he was angry, sad, or scared? Jimmy's fear intensified and a sense of injustice was brewing. Although everyone told him that he did nothing wrong, he was the one locked up in a stranger's home, while Andy, who did do something wrong, was free. In his new school, Jimmy hid what made him different but not special, which now also included being a foster child.

Weeks went by before Jimmy was able to visit with his mother. It was until after she began parenting classes, that she was allowed supervised visits to see her children. Each visit assured Jimmy that his mother was unharmed enough to make it there.

Adjudication

The next judicial stage of the dependency case is the adjudication, or the child abuse and neglect trial. Parents are not entitled to a jury trial in most states. The petitioning entity—most often the state's attorney, district attorney or child welfare agency—has the burden of proof to establish that the child was abused or neglected by a preponderance of the evidenceIn determining whether the child has been abused or, judicial findings are tied to the child and most courts can but are not required to assign responsibility to either or both parents for the harm or risk caused.[12] The following case law reveals the various approaches to determining whether a child is neglected due to domestic violence.

---

[12] 705 Ill. Comp. Stat. 405/2-21.

Courts have held that exposure to domestic violence does not automatically deem children maltreated and individualized and specific impact is required in order to deem a child neglected.[13] Specifically, a New Jersey court overturned a finding of neglect because "no evidence was introduced to support . . . a causal relationship between witnessing domestic violence and emotional distress in the young child."[14] Similarly, children have not been considered neglected based upon protracted predictions of future harm. A Florida court attempted to sever the needs of children from their mother based upon potential harm from the mother's possible future abusive relationships.[15] The appellate court overturned the finding that the children were neglected, citing evidence that the mother "grew up in an abusive home and had a history of abusive relationships" as insufficient.[16]

By buffering the impact of domestic violence, the protective steps of the adult survivor can also render children not neglected. Children were not deemed to be neglected in a West Virginia court because the adult survivor took "steps to protect" the children that were "reasonable in light of the threat posed by the batterer."[17] Likewise, a California court justified its "no neglect" finding based on the steps the mother had taken such as separating, limiting contact, calling the police, and obtaining a restraining order.[18] Importantly, when courts evaluate children's neglected status in consideration of the efforts the adult survivor made to parent and protect her children, their needs remain tied to one another.

Yet when harm to the child has occurred even amidst protective actions, many courts deflect responsibility punitively onto the morally constructed, nonoffending parent who is more amenable to complying with the juvenile court's requirements than the parent

---

[13] New Jersey Div. of Youth & Family Servs. v. S.S., 855 A.2d 8, 13-14 (N.J. Super. Ct. App. Div. 2004).

[14] *Id.*

[15] Fla. Dep't of Children and Families v. F.L., 880 So.2d 602 (Fla. 2004).

[16] *Id.* at 604–605.

[17] West Virginia, *Child Protective Services Policy*, Department of Health and Human Resources, 48 http://www.dhhr.wv.gov/bcf/policy/Documents/Child%20Protective%20Services%20Policy.pdf (citing *In Interest of Betty J.W.*, 179 W. Va. 605, 610 (1988).

[18] *In re* Jonathan B., 185 Cal.Rptr.3d 308, 313 (Cal. Ct. App. 2015).

who perpetrated the domestic violence. The existence of harm from domestic violence, therefore, tends to pit the needs of the child against the nonoffending parent. For instance, two Pennsylvania courts found that children were neglected by the nonoffending parents who continued to interact with the parent causing harm,[19] and neither requested assistance nor divulged that domestic violence was occurring.[20]

Even if particularized harm has not been identified, children have been adjudicated abused or neglected due to domestic violence when the domestic violence is severe, ongoing, and longstanding. In other words, the worse the domestic violence is, the more likely the children are to be deemed neglected regardless of the efforts of the nonoffending parent.[21] In Illinois, the sixty-two emergency room visits a mother endured and numerous beatings over a seven-year period witnessed by her children were sufficient evidence of domestic violence to support a finding of neglect.[22] The Florida appellate court upheld an adjudication of children as to the mother who had been victimized by the father's domestic violence for twelve years because the children may have been affected by domestic violence even if they did not see it.[23] When the grip of domestic violence so fiercely engulfed a mother, an Ohio court deemed this nonoffending parent neglectful due to her inability to extricate herself from the control of the violence, even though no other system could stem his violence.[24] The court immediately disconnected the children's needs away from their mother by viewing her apparent inaction as a result of unwillingness rather than as a product of living in constant terror, fear of lethality, and the constricted ability to take steps that appeared protective from the outside. Neglect findings that lead to prolonged separations of children from their nonoffending parents set in motion a trajectory

---

19 *In re* G.K., 2016 WL 1064397, at 6 (Pa. Super. Ct. Mar. 16, 2016).

20 K.C. v. Dep't of Pub. Welfare, 2012 WL 8685308, at 3–4 (Pa. Commw. Ct. Mar. 14, 2012).

21 S.V. v. People, 370 P.3d 1144, 1147-49 (Colo. 2016) (court deemed a mother neglectful because she continued a relationship with an abusive father).

22 *In re* A.D.R., 186 Ill. App. 3d at 393, 542 N.E.2d 487 (4th Dist. 1989).

23 D.W.G. v. Dep't of Children and Families, 833 So.2d 238, 240-41 (Fla. Dist. Ct. App. 2002).

24 *In re* Delfino M., 2005 WL 195488 (Ohio Ct. App. 2005).

that enables only half of the children in foster care to be reunified with their families.[25]

• • •

The court adjudicated Jimmy abused and neglected. He was considered abused because of the physical harm Andy inflicted upon him when he pushed him down and kicked him in the back. He was deemed neglected because his mother was not able to prevent the harm that Andy inflicted and because the domestic violence continued.

Disposition

The disposition hearing follows the adjudication and is best compared to a sentencing hearing where the consequences are not a loss of freedoms such as incarceration, but rather a temporary loss of the constitutional rights to the care and custody of one's children. At the disposition hearing, the judge makes a present-day finding regarding whether each parent is fit, willing, and able to parent,[26] and whether it is in the best interest of the child to be made a ward of the court.[27] (Some states, such as California, have statutorily eliminated the judgement-laden requirement of "fitness" and instead focus on the willingness and ability of parents to care for their children.) If a parent is fit, willing, and able, the child returns to the parent. If a parent is unfit, unable, or unwilling to parent, the court retains its power over the family, and children may or may not be allowed to return or remain with the parent.

By permitting children to remain with the adult survivor, even amidst complex circumstances, co-existing with domestic violence, and direct harm to the children, the children's best interest is preserved in connection with their mother, consistent with both the

---

[25] *See, In re* J.M., 2016 WL 5940454, 1 (Ohio Ct. App. 2016) (Children adjudicated neglected due to an "incident of domestic violence between the father and mother" who separated; children placed in foster care; mother visited children and participated in services; time passed where needs of children were severed from mother; the court found "the mere existence of a good relationship" insufficient to alter the status quo; court terminated mother's rights; children adopted by foster mother).

[26] 705 Ill. Comp. Stat. 405/2-23.

[27] 705 Ill. Comp. Stat. 405/2-22.

Greenbook and trauma-informed, strength-based, family-centered, and equity-focused practice.[28] In a California case, despite the father's severe domestic violence, physical and sexual abuse against the children, criminal history, and substance abuse, a child welfare agency recommended that the children remain with their mother at a domestic abuse shelter,[29] thereby recognizing that supporting the mother to meet her children's needs was the appropriate response to the harm her children experienced. At the disposition hearing, although the mother was not deemed fit, willing, and able to parent due to her own substance abuse struggles, the court held that it was in the children's best interest to remain with her as they were monitored and received services together.[30] From the beginning, the court avoided severing the connection as a reaction to the harm. Therefore, throughout the process, the children maintained an uninterrupted link with the source of their safety, stability, well-being, and healing.

While courts have deemed adult survivors as fit parents capable of parenting, evidence of ongoing domestic violence has substantiated findings of parental unfitness.[31] In Massachusetts, a mother, but not the father, was deemed unfit at the disposition hearing due to "her inability to break the pattern of abuse that m[ade] her currently unfit to the parent the children."[32] The child welfare agency first became involved with the family in 2006 after an incident of domestic violence perpetrated by the father against the mother. The parents later separated. The mother's new boyfriend threatened to kill the mother in front of the children. The three fled to a neighbor's house, and the police were called. The children were removed from their mother based upon the boyfriend's actions. At the disposition hearing, the court found that the father "engaged in services and completed all of his service plan tasks" and was fit, while the mother was found to be unfit due to a "continued pattern of neglect by permitting domestic violence in the home."[33] Although the mother had recently acknowledged the negative effects the domestic abuse had on her children's

---

[28] *In re* E.B., 184 Cal.App.4th 568 (Cal. Ct. App. 2010).
[29] *Id.* at 571.
[30] *Id.* at 574.
[31] *Care and Protection of Polly,* 87 N.E.3d 1201 (Mass. App. Ct. 2017).
[32] *Id.*
[33] *Id.*

lives, the judge found that insufficient time had passed to establish that her past pattern of conduct (i.e., permitting domestic violence in the home) had changed and that it was still likely to continue in the future. The court rejected the application of the *Nicholson* holdings that parental unfitness cannot be based solely on a child's exposure to domestic violence.

• • •

The juvenile court similarly deemed Carol unfit to parent her children due to the past and ongoing domestic violence that Andy perpetrated. While Carol remained willing to keep Andy away, she was not able to do so. Andy would return to the house to abuse and torment Carol. She would flee, lock the door, or call the police, but despite her efforts, Andy always made his way back in. Jimmy and his sisters were made wards of the court.

Permanency Planning

The objective of juvenile court proceedings is to achieve permanency for children. No federal definition of permanency exists although permanency is lauded as the primary end-game of dependency cases. Under most state law, permanency is not defined in principle but rather is understood in terms of the preferred order of permanency goals. After wardship has been established at the end of the disposition hearing, the judge assigns a permanency goal that is consistent with the best interest of the child. Most states list a hierarchical list of permanency goals such that the preceding goals are preferred over subsequently listed goals. Examples of permanency goal preferences include reunification, adoption, guardianship, and relative care.[34] When a judge selects a permanency goal lower on the list, the judge is typically required to explain why the goals higher on the list were ruled out.[35] Some cases are also assigned a goal of long-term substitute care, which leads children to eventually age out of the system while living in a foster home, group home, or residential treatment

---

[34] Fostering Connections to Success and Increasing Adoptions Act of 2008 (P.L. 110-351); *see* Judge Leonard Edwards, *The Urgency of Placing Children with Relatives*, 42 THE GUARDIAN 4 (Winter 2000).

[35] *See* Illinois Juvenile Court Act, 750 ILCS 5/2-28.

facility, thereby denying children permanency under the law.[36] Most often following dispositional findings of unfitness involving domestic violence, a judge will set an initial permanency goal of returning children home.

The service plan becomes the road map for reaching the permanency goal. Parents are required to engage in and make progress in the services outlined in the service plan. Despite the wishes of the parents where domestic violence has occurred, many courts will require parents to separate or mandate that adult survivors end relationships with abusive partners. Parents are also often required to maintain stable housing, employment, and address any other issues impacting their ability to parent such as substance abuse or mental health struggles. In addition, children will receive services to address any struggles they are experiencing, such as art therapy, to address the domestic violence they witnessed or educational supports aimed to compensate for academic deficits. Parent-child visits will likely occur which are vitally important to maintaining their connection and increasing their chances of reunifying.

At permanency hearings, typically held every six months, the judge will determine whether a parent has met the permanency goal, and if not, whether the services and placement are necessary and appropriate toward meeting the goal.[37] Parents' participation and progress in services and visits will be summarized in reports to the court as well as the through sworn testimony of service providers. If the judge determines that the permanency goal has been met, the children can be reunified with and returned to the care and custody of one or both parents. If the goal has not been met, the judge can provide the parents additional time to correct the conditions that caused the case to come into the system or change the goal. If grounds exist, a petition to terminate parental rights can also be filed. After the disposition hearing, the path toward often competing versions of permanency begins.

• • •

As part of the service plan toward the goal of reunification, Carol was required to participate and make progress in parenting classes

[36] Preventing Sex Trafficking and Strengthening Families Act of 2014 (P.L. 113-183).
[37] 705 Ill. Comp. Stat. 405/2-28.

and to keep Andy away from the house. She did not receive any other supportive services from her caseworker. Carol was trying to comply with the service plan, and Jimmy and his sister were returned home. But, Andy barged his way into their lives in ways that Carol could not stop. Jimmy and his sisters returned to foster care two more times.

Between the ages of nine and thirteen, Jimmy lived in five foster homes and switched schools multiple times. He began struggling in his classes, was diagnosed with attention deficit hyperactivity disorder, was prescribed medication, and was placed in special education classes. Jimmy's service plan required him to attend therapy. Therapy was scheduled on the afternoon that Jimmy played baseball with his friends from home. Not only did Jimmy have to miss the one activity that connected him to his life outside of foster care, he now had to start lying to his friends about why he could not play.

As his time in foster care lingered, Jimmy wished to speak with the judge. On the day his caseworker brought him to court, Jimmy was not allowed inside the courtroom. Jimmy witnessed through the window the little power his mother had in the system against them. The injustice he originally felt slowly evolved into resentment toward his mom. If the system was not going to keep Andy away nor force him to change, his mom was his last chance.

Reunification

The path toward reunification is fraught with needs tradeoffs, thereby proving to be an arduous, tenuous, and against-all-odds permanency outcome for many families. Following the initial removal that splits the children's needs from their families, parents are no longer seen as a primary, or valuable, source of meeting the children's needs and are denied the day-to-day opportunities to do so. As such, the pieces of the family are scattered and addressed separately only to possibly be brought back together with edges that fit less smoothly because of the challenge-filled time apart. The imposed and resulting disconnection becomes an obstacle to reunification that is exacerbated within the context of systemic hesitance, or even resistance, to returning children home. Trade-offs often surface between parents and foster parents.

Although reunification is the highest permanency goal on the hierarchy, the federal Adoption and Safe Families Act (ASFA) has made reunification more difficult. ASFA imposes condensed time requirements for parents to make progress in their services, provides financial incentives to foster care agencies to facilitate adoptions but not to return children to their families,[38] and requires child welfare workers to engage in concurrent planning.[39] Even when reunification is the goal, workers must locate a Plan B, which are often foster-adopt arrangements developed to minimize the number of placements that a child could experience. Intended to be a backup plan to achieve permanency quickly if reunification fails, finding and building relationships with foster parents who are willing to adopt in tandem with efforts to reunite the family can thwart reunification efforts. The existence of foster parents who are willing to adopt often causes caseworkers to shorten the duration of time parents are allotted to correct the conditions, sabotages opportunities to maintain the relationship between the children and their parents while in foster care, or prefer where the children could be going over from where the children came.

Placement in foster care and the role of the foster parent inherently generates competing needs toward reunification. Supporting the permanency goal is the cardinal rule for foster parents. Foster parents are supposed to care for a child like they would their own but are expected to hold back their desires and commitment to steadfastly dedicate themselves to raising the child, until that time may come. Foster parents who have committed to adoption, motivation stemming from the willingness or desire to have children live with them forever, may interfere consciously or subconsciously with their ability and inclination to support a permanency goal of reunification.

Stable placements for children with foster parents who want to adopt them create significant hurdles for parents who are fighting for the return of their children. Parents want their children to

---

[38] The Adoption and Legal Guardianship Incentive Payments programs were originally established as part of the Adoption and Safe Families Act of 1997 and have been reauthorized through 2021 as part of the Family First Prevention Services Act (discussed in chapter 11). *Adoption*, Children's Bureau, An Office of the Administration for Children & Families (Nov. 1, 2019), https://acf.hhs.gov/cb/focus-areas/adoption. Under ASFA, child welfare agencies receive incentive payments—up to $4000 per child—for every completed adoption. ASFA reached its goal of doubling the number of adoptions from 1997 to 2002.

[39] Adoption and Safe Families Act, 42 USC 671 (1997).

be safe and cared for while out of their home but perversely, the opposite—frequent foster care moves, abuse, or neglect in a foster home—enhances their chances of reunification. Because best interest determinations are present moment considerations, pre-adoptive, unwavering, and loving homes where children's needs have been serviced for quite some time to the exclusion of their parents cause many children to never return to their families. David Berns, who administered and directed child welfare agencies in Michigan, Colorado, and Arizona, repeatedly observed that resistance to changing the status quo and comparisons to foster parents resulted practically in requirements beyond the legally required "minimum parenting standards" that impeded reunification, such that:

> Courts and agencies expect the home and parents to be nearly perfect before they consider reunification. The situation has to be really "bad" before a child is removed but the bar for reunification is much higher. Anything short of perfection makes reunification questionable.

Parents often appear to pale in comparison to the elevated status assigned to committed foster parents and their real-time track record, such that only unattainable perfection imposed upon parents brings sufficient assurance for reunification. This illusory high standard is made more difficult when progress toward perfection is measured in part by the existence of something not occurring—by not returning to or choosing an abusive partner, by preventing someone else's violence and coercive control.

Even before judges make decisions about reunification, child welfare caseworkers are the arbiters of the competing needs that have resulted—the needs of children to remain connected to their families while preserving the lives they currently know especially as time passes, of parents to establish that they can parent safely and then further prove their worth, and of foster parents who are dedicated to children who are docketed to eventually return to home. Caseworkers hold the power to make recommendations to the court regarding reunification, and the determinants of human relationships in child welfare cases cannot be underestimated. The caseworker may have differing allegiances and relationships among the parents and committed foster parents. Foster parents may appear more complaint while interactions with parents may center on problems or dissatisfaction. Caseworkers may feel grateful to have found a willing foster parent to care for a child while viewing the parent as the cause of the child's misfortune and need for the foster parent in the first place. Caseworkers are influenced by the culture of their office and lessons learned in prior cases that they carry forward and import to others. Caseworkers are less likely to recommend that a child should return home until the professional opinion of a service provider supports that recommendation. Often hard-won, the caseworker's recommendation then requires multiple levels of approval from a supervisor and often the attorney for the child welfare agency in whom the balance of power rests.

Although not guaranteed as the permanency stopwatch continues to countdown, as parents complete and make progress in service, reunification becomes more likely. Visitation between the parent and children typically increases from supervised to unsupervised day visits and then to unsupervised overnight visits which serve as a test of sorts to expose remaining risks of returning children home. To bring reunification to fruition, often the parent's attorney files a motion, although any party is permitted to file a return home motion. Motions for "return home" are strongest when there is consensus, yet contested hearings often ensue. In deciding to return children home, judges barter between needs—the present-day needs of children that have been met outside of their parents, lifetime needs of children to be connected to their families, and the constitutional right of parents to the care and custody of their children if they are fit, willing, and able to parent. In opposition to deferring to the status-quo, reunification requires the reunion of needs that have been separated oftentimes for years.

• • •

After over four years, the scale of needs tipped toward returning Jimmy and his sisters to their mother. Carol had begun domestic violence counseling, and her advocate proffered to the court that Carol had developed an understanding of domestic violence and its impact on her children. It was not in the professional bounds of the advocate to offer the court the guarantee of absentia they coveted that Carol would never let Andy back home or find another abusive partner. Nonetheless, considering Jimmy's experience of foster care instability and his minimal prospects of being adopted as a teenage boy, returning to his mother better met his needs than lingering in foster care.

Termination of Parental Rights

Although over half of the families who enter the foster care system are reunified, many families are not.[40] When reunification becomes unlikely or when the system abandons continued reunification efforts, petitions to terminate parental rights are often filed. Termination of parental rights is one of the law's most drastic measures. If parental rights are terminated, parents and children lose their legal relationship with each other and children lose their legal relationship with siblings and extended family members.[41] Terminations sever children's needs from their family with finality. Termination of parental rights may be voluntary or involuntary.[42] Parents who wish to place their children for adoption may voluntarily relinquish their rights. When addressing whether parental rights should be terminated involuntarily, most states require that a court determine (1) by clear and convincing evidence that the parent is unfit and (2) determine by a preponderance of the evidence that severing the parent-child relationship is in the child's best interests.[43,44]

---

40 More than half (51%) of the children who exited foster care returned to a parent or principal caregiver.

41 In some states and under certain circumstances, a judge can reinstate parental rights. *See* 705 Ill. Comp. Stat. 405/2-34.

42 Child Welfare Information Gateway, *Consent to Adoption*, https://www.childwelfare.gov/topics/ system wide/laws-policies/statutes/consent/ (state-by-state details on voluntary relinquishment). *See In re* M.M., 156 Ill. 2d 53 (Ill. 1993) (holding no right to sibling visitation after the termination of parental rights); Aristotle P. v. Johnson, 721 F. Supp. 1002 (N.D. Ill. 1989) (recognizing sibling visitation for children in foster care is important, but not recognizing a liberty interest in such visitation).

43 The U.S. Supreme Court, in Santosky v. Kramer, 455 U.S. 745 (1982), set the standard of proof in termination of parental rights proceedings at clear and convincing evidence.

44 Child Welfare League of America, *Grounds for Involuntary Termination of Parental Rights*, 1, https://www.childwelfare.gov/pubPDFs/groundtermin.pdf#page=1&view=Introduction.

Under the law of many states and the reality of practice, if a case proceeds to termination and passes the unfitness stage, reconciling the needs of the children with their parents at the best interest phase is often insurmountable because they have been severed for so long.

Following termination of parental rights, children become eligible to be adopted.[45] Once the adoption process is finalized, adoptive parents have the same constitutional rights as biological parents to make decisions regarding the care, custody, and protection of their children without the interference of the state.[46] Parents, including adoptive parents, cannot be forced to allow visitation between their children and others.[47] Therefore, contact with the child's biological family is at the mercy of their adoptive parents. Judges cannot bindingly require visitation between adopted children and their biological parents, siblings, or relatives.

Families experiencing domestic violence face the risk of forever losing their legal relationship and future contact. Although no state specifically designates domestic violence as a ground for unfitness, the parental rights of nonoffending parents can be involuntarily terminated due to circumstances surrounding domestic violence. In addition, due to the amount of time that often transpires when a nonoffending parent endeavors to find enhanced safety and stability,

---

[45] Some children are not adopted following the termination of their parent's rights and become legal orphans. There are nearly 100,000 legal orphans in the country and their fate often depends upon aging out of the foster care system where they are more likely to experience homelessness, criminality, reduced employment, food insecurity, and poverty. Honorable Sharon McCully & Elizabeth Whitney Barnes, *Forever Families: Improving Outcomes by Achieving Permanency for Legal Orphans*, National Council of Juvenile and Family Court Judges (2013) http://www.ncjfcj.org/sites/default/files/LOTAB_3_25_13_newcover.pdf. Has the intervention measured up to meeting children's needs when the state takes away their family and is unable to provide them with a legal connection to a permanent family?

[46] *See* Simmons v. Simmons, 900 S.W.2d 682, 684 (Tenn. 1995). "[T]he relationship between an adoptive parent and child is no less sacred than the relationship between a natural parent and child, and that relationship is entitled to the same legal protection."

[47] Troxel v. Granville, 530 U.S. 57, 66 (2000) (aka the grandparent visitation case). Parents have the right to decide who shall have access to their children and that courts must give special weight or deference to parental decisions to deny or curtail the child's visits with nonparents; parents cannot be forced to allow their children to visit with grandparents.

ASFA's federally outlined timeframe about the length of time children have been in substitute care as an unfitness ground often triggers termination petitions.[48]

Failing to complete services or the continuation of the abusive relationship through the pendency of the dependency case can form the basis of an unfitness determination. In Pennsylvania, an abused mother lost her parental rights because she failed to complete domestic violence counseling and repeatedly denied the abuse.[49] A Nebraska court terminated the rights of a nonoffending parent because she continued a relationship with a violent partner following the removal of her children.[50] In Rhode Island, although the court acknowledged that it may not be the mother's fault, her rights were terminated because the ongoing domestic violence created an environment in which the mother's own safety was in constant jeopardy.[51] While most courts will not terminate a mother's rights because of her status as a victim of domestic violence, survivors of domestic violence may lose their parental rights for reasons related to their experiences of domestic violence, the resulting trauma, and obstacles stemming from the abuse.[52]

Following an unfitness determination, tradeoffs often occur at the next stage of the bifurcated termination trial, the best interest phase. For instance, in Arizona, the child's timely need for circumstantially defined permanency was traded against the mother's need for more time to find enhanced safety, stability, well-being, and healing.[53]

---

48 Adoption and Safe Families Act, P.L. 105-89, amended title IV-E of the Social Security Act, which establishes guidelines that States must comply with as a condition for receiving Federal title IV-E funds. The Adoption and Safe Families Act (ASFA) requires State agencies to file a petition to terminate parental rights, with certain exceptions, when a child has been in foster care for 15 of the most recent 22 months.

49 *In re* X.E., 2015 WL 6701749, at 7 (Pa. Super. Ct. Aug. 11, 2015).

50 *See In re Interest of Eli S.*, 2013 WL 6244136 (Ct. App. Neb. 2013) (affirming termination of mother's parental rights based on mother's "failure to take steps to protect her children from threats and domestic violence from her partner, continuation of a relationship with such partner, and such partner's refusal to modify behavior or attend a batterer's rehabilitation program"); *see also In re Jay S.*, 2011 WL 5433695 (Ct. App. Neb. 2011).

51 *In re* Natasha M., 800 A.2d 430, 431 (R.I. 2002).

52 *See, In Matter of Dependency of D.L.B.*, 379 P.3d 1099 (Wash. 2016).

53 Alma S. v Dept. of Child Safety, No. CV-17-0363-PR (2018).

Despite the child's strong bond with his mother, a Pennsylvania court scarified the child's relationship with his mother in exchange for the relationship with the foster parents who wanted to adopt.[54] The value of the past was traded for the potential of the future for another mother in Pennsylvania who similarly lost her parental rights to her children.[55] After the court deemed her unfit because she failed to adequately remedy or address the domestic violence "issues" that led to the children's removal, the court found that it was in the children's best interest to lose any protectable connection with their mother.[56] Despite not living together for three years, the court acknowledged the positive interaction between the mother and her children during their visits but relied upon testimony that the children were more attached to the foster parents who had the opportunity to meet the children's daily needs instead of their mother.[57] The fate of this family began with the initial removal and ended in the permanent legal severance of their relationships. he initial removal ultimately placed the needs of the children to be metoutside their mother forever more, predicating the case to become a barter between the passage of time and the present stability found in the foster home. That initial removalpriming the case for termination, occurred three years later.What if instead, the mother would have felt supported in the child welfare intervention by exploring the risks she faced while simultaneously identifying places of strength and promise? What if the mother and her children had been able to journey toward safety, stability, well-being, and healing together?

• • •

A legally terminated relationship was not Jimmy and his sisters' fate with their mother, but their relationships were devastated nonetheless. After the judge ordered Jimmy and his sisters to be returned to their mother, the case remained open for supervision. The caseworker warned Carol, "If you or these kids get hit again, you will lose them forever." Fearful, Carol admonished Jimmy, "You can't get

---

[54] *Adoption of Bianca*, 75 N.E.3d 1140 (Mass. App. Ct. 2017).
[55] *In re* X.E., 2015 WL 6701749 (Pa. Super. Ct. 2015).
[56] *Id.* at 7–9.
[57] *Id.* at 9.

in the middle of our fights. If you would just keep your damn mouth shut, you won't get hit and you won't get taken into foster care." After all Jimmy had done to protect her and be the champion his family needed, those words, more than anything else, destroyed the sense of purpose and connection that had propelled Jimmy through. The juvenile court had damaged the relationship that Jimmy needed the most and severed his needs from his mother for so long that their time apart had primed them for this strain. The relationship was left so tenuous that such words cloaked in anger while masking hurt and guilt, could cause Jimmy's needs to further detach from his mother.

Andy's reappearances remained inevitable, but fearing further intervention by the system, no one ever called the police again or spoke of what was happening in their home. Jimmy and his sisters felt even more scared because now they could not reach out for help lest they be removed from their mother for good. Six months after returning home, without any new incidents of domestic violence or injury to any of the children coming to the caseworker's attention, the juvenile court case closed, yet their lives carried on worse than they were before the four years of juvenile court involvement.

Despite resources spent on Jimmy's family, including the high cost of foster care, the intervention made them feel more shameful and alone rather than empowered or strong, and Carol fell into a deep depression. Because Andy's only consequence was that he was not allowed to stay in a home he did not want to live in anyway, the juvenile court intervention did not foster accountability for the harm he caused. Armed with the power of this implicit getaway, Carol became safer not because of the system's intervention, but because Andy moved away and focused his abuse on someone else and her children.

In the end, if Jimmy and his sisters were ultimately returned to their mother, could their removal have been avoided by supporting Carol? If not, how could the juvenile court intervention be repaired with gold instead? Consistent with trauma-informed, strength-based, family-centered, and equity-focused approaches to meet the needs of families experiencing domestic violence upfront rather than in an often self-defeating contest later, kinship care, guardianship, and interdisciplinary models of parental representation are ways to overcome the challenges that Carol and her family faced in the lengthy and disintegrating juvenile court process.

Kinship Care and Guardianship

Kinship care, or placing children with family members instead of in nonrelative foster care, better avoids the tradeoff of needs that develops as the juvenile court case endures. Kinship care enables children to remain in their family networks when they cannot reside with their parents, thus protecting those attachments and cultural connections while bringing children in closer contact with their parents who are deemed noncustodial at the time. Judge Edwards strongly supported kinship care in his courtroom and has written extensively about the importance of forming, maintaining, and strengthening children's connections. In 2017, nearly 141,000 youth were in kinship foster care across the country, representing 32 percent of all children in foster care.[58] Through his current advocacy efforts, Judge Edwards has set a goal that 60 to 80 percent of children removed from their homes should be placed with relatives.[59]

Most kinship care providers are over the age of fifty, such that grandparents raising their grandchildren is a common kinship care arrangement along with adult siblings caring for their younger siblings. Some states require kinship foster care providers to become licensed as foster parents. Most states provide a subsidy to kinship providers, although in some states the subsidy is less than the nonrelative foster care board rate. If children are removed from their parents without apparent kinship care options, child welfare agencies should use family search tools to locate potential kin.[60]

Kinship care programs exemplify trauma-informed, strength-based, family-centered, and equity-focused practice. As Judge Edwards expounds on the neuropsychiatric benefits of kinship care, "the source of self-understanding, inner strength, and character is based upon the reciprocal connections a person has with others.

---

[58] *What Is Kinship Care?* Annie E. Casey Foundation (Aug. 7, 2019), https://www.aecf.org/blog/what-is-kinship-care/. Privately, nearly 2.7 million children are in kinship care in the United States.

[59] Los Angeles and Omaha have met this goal, doubling the national average of the percentage of children in out-of-home placements that are residing with relatives.

[60] *See* Judge Leonard Edwards, *Family Finding and Relative Placement for Children Entering and in Foster Care* (Aug. 16, 2018) (available on YouTube); Kate Welti, Esther Gross, Alexandria Wilkins, & Karin Malm, *Evaluation of the Upfront Family Finding Pilot, Final Report*, Child Trends (Nov. 2018).

A person without connections is not living."[61] Kinship placements maintain connections that exist prior to removal and strengthen connections that will likely persist after the juvenile court case closes. Children experience less trauma from removals when they are placed with someone they know, care about, or who is connected to their family. Healing can begin in this caring and connected relationship, especially when the kinship care provider represents a connection to their parent where the deepest source of their healing lies. Being kept with relatives sends the message to children that there is still value in the places from where they came and any struggles are not deficits that they should internalize. Strength and promise can be found both in themselves and their family, even if they cannot live with their own parents. When children remain within their family networks, communities are not robbed of their children, and the additional support that kinship care providers receive may help to strengthen the broader community in which the families exist. The needs of children, parents, and kinship care providers are more often aligned although family conflicts and aspirations to adopt can also strain kinship care arrangements. Kinship care providers may be more prone to supporting the permanency goal than nonrelative foster parents because if the child returns home, the kinship care provider is less likely to lose all contact due to their preexisting relationship. Kinship care providers, therefore, are more naturally able to support the goal of reunification while committing to the long-term care of the children if needed.

Like the balancing of needs that can better occur through kinship care, guardianship is a permanency outcome that does not demand such exacting tradeoffs when children are not reunified with their parents. Typically, guardianships evolve from kinship care arrangements, but nonrelative foster parents can become guardians, too. Guardianship is a judicially created relationship between the child and a caretaker that gives the guardian legal rights in order to take responsibility for the child's care. The guardian has the legal

---

[61] Edwards, *supra* note 1; *see also* Dr. David Arredondo, Hon. Leonard P. Edwards, *Attachment, Bonding, and Reciprocal Connectedness: Limitations of the Attachment Theory in the Juvenile and Family Court*, J. OF THE CENTER FOR FAMILIES, CHILDREN & THE COURTS (2000).

authority to make virtually all decisions on behalf of the child, but parents retain the right to visit the child, consent to adoption, and retain some obligation to support the child financially.[62] Thirty-nine states provide for subsidized guardianship. Like subsidies given to adoptive parents, subsidized guardians receive financial assistance to support the children they have committed to caring for indefinitely. Most importantly, judges can order and enforce continued contact between children placed in guardianship and their parents, siblings, and relatives. Children's expectations of permanency are grounded in the continuity of their relationships, not legal labels.[63]

Continued contact often meets the needs of children.[64] Maintaining connection with noncustodial parents, siblings, and relatives has emotional, behavioral, and psychological benefits to most children that helps to mitigate the harm resulting from living away from their families.[65] Contact with their families contributes to the stability of the placement, and in turn fosters an environment that is more conducive to meeting their needs.[66] Guaranteed and protected visitation may help children feel more in control of their environment and facilitate their long term adjustment.[67] Severance of contact with families

---

62 Susan L. Brooks, *The Case for Adoption Alternatives,* 39 FAM. & CONCILIATION CTS. REV. 43, 47 (Jan. 2001).

63 *See* Marsha Garrison, *Parental Rights vs. Children's Interests: The Case of the Foster Child,* 22 N.Y.U. REV. L. & SOC. CHANGE 371, 378 (1996).

64 Situations exist where ongoing contact would not be beneficial and may even be harmful to children such as when the parent is a danger to the child.

65 *See* Garrison, *supra* note 63, at 383. When visitation would not be harmful to the children, psychological research demonstrates that visitation and contact enhanced the intellectual, psychological, and physical development of children with the biological family. *Id.* This reasoning was adopted in one of the first cases in support of open adoption. *In re* Anthony, 113 Misc.2d 26, 29-30 (NY Fam. Ct. 1982). Open adoption is not legally enforceable in most states.

66 JOSEPH P. ALLEN & DEBORAH LAND, ATTACHMENT IN ADOLESCENCE 319-25 (Jude Cassidy & Phillip R. Shaver, eds. of Handbook of Attachment: Theory, Research, and Clinical Applications, The Guilford Press) (1999); Annette Ruth Appell, *Blending Families Through Adoption: Implications for Collaborative Adoption Law and Practice,* 75 B.U. L. REV. 997, 1017 (1995). Delinquency and depression are examples of behavioral issues that children with insecure attachments experience.

67 Judy E. Nathan, *Visitation After Adoption: In the Best Interests of the Child,* 59 N.Y.U. L. REV. 633, 662 (1984). Most adoptions do not involve older infants but, rather, concern older children who have lived with multiple families; *See* Annette

can make it more difficult for children to develop psychological relationships with members of their current placement.[68] If children have continued and protected visitation, they understand and believe that they can have relationships with both sets of families and that their new family can endure. When the court cannot provide enforceable visitation provisions (like in adoptions), children are forced to play the precarious role as middlemen if they want to maintain contact with their parents, siblings, or extended family. Where children come is integral to their sense of identity, so when their new placements accept and respect their biological families, children will feel accepted and respected too.[69] Children who have contact with their biological parents report higher satisfaction in their placements.[70]

Guardianship should be a preferred permanency goal over adoption for children exiting the child welfare system. Under federal and state laws is a statutorily inferior permanency goal to adoption. Yet, guardianship achieves a form of permanency that embraces, preserves, and protects the continuity of all of a child's relationships, thereby meeting the panoply of children's needs inclusive of the need for safety and stability as well as family connections. As such, guardianship is arguably more permanent. Adoption is lauded as more ironclad than guardianship, but it is equally as permeable. Adoptions are not immune from unraveling which dissolves the once glorified permanency goal. Indeed, adoptions and guardianships unravel at nearly identical rates. Both adoptions and guardianships are often disrupt because youth runaway to their families of origin. Adoption and guardianships can both be subjected to later legal challenges as mechanisms exist in some states that enable biological parents to regain the rights to their children following both adoptions and guardianships.[71] Despite guardianship's similar prospects for permanency

---

R. Appell & Bruce A. Boyer, *Parental Rights vs. Best Interests of the Child: A False Dichotomy in the Context of Adoption,* 2 Duke J. Gender L. & Pol'y 63, 81 (1995).

[68] Nathan, *supra* note 67.

[69] *Id.* at 662.

[70] *Id.*

[71] A few states allow biological, nonlegal parents to later petition the court to unterminate their rights, reinstating legal status and likely custody. In other states, terminated parents can petition the probate court to appoint them as the guardians of their biological children, and although their fundamental liberty interests

and durability, the preference for adoption is based in part upon its redemptive symbolism of rebirth and starting anew, therein lies the desire for adoptions to abolish the connection to the children's past and the supposition that their needs can only and should only be met elsewhere and outside of those prior relationships. When children have a relationship with a parent who is not able to be custodial, guardianship avoids the all-or-nothing permanency preferences between reunification or termination/adoption.

Elevating guardianship in the hierarchy of permanency goals would make the option of continued contact and preservation of parent-child relationships a strong likelihood at the conclusion of most juvenile court cases. Preserving connections as an expected aspect of permanency would influence all the proceeding steps. Placing unwavering value on a child's family and believing in the promise and prospect of the family to meet the children's needs, either fully or partially butnonetheless in some connection to each other would impact juvenile court cases in the following ways:the initial removal may be reevaluated;genuine commitment to the prospects of reunification would strengthen; respect for the child's family would endure even despite serious struggles and potential mistakes visitation and more natural contact would be preserved; parents would not be measured against to whom and where children could be going; and support would be provided upon the children's return home, thereby meeting the needs of children and parents together and throughout a gold-infused juvenile court process.

• • •

Jimmy and his sisters were returned to their mother after spending four years in nonrelative foster care, a reunification closely tied to the dearth of adoption prospects. When Jimmy's Aunt Mona was uninterested in the government bureaucracy of becoming a kinship care provider, the caseworker did not explore other family members as placement options. Placing Jimmy with family would have met his needs to be safe, live amidst the familiar, and maintain predictable and regular contact with his mother, his anchor, both directly and

---

in the care are not returned, parents do regain a semblance of legal status toward their child.

indirectly through those connected to her. Intuiting that temporary separation often begets permanent separation, as time in foster care went on, termination and adoption loomed as a threat for Carol, Jimmy, and his sisters. Had guardianship been a viable permanency option, amid all of the fear that Andy perpetuated, Carol, Jimmy, and his sisters would not have had to also fear losing their connections to each other. If Jimmy had been adopted, this new legal status would not have erased his mother but rather created the nearly impossible feat of mourning her even though she was still alive. For Carol, amdist the fear of Andy and of losing her children indefinitely, Carol felt the oppressive sense of being alone in her fight to preserve her family and herself.

Interdisciplinary Models of Parent Representation

The form and quality of legal representation that parents receive during dependency cases is an essential bridge to meeting the needs of both children and their parents. Legal representation, known as family defense, is critical to both parents' experiences during the juvenile court case and positive outcomes for their children. In an adversarial system that pits parents against the state, the child welfare agency, and often against the attorneys or *guardian ad litems* for their children, no longer is high-quality parent representation viewed as a risk to the child. Rather, effective advocacy on behalf of the parents reinforces the shared goals of "prompting timely permanency at no cost to child safety."[72]

Thirty-nine states provide a categorical right to counsel for parents who are respondents in abuse and neglect proceedings.[73] In over ten states, however, parents may have to navigate the confusing child welfare case on their own, facing biases, burdensome service plans, restricted visitations, obstacles toward participation and progress,

[72] Lucas A. Gerber, Yuk C. Pang, Timothy Ross, Martin Guggenheim, Peter J. Pecora, Joel Miller, *Effects of Interdisciplinary Approach to Parental Representation in Child Welfare,* 102 Children and Youth Services Review 42, 52 (2019).

[73] Right to Counsel Map, National Coalition for a Civil Right to Counsel (2016), http://civilrighttocounsel.org/map.

and resource deficiencies.[74] In the states that create a statutory right to representation, if a parent cannot afford a lawyer (based upon income restrictions in accordance with federal poverty guidelines), a lawyer will be provided for the parent. These lawyers may work in a state-funded office of defense (such as the office of the public defender), a nonprofit legal services organization, or be contracted through a panel or rotating bar of attorneys. While experienced litigation skills are important, critical advocacy needed on behalf of the parents also occurs outside of the courtroom to support the parent during the arduous and emotional process, to advocate for realistic and appropriately tailored services, to respond to barriers to participation and progress, to maintain contact with children while they are in foster care, and to rally support from service providers on behalf of the parents and their children. In other words, out-of-court advocacy conditions the case for success in court. As the American Bar Association (ABA) concluded, "the dearth of quality representation is one factor that may lead to parents and their children experiencing unnecessary removals into foster care and needless, lengthy, and often devastating delays in reunifying."[75]

Support for enhancing the quality of parental representation exists. Family defense has become a recognized area of defense work. The ABA has promulgated practice standards to promote quality and uniformity of practice for parents' attorneys in abuse and neglect cases which includes caseload limits, encouraging the early appointment of lawyers in proceedings, and engaging with parents outside of court.[76] The ABA also supports holistic models of representation through interdisciplinary approaches. Interdisciplinary approaches to parent representation have developed in jurisdictions across the

---

[74] Vivek Sankaran, *A National Survey On Parent's Right to Counsel in Termination of Parental Rights and* Dependency *Cases*, http://youthrightsjustice.org/Documents/SurveyParentRighttoCounsel.pdf.

[75] *Legal Representation for Parents in Child Welfare Proceedings: A Performance-Based Analysis of Michigan Practice,* American Bar Association Center on Children and the Law (2009), https://courts.michigan.gov/Administration/SCAO/Resources/Documents/Publications/Reports/2009ABAParentRepresentationReport.pdf.

[76] *Standards of Practice for Attorneys Representing Parents in Abuse and Neglect Cases*, American Bar Association (2006), https://www.americanbar.org/content/dam/aba/administrative/child_law/aba-parent-rep-stds.pdf.

country, including New York City, Washington, and Oregon. As family defense work has professionalized and evolved into a distinct practice area, interdisciplinary defense teams have proven to be the most effective structure to safeguard the needs of both parents and their children in abuse and neglect proceedings.

Interdisciplinary representation involves a team on behalf of the parent that typically includes an attorney, a social worker, and/or a parent advocate.[77] Each member of the representation team has a specific role, yet together they work to support parents in achieving the permanency goal and meeting the additional needs of parents and their children. For instance, the lawyer navigates the legal terrain and strategy, presents evidence, and makes arguments in court on the parent's behalf bolstered by the work of the social worker and parent mentor. The social worker assists the parent to identify needed services and in securing needed resources such as transportation, public benefits, and housing. They also advocate for service plans that are practical, and help process the feelings of loss resulting from the separation from their children and of frustration stemming from disrespectful and patronizing interactions during the court case. Parent advocates help to mentor, support, encourage, empower, and instill hope in other parents based upon their own lived experience. Children of parents who receive interdisciplinary representation are more likely to be quickly, safely, and permanently kept together or reunified with their families than those of parents who receive representation from only an attorney.[78]

In the most comprehensive assessment of interdisciplinary representation to date, a 2019 study that examined 28,000 child welfare cases in New York City from 2007 to 2014 found that the interdisciplinary representation model involving an attorney, a social worker, and often a parent advocate shortened the time in foster care, enhanced reunifications, and staved off terminations. Families were reunited 43 percent more often (and more quickly) during the first year of cases and 27 percent were reunified within six months.

---

[77] The entire team is protected by attorney-client confidentiality, such that information can be freely shared amongst the team members but is immune from being forced to be shared with the outside.

[78] Gerber, *supra* note 72 at 43.

When children were unable to live with their parents, interdisciplinary representation enhanced short- and long-term kinship care and enabled children to be permanently released to relatives more than twice as often in the first year of a case and 67 percent more often in the second year, resulting in 40 percent more children with a permanent disposition of guardianship. The representation model reduced children's stays in foster care by nearly four months during the first forty-eight months following the petition filing and did not decrease the child's safety.[79] If New York City provided all children's parents with interdisciplinary representation, children would spend approximately 470,000 fewer days in foster care.[80] As Martin Guggenheim, an innovator of the interdisciplinary representation approach and one of the authors of the study explained, "these families may otherwise have been permanently dissolved or the children may have spent their childhood separated from their family and aged out."[81] Providing parents with an interdisciplinary representation team would reduce the foster care population by 12 percent, yielding an annual savings of almost $40 million dollars for a fully implemented program.[82] In reducing foster care stays and cost, no indication exists that children are coming home too soon or too fast as interdisciplinary representation did not lead to an increase in subsequent substantiated reports of child maltreatment during the twenty-four months following the petition.[83] Consistent with the central tenet of the Greenbook, supporting parents in turn supports the safety, stability, well-being, and healing of their children, and the interdisciplinary parent representation enhances the connection of their share needs.

The parent advocate is an evolving and important member of the interdisciplinary representation approach. Parent advocates are also

---

[79] *Id.* at 52.

[80] Press Release, *Providing Parents With the Right Kind of Legal Representation in Child Welfare Cases Significantly Reduces The Time Children Stay in Foster Care, New Study Finds* (May 7, 2019) (on file with author).

[81] Email from Martin Guggenheim to the American Bar Association Parents' Attorneys List Serve (May 2019) (on file with the author).

[82] Gerber, *supra* note 72 at 53.

[83] *Id.*, see also Kevin Penton, *Why An Attorney May Not be Enough in Child Welfare Cases,* Family Justice Initiative (July 14, 2019), https://familyjusticeinitiative.org/blog/why-an-attorney-may-not-be-enough-in-child-welfare-cases/.

known as parent allies, mentors, partners, and liaisons and have been involved with the juvenile court system themselves. Parent allies can exist in formalized interdisciplinary teams or as standalone individuals or programs that can be accessed by a parent or the parent's attorney. Parent allies have become routine and accessible in some parts of the country while they do not exist in other parts.[84] Many parent allies are compensated financially for their time, and some programs innovatively credit hours of mentorship against the cost of attorney representation that the organization provided the parent allies during their own juvenile court cases. Standards or certifications do not currently exist governing the qualifications or credentials of parent allies, but most receive nonuniform training that supplements their lived experience.[85]

As the Casey Foundation described, involving parent allies is a strategy for meaningful family engagement.[86] Within a system of inherent power differentials between parents, caseworkers, judges, and even their own lawyers, parent allies "serve to bridge the gap between parents and a complex, often challenging, and overwhelming system."[87] Through the hope-filled message of "if I can get through this, so can you," the lived experiences of parent allies help pave a pathway toward meeting the parents' needs by bestowing knowledge of and links to community support programs, innovatively navigating intersecting systems, and demonstrating proof that changing perpetuating patterns is possible. In service and connection to others, parent allies often find meaning in their experiences of trauma and separation and deepen their own healing and restoration. How would Carol and her children's experience in the juvenile court system improve had Carol worked with a parent ally like Heather Cantamessa?

---

[84] For instance, in addition to programs elsewhere, parent mentor programs exist in jurisdictions in California, Kentucky, Iowa, New York, Washington, Oregon, and Ohio.

[85] Parent-to-parent supports have precedent in the education, mental health, substance abuse, and veteran contexts *How Do Parent Partner Programs Instill Hope and Support Prevention and Reunification?* Casey Foundation (June 4, 2019), https://casey.org/parent-partner-program.

[86] *Id.*

[87] *Id.*

A Child-Stripped Mother

Heather Cantamessa's journey to becoming a parent ally, running her own parent ally organization, and speaking nationally and internationally about the benefits of parent ally programs began as a child sexually abused and exposed to domestic violence, labyrinthed through fifteen years of drug addiction and domestic violence, and culminated in nearly losing all five of her children to the child welfare system.

As a young child, Heather always went to bed scared and struggled to sleep because at night her stepfather molested her and was violent toward Heather's mother. Heather and her mother were able to escape by moving from one city to another. Heather's mother worked two jobs, and she and Heather became addicts together, nursing their trauma and ongoing fear with alcohol and marijuana. Heather attended nearly twenty schools before she eventually stopped going. Filled with anger and self-loathing by fourteen-years-old, her life revolved around getting more drugs and getting them faster. When Heather was sixteen, she became pregnant and her son was born drug-exposed. Over the next nine years, Heather would give birth to four more children, cycle through drug treatment programs, relapses, and periods of being clean, endure near-fatal domestic violence by her husband, and weave through the juvenile court system that returned and removed her children several times.

In 2007, with three of her children in her custody, the police were monitoring her house because of her husband's criminal activity. When he returned one day, the police arrived and so did the child welfare worker. Heather watched as her children were taken into state custody. She thought to herself, "My kids are safe now. I should be happy." Over the next six months, Heather was homeless, living on the street, and nearly destroyed herself. She used drugs heavily, put herself in very dangerous situations, and attended visits with her children high on drugs. Heather could not connect with her children, yet she dreaded saying goodbye. Heather was told they regressed after seeing her. Then she stopped going to the visits.

The depth of the emptiness Heather felt compelled her into an inpatient treatment program. She told herself to behave, follow the rules, listen, stay focused, and keep her eye on the prize—sobriety. When she finished the program, it had been eight months since she had seen her children. Heather moved into a recovery house that provided her with an opportunity to sustain a clean and sober way of life. She was ten months clean when she was asked to open a recovery house for women and children.

Then, after Heather's daughters had been in foster care for two years, her lawyer called her to tell her that her daughters were being abused in their foster home and asked, "Heather, are you an option?" An option was the best way to describe how Heather felt. Yes, there was the option she could be what her children needed and deserved. Scared that she may not be able to maintain her sobriety and care for others, she agreed to reengage in services. She was also told that in order for her daughters to return to her, she had to relinquish her rights to her boys, who had remained with their aunt who wanted to adopt them. Anguished to choose between her children, Heather acquiesced. Heather was eighteen months clean which was the longest she had been sober since she was thirteen years old, and her daughters were returned to her. Twelve years after her oldest son was born drug-exposed, Heather's final dependency case closed.

As Heather focused on remaining sober and parenting, Heather's friend attended a statewide meeting in 2008 in which the discussion was beginning to recognize that parents who had experienced the child welfare system could contribute to systemic improvement and reform. Calling upon themselves to act, Heather and her friend began a local parent advocacy committee with child welfare workers who wanted to make the system better. Sensing that the work was cementing rather than jeopardizing her sobriety, Heather started working at a program for women who used drugs or alcohol during pregnancy in order to educate them about the child welfare system and support their efforts to lead clean lives during pregnancy and after. Believing for the first time that she herself was the right person to lead, Heather then applied and was hired to implement a Parents for Parents Program as part of the Spokane County juvenile court that provided outreach and education to parents.

Trailblazing, Heather then expanded parent ally work to become part of the parent representation team. She now works with the Washington State Office of Public Defense and is contracted as a parent ally with the defense team. As a parent ally, Heather advocates to secure conditions and advocate for home placements, facilitate quick engagement in services, and help parents identify, navigate, and address the obstacles they face, all while fostering connection based upon shared lived experience. Heather pushes the lawyers to think creatively beyond the expected strategy. Heather works to hold the child welfare agency responsible by pushing for what the parent needs as a way of also meeting the needs of their children. Even when children are separated from their parents, Heather is adept at preserving the unified needs of children and their parents at the forefront of the intervention both by humanizing the parent and by assertively advocating for reunification services and visitation.

On her own ongoing journey of healing and repair, Heather remains dedicated to working with parents who are now where Heather once stood.

• • •

Heather once stood where Carol did before and during the juvenile court case. Like Heather, Carol loved and was committed to her children but was at the mercy of something much bigger than herself—Andy's violence and coercive control. For four years, Carol navigated the juvenile court case ostensibly alone with a lawyer she only spoke with minutes before the judge called the case to be heard. Had Carol been connected to a parent ally, both the process and outcome of the juvenile court case could have been a golden adhesive joining the needs of Carol and her children. Heather could have served as a counterpoint to Andy's abusive diatribes and a translator of the complicated and bureaucratic system Carol was traversing. By sharing Heather's own experience of overcoming significant obstacles, Carol could have begun to hope that there is a way to live outside of the abusive relationship envisioning and paving the path toward reuniting with her children more possible. Heather could strategize with Carol to find greater safety and buffer the risks for herself, and in turn for her children upon their return. Heather could have helped Carol access domestic violence services years earlier. Heather would have advocated with the local law enforcement to prepare them for the danger Carol might face in separating from Andy. Heather could advocate to seek, integrate, and elevate Carol's needs and goals into the service plan. Heather could creatively suggest ways for Jimmy to communicate and visit his mother. Such support could have prevented the removal altogether or led to a quicker and less destructive four years in the system leaving Carol and Jimmy together unbroken rather than weakening their safety, stability, well-being, and healing as it did.

• • •

At thirteen years old and when the juvenile court case closed, Jimmy moved to Aunt Mona's farm where he finally felt safe. Aunt Mona gave Jimmy a dog and a horse of his own that he cared for. Among the horses and the dogs, Jimmy began to unravel the trauma that both the domestic violence and the juvenile court intervention had caused. Jimmy did not believe in himself in any other area of his life, but on a horse, he knew he was a respectful and respectable rider. After years of being in a fight or flight state due to the ongoing trauma he experienced, his responses had become big, reactive, and harmful to himself and others. But on a horse, he could maintain his balance. After high school, Jimmy chose to enter a residential program. Jimmy did not have to hide what made him different. He began constructing his narrative of trauma that named his strengths amidst his struggles and was compelled to recognize that his past does not define his present. Jimmy began to heal.

Jimmy then went to college to become a social worker. After achieving his master's degree in social work, Jimmy became a special needs probation officer and was later asked to direct the criminal probation docket for domestic violence offenders working with men like Andy. Jimmy abided by the doctrine that working to develop offender accountability can and must center on the needs of the people who have been harmed. Those harmed needed to experience a community that cared about their safety, and the offenders needed to see a community standing behind the person who was hurt. Jimmy refused to allow the probation system to be a tool of further abuse like the child welfare system had been for Andy.

Jimmy approached his work with domestic violence offenders in ways he wished the child welfare system would have responded to his family. He sought to understand and reconcile the needs of each individual and the collective family in respectful and creative ways as Heather strives to achieve too. The child welfare intervention replicated the dynamics of abuse Jimmy, his mom, and sisters were experiencing at home by stripping them of their autonomy and the ability to make decisions about their own lives and well-being.

Rather than divesting power from people already with less power, juvenile court proceedings should seek ways to return control to children and their parents by building upon their strengths and creating pathways for their self-identified goals. Had he been asked, Jimmy would have made it clear that what he wanted, actually what he needed, was to see his sisters and have direct and unlimited access to his mother, such that Jimmy was not at the mercy of Carol earning the privilege of seeing her own child. The caseworker should have asked Jimmy what services he felt he needed. Jimmy may have been receptive to talking with a group of other teens on a day he did not have baseball, or he might have suggested horseback riding lessons or a tutor.

In asking Carol what she needed, she would have replied that she needed Andy to stop abusing her and to care for her children at home. Andy may have stopped abusing Carol had the judge held Andy in contempt of court for not complying with the orders to cease harming Carol while also offering him services, such as a batterer intervention program. Had the intervention engaged with Andy in this way, Carol and her children would have seen that Andy was experiencing consequences, too, that might foment a motivation to change—a possible pathway to his accountability and their safety. Then, Jimmy, his mom, and sisters would not have been the only ones saddled with the costs of the intervention. Because the best way to meet the needs of children is to support their parents in meeting their needs, when asked, Carol also would have shared that she had a need to finish college and secure a professional job in order to independently support her children. Helping Carol to become economically independent would have been one of the most effective ways to support her in caring for her children. Instead, for years following the closure of the child welfare case, Carol struggled with debilitating depression.

The family did not come to the attention of the child welfare agency again because each person learned to avoid involvement with the system at any cost not because their struggles had resolved. While the success of child welfare interventons is often measured by the lack of subsequent child welfare involvement, here success rather would have been a juvenile court process that met Carol and her children's needs by maintaining the family's personal and communal connections as a source of strength, resilience, and healing while creating possible avenues for accountability rather than becoming another obstacle for the family to overcome.

Jimmy now lives on the farm surrounded by eighty-eight acres, forty horses, and twenty dogs. The farm is now bigger than the one he lived on with Aunt Mona, and it's different but different in a way that makes him feel peaceful, whole, and special in a way that satisfies his measured need to be home.

8

Parallel Process for Families: Collaborative Practice between Domestic Violence and Child Welfare

The essence of effective child welfare intervention into the lives of families experiencing domestic violence is partnering with each member of the family, the adult and child survivors and the person who uses coercive control and violence, to enhance their safety, stability, well-being, and healing through trauma-informed, strength-based, family-centered, and equity-focused approaches. Yet the effective ingredient, namely partnering together, remains difficult.

Obstacles are inherent to developing a partnership between child welfare workers and families experiencing domestic violence. Child welfare involvement is often unwanted and viewed as a fear-provoking intrusion. The adult survivor is forced to confront the abuse before she may be ready. Child welfare recommendations or mandates may compromise her family's safety or question her parenting. Although they are expected to be experts in wide-ranging issues, the workers may be ill-equipped, often self-admittedly, to understand the dynamics of domestic violence at play. Engaging with the person using violence and coercive control may feel scary, intimidating, or confusing, especially if charisma or manipulation surface. Determining the risk and impact of abuse on the child survivors may seem amorphous, obtuse, and unclear. Figuring out how to actually help a family may be overwhelming when the family faces so many challenges and sources of oppression. The antidote to this acrimonious context is its opposite—collaboration.

Indeed, the places in which collaboration is often needed the most are amidst relationships with the most pervasive and longstanding rub. Parallel processing provides the solution, albeit no panacea. Parallel processing is premised on the notion that one can only give what one has within or has received. The adages of one cannot serve from an empty vessel, practice what you preach, and be the change you want to see could be simplistic taglines for the case of parallel processing. If the end goal is partnerships with families that lead to safety, stability, well-being, and healing, the foundation of these outcomes must start before the interactions between child welfare workers and families occur. As such, the ability to partner meaningfully with families derives from meaningful systemic partnerships. Likewise, meaningful systemic partnerships nurture the environment and the conditions for partnerships with families. Collaboration must exist in the structure of the interventions itself, passed down from the leadership level to the casework level to the family level. Such collaborative practice between child welfare and domestic violence professionals has become a centerpiece, or at least a strategy, in many states to meet the needs of families experiencing both domestic violence and the child welfare system.

Collaboration between child welfare and domestic violence camps has manifested in many forms. Collaborative practices include creating Domestic Violence Specialists among child welfare staff, co-locating domestic violence advocates in child welfare offices, bringing together child welfare and domestic violence personnel in community centers, using statewide domestic violence coalitions to provide support and assistance to child welfare, and cross-training child welfare and domestic violence staff together. The first formalized domestic violence program within a child welfare agency, the Massachusetts Domestic Violence Unit, will be thoroughly explored to understand the history, evolution, practice, and benefits of collaborative interventions. The various above-mentioned collaborative approaches will then be explored, spotlighting a co-location collaborative program in New Jersey. Above all, as learned from the Greenbook demonstration sites, collaboration is not a goal in and of itself, but rather a means to improve outcomes for families and communities. With the essence of parallel process as the guide, a collaboration between child welfare and domestic violence professionals not only mirrors the partnership needed with families, but creates a culture, priority, motivation, and pathway for doing so, and in turn increases the opportunity for trauma-informed, strength-based, family-centered, and equity-focused interventions that enable families to remain unbroken together.

The Sisterhood of Parallel Process

As their predecessors had done through sisterhood in the early days of the battered women's movement, a sisterhood of women aimed to dissolve the divide between those working in the fields of domestic violence and child welfare in the name of better serving families. The sisterhood became the originals in the Domestic Violence Unit of the Massachusetts Department of Children and Families (DCF), a specialized domestic violence unit within the state's child welfare agency.[1] Lonna Davis, Susan Hubert, Isa Woldeguiorguis, Crystal Jackson, Shellie Taggart, Katchi Lessard, Tammy Mello, and others all found their way there,[2] and Andrew Rome and Sue Englaish continue to strengthen this community of collective cultural norms and evolving practice thereby sustaining the legacy of the collaborative sisterhood for the betterment of families.[3]

---

1 When the Domestic Violence Unit began, the state agency was called the Massachusetts Department of Social Services and became the Department of Children and Families (DCF) in July 2008. For ease here, DCF will be used.

2 Other Domestic Violence Specialists in the early days included Brenda Lopez, Spring Redd, Janet Fender, Sue Ash, Stacy Cabot, Evanice Cerelli, Sandy Galindo, Sandy Goodman, Susan Hoye, Antonia Chronis, Laurie Coombs, and Linda Enerson.

3 Reminiscent of the early days of the battered women's movement, Susan Schechter wrote, "As a reaction to isolation and as an affirmation of women, activists

• • •

After the lengthy and dangerous process of leaving an abusive relationship with the support of her family, in Boston Lonna Davis began the first children's program at the second oldest domestic violence agency in the country. In designing the program, Lonna recognized the critical role that mothers in shelters played in helping their children. She also witnessed the burdens that these mothers experienced, especially when they also had a child welfare case.

Many mothers faced impossible ultimatums imposed by the child welfare workers and case plans: end the abusive relationship (as if it were that easy, the mothers and Lonna thought) or lose the children; stay in a shelter or lose the children; obtain housing, food, and medical care without a breadwinning abuser or lose the children; comply with services and maintain a job or lose the children. As a first attempt to address these divisions, Lonna reached out to the local child welfare office offering to provide training on domestic violence but received no invitations.

At the same time, Susan Schechter's program Advocate for Women and Kids in Emergencies (AWAKE) at Children's Hospital Boston had released its first findings that in nearly 50 percent of the cases referred to the AWAKE domestic violence advocates, the children did not enter foster care. Equipped with some of the first evidence of the effectiveness of cross-system collaboration around domestic violence and child welfare, Susan approached the Massachusetts DCF to integrate collaboration into child welfare practice. A needs assessment of the current cross-system work became the next step. Motivated to address the systemic challenges impacting the families with whom she worked, Lonna was hired to conduct the needs assessment, and Susan became Lonna's supervisor. In authoring the needs assessment, Lonna concluded that the divide between the outside systems, especially child welfare, and the domestic violence community was expansive but that crossing the divide would benefit families facing complicated and precarious circumstances. In other words, no one system or provider could be expected to do it all, and doing it together could enhance positive outcomes for families.

---

tried to form a sustaining sisterhood, a community with new cultural norms." Susan Schechter, Women and Male Violence, (1982).

Based upon the identified need to work together for the benefit of families, in 1990 Susan and her child welfare colleagues, Linda Spears and Pamela (Pam) Whitney,[4,5] started what would become the Domestic Violence Unit at DCF. Pam hired Lonna, and together they translated Susan's model born at AWAKE to child welfare. Lonna became the first domestic violence advocate co-located in a child welfare office. The vision for this integrated position was to build the capacity of child welfare staff to understand domestic violence, to support the family through the intervention, and to build bridges between the domestic violence advocacy community and child welfare. If the findings from AWAKE were predictive here, such collaboration could increase outcomes for families such that fewer children who experienced domestic violence would be in foster care, and families would be safer and more stable following child welfare interventions. Little guidance existed about what collaboration should and could be, but two principles guided Lonna's work—every action must be safe (i.e., not increase risk) to the adult survivor and her children, and the intervention should strive for the parent causing harm to be accountable.[6] At the core of developing collaborative practice existed Lonna's "Golden Rule of Parallel Process"—do unto others as you would have done unto yourself so that others can do unto others to come.

Without a model elsewhere, Pam and Lonna wrote the department's domestic violence in child welfare protocols. In search of appropriate terminology, Lonna met with Susan and the DCF general counsel at the time to identify a term that would both identify a parent's experience of domestic violence and connect her to her children. Following the discussion, Lonna coined the now widely used term nonoffending parent to describe the adult victim who is involved in the child welfare system due to domestic violence perpetrated against her.

---

4 Linda Spears was the vice president of the Child Welfare League of America since 2015, has been the commissioner of the Massachusetts Department of Children and Families, and testified as an expert on behalf of the plaintiff class in the class action Nicholson v. Williams discussed in chapter 5.

5 Pamela Whitney was an assistant commissioner of DSS and was instrumental in forming the Domestic Violence Unit. A staunch advocate for women, children, and families and an innovator in helping families, Pamela passed away in 2010.

6 Diane Dipanfilis wrote a short guide in the 1980s that helped to shape Lonna and Pam's thinking about collaboration.

Pam and Lonna published an article in the *Journal of Child Maltreatment* about institutionalizing domestic violence practice in a child welfare setting. From the early lessons learned, their article explained the benefits to child welfare workers and families when a domestic violence advocate is involved. The co-location model began to grow as federal Family Violence Prevention Service Act dollars funded the program from two to four Domestic Violence Specialists and the Domestic Violence Unit formed.

The new unit needed highly qualified advocates, but the domestic violence community was distrustful of DCF and resisted. Through Lonna's persistence and persuasion, the domestic violence community began to appreciate that if they were not willing to work with child welfare, they could not expect child welfare to effectively work with families they both touched. Because all funding for domestic violence programs passed through DCF, the power of the purse compelled some to listen. Believing in the mission of her work, slowly and steadfastly, Lonna persuaded the domestic violence community about the potential impact of collaboration and recruited effective advocates who came aboard. The unit grew and a sisterhood formed.

Although the women of the sisterhood came to the unit through different paths, they were united in their core beliefs. To the sisterhood, the women brought their own experiences of or feminist perspectives on domestic violence yet were all rooted in the view that the personal is political, a belief in the value of family, the importance of responding to the needs of children, the commitment to survivor-driven safety, the worth of locating pathways for offender accountability, and a passion for making systems work better.

As an advocate in a battered women's shelter, Susan Hubert stood next to a mother as her children were taken from her in the shelter parking lot to be placed in foster care. All of the issues important to Susan—women's liberation, family, children's well-being, acceptance, tolerance, fairness—seemed in conflict with what she had witnessed. Years later, as the director of a new domestic violence agency, Susan heard Lonna speak about her new position working in child welfare. Concerned about holding the roots of her domestic violence work within an outside system yet motivated by the need to advance the response of the child welfare system, Susan became a Domestic Violence Specialist in 1994 with Lonna as her supervisor.[7]

Isa Woldeguiorguis began her career as a child welfare worker in her childhood neighborhood. Isa then moved to Massachusetts to work in an alternative sentencing program for women who had killed their abusers. Through the women there, Isa recognized the intergenerational legacy of violence they had experienced from childhood sexual abuse to exploitation as young women to domestic violence and substance abuse as adults. With a view of the trajectory of violence over a lifetime, Isa joined the Unit in 1994.[8]

Crystal Jackson worked as a legal advocate in the county assisting domestic violence survivors seeking protective orders. Crystal learned to navigate a system and its personnel whose disrespectfulness and frustration often exacerbated the angst of her clients and failed to meet their needs. Crystal met Lonna during one of the meetings in which Lonna was speaking with domestic violence programs in the area to discuss strategies for connecting with the local DCF child welfare office. To Crystal's shock, her colleagues stood up and left. Crystal stayed and agreed to do a training sessions for the local DCF

---

7 Susan Hubert remained a Domestic Violence Specialist in the western part of the state for three years. Isa then became her supervisor. Susan moved to the southern region as a Domestic Violence Specialist for another two years, until becoming a supervisor in 1998. In 2015, Susan became the director of the Domestic Violence Unit following Lonna and then Isa. Susan inherited a unit that was understaffed (from fourteen specialists down to five specialists). When Linda Spears became the commissioner of DCF, funding stabilized to provide for nine specialists, two supervisors, and the unit director. Susan is the current director of the Domestic Violence Unit at the Massachusetts Department of Children and Families.

8 Isa worked at DCF for a total of thirteen years, from a Domestic Violence Specialist to a supervisor. When Lonna left, Isa became the director of the unit and then the assistant commissioner of DCF. Isa left DCF to work at Jane Doe, Inc., the Massachusetts Coalition Against Sexual Assault and Domestic Violence. Isa then worked on a national initiative called Defending Childhood that focused on the intersections of all children's exposure to violence. In 2012, Isa became the executive director of The Center for Hope and Healing, an agency providing prevention, intervention, and rape crisis services to sexual assault survivors, thereby continuing Isa's career in the field of anti-violence. Isa was a member of the Quality Improvement Center on Domestic Violence in Child Welfare National Advisory Committee administered by Lonna Davis and Shellie Taggart of which Massachusetts (along with Illinois and Allegheny County, Pennsylvania), under the leadership of Susan Hubert, became a Research and Capacity Building Project.

office about domestic violence. Workers then began calling Crystal when they had challenging cases involving domestic violence. Dismayed by the developing response of her domestic violence agency to the poor women of color who were replacing the white, middle-class women who had been entering shelters over the past decade, Crystal joined the Domestic Violence Unit.[9]

Following her five years of service as an officer in the U.S. Air Force, Shellie reflected back on her early experience in an abusive relationship and began working at a domestic violence agency as one of the earliest legal advocates in the country. Through helping people file for civil protection orders, Shellie observed that the issues affecting their families included violence that never began or ended at the courthouse, and by collecting data she found that around 85 percent of the petitioners never contacted a domestic violence program. It seemed that both systems and agencies were not fully meeting the needs of families. The underutilization of domestic violence agencies appeared to rest in a discomfort about the inequitable delivery of services and the unwillingness to consider all members of the family (i.e., the men who use violence). Shellie began volunteering at the Men's Resource Center with Juan Carolos Areán. There she developed a belief that men could change, grow, and become healthier parents and partners. Shellie sought an opportunity to address the issue of domestic violence from a broader and intersecting vantage point and became a Domestic Violence Specialist under Isa's supervision.[10]

---

[9] Crystal worked for DSS for twenty-one years as a Domestic Violence Specialist, training coordinator, and supervisor (of Shellie's team). Recognizing the connection between economic stability, freedom from abuse, and safety in the broadest sense, Crystal now directs the Domestic Violence Unit of the Department of Transitional Assistance, in which over twenty domestic violence advocates are co-located in public benefits offices across the state. These advocates help ensure that the benefits are actually improving the lives of families (e.g., providing a domestic violence survivor more time to fulfill the work requirement of her case plan if she is in crisis), avoiding harmful policies and practice (e.g., requiring a domestic violence survivor to pursue child support if it would be dangerous), and connecting family to useful services.

[10] Shellie worked in the Domestic Violence Unit of DCF for seven years. She then became a consultant on domestic violence and child welfare, and following *Nicholson*, helped New Jersey start its child welfare Domestic Violence Liaison program. When the Children's Bureau selected Futures Without Violence to lead the Quality Improvement Center on Domestic Violence in Child Welfare, Lonna

Kate "Katchi" Lessard immigrated to the United States from Brazil. She moved in with her aunt, uncle, and cousins in their home yet moved out because the abuse her uncle inflicted upon her aunt was traumatic to witness. In 1994, Katchi began working for DCF as a child welfare investigator. So many of Katchi's cases involved domestic violence yet punitive victim-blaming and offender invisibility functioned as barriers to effectively helping the family. Wanting to further improve the way DCF responded to domestic violence, Katchi transitioned to become a Domestic Violence Specialist two years later.[11]

Tammy Mello became a child welfare worker with DCF when the Unit was in its infancy. Many of Tammy's colleagues thought that the Domestic Violence Specialists only cared about the mothers to the detriment of the children. Tammy was assigned a very challenging case involving domestic violence and consulted with the Domestic Violence Specialist. Tammy feared that her involvement with the family would make the situation worse if she adhered to the typical DCF response, which destabilized families with one-size-fits-all punitive approaches that diminished accountability and sustainable well-being. Through many consultations to come, Tammy came to understand the dynamics of domestic violence and began developing her own skills. Viewing herself as an advocate within the system, Tammy joined the Domestic Violence Unit.[12]

• • •

Davis called her former co-worker, and Shellie became the program director of which Massachusetts (and Illinois and Allegheny County, Pennsylvania) was a Research and Capacity Building Project.

11 Katchi remained a Domestic Violence Specialist for five years. She then left DSS, obtained her Master's degree, worked with Brazilian women experiencing domestic violence, worked for Isa at the sexual assault agency that Isa currently directs, and returned to DSS in 2015 as an area supervisor of DSS child welfare social workers with Domestic Violence Specialists in the offices under her supervision.

12 Tammy left the Domestic Violence Unit to join a local domestic violence program overseeing a supervised visitation center and a homicidal bereavement program. She then returned to DSS as a Program Coordinator that oversaw the passage of state funds to domestic violence programs. After Isa and before Susan, Tammy directed the Domestic Violence Unit for nearly five years. Tammy then joined the Massachusetts Health and Human Services Domestic Violence Prevention, ran the Governor's Council on Domestic Violence and Sexual Assault, and headed the Children's League of Massachusetts.

Lonna, Susan, Isa, Crystal, Shellie, Katchi, and Tammy all worked together at overlapping times during the first decade of the DCF Domestic Violence Unit, forming a supportive sisterhood grounded in parallel processing that enabled them to respond to the complexities of domestic violence in the child welfare system. The advocates highlighted here reunited to participate in a group interview. Through laughter, tears, and reflection, they shared their wisdom and experiences about why cases at the intersection of domestic violence and child welfare are so hard, the importance of collaboration, the key principles of effective collaboration, the evolution of their collaborative practice, the practical influence of collaboration on interventions, the impact of collaboration for families, and the persisting challenges.

Why These Cases are So Hard

As Crystal said, "If I had a dollar for every time I heard that domestic violence cases were the hardest [cases] in the twenty-one years I worked for DCF, I would be a rich woman." Child welfare cases involving domestic violence are challenging, and the hard questions exist and persist because no one model of intervention applies. Social work, criminal justice, and advocacy models all influence child welfare interventions but no one approach governs. The social work principles of meeting families where they are and allowing individuals to direct the course of their lives struggle to co-exist in a system that has the power to remove someone's children and impose mandates. Being incident-driven, like the criminal justice system, often obscures the important context of the continuum of domestic violence which may cause them to misunderstand the roles and dynamics present, miss circumstances that actually pose a real threat of harm to children, and obscure opportunities to build upon the protective capacities already there. Advocacy requires knowledge of domestic violence and available services, yet child welfare workers are not experts in all the issues families coming to their attention face, especially with a workforce that experiences high turnover.

Amidst the conflation of various fields coming together in child welfare, the system itself has limitations. Riding philosophical pendulum swings between saving kids and preserving families leads to confusion for systems that are not nimble enough to respond to emerging knowledge or shifts in institutional culture. Although the child welfare system holds the power of removal, it lacks the corollary power to create sustainable change; sustainable change cannot be coerced but rather must be fostered through support and partnership. Even when child welfare workers are not hampered by the moral constructions of individuals and can identify the intersecting needs of the family, it might be impossible to actually give families what they need. Limited supports, resource deserts, time constraints, liability, caseloads, and inevitable public criticism weigh heavily on stressed and fatigued workforces trying to do difficult work. Collaboration is necessary so these various models can co-exist, rather than crash and bang into one another, as Susan said, resulting in inequitable systems that breed confusion and conflict.

The Importance of Collaboration

Without collaboration, those who work with families experiencing domestic violence have to pick teams amongst family members. As Lonna described, by working in the child welfare system, the violence and harm inflicted upon children surfaces and experiences of the parent survivor fade from significance. Likewise, by working in the domestic violence field, the harm inflicted upon the parent survivor surfaces, and the experiences of the children fade from focus, and in both fields, addressing the person who causes the harm becomes ignorable or insurmountable. Through the mutual growth that evolves from collaborative practice, child welfare partnerships enable domestic violence providers to have a broader view of their service, while philosophies and approaches that connect the needs of children within their families are integrated into child welfare interventions. Responses become less siloed and addressing the needs of the family members becomes less isolated and disconnected from one another thereby focusing on the family as the fundamental and primary realm in which these relationships exist—the place where interests align even amidst struggles.

Rather than segmenting each family member apart from the other, collaboration enables child welfare and domestic violence advocates to hold whole the entire experience of the family—the nonoffending parent, the parent who uses violence and coercive control, and the children. The collective effort is for the betterment of the family driven by the safety and well-being of the adult and child survivors. Individual needs are not ignored within the context of the family but collaboration supports interventions that respond to each member with the goal of helping families become safer and stronger together.

Bringing both parents and children together into focus, a governing mantra of the Domestic Violence Unit is that every family has value. The professional orientations influencing child welfare practice thereby come together around a trauma-informed, strength-based, family-centered, and equity-focused approach, using the most effective elements from the various fields to best operationalize this unifying guide star. Keeping families together or getting families back together if the children were removed as a last resort is the lens through which decisions are filtered. For Tammy, she has remained in this field for so many years because of the powerful and irreplaceable love between children and their parents. The value of all families, even those with harmful struggles, guides and motivates her. She recognizes the responsibility she has and the system's role in enhancing (or at least not impeding) these invaluable ties. In this way, the sisterhood of Domestic Violence Specialists identified as supporters of the family.

Key Principles of Collaboration

Core principles of nonjudgmental respect, knowledge sharing, listening, learning, teaching, and self and systemic reflection ground the collaboration and serve as the values to replicate in interventions. Every interaction, discussion, and disagreement between the Domestic Violence Specialist and a child welfare worker must be respectful and nonjudgmental. The collaboration dynamics set the tone and approach for interacting with families with dignity and humanity, thereby potentially creating or reinforcing the demand for and manifestation of such treatment in the families' own lives and relationships.

Because power dynamics are unavoidable even in thoughtful and strong collaborations,[13] the sharing and exchange of knowledge becomes the equalizer. Valuable sources of knowledge exist among all involved. The specialist is an expert in domestic violence; the child welfare worker is an expert in child welfare; each parent and child

[13] This was an important lesson learned from the Greenbook Demonstration Sites.

are experts in their experiences, needs, and aspirations. No knowledge source has value over the other. Shellie recognized the expertise in those around her, listened to the knowledge of others in every interaction, and integrated information from all sources. If those intervening value the knowledge and perspective of each other, then they will be primed to value the knowledge and perspectives from the families themselves. By sharing and listening to others' knowledge, each partner becomes a learner and a teacher. Susan describes this duality as confidence with humility. As Crystal said, "Being an expert means you see the expertise in others." The exchange, debate, brainstorming, and problem solving through collaboration enhance the undergirding principle that strength exists amidst struggle and reinforces the practice of seeking, elevating, and integrating the voices of all members of the family, thereby serving as the means toward better outcomes.

The collaborative partners must reflect and be honest about the system's flaws and dangers while still believing in the potential of the system to operate radically differently. Willing to work toward better systemic responses, Isa reiterated that at the core of ending domestic violence is increasing equity not just in systems but in every fold of society. She shared that the child welfare system seems like the unlikely vehicle toward this end because it is plagued by institutional racism and systemic oppression from its inception through the present and utilizes policing powers that are contraindicated for effective responses to domestic violence. The collaboration, however, Isa opined, can hold the system accountable to families to meet their needs and demand transformation. "For a system that is not going to cease to exist," Isa continued, "the more people repel against or isolate away from the system, the more the system inoculates itself from change."

The Evolution of Collaborative Practice

Toward the aim of collaborative practice based upon the mutual transference of information and understanding, the role of the Domestic Violence Specialist has evolved. When Lonna became the first domestic violence advocate co-located with DCF, her role functioned like a superimposed domestic violence advocate working with individual survivors, only in the child welfare context. As the unit grew, Lonna,

Isa, Crystal, Shellie, and Susan recognized that building the capacity of the child welfare staff to effectively respond to all members of the family was needed.

Within this shift, relationships began to form when the Specialists were able to demonstrate their timely responsiveness and helpfulness, especially on hard cases and in the field. Months after being hired and without any consultations, a supervisor and six investigators consulted with Susan on a particularly dangerous case to make a plan to talk with the survivor and meet with the children while working around the control and dangerousness of the father. The plan transpired over three days, and Susan stood by her colleagues' sides the entire time. Suspicions of each other faded when the child welfare workers experienced that Susan listened, offered helpful ideas, and was part of the team effort to assist and protect the family and when Susan observed that the child welfare workers wanted to be effective and avoid causing harm but were unsure of how to do so. Developing relationships between Domestic Violence Specialists and child welfare workers became the starting point of front-line collaborative practice.

While dynamics differed in each office and among personalities, Isa reflected that "At first no one wanted us, but soon everyone wanted us." Each consultation became an opportunity to assist child welfare workers to better understand the dynamics of abuse, assess and plan for safety, address any harm to children, strategize ways to foster offender accountability, and link the family to services and support. Crystal helped her colleagues identify the spectrum of coercive behaviors that constitute domestic violence, interpret confusing reports about injured perpetrators and violent victims, recognize the many faces and reactions of survivors as people who fight back or do not, who are scared or may not be, or who could be more apt to be angry than cry, and dismantle stereotypes of people who cause harm. Guiding nuanced assessments of past harm and future risk, Susan's practice involved relying upon specific details, rather than resting on general descriptions of behavior and presumptive risks to avoid unnecessary and intrusive interventions as well as missed opportunities to respond to the specific needs of the individuals and families. When DCF took actions that were inconsistent with the nonoffending parent's wishes and directives, Katchi tried to help the nonoffending parent understand the child welfare worker's concerns so that she could offer alternatives or feel a sense of control over decisions she did not face willingly,. With the child welfare worker, Katchi highlighted the trade-offs nonoffending parents regularly face both with and without child welfare intervention. By the mid-1990s, the Domestic Violence Unit had consulted on nearly 11,000 cases, close to one-third of the total DCF caseload, and systemic capacity was developing.

The Influence of Collaboration on Partnership and Engagement

Collaboration amongst the specialists and child welfare workers elevated partnering with the nonoffending parent and engaging with the person causing harm not only as priorities but also as practical methods for enhancing the safety, stability, well-being, and healing of the family by building upon strengths, buffering risk, and cultivating protective factors. Crystal encouraged her child welfare colleagues to assume that the adult survivor is a natural ally of her children and to work with her as a resource rather than a liability. Just as Shellie built upon the strengths of her child welfare colleagues, so did she guide them to identify the protective steps the nonoffending parent took and built upon those efforts as a strategy for mitigating risk. Tammy assisted the child welfare workers in identifying sources of resilience in children and creatively sought sources of additional feathers. All of the specialists guided child welfare workers to ask what the family needed rather than impose or assume their own projections in order to uncover the key elements that could lead to sustainable safety, stability, well-being, and healing.

The specialists and child welfare colleagues committed to listening to survivors who voiced the importance of not ignoring the person who used violence and coercive control. Less accustomed to working with those who perpetrate domestic violence, from the beginning of her work in the unit, Lonna enlisted outside expert guidance from Lundy Bancroft, David Adams, and Fernando Mederos to centralize the importance of and develop the skills for fostering avenues of accountability with those who cause harm. Susan cultivated the belief in the positive attributes (e.g., capacity for empathy, desire to cease harm provoking conduct, belief in positive fatherhood) of those who use violence and coercive control and strove to build upon those sources of strength as ways to reduce the risk they posed. To engage parents who cause harm, Isa helped her child welfare colleagues commit to meaningful engagement and plan for conversations to encourage information sharing and commitment to changing behaviors. Crystal emphasized the important bi-directional accountability—the practice of both creating pathways for offender accountability toward his partner, children, and community as well as systemic accountability toward the families and each of their members to foster interventions that meet their needs.

Each specialist saw it as the responsibility of every person involved to contribute to the fostering of protective factors for the family. Every interaction became an opportunity to strategize for safer and more stable conditions, facilitate social, cultural, and spiritual connections, contribute to resilience and a growth mindset, nurture the parent-child relationship, and reinforce social and emotional abilities.[14] To respond to the specific needs of adult and child survivors as well as foster mutual accountability, the specialists served as a link to community-based services and concrete supports. Susan regularly explored ways to develop relationships with community-based organizations. Tammy emphasized the importance of ensuring that state agencies were funding the right kind of services for children to help them heal and to keep children home.

Successes

Through collaborative domestic violence informed child welfare practice at DCF, more children were able to heal in safer and more

[14] These five protective factors were defined years later in 2019 through the Quality Improvement Center on Domestic Violence in Child Welfare that Futures Without Violence led by Lonna Davis and Shellie Taggart through a cooperative agreement with the U.S. Department of Health and Human Services, Administration for Children and Families, Children's Bureau. *Adult & Child Survivor-Centered Approach for Addressing Domestic Violence,* Quality Improvement Center on Domestic Violence in Child Welfare, (March 2019), dvchildwelfare.org. While the specific articulation of these interrelated domestic violence protective factors did not occur during the early years of the unit, even without this defined direction, the specialists' aimed to create these conditions in partnership with families and the community, and their actions helped to later inform the articulation of this framework.

stable homes with their families, adult survivors were more likely to experience the child welfare system as a potential source of support rather than a barrier, pathways for accountability increased, and connections with services and concrete supports developed. Yes, success was not confined to measurable outcomes.

Important moments for Lonna occurred when people felt seen and heard—her fellow Domestic Violence Specialists, her child welfare colleagues, adult and child survivors, and those who use violence and coercive control. When a mother was killed by her partner, Lonna sat with the child welfare worker who was in pain, mourning, and second-guessing herself. Lonna's presence served as a fortification of their shared humanity and defiance of invisibility that penetrated the worker's devastation and equipped her to do the same for others.

Isa found success in building community bridges. When a domestic violence-related homicide and a second suicide-homicide occurred within months of each other with children in both homes, the Domestic Violence Specialists acted as a resource for the entire community by guiding discussions and reflections about how the community response to the families could have differed in ways that may have led to nonlethal outcomes.

Success also occurred when the system followed the lead of the survivor, responded in the moment, and mobilized to meet her and her children's needs. Shellie recalled a mother who came to a DCF meeting and reported that her partner was standing outside of the front door and that she felt unsafe. Shellie and her colleagues took her and her children out the back door and drove them to a domestic violence shelter where the mother wanted to go.

Defying expectations made Susan proud. By holding and overcoming their own fears rooted in feeling helpless, Susan and her child welfare colleagues helped a mother facing grave danger leave the state with her children rather than remove her children from her. The mother later said, "I never could have imagined that DCF would interact with me in this way. I figured the next time DCF showed up, they would take my kids because *I* cannot figure out how to stay safe."

Tammy saw success in the creativity that resulted from working together, which contributed to the longevity and integration of the unit into DCF practice. Crystal valued the way the system embraced the feminist-oriented approach to domestic violence, seen when supervisors consulted before deciding to remove a child or when a lawyer argued a domestic violence case differently.

Katchi attributes the progress she has witnessed to the process of fostering strength and respect at every level of intervention interactions—amidst Domestic Violence Specialists, between child welfare colleagues, with families, and among the community—constituting the heart and legacy of the sisterhood of parallel process.

Persistent Challenges

Amidst the unit's integration, longevity, and multiple measures of success, challenges remained. Gauging, anticipating, and planning for capacity proved difficult. Offices across the state did not consistently access the specialists. Additionally, the specialists did not always have the capacity to meet the demands of the child welfare staff, and consultations were not always utilized in the most effective way (e.g., consultations that occurred on the eve of a case closing). High turnover among child welfare staff hindered long-term relationship building, knowledge acquisition, skill development, and systemic capacity growth. Remaining committed to their orientation as advocates for the family within the child welfare system, specialists were challenged to resist being co-opted by the host system. Capturing the lessons learned in the unit to replicate for new staff was difficult. Susan often wondered, "How do we know how to do what we do? How did this group learn to do what we did so well?" Evaluating the outcomes for children and families that result from collaborative practice was also challenging, and anecdotal success was easier to describe than evidence-based data.

While the collaboration constituted a significant step toward greater community coordination to families experiencing domestic violence, fragmentation, inconsistency, and distance between systems persisted and the collaboration could not fix deficits in each system. The collaborative practice revealed and confirmed concerns about the provision of services among domestic violence agencies. Shellie met many women involved in the child welfare system who said they would never go to a domestic violence program, revealing that despite vital work, domestic violence providers were not meeting the needs of many. The specialists wished to extend the sisterhood of their unit to the broader provision of domestic violence services yet many remained uninterested. Disproportionate representation of families of color and those experiencing poverty in the child welfare system endured, in spite of the targeted efforts of the unit. The specialists experienced vicarious trauma both in the stories they witnessed every day, the high stakes of the interventions in which they were involved, and the occasional yet heartbreaking calamity.

The sisterhood within the Domestic Violence Unit served as the antidote to many of these challenges. Their connection enabled the evolution and durability of the unit. As Crystal explained, "Growing was not easy—it had its moments of confusion, pain, and questioning. But a strong bond continued when we understood where each other came from and where we envisioned going. We were just a small group that did this work and it mattered a great deal."

Sustained Impact

After a decade of building relationships and innovative collaboration amidst trauma and tragedy born from the involvement of the unit on nearly 30 percent of all DCF cases, Lonna turned the Domestic Violence Unit over to Isa.[15] Lonna left a collage filled with magazine clippings that synthesized the spirit, humor and all, and philosophy of the sisterhood with the following words:

> Just say what you need; Shift the Practice; Lessons Learned; Safety; Help for the Helpers; Think of the Possibilities; Knowl edge, Vision, Community; Child Safety; The Sacrifice and persistence of a small group of concerned citizens; Compassion; Family Advocates; Screaming Divas; N-O Spells No; Race, Culture, Class; un-Conventional Wisdom; Put on the Gloves; Courage; Thanks; Somewhere in the Middle; Prevention; Pick Your Battles; Take a Day Off; Start the Conversation; Put on the Gloves; Teamwork; Big Picture; Love That! Hate That!; Whadja do that for?; You don't have to know the answers, you just have to where to turn; It's your future, don't leave it blank;

[15] Lonna was recruited by Futures Without Violence to work on the Greenbook Demonstration Site project. Susan Schechter remained Lonna's mentor.

Choice; Resources; Integrate; Listen; Respect; Be a Model (Or just look like one) . . . Parallel Process.

The unit has remained an integrated and respected part of DCF. Although the number of advocates has fluctuated amidst funding allocations, the leadership at DCF continues to send a clear message to supervisors and front-line workers that the unit is a valued resource, worthy of involvement and consideration on cases.

Current General Counsel for DCF, Andrew Rome, has experienced first-hand the professional growth that occurs through collaboration. Early on, Andrew and specialist Sue Englaish,[16] together grappled with the legal and practical complexities of the hard questions—how to ensure a child's safety when the risk of domestic violence exists and/or if the relationship continues, avoid punishing the victim while enabling her to protect her children, and foster greater safety while providing a mechanism of accountability for the person who uses violence. As Andrew experienced, each conversation with Sue was a teachable moment, rather than a didactic mandate. Andrew learned about domestic violence through both theoretical and case-specific conversations with Sue through her active listening, probing questions, and outline of options. Despite often lively exchanges, Sue never judged Andrew when he expressed exasperation, for instance, that a mother had returned to her children's abusive father for the fourth time. Sue was able to frame the reality of that mother's decision not as a choice involving free will or "choosing the father over the children" but rather as a weighing of tradeoffs around the safety of her and her children and their well-being now and in the future. Listening and sharing with compassionate honesty, Andrew articulated the safety risks that the continued domestic violence posed to the children. Together, Sue and Andrew creatively identified solutions, like helping the mother enroll in a cosmetic certificate program

[16] Sue Englaish joined the DVU in 2001 as a DV Specialist in the Western Region after working in the domestic violence field. For several years Sue worked collaboratively with the District Attorney's Office and local police to ensure the safety of survivors and children. It was through this work that she learned the value of listening and collaboration, which continues to be a part of her work at DCF as a supervisor within the DVU overseeing the specialist in the western, central, and Boston Regions.

like she desired to gain financial independence to mitigate the risk of returning to her breadwinning abuser. In working with Andrew, Sue modeled the respect, trust, openness, and compassion that DCF should embody when working with families. Andrew now identifies a successful child welfare intervention into the lives of families experiencing domestic violence as a vehicle toward sustainable change that meets the needs of the family individually and collectively as a result of nonjudgmental and nuanced interactions that promote safety, stability, well-being, and ultimately healing.

Other Forms of Collaborative Practice

As Massachusetts demonstratives, collaboration is beneficial to families, domestic violence and child welfare workers alike, systems, and communities.[17] While the specific form of collaboration is unique to the needs and dynamics of each jurisdiction, additional models and methods of collaboration have developed.

Co-Location

Rather than cultivating domestic violence experts within a child welfare agency, other states have adopted a co-location model of collaboration between child welfare and domestic violence professionals and systems. More common in hospitals and police stations, co-location in the child welfare context places domestic violence advocates who are employed by domestic violence agencies in child welfare offices. Like the Domestic Violence Specialists in Massachusetts, co-located advocates are typically charged with both enhancing the capacity of the child welfare system to effectively respond to families experiencing domestic violence and supporting families during the child welfare intervention. Co-location also provides support to

---

[17] Like Massachusetts, Vermont also has an internal Domestic Violence Unit in which a Domestic Violence Specialist is positioned in each of its child welfare offices. Brittany DiBella, Judy L. Postmus, Cassandra Simmel, Catherine Buttner, & Caitlin Eckert, *From Research to Practice: An Overview of Systems of Collaboration Efforts to Address the Co-Occurrence of Domestic Violence and Child Welfare*, Rutgers University School of Social Work, Center of Violence Against Women and Children 8 (July 25, 2019), https://safeandtogetherinstitute.com/wp-content/uploads/2018/01/RUTGERS_DV_BRIEFING_061517.pdf.

child welfare workers so they can better support families who in turn support healing together.

Arizona,[18] California, Connecticut,[19] Delaware,[20] Iowa,[21] Maine,[22] New Hampshire,[23] Florida,[24] North Carolina,[25] Oregon,[26] South Carolina,[27] New York State, and New Jersey have (or have had) co-location collaborations.[28] A 2014 evaluation of the State of New York's Advocate Co-Location program revealed that in the

18 Domestic violence advocates in Arizona are co-located in child welfare offices but not in every county. Rutgers, *supra* note 17.

19 Connecticut's Domestic Violence Consultation Initiatives have placed thirteen consultants in child welfare offices starting in 2006. *Id.*

20 Delaware's Domestic Violence Liaison program was piloted in 2002, and now five Domestic Violence Liaisons are co-located in five counties. *Id.*

21 The Quad-Cities in Iowa have had a co-location program with child welfare that has been jeopardized by funding cuts.

22 Domestic Violence Liaisons are located in medical centers and child welfare offices in some counties. *Id.*

23 New Hampshire's Family Violence Prevention Specialist Program is a partnership between the Department of Children and Family Services and the New Hampshire Coalition Against Domestic and Sexual Violence, and one specialist is co-located in each district office statewide. *Id.*

24 Florida has a statewide co-location program in which over sixty domestic violence advocates are working in nearly every investigative child welfare office in the state. *FCADV's Child Protection Investigations (CPI) Project*, Florida Coalition Against Domestic Violence (July 28, 2019), http://www.fcadv.org/projects-programs/child-welfare/cpi-project; *FCADV Child Protection Investigations Project Standards Manual*, Florida Coalition Against Domestic Violence (July 28, 2019), http://www.fcadv.org/sites/default/files/CPI%20Project%20Manual%202015.pdf.

25 North Carolina's co-location program refers to its advocates as Domestic Violence Consultants. *Id.*

26 In Oregon, Intimate Partner Violence Specialists are co-located in the Department of Human Services' offices and "provide advocacy to victims, information, training, and consultations to case social workers in various counties. *Id.*

27 South Carolina has had a Domestic Violence Liaison Program in the Department of Social Services since 2001. *Id.*

28 Some of the domestic violence co-locations have been evaluated. *See also, Leading Florida Higher, Lifting Survivors Upward, Florida's Commitment to* Ending *Domestic Violence and Saving Lives,* Florida Coalitions Against Domestic Violence (2019); *Domestic Violence Liaison Program Evaluation—Final Report*, Center of Violence Against Women and Children, Rutgers University School of Social Work for The New Jersey Department of Children and Family Services (2017); *Evaluation of Co-Locating Domestic Violence Advocates in New York State Child Protective Services Offices, Final Report,* Center for Human Services Research, University of Albany, State University of New York (2014).

37 percent of local child protection districts, the collaboration enhanced responses to adult survivor needs, helped parents better understand the child welfare process, and increased empathy among case workers.[29] Specifically, the collaboration between co-located advocates increased cross-system communication, victim referrals to domestic violence programs, caseworker knowledge around the dynamics of domestic violence, domestic violence advocates' knowledge about the child welfare system and child safety issues, and decreased neglect findings against adult survivors.[30] To realize similar outcomes, New Jersey's Domestic Violence Liaison Program, spearheaded by Barbara Price, journeyed from its beginnings in 2007 to a statewide program demonstrating the benefit of institutionalized relationships to effectuate and sustain collaborations.

Collaboration Begetting Collaboration

As Barbara Price witnessed as a volunteer in a domestic violence shelter, needing to uproot and disconnect from one's life is not an equitable way to find safety. Acting upon the need to equalize support for women in times of need and address systemic inequities, Barbara served as the director of the New Jersey Coalition Against Domestic Violence (NJCADV) from 1989 to 2009 and developed a co-location program between NJCADV and the New Jersey Department of Youth and Family Services (DYFS).

The relationship between NJCADV and DYFS laid the groundwork for the co-location program that later arose from the national response to the intersection of domestic violence and child welfare. In the early 1990s, connections between NJCADV and DYFS existed. The funding for domestic violence agencies passed through DYFS, NJCADV provided training to DYFS on domestic violence,[31] and DYFS created a program for children at domestic violence shelters.[32] Amidst these sources of institutionalized connections between

---

29 *Evaluation of CPS/DV Co-Location*, University at Albany, Center for Human Services Research (July 25, 2019), https://www.albany.edu/chsr/csp-dv.shtml.

30 Rutgers, *supra* note 17 at 8.

31 In 1987, NJCADV began providing training on domestic violence to child welfare social workers.

32 In 1998, DYFS created the Peace: A Learned Solution (PALS) program for domestic violence providers to administer at their agencies, consisting of a six-month

DYFS and the domestic violence community, the Greenbook was published in 1999. Then in 2004, the New Jersey Superior Court issued its decision in *DYFS v. S.S.* and quoted *Nicholson* as persuasive authority in overturning the trial courts' decision to presume a child is neglected because of his exposure to domestic violence and substantiate a neglect finding against his abused mother. From *S.S.*, it became clear to the judiciary that the tenets of the Greenbook were not taking root in New Jersey's child welfare practice. In 2007, as out outgrowth of the interest in using the Greenbook to improve practice in New Jersey, the New Jersey Superior and Municipal Court judges created a joint task force, of which Barbara was a part, that recommended the creation of a co-location program between DYFS and domestic violence agencies that NJCADV would spearhead. Barbara hired Shellie Taggart, who had recently left the Domestic Violence Unit of DCF, to both implement and evaluate the new collaborative program.

In 2008, the Domestic Violence Liaison Program was launched in seven New Jersey counties. The Domestic Violence Liaisons were met with differing responses in the various DYFS offices. Some offices embraced the Liaisons and others did not even give the Liaisons a desk to use. The Liaisons spent four days per week in the DYFS offices. The one day per week at their domestic violence agency enabled them to retain their connection to their colleagues, teach their colleagues about child welfare, strategize, problem solve, share successes, and avoid becoming co-opted by their host offices. Despite the challenges, relationships between the two systems formed, the DYFS workers began involving the Liaisons in cases, and the Liaisons were able to support both the workers and families through these challenging interventions. Federal money from the Violence Against Women Act was accessed to expand the program statewide, equalizing the experiences of children and adult survivors of domestic violence during DYFS interventions across the counties. Twenty-three Domestic Violence Liaisons and their domestic violence agencies now work with DYFS.

---

program for children that began when they arrived at the shelter and extended beyond their shelter stay, demonstrating the benefit of working in conjunction with multiple systems to address the needs of children and families.

Barbara shares that by strengthening front-end child welfare interventions through the improved practice that the collaboration facilitates, fewer children entered foster care. The co-location program, therefore, became an important prevention program that saved money by avoiding the steep costs of out-of-home placements and court cases without jeopardizing child safety. Systemically, merging the lanes of those who interact with families experiencing domestic violence sent the message that the community has a shared responsibility for the safety and well-being of its members, and such responsibility cannot fall on the lone shoulders of just one. Institutionalizing partnerships for the betterment of families that exist beyond individual tenure and can infiltrate institutional culture takes time and patience yet is reinforced by the benefit of collaboration.

Community-Based Collaborations and Multi-Disciplinary Teams

Bringing together child welfare and domestic violence providers along with other community-based services is another strategy that some states have used to enhance outcomes for families experiencing domestic violence. Resembling multi-disciplinary teams or components of an effort toward coordinated community responses, Iowa, Connecticut, Rhode Island, and Washington have programs that foster collaboration between child welfare, domestic violence, and other community partners. For instance, Iowa implemented the Community Partnerships for Protecting Children Model by placing domestic violence advocates, child welfare workers, and other services providers in community centers in neighborhoods to serve families impacted by domestic violence.[33] In this way, domestic violence and child welfare professionals were both co-located in places in which they could reach and serve families.

Providing a broader collaborative environment surrounding its domestic violence co-location program, the Child Development—Community Policing Intervention Program (CDCP) was created in New Haven, Connecticut in 1992 by the Child Study Center at Yale University School of Medicine and the New Haven Police Department. This initiative convened community police officers, service providers, and

[33] Rutgers, *supra* note 17 at 6.

mental health clinicians to provide joint responses to victims of domestic violence and their children. Law enforcement officers were trained to identify children exposed to violence and refer them to mental health providers for further assessment. Police officers connected victims with domestic violence services. The U.S. Department of Health and Human Services identified this project in a 2003 publication as a model initiative for intervention to address child maltreatment and domestic violence.[34] Similarly, the police department in Providence, Rhode Island uses this collaborative model through Providence Police Go-Teams to provide crisis intervention to children and families.[35]

In 2007, the Children's Domestic Violence Response Team began in Seattle, Washington as a collaboration among mental health service providers and a domestic violence advocacy organization to provide a coordinated team response to nonoffending parents and their children. Domestic violence advocates conducted initial screenings, while the mental health clinician engaged in a strengths-based family assessment when needed. During wrap-around meetings, the team worked with adult survivors to develop a service plan that may include therapeutic services shown to be effective for child exposure to domestic violence and/or other trauma, thereby helping children and their mothers heal together.[36] These various models demonstrate that collaboration among various systems is often the means to meeting the needs of families without invasive and often harmful child welfare interventions.

Domestic Violence Coalitions

As collaborations themselves, statewide domestic violence coalitions are in unique positions to facilitate connections and partnerships between their member domestic violence organizations and child welfare agencies. Domestic violence coalitions have both a bird's-eye-view of issues as well as an on-the-ground insight about the practice

---

[34] LIEN H. BRAGG, CHILD PROTECTION IN FAMILIES EXPERIENCING DOMESTIC VIOLENCE, (2011).

[35] *Police Partnerships,* FAMILY SERVICES OF RHODE ISLAND (July 28, 2019), www.familyserviceri.org/partner_police_help.asp.

[36] *What do Kids Need? Programs,* PROMISING FUTURES (July 28, 2019), http://promising.futureswithoutviolence.org/?program=childrens-domestic-violence-response-team-cdvrt-2.

and challenges informed by their member organizations. Coalitions have the ability to bring their domestic violence member agencies to the table on both a broad scale and on localized projects. In this role, coalitions can act as a bridge between their domestic violence communities and the child welfare system.

Statewide domestic violence coalitions in the following states have identified themselves as having a collaboration or program with the state's child welfare agency: Arizona, Colorado, Connecticut, Florida, Georgia, Idaho, Illinois, Iowa, Maine, New Hampshire, New Jersey, Ohio, Rhode Island, Texas, Vermont, West Virginia, and Wisconsin.[37] Like the NJCADV, domestic violence coalitions can take an active role in launching and implementing co-location programs, as has occurred in Illinois too. The domestic violence coalitions in these states are providing training to child welfare agencies, as-needed case consultation, and participation in regular stakeholder meetings. For instance, in Iowa advocates from member programs serve on Connect and Protect teams to consult on child welfare cases, and the Colorado coalition hosts monthly calls for a work group focused on expert testimony in dependency cases.[38]

Elsewhere statewide coalitions have been at the forefront of collaborative efforts that have led to significant legislative changes. The Survivors with Children Workgroup of the West Virginia coalition collaborated with the Department of Health and Human Resources and the West Virginia Supreme Court Improvement Project. The workgroup evaluated how state law and policy impacted victims of domestic violence and their children, leading to the elimination of the use of the term failure to protect from child welfare policy, practice, and law. In addition, as a result of the workgroup, West Virginia law was amended to now permit adult survivors to co-petition with the state in dependency cases against the person who causes harm and allows the state to offer a "no-fault battered parent adjudication" in cases when co-petitioning is not appropriate.[39]

---

[37] *Survey to Coalition Members, Topic: Partnerships/Programming with Child Protective Services,* National Network to End Domestic Violence (2019) (on file with the author).

[38] *Id.*

[39] *Survivors with Children Workgroup*, West Virginia Coalition Against Domestic Violence (July 28, 2019), http://wvcadv.org/?page_id=2596; *System*

In addition to focusing on improving and reforming child welfare's response to families, coalitions have also enhanced the response of domestic violence agencies to the needs of children. For instance, the Connecticut Coalition Against Domestic Violence engaged with Betsy McAlister Groves to address the needs of children, resulting in an assigned specialized child advocate to every member domestic violence program.[40] The leadership of coalitions can drive the importance of addressing the needs of adults and children together for its domestic violence member and child welfare partners.

Cross-Training

Training child welfare workers and domestic violence advocates together is another opportunity to develop a shared understanding and build foundations for collaborative practice. Cross-trainings develop consistent approaches, contend with power dynamics, and decreases defensiveness as both sides learn about the fields of the other and create opportunities to experience working together in the safe and brave zones of training exercises. Involving child welfare and domestic violence professionals, as well as additional stakeholders in cross-training opportunities, further nurtures unity in the commitment to families experiencing domestic violence.

Shared experiential learning helps to foster empathy, dismantle divisions, and prompt the need to identify alternatives together to meet the needs of families. *In Her Shoes* is an opportunity for "learning by feeling" developed by the Washington State Coalition Against Domestic Violence.[41] The experiential training confronts the often-asked question, "why doesn't she just leave." *In Her Shoes* is a powerful exercise to experience the visceral response to the struggles domestic violence

---

Change in West Virginia's Child Protection System, Battered Women's Justice Project (July 28, 2019), http://www.bwjp.org/resource-center/resource-results/system-change-in-west-virginia-s-child-protection-system.html.

40 *Project Initiatives—Children,* Connecticut Coalition Against Domestic Violence (July 28, 2019), http://www.ctcadv.org/projects-initiatives/children/.

41 *In Her Shoes Training Kits,* Washington State Coalition Against Domestic Violence, (Jan. 2000), https://wscadv.org/resources/in-her-shoes-training-kits/. *In Her Shoes* has been adapted with an economic justice lens to capture the struggles of domestic violence survivors when they are poor and also includes the experiences of the person who uses coercive control and violence. *In Their Shoes* has also been created for teen dating violence, and additional nuanced iterations for specific populations of survivors would be helpful.

survivors face in both living with and trying to live away from an abusive partner, as the group participants move, act, think, and make "choices" as a person experiencing domestic violence. Based upon actual experiences of survivors, the facilitator reads nearly twenty events and incidents that capture the patterned escalation of domestic violence and other intersecting issues, and each participant then makes a decision about what she or he can do within the given circumstances and resources. One of the most powerful moments occurs when a participant stands in the center of the room, surveys the options, and realizes there is nowhere to go. *In Her Shoes* concludes with a personified sense of despair in which most participants are homeless with their children in foster care. Debriefed afterward, participants often describe being frozen, trapped, and lost. No one finds themselves in a position of greater strength, control, or betterment than when the exercise began and all encountered the risks attendant to both staying or leaving over which they felt little power to change.

When child welfare and domestic violence workers engage in an *In Her Shoes* training together, dual boundaries between "them and us" seem to dissolve. Standing in her shoes becomes a profound shared moment that develops both the empathy and the will to strategically work better, differently, and in partnership to enhance safety, stability, well-being, and healing that feels strikingly personal. *In Her Shoes* can become the kernel that shifts cross-system orientation away from victim-blaming to needs-based support in partnership with families. Recalling their individual and shared experiences during *In Her Shoes* reinforces ongoing commitment to supporting families together.

Collaboration fosters parallel processing at the community, systemic, familial, and individual levels that in turn impacts individuals, families, systems, and communities. Working across the line with other professionals models the partnerships needed with families, fosters connections that better harness resources and support, and generates more consistent, coherent, and holistic responses to families impacted by domestic violence.

Benefits of Parallel Process for a Family

Regardless of the selected collaboration program, the intentional and thoughtful partnership between domestic violence and child welfare professionals enhances the likelihood that interventions will be trauma-informed, strength-based, family-centered, and equity-focused because the magic of parallel process replicates the necessary positive and supportive interactions that facilitate greater safety, stability, well-being, and healing. Returning to the work of Sue Englaish, a Domestic Violence Specialist in the Massachusetts DCF Domestic Violence Unit, demonstrates the tangible and concrete impact of collaboration on the life of a family.

Sue began her work in the Massachusetts civil court system helping survivors obtain protective orders. Many times, women appeared in court reporting that their child welfare worker had sent them to get a protective order even when it was evident that the survivor did not want the order, did not think it would keep her and her children safe, or worried that the order might put them in more danger due to the abusive partner's responsive anger and retaliation. As a court advocate, Sue began working with Shellie Taggart, the DCF Domestic Violence Specialist in her region, to curb this practice. Seeking to address these systemic challenges and others, Sue decided to apply to work in the Domestic Violence Unit. For nearly two decades as a Specialist, harnessing the power of the system to meet the needs of families continues to be Sue's definition of success on behalf of families like Paula's.

Paula was twenty-four years old, staying at a homeless shelter with her three-year-old child, and was pregnant. Paula and her child were spending time with her husband away from the shelter when he punched her in the face several times. Paula returned to the shelter, and the shelter staff informed her that as mandated reporters, they needed to call the abuse and neglect Hotline because the violence occurred in front of the three-year-old. The shelter also called the police, who then arrested the father. Paula obtained a civil protection order and relocated to a domestic violence shelter. The case remained open with DCF. Paula was engaging with her caseworker and in services, while her husband was not. Four months after her baby was born, a new call was made to the Hotline because the baby had unexpectedly died. A week after the death, it was determined that the baby had died of accidental causes.

Before the cause of death was determined, the child welfare supervisor consulted with Sue. The supervisor brought Sue into the case for the express purpose of convincing the advocate at the domestic violence shelter to provide an opinion on whether the three-year-old was safe in her mother's care now and in the future. Sue called the shelter and spoke with the executive director who, in accordance with the state's laws around confidentiality, would not confirm or deny that Paula was staying there without Paula's consent and relayed that it was outside of the scope of her professional opinion to conclude if Paula was a safe parent who would never return to her husband. Sue then called General Counsel Andrew Rome. Andrew and Sue concluded that even if DCF had the power to compel the agency to share, it was more beneficial to honor the confidentiality of Paula's work with the domestic violence program so that Paula would be willing to continue accessing the vital services there.

Sue then spoke with the DCF supervisor. Sue and the supervisor had established a trusting relationship over the years based upon mutual respect fostered by working together on other cases, which made this difficult conversation easier to have. Sue approached the conversation by inquisitively asking questions. The supervisor expressed an accurate understanding of the dynamics of domestic violence in Paula's relationship. Sue used shared language about prioritizing the entire family's well-being and the link between the safety of the child and Paula, reiterating that accessing supportive services enables Paula to provide increased safety and stability for her child. Sue actively listened and expressed her nonjudgmental understanding that the supervisor needed information to assess risk to the child in accordance with the supervisor's professional, legal, and moral obligations and that the domestic violence advocate had this needed information. Sue shared her knowledge that remaining in the shelter and participating in services reduces the risk to Paula and therefore her child; penetrating the confidentiality could increase the risk to both if Paula disengages. Sue acknowledged the supervisor's concern that if the child is hurt, the media will criticize her for trading confidentiality for safety. Sue offered to document the content of the consultation and her recommendations and committed to standing by the supervisor's side if harm to the child indeed occurred. Sue then suggested creative alternatives and reliable ways to assess the risk to the child, which focused on talking with Paula herself. The supervisor decided to refrain from demanding information from the shelter. The tone and intention of this difficult conversation between professionals modeled the tenor and aim of the effective conversations that then occurred between the supervisor and Paula and Paula's husband.

With input from Sue and with the consent and collaboration of Paula, the supervisor eventually developed separate intact family service plans for each parent and the child. Both parents engaged in services. In the end, the supervisor successfully closed the case without needing to remove the child into foster care. Through the collaboration with the Domestic Violence Unit, the supervisor weighed the risks of DCF's own intervention and chose a course that generated what the family actually needed, respect, connection, and support, which became the critical path toward increasing rather than decreasing the family's safety, stability, and well-being, making healing possible.

9
The Road to Reform in Illinois: A Story of a Mother and her Daughter

A mother and her daughter paved the way toward reform in Illinois. Ten years apart, Patricia Sevedo and her daughter, Alejandra Sevedo, separately laid the foundation to improve the law and practice regarding domestic violence and neglect and to strengthen protections for domestic violence survivors who receive services. Through strategies of individual representation, impact litigation, and collaborative practice, a child welfare system in Illinois underwent a decade-long progression, spurred by the parallel journies of Patricia, Alejandra, and their family - a testament to the power of survivor-driven advocacy and a system willing to evolve.

A Mother

Patricia Sevedo was born in a small town in Mexico to a father who abused her mother and who spent the little money he earned on alcohol rather than on food or clothes for his children. No matter their condition or size, Patricia squeezed into hand-me-down or scavenged shoes on her feet because, with shoes, she was able to go to school. Rather than having the required composition books for each class, Patricia shrunk her handwriting so she could pen multiple lines of writing in the space between the two blue lines in the one notebook she had. Patricia's father did not approve of Patricia being in school. Although he punished Patricia's dedication to her education with physical violence, Patricia found ingenious ways to pay for her school fees transportation fares, and the Coca-Cola that she stretched to last two days, the sugar and carbonation abating her hunger.

In school, Patricia was placed in advanced classes. She loved reading and science. In order to be ready for the university entrance exam, Patricia needed more money to pay for the preparation. She found a job in a little gift store and befriended a co-worker. They walked two miles every day together before reaching the bus home. While walking together one afternoon, three men attacked the pair. The men raped both of them. As the months progressed, Patricia discovered she was pregnant. Now that she was pregnant, doing well on the college entrance test and attending university seemed a dream too distant for even Patricia to make a reality. Patricia left school and prepared to care for her baby. Throughout her pregnancy, Patricia prayed that the baby would look like her, welding a connection that would obfuscate the circumstances of the baby's conception and solidify the baby's sense of belonging to her mother. Patricia gave birth to a baby girl, Alejandra, and her eyes, her smile, looked just like her mother's.

Not long after Alejandra's birth, Patricia took a job in construction. For four years, she learned to lay roofs, build walls, set floors, and paint, but most importantly, Patricia was able to provide for herself, her daughter, mother, and brothers. As Patricia's strength grew, however, her father's abuse intensified, and as Mexico entered a recession, construction dwindled. A pattern was developing in Patricia's life that as one challenge subsided, another one surfaced. Patricia and her sister Monica heard that factories in the north of the country were hiring. Desperate to provide for her daughter and mother once again, the sisters bussed north, intended to work, save money, and return home. Their plans changed when they were presented with an unexpected opportunity to go even further north, into the United States. They crossed the border into Arizona where a relative picked them up and brought them to Chicago. When Patricia left home to go north, she did not anticipate the goodbye to her daughter would be so long.

The sisters stayed with their relative and found a job cleaning the kitchen of a hotel. They received paychecks but were unable to cash them because they did not have a bank account. The relative pocketed all of their checks and later forced them to leave. The sisters slept on the streets at night, returning to work in the morning, until a coworker at the hotel learned about their situation and offered to rent them a basement apartment.

As Patricia left her cleaning shift at five in the morning, Raul Trigo began his shift in hotel catering. Raul befriended Patricia, often giving her food. Raul was thirty years Patricia's senior, so his gestures seemed like acts of kindness without romantic expectations attached. Soon he gave Patricia his telephone number, inviting Patricia to call him if she ever needed help. Then Raul started taking Patricia out for dinner, and he introduced her to his friends. Monica found a new job with daytime hours and as Patricia spent more time with Raul, they fell in love. Raul moved into the basement apartment with the sisters. Then, one day, Patricia received a call from a woman screaming at her that Raul was her husband. When Patricia confronted Raul, his denial also included a slap across her face. The security Patricia was starting to feel seemed worth the cost of that slap. Patricia and Raul married. Raul bought a bungalow under the flight pattern of a nearby airport, and although Raul did not allow Patricia's name on the deed, Monica moved in too. A month after their wedding, Patricia discovered she was pregnant. After all of the suffering she experienced providing for Alejandra, she would not let the same befall this new baby. Patricia gave birth to a girl named Angela, and three years later, their son David was born.

The roof continued over her children's heads and food remained on their table, but that first slap turned into more as Raul began treating Patricia like her father had treated her mother. He told Patricia he hated the food she "cooked like all of the Mexicans." He insulted her in ways that went to the core of Patricia's pride, calling her stupid and predicting she would never be anybody. He snubbed Patricia's requests to take English classes, so Patricia resorted to learning English from the television. Raul refused to teach Patricia how to drive, limiting her mobility, her ability to stray, her access to the outside world, and her freedom.

At home, whenever Monica would take the children out, Raul became more aggressive with Patricia. He demanded that Patricia maintain a spotless house and checked the dust on obscure surfaces to ensure she met his demands. One particular afternoon, Monica took the children to a relative's party. Patricia needed to stay home to clean, but Raul returned home before she was finished. He moved a chair she had not yet cleaned and pointed to the spot below that still was dirty. Patricia bent down to clean the floor and Raul started hitting her. When she stood up, Raul hit her so hard in the head that she lost consciousness. Alarmed, Raul picked her up, placed her on the sofa, and apologized when she awoke. The lull that followed gave her reprieve, for now. Even when the hiatus ended, as it always did, leaving Raul would come at too great of a cost to her children. Angela had a kidney disorder, and David had a musculoskeletal issue with his eyes. Patricia trusted that the medical care they received in the United States far surpassed the treatment they would receive back in Mexico. Returning home was not an option, and the options for providing for her children in the states apart from Raul, their father, were similarly sparse.

Yet part of Patricia always remained in Mexico with Alejandra. When a friend offered to take Alejandra along as she crossed the border herself, Patricia tepidly agreed. Patricia knew personally that the trip was fraught with danger and risk, but when Alejandra was ten-years-old, Patricia paid the transporters for her friend and her daughter's journey north. Finally, Patricia received the much-awaited call that her friend and Alejandra had arrived in Tucson, and the two took a bus to Chicago. Alejandra was headed toward her mother. After five years, Patricia finally embraced her daughter, stroking her hair, kissing her cheek, relishing in the gift of being able to mother her daughter who was no longer an apparition in her thoughts, her dreams, or in her heart. Raul did not prevent Alejandra's arrival because he expected Alejandra to cook and take care of the children. Patricia steadfastly protested, insisting her daughter would attend school, threatening to leave Raul if he forbade Alejandra from getting an education. Although Alejandra was immediately enrolled in school, the abuse against Patricia worsened. Patricia had all three of her children under one roof, yet she was punished for her assertion and resolve toward Alejandra's schooling, just as she had been toward her own schooling when she was Alejandra's age.

One night before work while Raul was drinking, he punched and hit Patricia very hard in the ribs and chest. He did not want the children seeing his abuse, so he hurt her in places Patricia could cover. At work the next day, Patricia asked her manager if she could leave because she was not feeling well. The manager asked Patricia what was wrong. Patricia showed her the bruises and through her broken English, explained their cause. Relieved that the first person she told about the abuse believed her, her manager let her leave work to go to the doctor and Patricia picked up Angela and David while Alejandra was at school. The doctor was patient with Patricia, listened to her, and also believed her. He took x-rays of her ribs and pictures of her bruises. A pediatrician arrived, and with Patricia's permission, examined and spoke with Angela and David. Despite the respect and validation she felt from the doctors, Patricia was not offered a referral to a domestic violence agency or counseling for her and her children. Nonetheless, reaching out for help, to these mandated reporters who engaged in "mandated supporting,"[1] felt affirming and supportive.

In 2007, Angela was recovering from kidney surgery. Patricia had taken six weeks off from work to care for her daughter. Early in the evening before she was to return to work, Raul began relentlessly insulting Patricia, calling her degrading names. Patricia decided to go to the grocery store hoping that when she returned Raul would stop ridiculing her. When she returned home, she carried David into the kitchen and Raul was sitting quietly at the table, drinking a beer while Angela was coloring next to him. Alejandra was in the basement. Patricia was preparing and washing broccoli, cutting the stems from the florets. She picked David up and was holding him in her left arm with his head facing away from her while she made his bottle in the sink with her right hand. Raul resumed his insults, this time smiling and laughing, so Angela would not be disturbed from her coloring. While preparing his bottle, Patricia accidentally dropped a plate in the sink. Raul began yelling at her. Patricia turned around and Raul threw the glass beer bottle in her direction. It happened

1 "Mandated supporting" is a term coined by Futures Without Violence.

suddenly, but she lifted her arms to protect David. When she heard David cry, she realized the bottle had hit her son. She turned David toward her, did not see any injury, and pressed David's face into her body to comfort him. Raul got up and not knowing what he was going to do, Patricia threw a freshly cut broccoli floret at him. Patricia reached for the phone but Raul took it out of her hands. Patricia called down to Alejandra to call the police, and Alejandra dialed 911. Patricia took all three children outside to wait for the police to arrive.

The police arrived and arrested Raul. The next day, Patricia contacted a domestic violence agency for counseling for her and her children. She also went to civil court and obtained an Emergency Order of Protection against Raul. The protection order prohibited Raul from having any unlawful contact with her and the children and prohibited him from returning home. Raul went to stay with a relative. Patricia participated in the criminal case, and Raul was found guilty of misdemeanor domestic battery and was sentenced to probation. The evening that Raul was arrested, police officers had also called the Department of Children and Family Services (DCFS) Child Abuse and Neglect Hotline.

Patricia received written notification in Spanish that she was being investigated by DCFS for abusing and neglecting her children. Patricia was forthcoming with the Spanish-speaking investigator. She described what happened during this incident and shared the history of abuse. The investigator completed a domestic violence screen that designated Patricia as a victim of domestic violence and acknowledged that only Raul had been arrested. The investigator completed a safety assessment and concluded that all of the children were safe. The investigator also spoke with Raul, who claimed that the beer bottle slipped out of his hands when he slammed it down and that Patricia used David to shield her own face from being struck by the bottle. The investigator documented the steps of her investigation and concluded that Patricia had "engaged in domestic violence," "provoked" her husband to throw the bottle, and protected herself at the expense of her young son.

Patricia received a letter in the mail telling her that she had been indicated for abuse and neglect. Specifically, both Patricia and Raul were indicated for the abuse allegation for causing a "cut, welts, and bruises" to David and for the neglect allegation of creating an environment injurious to the welfare of all three children. On account of being a victim of domestic violence and as a result of reaching out to the police for help, Patricia was now designated an abusive and neglectful parent whose name would be retained on the State Central Register. Staring at the paper was like looking into a mirror revealing a reflection that was not hers. She loved her children with her entire being and sacrificed her own happiness and well-being for theirs. Her loveless and frightening marriage to Raul provided a roof over her children's heads, food on the table, medical care especially important for Angela and David, and education for all three—so much more than she feared she would be able to give them alone as an undocumented mother with limited English, despite her fierce intelligence and ability to navigate both the rural and urban streets of her life. She reminded herself that she still believed in the opportunity her children could have in America that she never had.

The bottom of the letter from DCFS outlined her appeal rights. Through the hundreds of phone book pages, Patricia called over 200 organizations for help. Some could not understand her because she only spoke Spanish, others did not handle DCFS cases, and others were able to provide her with some referrals for agencies they thought might help.

The Appeal that Began It All

Lawyers at the Legal Assistance Foundation of Metropolitan Chicago, the largest civil legal aid provider in her county, became Patricia's counsel.[2] Providing holistic legal representation to Patricia, a civil court granted her a two-year protective order that prohibited Raul from having unlawful contact with her and the children, allowed him to stay at home, and required him to complete a certified batterer intervention program. As a matter of right, Patricia's abuse and neglect appeal was tried before an administrative law judge employed by DCFS. A four-day trial ensued. DCFS called Patricia, Raul, and the investigator as witnesses in its case in chief, who all testified consistently with the information conveyed during the investigation. In

---

2 The author of this book was Patricia's lawyer as a Skadden Fellow at the Legal Assistance Foundation of Metropolitan Chicago (now Legal Aid Chicago). Patricia has provided her informed consent to the information shared in this chapter.

order to explain the important context of domestic violence, Patricia's attorney tendered Patricia's domestic violence advocate as an expert witness on domestic violence.

In her written opinion, the administrative law judge made the following findings of fact:

1. A domestic disturbance began verbally in the household, escalated over a period of hours, erupted into physical violence in which infant David was injured on his face;
2. Both parents participated in the dispute—the verbal disagreement and the physical disagreement that ensued;
3. Neither Patricia nor Raul testified credibly or consistently about whether the bottle or the broccoli were thrown first;
4. Patricia lifted her arms up and the bottle hit her son's face;
5. Patricia was free to come and go from the house;
6. Patricia created an ongoing environment of unpredictable domestic violence;
7. Patricia was not remorseful and did not demonstrate care or concern for her children;
8. The testimony of the domestic violence counselor was given careful consideration and was accepted and understood as an advocate for Patricia.

The administrative law judge recommended to the Director of DCFS to expunge the abuse finding but retain the neglect finding against Patricia.[3] At the time of the hearing, the administrative rule, which has the force of law, relevant to the remaining indicated finding was "Allegation #10/60, Substantial Risk of Physical Injury/Environment Injurious." Circumstances involving domestic violence were subsumed in this general catchall category of neglect. In its definition of Allegation #10/60, the rule differentiated between abuse and neglect.[4] The rule explained that substantial risk of physical injury "means that the parent . . . has created a real and significant danger of physical injury that would likely cause disfigurement, death, or

[3] The administrative law judge presents a recommended decision to the director of DCFS who issues a final ruling. 89 Ill. Admin. Code 336.120(b)(15), 336.220(a)

[4] 89 Ill. Admin. Code 300, Appx. B.

impairment of physical health or loss or impairment of bodily functions (abuse)."[5] The rule further stated, "this allegation of harm also includes . . . placing a child in an environment that is injurious to the child's health and welfare (neglect)."[6] Such environmental issues may include "domestic violence in the home when the child has been threatened and the threat is believable, as evidenced by a past history of violence or uncontrolled behavior (neglect)."[7] DCFS procedures listed the following factors to consider in determining whether domestic violence created an injurious environment: history of past incidents of domestic violence, nature of domestic violence, use of weapons, level of involvement of children, and ability of the victim of domestic violence to use a support system.[8]

Despite the evidence presented, above all else, the administrative law judge failed to accurately identify the existence of domestic violence, thus skewing the conclusion of Raul and Patricia as responsible co-equals, and disregarding the legal significance of the steps Patricia took before, during, and after the incident to protect her children. Patricia appealed the denial of her request to expunge the indicated finding of neglect to the Illinois circuit court, which sits as a reviewing court of administrative decisions.[9]

On appeal to the district court, the Illinois Attorney General's office represented DCFS and both sides filed memorandums of law in support of their positions alleging that the administrative decision was correct or incorrect. The memorandum of law in support of Patricia's request highlighted important factual arguments including that the incident was part of a pattern of domestic violence, rehabilitated Patricia's credibility, and reconciled the various sequences of events. The memorandum also utilized *Nicholson* as persuasive authority to argue that indicating Patricia for neglect violated the U.S. Constitution and to harness public policy in support of Patricia. The memorandum then presented a novel statutory argument that the allegation of neglect used to indicate Patricia was unauthorized

---

5 *Id.*

6 *Id.*

7 *Id.*

8 DCFS Procedures 300, Appx. B.

9 Administrative Review Law, 735 ILCS 5/3-101.

under the law and therefore void and unallowable as a basis for an indicated finding. Excerpts from the memorandum of the *Nicholson* and statutory argument are below:

> Substantive Due Process and Public Policy Require Child Welfare Agencies to Unfound Reports of Child Neglect Against Abused Mothers When the Sole Allegation is Domestic Violence in the Home.
>
> Although not binding, this Court should recognize as persuasive the United States Court of Appeals' important ruling in *Nicholson v. Williams* and reverse the Director's decision to refuse Ms. Sevedo's request to expunge the indicated finding of neglect. In *Nicholson,* the District Court certified a class of mothers who were involved in the child welfare system because of domestic violence. *Nicholson v. Williams,* 205 F.R.D. 92, 101-02 (E.D.N.Y 2001); *see Nicholson v. Williams*, 203 F.Supp. 2d 153, 168-93 (E.D.N.Y. 2002) (detailed description of class members).[10] There were no other allegations that the children were being neglected by the mother other than by virtue of the mother's status as a victim of domestic violence. *In re Nicholson,* 181 F.Supp. 2d 182, 183 (E.D.N.Y. 2002); *see Nicholson,* 203 F.Supp. 2d at 163-64. The court then enjoined the child welfare agency, requiring that reports should be unfounded where
>
> 1. the sole basis for the report against the mother is that she has been a victim of domestic violence or
> 2. she has "engaged" in domestic violence where the sole basis for the allegation is that the mother has been the victim of domestic violence.
>
> *In re Nicholson,* 181 F.Supp. 2d at 190; *see also Nicholson,* 203 F.Supp. 2d at 258 (over 100-page elaboration of grounds for the injunction and holding that the preliminary injunction

[10] The class of abused mothers was predominately comprised of mothers whose children were removed from them because the children lived in homes where there was domestic violence.

issued in this case remains in effect).[11] The court Upheld the injunction based on Fourteenth Amendment substantive due process grounds. *Nicholson*, 203 F.Supp. 2d at 250-51. The court's rationale was that the child welfare agency's conduct substantially infringed on fundamental liberty interests of mothers and children without advancing a compelling or substantial state interest. *Id.* The court found in part that abused mothers should not be deemed neglectful for failing to stop abuse over which they had little or no control. *Id.* At 201. The mothers, like Ms. Sevedo, did not cause the abuse; the batterer did, so the harm to the child could not be linked to the actions of the mother. *Id.* The court also found that holding the victims responsible reinforces the power of the batterer and that it violates fundamental principles of justice to hold the victim responsible for the crime committed against her. *Id.* At 201, 252. The indicated finding against Ms. Sevedo, therefore, violates public policy.

DCFS' "environment injurious" Finding Cannot Stand Because This Definition of Neglect Is Not Authorized by Its Authorizing Statute, ANCRA.

The Department's rules and regulations defining its abuse and neglect allegations are governed and bound by the definitions in the Abused and Neglected Child Reporting Act (ANCRA). 89 Ill. Admin. Code 300.20 (cross references ANCRA) and 336.100 (the report must be maintained in a manner consistent with ANCRA); DCFS Rule 300, Appx. B; 20 ILCS 505/5(l) (Children and Family Services Act, creates DCFS; ANCRA governs DCFS investigations of suspected child abuse and neglect); ANCRA, 325 ILCS

---

[11] The court enjoined the New York child welfare agency based on New York State law and constitutional grounds, focusing on the unconstitutionality of removing children from abused mothers. *Nicholson,* 203 F.Supp.2d at 250; U.S. Const. amend. XIV; 42 U.S.C.A. § 1983; N.Y.McKinney's Family Court Act § 1011 et seq. Although this opinion describes in length and detail the legal impermissibility of removing children from their abused mothers, the injunction still stood requiring state officials to unfound reports against abused mothers where the sole allegation is domestic violence. *Nicholson*, 203 F.Supp. 2d at 258.

5/7.12. DCFS' definitions of abuse and neglect, therefore, must be within the authority of ANCRA. To the extent that an administrative rule conflicts with a statute, the rule is invalid. *Cappitelli v. Rodewald*, 171 Ill. App. 3d 875, 878 (1st Dist. 1988). A child who is an "environment injurious" is not part of the definition of a neglected child. Because "environment injurious" is not part of the ANCRA definition of a neglected child, DCFS' neglect allegation of "environment injurious" is void . . .

"Environment injurious" is missing from ANCRA's definition of a "neglected child" because the Illinois legislature deliberately excluded it. *See* 325 ILCS 5/3. This exclusion was an intentional decision of the Illinois legislature four years after the enactment of ANCRA. When ANCRA was first enacted in 1975, the definition of neglect included subjecting a child to an "environment injurious." Pub. Act No. 79-65, § 3 (approved June 26, 1975) (*see* Exhibit 2, page 147). In 1979, the legislature amended ANCRA and purposefully removed "environment injurious" from the neglect definition. Pub. Act No. 81-1077; *see* Illinois Legislative Synopsis and Digest for 81st General Assembly (*see* Exhibit 3, page 737). Specifically, House Amendment No. 8 deleted from the definition of a neglected child one "who is subjected to an environment injurious to his or her welfare." *Id.*

The following statements evidence the legislature's clear intent to remove "environment injurious" from ANCRA's neglect definition. During the floor debates, Representative Peters, the House Sponsor of Amendment #8, further elucidated the legislature's reasoning behind erasing "environment injurious" from ANCRA when he said:

> Amendment #8 is again an attempt to reach an agreement between the various associations and groups that have come into play in working on this comprehensive reform of the Act. What Amendment #8 would do is to remove from the definition of neglected child the words "subjected to an environment injurious to his or her welfare" and the reasons we are removing that is the concern

> over the interpretation of what environment injurious may mean. We are fearful that it may end up in a lot of litigation, a lot of misunderstandings and until such time that we can arrive at a more clearer, concise kind of definition to address this kind of problem, we think it's better to remove this from the Bill. 81st Gen. Assem., House Transcription Debate 100 (Ill., June 22, 1979) (statement of Rep. Peters, Sponsor of the Bill)

> Further underscoring the legislature's primary motivation in deleting "environment injurious" from ANCRA, Senator Daley explained, "We need it a little more specific, so people understand what abuse and neglect is." 81st Gen. Assem., Senate Transcription Debate 202 (Ill., May 25, 1979) (statement of Sen. Daley).
>
> For nearly thirty years, the legislature has left "environment injurious" out of ANCRA's definition of neglect. Thus, the plain language of ANCRA reveals the legislature's continued intent to define neglect without "environment injurious." *See People v. Galan*, 229 Ill. 2d 484, 520 (2008) (the best indication of legislative intent is the statutory language, given its plain and ordinary meaning). Nevertheless, in direct conflict with the language and intent of ANCRA, DCFS' current rules define a neglected child as one whose parent creates an environment injurious to the child's welfare; Ms. Sevedo was indicated under this erroneous rule. 89 Ill. Admin. Code 300; DCFS Rules 300, Appx. B.
>
> DCFS' rule defining neglect to include a parent who placed a child in an "environment injurious" must be set aside because it exceeds the statutory authority conferred by ANCRA. *Cappitelli*, 171 Ill. App. 3d at 878. The indicated finding against Ms. Sevedo, therefore, cannot stand.

Following oral argument and after over a year of litigation, Patricia won her appeal. In its opinion, the circuit court found:

> This Court agrees with Sevedo that the "environment injurious" allegation is not authorized by statute. In fact, it has not been part of the neglect definition for almost 30 years now.

> This court also looked to the Department's rules and procedures that outline factors to consider in evaluating whether a victim of domestic violence created an injurious environment for her children. In the current case, the children were not threatened by Mr. Trigo and there were no use of weapons during the incident. Sevedo reported that Mr. Trigo had pushed and hit her in the past but never threw anything at her or in her direction. Furthermore, once the incident occurred, Sevedo immediately removed the children from the room and called the police which resulted in Mr. Trigo's arrest. Thereafter, Sevedo sought an order of protection, participated in counseling sessions with the children, and brought David to the hospital to check for injuries. This Court finds that Sevedo took all of the necessary steps to protect her children from an injurious environment. Therefore, the indicated finding of child neglect should be expunged.
>
> Sevedo's complaint for Administrative Review is granted. The final administrative decision is reversed and the indicated finding of "environment injurious" shall be expunged.

The court ruled on both statutory and factual grounds. Significantly, in the first case that tested the statutory argument, the court concluded that the environment injurious ground of neglect could not be used in this particular case. The court, however, did not dismantle the allegation from being used in future cases, thus laying the runway for future litigation. In addition, by applying the facts to the law, the neglect finding was overturned; Patricia was no longer a neglectful mother under the law, as she felt she had never been in life.

For years, Patricia had lost her sense of smell, perhaps her body's response to protecting itself from loss, pain, or fear by closing off one of its senses. When she received a call from her attorney that she had won her appeal of the indicated finding, Patricia was standing by the commuter train, and it was raining. For the first time in a very long time, Patricia smelled the rain, cleansing her of her deepest fear that her children would be taken from her,and washing her with hope in a way forward.

Her Sister's Keeper

Following the resolution of her appeal, Patricia was able to file for immigration relief for herself and Alejandra. Throughout their marriage, Raul refused to file a petition to adjust Patricia's immigration status based upon their marriage.[12] Leaving Patricia undocumented was a tactic of Raul's abuse that increased her dependence on him, reduced the likelihood that she could leave him with her three children, and deterred her from seeking help from authorities or systems. Under the Violence Against Women Act amendment to the Immigration and Nationality Act, spouses, children, and parents of a U.S. citizen or lawful permanent resident can self-petition to adjust their immigration status based upon domestic violence.[13] With the neglect finding erased, Patricia felt immense relief in being able to establish her "good moral character" in her application; in this way, her VAWA application reflected how she saw herself. Patricia and Alejandra's applications were approved; they were no longer deportable. Alejandra was eligible for federal college financial aid; they could become citizens of the United States over time, and Raul was none the wiser.

Rid of the crucifixion neglect finding and armed with clandestine knowledge of her legal status in this country, Patricia felt a renewed sense of agency, of hope, a quiet shield against the abuse she continued to endure. When Patricia learned that a neighbor and two young children were being abused, Patricia persuaded them to hide in her basement. Reminiscent of the original feminist response to domestic violence, Patricia intuitively made her home into a "safe house," until they were able to safely relocate three weeks later. Raul never knew that a mother and her children like his own had gone underground under his own roof. Patricia's profound impact on those three lives mirrored the impact she would soon have on the law and practice throughout the state.

The Spark of Reform

The statutory argument in Patricia's appeal became the spark of future litigation to help thousands of people like herself and her children. The neglect allegation of "Allegation 60/environment injurious" was the most common allegation used to indicate parents, and as the legislators had warned in 1979, the allegation was an overly broad catch-all, meaning everything and, at the same time, nothing at all. Allegation 60 often applied to situations involving domestic violence,

---

12 See INA 319(a). See 8 CFR 319.1.

13 *Battered Spouse, Children and Parents,* U.S. Citizenship and Immigration Services (Feb. 15, 2019), https://www.uscis.gov/humanitarian/battered-spouse-children-parents.

as well as circumstances concerning substance misuse or abuse and mental health. As a result, Allegation 60 disproportionately impacted mothers, especially mothers of color,[14] many of whom were indeed struggling yet trying to do right by their children.

As seen in Patricia's case, the current version of Allegation 60 led to erroneous indicated findings whose toll exacted more than the resources and time required to overturn the unjust finding. The allegation as written led to interventions centered on the conclusion that the worse the abuse was, the more likely the victim was to be deemed neglectful. The allegation was without a proscriptive focus on whether the harm to the child rose to the level of neglect or directive emphasis on how to locate the nonoffending parent's responsibility, if any, by looking at what she did to protect her children despite often severe domestic violence. Pinning these mothers with

---

[14] Testing pregnant or postpartum women and infants for drugs can be a gateway into the child welfare system, and the decision to test is influenced by gender, race, and class. Women, not men, are tested for illicit drugs in neonatal settings. Black women are more likely to be tested for drugs in the course of obstetric care and perinatal settings. *See The Public Health Disparities Geocoding Project, Harvard School of Health*, (Feb. 20, 2019), www.hsph/harvard.edu/thegeocodingproject/webpage/mongraph, (black women were more likely to be tested in the course of receiving obstetric care); Hillary Veda Kunins, M.D., Era Bellin, M.D., Cynthia Chazotte, M.D., Evelyn Du, Ph.D., & Julia Hope Arnsten, M.D., *The Effect of Race on Provider Decisions to Test for Illicit Drug Use in the Peripartum Setting*, 16 J. Womens Health, 245, 245 (2007) (Black women and their newborns were 1.5 times more likely to be tested for illicit drugs as nonblack women in a multivariable analysis). In addition, "markers of lower socioeconomic status, including being married, having less than a high school education, being unemployed, or having Medicaid or no insurance, were independently associated with testing for illicit drugs." *Id.* In states like Illinois, individual hospitals determine policies as to which infants should be tested and screened. "Testing women or their newborn infants for illicit drug use in the peripartum setting . . . is a special case that may expose women who test positive for illicit drugs to severe legal and social consequences, including loss of parental rights and criminal prosecution." *Id.* Several studies have demonstrated the existence of racial disparities in infant referral to and action by child protective service agencies, despite the federal Child Abuse Prevention and Treatment Act of 1974 requiring healthcare providers to make reports to child welfare agencies about all infants affected by illegal substance abuse. *See* IJ Chasnoff, HJ Landress & ME Barrett, *The Prevalence of Illicit-drug or Alcohol Use During Pregnancy and Discrepancies in Mandatory Reporting in Pinellas County, Florida*, 332 N Engl J Med, 1202, 1203 (1990); DR Neuspiel, TM Zingman, VH Templeton, P DiStabile, & E. Drucker, *Custody of Cocaine-Exposed Newborns: Determinants of Discharge Decisions.* 83 Am J Public Health 1726, 1727 (1993).

a punitive, scarlet neglect finding only made it harder for them to overcome their struggles and care for their children in ways they so desperately wanted to do. Indicated findings psychologically distort self-views of parental agency and competency, tangibly limit employment opportunities and potential immigration relief, and freeze outside help-seeking behaviors. The allegation, therefore, was leading to interventions that weakened, rather than strengthened, the nonoffending parent's ability to parent in safety and stability, and therefore needed to change. Litigation became a strategy in dismantling the ineffective allegation, and the statutory argument conceived in Patricia's case evolved as a critical tool of that strategy.

Following Patricia's successful appeal, the statutory argument that the environment injurious allegation was unauthorized under the law and therefore void was shared among lawyers who commonly represented parents in appeals of indicated findings and became a routine centerpiece of these appeals. Because courts prefer to rule on the narrowest grounds, most of the appeals were decided on factual grounds, and therefore courts could avoid the earthquake of undoing DCFS' most commonly used neglect allegation. However, one case reached the Illinois Supreme Court. In *Julie Q. v. DCFS,* the highest court in Illinois held that Allegation 60 is legally void from the start, or *void ab initio,* thus ushering in critical reform in the state.

While *Julie Q.* was pending in the Illinois Supreme Court, DCFS sought relief in the legislature to reinsert environment injurious as a ground of neglect into the authorizing statute, ANCRA. Together with DCFS and the Office of the Public Guardian, Julie's counsel along with advocates at other legal service organizations, including Patricia's former lawyers, discussed ways to draft the environment injurious neglect allegation so as not to replicate the same concerns that prompted the legislature to remove the ground years before. In July 2012, a more clear and narrow amendment to ANCRA defined a neglected child as "one who is subjected to an environment which is injurious insofar as (i) the child's environment creates a likelihood of harm to the child's health, physical well-being, or welfare and (ii) the likely harm to the child is the result of a blatant disregard of parent, caretaker, or agency responsibilities."[15] Blatant disregard was defined as "an incident where the real, significant, and imminent risk of harm

[15] Pub. Act. No. 97-803 (eff. July 13, 2012); ANCRA, 325 ILCS 5/3.

would be so obvious to a reasonable parent or caretaker that it is unlikely that a reasonable parent or caretaker would have exposed the child to the danger without exercising precautionary measures to protect the child from harm."[16] The definition now required a real showing of a likelihood of harm and specified the parameters of expected parental conduct.

Although ANCRA now included environment injurious, the Illinois Supreme Court proceeded with the *Julie Q.* case and grappled with the very issue developed in Patricia's appeal—whether DCFS exceeded its previous statutory authority in promulgating Allegation 60 and using it to indicate the mother Julie Q.[17] Four years after Patricia's case established this argument, the Illinois Supreme Court issued a sweeping holding:

> ... When the legislature has specifically removed the environment-injurious language from its definition of neglect, DCFS was without authority to reestablish the environment-injurious definition of neglect. Therefore, Allegation 60 exceeds DCFS's authority under the Act and it is void.[18]

As a result of this decision, DCFS sent letters to the 19,000 parents and guardians who registered indicated findings for Allegation 60.[19] The letters told them that their findings were being expunged from the State Central Registry.

Following *Julie Q.*, Illinois had a new definition for environment injurious in ANCRA but an old and now inconsistent, unauthorized, and void administrative rule defining Allegation 60. *Ashley M. v. DCFS* was a class action lawsuit that aimed to protect those who were still being indicated under the nonconforming Allegation 60 definition and to induce DCFS to promulgate a new Allegation 60 rule consistent with the amendments to ANCRA.[20]

---

16 *Id.*

17 Julie Q. v. DCFS. at 6.

18 *Id.* at 12.

19 Diane Redleaf, *Julie Q. Rule Changes: The Long Road to Ending the Overcharging "Environment Injurious" Neglect Claims,* The Family Defense Center (Feb. 18, 2019), https://www.familydefensecenter.net/category/news/julie-q.

20 The author of this book has been employed by the legal services law firm, The Family Defense Center, that represented the plaintiff-class in Ashley M. v. DCFS.

While *Ashely M.* was pending, DCFS filed an emergency rule, attempting to draft Allegation 60 to be consistent with the definition of environment injurious in ANCRA. The attorneys for *Ashley M.* and others including Patricia's former counsel submitted two letters to the Illinois Joint Commission on Administrative Rules (JCAR) that proposed language for the new rule to Allegation 60. The comments cited the Greenbook as support for the proposed language that was consistent with the established best practice tenets for effective child welfare intervention into the lives of families experiencing domestic violence.

JCAR approved the proposed rule, replacing the old Allegation 60. The rule that went into effect more clearly distinguished the difference between the environment injurious allegation of neglect (Allegation 60) and its abuse corollary, "substantial risk of physical injury" (Allegation 10), thus increasing clarity for both parents, practitioners, and DCFS personnel.[21] The rule also addressed how the allegation specifically pertains to domestic violence as well as substance abuse and mental health, thereby decreasing ambiguity around the most common fact patterns netted by environment injurious allegations. The rule imports the definition of domestic violence from the Illinois criminal code, hence enhancing consistency in language across systems.[22] Most significantly, the rule establishes a threshold for neglect and the only presumption *against* neglect in all of DCFS' rules. Specifically, the Allegation 60 rule states:

> An incident of past or current domestic violence may qualify for an allegation of environment injurious if the domestic violence creates a real, significant, and imminent risk of moderate to severe harm to the child's health, physical well-being or welfare, and the parent or caregiver has failed to exercise reasonable precautionary measures to prevent or mitigate the risk of harm to the child.
>
> Domestic violence is also referred to as "intimate partner violence." The adult victim of domestic violence, who is the non-offending parent or caregiver, is presumed to be not neglectful or to have created an environment injurious to the child so long

---

[21] 89 Ill. Admin. Code Chapter III, subchapter b, Part 300, App. B. Allegation 60.

[22] Illinois Criminal Code of 2012, 720 ILCS 5/12-4.4a.

> as he or she has exercised precautionary measures to prevent or mitigate the real, significant, and imminent risk of moderate to severe harm to the child.

In simple terms, this new rule defines the level of exposure that constitutes neglect and locates parental responsibility. Because not all exposure to domestic violence rises to the level of abuse or neglect, the rule sets the bar at domestic violence that "creates real, significant, and imminent risk of moderate to severe harm to the child's health, physical well-being or welfare." Significantly, the nonoffending parent is not responsible for the neglect if she took precautionary measures to keep her children safe, even if those steps did not achieve safety for her children. Precautionary measures are consistent with the lived experiences of the majority of mothers, like Patricia, who take creative and courageous steps every day to care for their children and try to keep them safe amidst the abuse they are enduring. This standard is the appropriate measure of determining neglectfulness, instead of the severity of the abuse imputing neglect if mothers cannot stop the abuse or leave. The ancestral path of this new rule hails directly from the Greenbook and the legal theories of *Nicholson,* yet would not have come into existence without Patricia's enduring commitment and courage to challenge a neglect finding that was incongruent with the realities of her motherhood.

A Daughter

As the *Julie Q.* and *Ashley M.* cases generated hope and expectations that the new law and rule would effectively shift practice around the intersection of domestic violence and child welfare, Raul's abuse worsened. Then, his kidneys began failing. Weakened and in need of weekly dialysis, Patricia became safer as her daughter's life unraveled. Like her mother, Alejandra's early years in the United States were riddled with both happiness and sorrow, near defeat, and triumph. While Alejandra's performance in school enabled her to be college-bound, she started dating a new boyfriend. He quickly became controlling and violent. The love Alejandra felt from her mother was the undercurrent of her own self-respect and strength, and Alejandra knew that she deserved more, just as she knew her mother did, but she quickly felt trapped and scared. The abusive relationship continued as she began college.

One day, Alejandra was at home and reported to her boyfriend that she was going to the pharmacy to pick up a prescription. He insisted on coming with her. Alejandra drove, and on the way, her boyfriend saw a friend and forced Alejandra to pick him up. While she was inside the pharmacy, her boyfriend and his friend crossed the street and approached two teenagers at the bus stop. As Alejandra was paying for her medication, her boyfriend and his friend stole their wallets and phones. As Alejandra walked out of the pharmacy, she saw her boyfriend and his friend running toward her car. She quickly knew that something was wrong, and she frantically got into her car, trying to drive away without them. She was able to pull out of the parking lot and drove down an alley thinking she could leave them behind, but when the street unexpectedly reached a dead-end, they caught up to her car. She refused to unlock the doors; nevertheless, her boyfriend climbed in through the window and unlocked the car door for his friend. Shaking with fear, Alejandra drove toward her home, and relief washed over her once inside. A week later, however, Alejandra was arrested, her license plate connected to the crime her boyfriend and his friend committed.

At the police station, Alejandra cooperated, explained what had happened, and provided the identities to the officer, but the hours in custody morphed from being treated as an informant to a criminal. When Patricia finally learned that Alejandra had been arrested, she rushed to the police station. She was told that her daughter would be released later and to come back then. The next morning, Alejandra was transferred to a large county jail. That same day, desperate to see her daughter, Patricia again went to the police station and was informed that Alejandra had been transferred. That day, Alejandra's second day behind bars, she was sexually assaulted by two police officers.

At the arraignment, Patricia paid the bond and watched her daughter barely able to walk through the door of the police station and into her car. Alejandra told Patricia what happened to her, and Patricia took her daughter to the emergency room, which revealed injuries so severe that the doctor predicted that Alejandra would not be able to have children. Alejandra made a police report, yet as she faced a criminal prosecution, the police officers were never disciplined or charged.

The trauma Alejandra experienced following her arrest deposited her in a state of paralyzing depression, profound post-traumatic stress disorder (PTSD), and suicidality. Patricia scoured the city trying to find help for her daughter. Patricia connected Alejandra with a domestic violence agency. After a few counseling sessions, the domestic violence advocate attended court with Alejandra as the criminal case progressed.

Alejandra was accused of armed robbery based upon accomplice liability for allegedly driving the getaway car, and a bench trial commenced. Alejandra sat through the trial against her with her mother and her domestic violence advocate in the first row of the gallery seats behind her. She listened to the police detective, the same one who had assaulted her, testify as a witness for the state.[23] That afternoon, Alejandra spoke with her domestic violence advocate in reflection about the day of trial. As she described the pain she felt listening to the police detective who had so damagingly hurt her testify against her, Alejandra expressed a desire to hurt the police officer and his family, like he had hurt her and her family. Without asking further questions, the domestic violence advocate interpreted these statements as a desire to kill the officer and his family with a plan for doing so.

Domestic violence advocates in Illinois are legally bound to protect the confidentiality of their client's information. In Illinois, this protection is strong. Specificallyinformation, including records, from a domestic violence survivor conveyed to a domestic violence advocate who is employed by a domestic violence program in the course of providing domestic violence information, counseling or advocacy is privileged information that must be kept confidential.[24] Domestic violence advocates have a state and federal statutory obligation to not disclose such information without the client's consent and cannot be examined as a witness in criminal or civil proceedings,[25] underscoring that confidentiality protections are essential to the very

---

23 People v. Sevedo, 2017 IL App (1st) 152541 at 2.

24 750 ILCS 60/227 (a).

25 750 ILCS 60/227 (b). As a recipient of funds under the Violence Against Women Act, the domestic violence agency was also bound by the federal law's prohibition against disclosing privileged communications. Violence Against Women Act, 42 U.S.C. III, Title IV of P.L. 103-122 (1994); Violence Against Women Reauthorization Act, P.L. 113-4 (2013). In Illinois, domestic violence advocates can be subpoenaed to provide testimony and documents in juvenile court proceedings.

structure and efficacy of domestic violence services. While the privileged nature of these communications is well-founded and robust under the law, domestic violence advocates may disclose privileged information without the domestic violence victim's consent when there is reasonable suspicion that a child has been abused or neglected or in cases where failure to disclose is likely to result in imminent risk of serious bodily harm or death of the victim or another person.[26] Believing that Alejandra could likely cause serious harm or death to the officer and his family and that this harm could be prevented by sharing the information, under this exception and without Alejandra's consent, her domestic violence advocate reported Alejandra's statements to the police.

Alejandra was ultimately acquitted of armed robbery, yet a few weeks following Alejandra's acquittal, the state filed a complaint concerning her alleged threat to the police officer.[27] Eight days later, a grand jury indicted Alejandra for threatening a public official and issued a subpoena for the documents of the domestic violence agency and reports related to the threats Alejandra allegedly made. Under the rules of evidence, the state's case rested on the records and testimony of the domestic violence advocate. The court ordered the domestic violence agency to provide the documents to the court for *in camera,* meaning the judge would review the documents in private to determine whether privilege protected these documents from discovery. The domestic violence agency refused, arguing that reporting the perceived threat did not create an opening to penetrate the confidentiality privilege.

After filing a motion to reconsider, the domestic violence agency through its executive director remained steadfastly committed to their interpretation of the law and duty to their clients. The executive director of the domestic violence agency attended the hearing prepared to be held in contempt of court and arrested. Her unwavering refusal to turn over the records was unexpected. Much discussion ensued. Ultimately, the domestic violence agency agreed to provide the documents under seal with the chief deputy of the criminal court building, meaning that no one from this courtroom or their offices would be able to view the

---

[26] *Id.* In Illinois, domestic violence program personnel are mandated reporters. 325 ILCS 5/4 (Persons required to report).

[27] People v. Sevedo, 2017 IL App (1st) 152541 at 3.

records. The judge denied the motion to reconsider, found the domestic violence agency director guilty of contempt, and fined the agency $500 per day. The denial of the motion to reconsider became an issue that the domestic violence agency could now appeal. The domestic violence agency brought the sealed documents to the clerk's office, and the fine was stayed pending the appeal.[28]

The Illinois Appellate Court agreed with the domestic violence agency and disagreed with the state. Ultimately, the court found that "the advocate-victim privilege is absolute in nature."[29] The exception expires once the imminent risk disclosure is made, leaving the privilege intact, and now, absolute. The court further held that the privilege provides protection for a broad scope of communications, including those that are "not related to instances of domestic violence or services provided by the advocate."[30] Therefore, Alejandra's statement made to her domestic violence advocate at a criminal courthouse about her criminal trial for armed robbery qualified as a privileged communication and was inadmissible as evidence. Because of the danger that disclosing information can pose, the court acknowledged that the advocate-victim privilege is even stronger and more comprehensive than the mental health therapist-patient privilege.[31] The appellate court reversed the judgment of contempt against the director of the domestic violence agency and vacated the fines. The criminal threat charges were dropped against Alejandra because the state did not have any evidence to present to the court. On appeal, Alejandra's threat and the resoluteness of the executive director from the domestic violence agency enabled the advocate-victim privilege to become ironclad across Illinois.

Alejandra and the domestic violence agency made a momentous contribution to the ability of survivors of domestic violence to receive the help they need from domestic violence providers. Now, thousands of men, women, and children will benefit from the assurance that they can share difficult, personal, scary, and traumatizing information with their domestic violence advocate, and it cannot be shared because sharing such information could put survivors in danger. Having a

[28] *Id.*
[29] *Id.* at 10.
[30] *Id.* at 8.
[31] *Id.* at 10. Mental Health and Developmental Disabilities Confidentiality Act, 740 ILCS 110/10, 11 (2014).

protected relationship with a helpful and supportive domestic violence advocate can be critical to survivors' ability to navigate the risks of domestic violence, build upon their protective strengths, and find enhanced safety and stability for their children. Likewise, the nearly 43,000 adult survivors and over 8,000 child survivors of domestic violence who receive domestic violence services in Illinois will feel comfortable discussing the myriad of issues that intersect with their experience of domestic violence on their journey toward healing.[32]

As Alejandra contributed to the conditions of the healing for others, the trauma she had experienced still tormented her mind, body, and soul. Patricia was determined to find pathways for her daughter's healing. Patricia bought Alejandra a dog, Coco. When Alejandra cried, Coco would nestle in her neck. If Alejandra did not wipe aside her own tears, Coco would lick them away. When Alejandra was unable to hear anyone's voice to wake up from a depressive sleep, Coco would pat her shut eyelids with her paws. Responding to Coco's needs, Alejandra would rise to take Coco outside. Needing to care for Coco, a dog she loved, gave Alejandra something to live for. Patricia also found a hospital that seemed fitting for her daughter, and Alejandra spent a month there. Following the hospital stay, Alejandra's life began feeling less constricted. As she ventured outside of her home, she always took Coco with her. Patricia often held Coco's head in her hand and said, "Thank you, little Coco, you are a beautiful creature, thank you for saving my daughter's life." When the appellate court issued its decision, Alejandra was actually able to feel—to feel relief, to feel happiness, to feel pride, just like her mother who, with the appellate court decision in hand, was finally was able to smell the rain. Understanding her contribution to survivors like herself bolstered Alejandra's healing, just as her mother's impact continued to reverberate beyond her family.

Resulting Reform from a Mother and Daughter

During the time of Alejandra's odyssey through the criminal court system, the new and promising environment injurious allegation

---

[32] *Illinois Domestic Violence Service Statistics, 2018,* Illinois Coalition Against Domestic Violence (Feb. 15, 2019), http://www.ilcadv.org/resources/statistics/FY18DataSheet.pdf.

rule was not translating into improved child welfare practice—a classic example that a law on the books is only as effective as it is implemented.

Over a year after the new rule went into effect, the newly appointed director of DCFS at the time, Director George Sheldon, invited the community to come forward to voice input about how the Department could better serve families. Accepting this invitation and mobilizing the gender-based violence advocacy community, Patricia's former attorney and advocates from the Chicago Metropolitan Battered Women's Network formed the Domestic Violence Child Welfare Resource Coalition (DVCWRC) in January 2015.[33] The DVCWRC was comprised of over thirty domestic violence and sexual assault social and legal service agencies in the Chicagoland area. The DVCWRC aimed to translate the reform of Allegation 60 from policy into practice and posited itself to be a partner with DCFS in the path toward improvement. The DVCWRC convened over the course of nine months in order to be a strong, unified voice identifying issues and proposing solutions.

Through submitted, written comments to DCFS' Strategic Plan, the DVCWRC identified the following obstacles that front-line advocates at domestic violence agencies were commonly observing during DCFS interventions into the lives of families experiencing domestic violence:

1. Judgment, bias, stereotyping, and lack of cultural competency;
2. Lack of understanding about the dynamics of domestic violence and stated inaccuracies such as "parents engaged in domestic violence" or "mutual domestic violence;"
3. Measuring the nonoffending parent's worth as a mother on whether she "stayed or left;"
4. Mandating the nonoffending parent to obtain a protective order when there may not be legal grounds to do so, when the survivor did not want it, or when it could put the family in increased danger;
5. Implementing a safety plan that places the children with the offender's family;

[33] This organization is now named The Network: Advocating Against Domestic Violence.

6. Inappropriate referrals to services, such as anger management rather than a batterer intervention program for domestic violence offenders; and
7. Childcare workers who lose their jobs due to DCFS involvement and become even more reliant on abusive, yet breadwinning, partners.

The letter punctuated that these flaws often weaken rather than strengthen the nonoffending parent's ability to parent in safety and stability and are, therefore, harmful to the well-being and healing of the children who have experienced domestic violence. The letter further explained that punitive or ineffective child welfare interventions do not cause long-term sustainable change for families, act as a deterrent to reaching out for help in the future, and increase danger for the mother and her children by validating the offender's use of power and control over his partner. The current climate was directly reminiscent of Patricia's experience with DCFS, despite significant subsequent changes in the law.

The DVCWRC expressed its commitment to partnering with DCFS and received invaluable assistance in formulating ideas for improving practice. The National Council of Juvenile and Family Court Judges, the publisher of the Greenbook, provided technical assistance and support to the DVCWRC. As learned from the Greenbook, the DVCWC believed that collaboration between the domestic violence and child welfare communities was a critical pathway toward improving practices and outcomes for families. The National Council surveyed the country and provided the DVCWRC with a summary of the collaborative efforts between child welfare and domestic violence occurring in other states. A domestic violence program in Florida specifically compelled the DVCWRC.

The Florida Coalition Against Domestic Violence administered a statewide domestic violence co-location program called the Child Protection Investigations (CPI) project. Like the Domestic Violence Liaison program in New Jersey, in Florida domestic violence advocates employed by most local domestic violence agencies worked in child welfare offices in order to build the capacity of child welfare staff to effectively intervene and to support families through the intervention.[34] After three phases of expansion, the CPI reached all sixty-seven counties in Florida; over forty domestic violence advocates were co-located in child welfare investigative offices, and nearly all of the Florida's domestic violence agencies participated in the CPI.[35] The ultimate goal of the CPI project was to bridge the gap between child welfare and domestic violence service providers to enhance family safety, create permanency for children, reduce the removal of children from nonoffending parents, and foster accountability for the parents causing harm.[36] By strengthening families, the CPI served as a foster care prevention from into foster care program, saving the state over $26 million per year in placement services.[37] In a letter sent directly to Director Sheldon, the DVCWRC proposed a similar domestic violence co-location program in Illinois. Hailing from Florida, Director Sheldon was familiar with the breadth and impact of his home state's, statewide program. He convened meetings between representatives of the DVCWRC and key leaders and administrators of DCFS to discuss the possibility of piloting a co-location program in Illinois and conversations progressed.

In early 2017, while the appellate court was considering and deciding the advocate-victim privilege issue in Alejandra's criminal case, leaders at DCFS and the DVCWRC conducted a site visit in Florida that the National Council sponsored. The site visit solidified the commitment to piloting the domestic violence co-location program in Illinois.

To bolster commitment for the pilot program, members of the DVCWRC in partnership with DCFS drafted a bill that authorized the Domestic Violence Co-Location Program (DVCLP).[38] SB 646 defined the DVCLP and set forth requirements of partnering with agencies outside of DCFS, data tracking, and developing training, rules, and

---

[34] *Child Protection Investigations (CPI) Project Standards Manual*, The Florida Coalition Against Domestic Violence, (Feb. 20, 2019) http://fcadv.org/sites/default/files/CPI%20Project%20Manual%202015.pdf.

[35] *Id.*

[36] *Id.*

[37] *Id.*

[38] Statutory authority was not required to authorize the DVCLP, but the statutory codification bolstered the importance of the program and solidified its existence in anticipation of leadership changes at DCFS, which indeed occurred.

procedures during this five-year pilot program.[39] The bill was explicit that the DVCLP does not breach the advocate-victim confidentiality protections that the appellate court was concurrently considering in the contempt case of the domestic violence agency regarding Alejandra's statements. SB 646 passed unanimously in both houses of the Illinois state legislature, and the governor signed the bill into law in August 2017.[40]

In the fall of 2017, Illinois applied for and was awarded a federal research grant in support of the DVCLP. More specifically, the Children's Bureau, a part of the Administration for Children and Families of the U.S. Department of Health and Human Services, launched the national Quality Improvement Center on Domestic Violence in Child Welfare (QIC-DVCW) to test interventions to improve how child welfare agencies and their partners work with families experiencing domestic violence.[41] The creation of the QIC-DVCW and its targeted research was a long-awaited follow-up to the conclusion of the federally funded Greenbook Demonstration Sites. The Children's Bureau selected Futures without Violence to lead the endeavor of the QIC-DVCW.[42]

The QIC-DVCW selected three Research and Capacity Building projects to implement and test a specific approach that layers guidance for practice atop the premise that effectively addressing domestic violence in child welfare requires collaboration. The Illinois Department

---

[39] Pub. Act. 100-406, eff. 1-1-18.

[40] ANCRA, 325 ILCS 5/7.41 (domestic violence co-location program).

[41] *Quality Improvement Center on Domestic Violence in Child Welfare*, FUTURES WITHOUT VIOLENCE (Feb. 20, 2019), https://www.futureswithoutviolence.org/children-youth-teens/quality-improvement-center-domestic-violence-child-welfare-advancing-adult-child-survivor-centered-practice/.

[42] To administer the QIC-DVCW, Futures without Violence partnered in part with the National Council of Juvenile and Family Court Judges, Caminar Latino, the Center for the Study of Social Policy, the University of Kansas School of Social Welfare, and the Center for Health and Safety Culture at Montana State University, accompanied by a robust National Advisory Committee, including Juan Carlos Areán (chapter 4), Ruby White Starr (chapter 4), and Isa Woldeguiorguis (chapter 7). Many of the originals of the DCF Domestic Violence Unit (chapter 7) in Massachusetts originals are instrumental to the QIC- DVCW. Lonna Davis directs the department at Futures overseeing this project; Shellie Taggart is the director of the QIC-DVCW; Susan Hubertleads the Massachusetts' Research and Capacity Building site.

of Children and Family Services was selected in the company of Allegheny County Office of Children, Youth, and Families in Pennsylvania and the Massachusetts Department of Children and Families as the three Research and Capacity Building Projects.[43] The specific collaborative practice models differ among the three projects as collaboration must fit within the structural, political, funding, and community needs of each locale. In each project site, collaboration was designed to include the triad of the Greenbook—domestic violence organizations, child welfare agencies, and the courts—as well as expand to other stakeholders, such as community-based service providers, law enforcement, and mental health and substance abuse treatment providers.

As was learned from the Greenbook demonstration sites, collaboration is not an end-goal in itself, but rather a means, a process, a pathway toward more effective interventions that lead to better outcomes for families. The Adult and Child Survivor Centered Approach (the Approach)—that which QIC-DVCW was testing—became the conduit for translating collaborative practice into enhanced safety, stability, well-being, and healing for families. To guide collaborative practice, the Adult and Child Survivor Centered Approach builds upon more than twenty-five years of work by child welfare and domestic violence practitioners and policy makers and is grounded in research on violence prevention, human development, trauma, and resilience. The Approach is not prescriptive nor a checklist or protocol yet is more than mere theory and philosophy. The Approach is a common vision and framework advanced through collaborative practice between child welfare and its community partners. In translationally connecting research with practice, the Approach is grounded in the tenets that Susan Schechter and Jeffrey Edleson established in the Greenbook that the safety and well-being of child survivors of domestic violence are inextricably linked to the safety and well-being of the adult survivor of domestic violence.[44] The Approach prioritizes partnership with the adult survivor in buffering risk and building upon strength with

---

43 *Announcing the Research and Capacity Building Projects,* Quality Improvement Center on Domestic Violence in Child Welfare (Feb. 20, 2019), https://dvchildwelfare.org/announcing-the-research-and-capacity-building-projects.

44 *What is the QIC-DVCW, Advancing an Adult and Survivor Centered Approach,* Quality Improvement Center on Domestic Violence in Child Welfare (Feb. 20, 2019), https://dvchildwelfare.org.

support. The Approach deepens the commitment to engaging with people who use violence and coercive control through reparative avenues of accountability. The Approach places great value on the importance of relationships in the experience of and recovery from trauma. The Approach locates sources of resilience in all family members. Equity is woven into every principle and framework of the Approach. Respect, dignity, and cultural sensitivity also permeate the fiber of the Approach. The Approach is guidance toward trauma-informed, strength-based, family-centered, and equity-focused interventions.

In Illinois, two co-located domestic violence advocates of the DVCLP were funded to work in DCFS offices in two separate counties in the northern region of Illinois to support investigation, intact, and permanency for child welfare workers and families. One site advanced the Approach while the other site was not equipped with this tool in order to serve as a comparison site for the tested intervention. The federal evaluation and research aim to (1) establish whether the Approach improves safety, child permanence, and family well-being, for which families and under what circumstances, (2) determine the factors necessary for implementation and sustainability, and (3) ascertain cost associated with maintaining the Approach.[45] Potentially established as evidenced-based practice, with will and resources, the DVCLP-Approach aspires to expand statewide, broadly applying the benefits of parallel process that principled collaborative practice generates for systems and families. In partnership with other systems, communities, and families, this collaborative model is the way to move the systemic needle toward more effective child welfare interventions in Illinois. Great change is to come.

This decade-long journey is a testament to a child welfare system that is open and responsive to change, self-reflection, and commitment to improvement. This is progress. Patricia is the founding mother of this progress, this hope, this future for Illinois. A decade earlier, Patricia planted the seed for this reform by being the impetus for changing the law that set in motion efforts to shift practice. Because of her, and consistent with her spirit as a person, thousands of mothers, fathers, and children could experience more supportive,

45 The QIC-DVCW research was not yet released or published at the time of this book's publication.

respectful, and helpful child welfare interventions than she did. Because of her daughter, those who seek help to overcome crisis and heal from domestic violence can do so knowing that the necessary element of effective domestic violence services, privacy, is safeguarded.

A Mother and her Children

Walking out of the house to David's middle school graduation, Raul collapsed from a heart attack and died. Patricia does not feel sad, and for that, she feels guilty. But now she feels free. Before his death, unaware that Patricia had legal status in this country, Raul still refused to file to adjust her undocumented status, but he paid off the house. The house became his olive branch to Patricia to contend with his wrongdoings.

Within the home's walls, love and trauma have coexisted. A watercolor portrait that Angela skillfully painted of her mother is framed on the dining room wall. Angela captured her mother's knowing and eager eyes, warm smile, and spirit of kindness and love. Improvements to the house were the product of David and Patricia's hard work, including display cabinets they built together in his bedroom exhibiting his love of airplanes inspired by growing up in a house over which planes fly so close overhead, filling him with a soaring feeling each time. Sitting next to her mother in the kitchen where Raul threw the glass bottle, Alejandra looks at her mother with a love as deep as the pain she once felt. Tears now come as a surprise rather than as a prophecy when she thinks about all that her mother has been through, and still to this day, her mother, with an encouraging and reassuring smile, helps her breathe. Alejandra calms and with affection and gratitude strokes her mother's hair; Alejandra could not have survived without her. On the main wall of the living room, framed pictures of U.S. Marines are displayed with prominence and pride, with Alejandra's new husband's portrait featured at the top.

And finally, after miscarrying many times, Alejandra defied the premonition, and Patricia awaits becoming a grandmother to her daughter's child. As Alejandra prepares to welcome her own baby into this world, the collaborative pilot program that was seeded with her call to the police when she was thirteen-years-old is being born.

10
Together Unbroken: Healing from Trauma and the Child Welfare System

Without healing, the cycle of violence moves through generations, lives become stymied, individuals struggle in perpetuity, families lose connection, and communities weaken. With healing, individuals, families, and communities together become unbroken. Most families involved in the child welfare system are in need of an unobstructed path toward healing. To meet this need, child welfare interventions should, at least, neither hinder healing nor compound the reasons healing is needed and, at best, foster conditions for healing—the greatest indication that families are better off after interventions than before. The child welfare priorities of enhancing safety, well-being, and stability are prerequisite conditions for healing. Whether child welfare interventions facilitate or thwart healing for all families, the individuals, and their collective is a measure of either the effectiveness of the systemic response or the need for improvement, reform, and even radical transformation. The process and practice of healing from trauma must be understood so that child welfare interventions enhance, rather than impede, the ability of families to heal.

survivors are alchemists
transmitting pain into joy,
violence into love.
the difference between us
and victims
is we have tasted triumph
on the internal battlefields
of mind and spirit.
we know how to heal ourselves,
and our world,
together.

magic warriors, @amitaswadhin

Deriving the Alchemy of Healing

Healing from trauma requires safety, voice, and connection.[1] Psychiatrist, Dr. Judith Herman, derived this three-part alchemy of healing from trauma—an attainable aspiration for a trauma-informed, family-centered, strength-based, and equity-centered child welfare system to cultivate and not encumber. This alchemy of healing arose from the thread of connections in Judith's experiences as the granddaughter of Jewish immigrants fleeing anti-Semitism and oppression, a daughter of leftist intellectuals who suffered political persecution under McCarthyism, an "outside agitator" and college student in the Deep South during the Freedom Summer of 1964, a female medical student outnumbered amidst a class of men, and a member of a feminist consciousness-raising group where the truth of violence was revealed and indoctrinated to impact the lives of others.[2,3] Accepting the reality that violence is endemic to a social structure in which oppression occurs and fortified by the will to remain invested long enough to articulate a path for the process of healing, Judith dedicated her career in psychiatry to the alchemy of trauma, navigating the journey from violence and pain to life and meaning.

---

1 HERMAN, TRAUMA AND RECOVERY: THE AFTERMATH OF VIOLENCE—FROM DOMESTIC ABUSE TO POLITICAL TERROR (1992).

2 Judith Herman was a member of the Bread and Roses Collective #9 in Boston at the same time as she began her residency in psychiatry.

3 Interview with Judith Herman (May 14, 2019).

Early in her psychiatric career, Judith encountered two women in an inpatient hospital who awakened Judith's exploration of the alchemy of trauma and its recovery. Following attempts to end their own lives, both women disclosed, nearly "confessed," a history of sexual abuse perpetrated by each of their fathers, and one resorted to suicide as an escape from lethal domestic violence. Because Judith believed them, they were able to talk; because she bore witness, they felt less shame; slowly, their symptoms of trauma began to abate. As Judith described,

> As clinicians, we were also privileged to witness the liberation that comes when the burdens of shame and fear are lifted. As our patients told their stories and were met with compassion rather than scorn, their despair gave way to renewed hope, and their isolation to a renewed sense of community. My work for the next forty years has been built on those initial discoveries of that revolutionary moment.[4]

When Judith finished her medical training, she became a psychiatrist at a free feminist-based clinic whose patients would influence the perception of trauma and healing forevermore. There Judith uncovered the hidden prevalence of incest amongst her patients. To cement these experiences in history's collective memory thereby bucking her own field's history of amnesiac cover-up and patriarchy's stronghold, Judith wrote a book entitled *Father-Daughter Incest,* which was published in 1981. Judith was then invited to join the faculty of the Harvard-affiliated Department of Psychiatry at Cambridge Hospital; her work through this public safety-net hospital advanced her understanding of trauma. There, Judith and a community psychologist colleague imported the knowledge of grass-roots feminist organization into the hospital, creating the Victims of Violence Program to respond to and support those whose experiences of violence were impacting their health.[5] Judith also joined a city-wide trauma group led by the former Department of Veteran Affairs psychiatrist, Dr. Bessel van der

---

4 Judith Lewis Herman, *Helen Block Lewis: A Memoir of Three Generations*, 20 PSYCHOANALYTICAL PSYCHOLOGY 528 (2013).

5 Betsy McAlister Groves would later begin a similar program in 1992 for young children, rather than adults, called the Child Witness to Violence Project at Boston Medical Center (discussed in chapter 5).

Kolk (discussed in chapter 4). The group gathered together a wide range of trauma practitioners working with abused children, combat veterans, battered women, and rape survivors to study the newly defined mental health disorder of post-traumatic stress disorder (PTSD) that had recently been added to the *Diagnostic and Statistical Manual of Mental Disorders (DSM-III)*.[6] The alchemy of trauma was crystallizing for Judith: violence is prevalent, the causes have roots in society, and ubiquity exists such that "oppression is oppression, trauma is trauma, whether in the political sphere of war and dictatorship, or in the private sphere of sex, intimacy, and family life."[7]

Universalizing both the understanding of trauma and the alchemy of transforming through trauma, Judith penned the book *Trauma and Recovery,* which quickly became the guidepost for the process of healing from trauma.[8] This time feminism, the opposite of oppression, fueled the social, political, and historical context that was willing to accept the realities of people's experiences with violence, never

---

6 Veterans from the Vietnam War were home from combat, but many felt as though they were still there. The combat had found a permanent bunker in their body and minds. Veteran "rap" groups were the predecessors of feminist consciousness-raising like those in Bread and Roses. There, veterans came together to share, discuss, and strategize around the symptoms they were experiencing from war and combat—flashbacks, difficulty remembering, numbness, hyper-vigilance, agitation, challenges connecting with loved ones whose very existence and support seemingly got them through the war, and "minds and brains that keep them frozen, trapped in a place they desperately wish to escape." These grassroots groups fostered the awareness, organizing, and advocacy necessary to begin understanding the symptoms that occur after trauma. Vietnam veterans along with a few psychoanalyst activists lobbied the American Psychiatric Association (APA) to create a new diagnosis that described the cluster of symptoms to describe the horror and helplessness people experienced following trauma. In 1980, the APA added post-traumatic stress disorder to the *Diagnostic and Statistical Manual of Mental Disorders (DSM-III)* as a recognized disorder with specific symptoms that could be diagnosed. Bessel van der Kolk, The Body Keeps the Score: Brain, Mind, and Body in the Healing of Trauma [STT] 50, 78 (2015).

7 Herman, *supra* note 3.

8 HERMAN, TRAUMA AND RECOVERY: THE AFTERMATH OF VIOLENCE—FROM DOMESTIC ABUSE TO POLITICAL TERROR (1992). At the time of its publication in 1992, the psychologist Phyllis Chesler, writing in the *New York Times*, described the book accurately yet rather ironically, as "one of the most important psychiatric works to be published since Freud." Laurel Graeber, *New & Noteworthy Paperbacks,* THE NEW YORK TIMES (Aug. 15, 1993), https://www.nytimes.com/1993/08/15/books/new-noteworthy-paperbacks-179693.html.

losing consciousness of the vastness or devastation of trauma while also deriving a way forward. Directly informed by the experiences of survivors with whom Judith worked for nearly two decades who struggled to survive as their own alchemists and with professionals, Judith's writing instills hope, as well as the will and the way toward healing. Judith's own articulations of the healing process are worthy of repeating here:

> Recovery unfolds in three stages. The central task for the first stage is the establishment of *safety*. The central task of the second stage is *remembrance and mourning*. The central task of the third stage is *reconnection* with ordinary life. Like an abstract concept, these stages of recovery . . . are an attempt to impose simplicity and order upon a process that is inherently turbulent and complex.[9]

> Trauma robs the victim of a sense of power and control; the guiding principle of recovering to restore power and control to the survivor.[10]

The parallels between the healing process for adults and children reveal the unisons of healing, nuanced for age, identity, and culture, as the healing journeys shared in this chapter demonstrate.[11]

Like many of Dr. Judith's patients, Amita Swadhin and Lenny Hayes both experienced childhood physical and sexual abuse, and like Johnny Rice II, also lived in homes where domestic violence occurred. Amita Swadhin's journey demonstrates the first two stages of healing—safety and recounting and mourning—and Lenny Hayes' and Johnny Rice IIs' experiences embody the third stage of healing,

---

[9] *Id.* at 395-96.

[10] *Id.* at 406.

[11] Betsy McAllister Groves identifies safety, providing a safe space for a child to talk about what happened, and a nurturing caregiving relationship as the three critical elements to children's recovery from trauma. BETSY MCALISTER GROVES, CHILDREN WHO SEE TOO MUCH: LESSONS FROM THE CHILDREN WITNESS TO VIOLENCE PROJECT (2002). At the time that post-traumatic stress disorder was added to the *Diagnostic and Statistical Manual of Mental Disorders* in 1980, children could not be diagnosed with PTSD. Id. at 34. Dr. Lenore Terr researched to determine whether children could suffer from PTSD and found that children experience a similar constellation of post-traumatic symptoms as adults. Id. at 34-35.

reconnection. Amita and Lenny became alchemists of their healing in spite of, rather than because of, the intervention of the child welfare system into their lives, while Johnny navigated reconnection in ways that located sources of accountability and connection through relationships and community rather than in punitive and paternalistic systems. Facilitating safety, storytelling, and connections for children and adults following trauma is both critical to their healing and the viability of their communities, as well as attainable for child welfare interventions.

The Becoming of Truth-Tellers and Magic Warriors

Amita Swadhin crafted parallel narratives, their[12] childhood a tale of many separate stories, fictions, that if converged would erase all that enabled their survival.

The intergenerational transmission of state-induced and individual trauma for Amita's family begins with the narrative of their grandparents and parents fighting and experiencing oppression and violence. Amita's grandparents met in the movement to liberate Goa, India from Portuguese control. Attracted to the freedom movement around civil rights occurring in the United States, Amita's grandmother left India for America with her doctorate degree, leaving her two daughters temporarily and her adulterous husband permanently behind. Amita's grandmother was unprepared to be racialized in a homogeneous midwestern suburb, despite her designation as a "desirable" immigrant. She became a professor at a state university and sent for her daughters.

Amita's mother was lonely in the United States. Even as a young girl, she felt like an outsider in the all-white town she lived in with an unmarried mother who was more interested in professionalism than maternalism. In high school, she found a place of belonging in evangelical Christianity, participating in both church revival camps and Bhangra

[12] Amita, pronounced Amitha, identifies as a genderqueer, pansexual South Asian American femme whose preferred pronouns are they/them/theirs. For more information about the use of preferred pronouns, please visit https://www.mypronouns.org/what-and-why.

dance performances. Amidst confusion, she entered college and met a handsome Indian man who had also converted to Christianity.

Amita's Punjabi father was born after Britain had partitioned its territories of India and Pakistan, arbitrarily drawing boundaries that ignored ethnic divides, sewing seeds for unrest and violence. Amita's paternal family had been displaced, along with 18 million others, and made the journey across the partition from Lahore, now Pakistan, to New Delhi, now India. Brutality on that journey marked the years before his birth, violence continued into his life, and he perpetuated the same pain he endured onto others. Amita's father was first raped by his older brother and later by neighborhood boys and servants. He then raped two cousins in India before moving to the United States, packing with him his view that his culture maintained children and women as the property of men.

Upon marriage, Amita's mother dropped out of college, embracing the domesticity her own mother rejected. Using Christianity as a wedge between his wife and her only support, Amita's father hit their mother for the first time before Amita's birth, and by the time Amita was born, their mother was already isolated and dependent. He treated his wife like a domestic servant, and he often punctuated verbal violence with physical violence. When his business skills failed to provide for his now family of four, he pushed his wife to re-enroll in school to become a medical technician. Working days and going to school at night left Amita in the care of their father.

Beginning at the age of four, and for eight more years, he raped Amita at least weekly and whenever he had unfettered access to Amita. Throughout the years of sexual abuse, Amita developed the story that their mother did not know her daughter was being hurt alongside the abuse she too suffered.

Amita developed multiple narratives of themselves and their experiences, thereby enabling their survival. Amita presented a narrative to the outside as a character like their strong, intelligent, and independent grandmother committed to liberation. Amita's father valued school, viewing education as a way to advance his family's status. Amita's constricted world expanded within the bounds of school, counterpoint narratives co-existed, and Amita excelled. Amita joined any extracurricular activity possible—choir, Girls Scouts, orchestra, student government, newspaper, debate. What Amita could not be at home, they could be at school. Fearful at home, Amita was confident in school. Losing a sense of self at home, Amita was extroverted at school. Obedient at home, Amita was precocious in school. Flooded with shame at home, Amita placed into academically and artistically gifted tracks. Amita's accomplishments thwarted most suspicion that Amita's life at home did not mirror their portrayal in school. Amita had attached themself to the idea that school was their refuge and salvation, and disclosure of their other narrative would dismantle the sanctuary and path toward freedom that Amita refused to jeopardize.

At home, Amita also wrote the narrative of being their sister's protector. Amita told herself that they endured the abuse so their sister would not have to. Amita was both the protector and the oppressed, the victim and the savior, crafing a narrative of heroic martyrdom. Although Amita endured and survived because of the belief, the story, that their sister was never directly harmed, a different form of trauma occurred when one sister repeatedly hears the other sister being tortured on the other side of their shared wall.

Amita does not remember the last time their father raped them because they did not know it would be the last. Amita menstruated for the first time on Christmas morning when Amita was twelve years old. Even Amita's father did not want to father his own grandchild, so he stopped assaulting Amita. Amita thought the narrative of their abuse had now ended, leaving space for only the narrative upon which Amita's freedom depended. The violence against Amita's mother's continued.

Early on in their freshman year of high school, Amita came home from school to find their father and sister lying next to each other in bed, playing video games. The memories of the grooming Amita's father perpetrated against Amita resurrected from the bed. Had he already harmed Amita's sister? Had Amita survived violence and torture on the false narrative they were sparing their sister? At that moment, putting words to their trauma and protecting their sister was worth the crashing of their worlds; Amita was willing to share the narrative she had hidden. But the series of people who responded to Amita's disclosure made Amita feel neither safe nor affirmed and Amita experienced years of unhealed struggling.

Amita gave themself until the next day to summon the courage to tell their mom. Amita's father and sister were at work and school respectively. Amita's mother was in the kitchen. Standing in the door frame, Amita spoke. "I need to talk to you. Dad abused me when I was little." The room stopped. Amita's mother replied, "Are you remembering what happened to you when you were four?" Not recalling the disclosure their mother revealed, Amita's narrative of her mother's unknowing shattered into a narrative of complicity. Amita's presence returned to the kitchen. Amita told their mother that they had endured "years and years of abuse." Amita did not label the abuse as rape, unwilling to confront that level of violence yet.

> on this day,
> legions of children
> worldwide
> realize
> the line between
> performing
> and
> existing
> is a fiction.
>
> -*father's day,* @amitaswadhin

Amita's mother cried. Amita cried. Parenting in a way that Amita had not experienced, Amita's mother called a therapist and briefly described why she was calling. The therapist was a mandated reporter of child abuse and neglect.

The First Two Stages in the Alchemy of Healing: Safety and Recounting

Dr. Judith Herman's alchemy of healing from trauma includes safety, recounting, and reconnection. The process of healing from trauma begins by establishing safety. Because trauma steals power and control from those victimized, safety entails gaining control over the traumatized person's body and then control over the environment.[13] Control is the antonym to inflicted violence - those who have control

[13] Herman, *supra* note 7, at 408.

over their bodies, spirit, and surroundings are not being harmed or hurt by others. Complete safety is rarely possible. Survivors must assess the "degree of continued threat and decide what sort of precautions are necessary" to becoming safer.[14] Attempts to dictate the survivor's choices or take action without her consent undermines her safety by disempowering her, replicating the dynamics in which she has already been powerless and thus unsafe.[15] The task of establishing safety when the relationship with the person causing harm still persists is "complex," but as Dr. Herman guided, "the guarantee of safety in an abusive relationship can never be based upon a promise from the perpetrator, no matter how heartfelt. Rather, it must be based upon the self-protective capability of the victim."[16] The people in the traumatized person's life can be "source[s] of protection, emotional support, or practical support."[17] Pure safety is often unattainable but the progression toward greater safety—feeling "safer," gaining more predictability, possessing more control—is the trigger of the healing journey, without which even desired healing becomes stagnant. Once greater safety is established, the traumatized person begins to believe she can trust and rely upon herself and others, and the glimmer of believing that she "deserves no less" begins to appear.[18]

Once the stronghold of the violence lessens its tangible grip on the survivor's body, mind, and environment recounting and mourning becomes possible. Communicating the trauma is central to retelling and using words directly defies the impact of trauma. Because traumatic experiences rob people of the ability to articulate the fragments of their traumatic experiences by cutting them off from language, speaking the trauma is an act of r,of that t reclamation of what the trauma stole.[19] Words that had not been used before can now be applied to the traumatic memories. The "restorative power of truth-telling" changes the abnormal biochemical processing of the traumatic memory, thereby relieving the severity and frequency of the

[14] *Id.* at 417.
[15] *Id.* at 420.
[16] *Id.* at 429.
[17] *Id.* at 413.
[18] *Id.* at 441–42.
[19] *Id.* at 149.

post-traumatic stress symptoms.[20] Most significantly, "the physioneurosis induced by terror can be reversed through the use of words."[21]

The goal of recounting the trauma is "integration, not exorcism," as the trauma story becomes "more present and more real," transforming into a "new story" about "dignity and virtue," rather than "shame and humiliation."[22] As Dr. Herman describes, "in the second stage of recovery, the survivor tells the story of the trauma. She tells it completely in-depth and in detail. This work of reconstruction actually transforms the traumatic memory, so that it can be integrated into the survivor's life story."[23] Until their experience is assimilated into the ongoing story of their lives, survivors continue to live in the place they wish to escape and are not fully alive in the present.[24] Uncovering, reconstructing, and integrating the trauma narrative into the survivor's unified life story often produces profound grief. Mourning all that was lost, all that could never be, all that cannot be replaced, yet on the other side of grief, "the trauma no longer commands the central place in her life."[25] Once they reclaim their own history, they can then engage with and rebuild life.[26]

Yet that reclamation, engagement, and rebuilding cannot occur until safety produces the comfort to integrate the narrative of trauma into the narrative of self. As survivors are finding the words to bring the "story into the room where it can be spoken and heard," those listening play the role of witness and ally in whose presence the survivor can speak the unspeakable.[27] If the listener is not such, the words will remain stunted, the truth in its entirety will remain unspoken, and the trauma will maintain its grip on the survivor.[28] Stagnation in narrative integration, as Amita's experiences reveal, delays healing.

• • •

[20] *Id.* at 460.

[21] *Id.* at 466.

[22] *Id.* at 460.

[23] *Id.* at 444.

[24] Bessel van der Kolk, The Body Keeps the Score: Brain, Mind, and Body in the Healing of Trauma (2015).

[25] Herman, *supra* note 7 at 495.

[26] *Id.* at 496.

[27] *Id.* at 450-51.

[28] *Id.* at 445.

Within forty-eight hours, a Department of Youth and Family Services (DYFS) employee was in the Swadhins' living room. Amita was scared. Amita knew about foster care. Amita did not want to leave their home, their mother, or their school and could not be pulled away from their sister who still needed their protection. Amita knew they would all be forced to deal with the aftermath—the potentially lethal response their father could unleash for involving outsiders into their family, no less the state.

A white man and woman from DYFS sat on the couch across from Amita. As a ninth- grader wearing an Ivy League university sweatshirt, the two investigators began asking questions about what Amita's father had done. The workers used slang and euphemistic names for anatomy and sex. Then the woman uttered, "You can trust us. We know this happens more often in your culture." Condescending, patronizing, and racist, Amita immediately perceived that it was not safe to share their narrative and retreated away from their truth; if these investigators were not going to be able to help them, jeopardizing the future upon which Amita steadfastly focused on would be futile and self-defeating. DYFS left that day, preserved the status quo, did not remove Amita's father from the home, offered no supportive services, made no connections to community resources, and referred the case to the criminal court. The violence over the next two years worsened.

A trauma-informed, strength-based, family-centered, and equity-focused child welfare intervention could have enhanced the safety of Amita and their family, giving Amita the space for their dual narratives to co-exist, and thus initiating the conditions for the process of healing. The investigators could have extended a twenty-minute conversation into an actual opportunity to connect with Amita, to get to know this dimensional teenager, to ask them about the aspirations embossed upon the sweatshirt they were wearing, to hear Amita, to listen. The investigators could have shared control and predictability with Amita by centering on their hopefulness that education would be the pathway to a different future and that their story would not shatter their privacy by being publicized. Grounded in the belief of strength amidst struggle, the investigators could have held the complexities of a teenager who both excels and suffers, alongside a mother who was insufficiently protective yet is central to her daughter's healing and a sister who was anguishing in silence. The investigators could have supported Amita's mother to meet the needs of her daughters by partnering with her to develop a strategy for her own safety, educating her about what her daughters needed to begin to heal, and connecting all three with effective and nuanced social service and community resources to address their trauma. In asking each what they needed, the investigators would have heard that the three needed to remain together but were desperate for a reprieve from the violence. Together, the three of them with the investigators could have discussed options for removing their father and sheltering them in place.

By holding the entire family at the center of the intervention, the investigators would not have ignored a central member of the family, Amita's father. The investigators could have strategized ways to engage him with the prospect of him developing accountability to himself, his family, and his community. Amita's mother could have shared that her husband's Hinduism was both a tool of his dominion over his family as well as a potential source of motivation to reflect and reform, to change. What if the child welfare workers could have provided a well-trained facilitator to hold a conversation with their extended family and friends in the Hindu temple where their father attended that centered on his family's safety and well-being? Instead, no one spoke with Amita's father. His violence escalated in retaliation for involving the state. The child welfare intervention decreased Amita's safety and pushed Amita further from speaking their truth, thus inhibiting the start of their ability to heal.

Similarly, the criminal justice system offered Amita scant safety, and their truth remained hidden. Later captured in a poem Amita entitled "state violence," Amita's father drove them to the courthouse to be interviewed by the prosecutors. There alone, a female officer sat in front of a double mirror and stayed stone-faced as Amita sobbed. Two white men asked Amita if they would make a good witness, threatened to prosecute Amita's mother, and asked if Amita had anything to add to Amita's father's statement that he had fondled his daughter once when Amita was four. Confronting another system that proved incapable of creating safety for Amita or their truth, Amita said nothing. Advised to plead guilty to something "minor," Amita's father was sentenced to five years of probation, remained at home, and became increasingly violent to Amita's mother.

After two years of enduring violence in the shadow of his probation, Amita's father nearly killed their mother by strangling her one morning before work. Amita's mother called the police, left the house, filed for divorce, and did not press criminal charges. As part of the divorce, Amita's sister wanted to visit with their father; Amita would not let her go alone. That year, their father began stalking their mother, lurking on her route to work, trying to drive her car off the freeway, and driving recklessly with them in the car. Amita's sister then refused to continue the visits, finally giving Amita space to close their father out of their life. Amita's father's absence created the safety—the tangible physical safety and a sense of control—that Amita needed to finally speak their full truth. For the first time, Amita told their mother the extent of his violence and used the word rape.

Through the New Jersey Office of Crimes, the Swadhins' were awarded crime victims compensation that paid for one hundred sessions of counseling for Amita and fifty hours each for Amita's mother and sister. Group therapy became transformative for Amita. Teenage girls, two of whom were East and South Asian, who had experienced incest and state intervention comprised the group therapy circle. Amita was the only one whose coping strategies, overachieving and perfectionism, were rewarded in a capitalist society; all of the others struggled with addiction, eating disorders, self-mutilation, or suicidality on top of the causes of their struggles. Within this group, Amita felt safe. Amidst the experiences of others, shame lifted when Amita realized they were not alone. Speaking and recounting their trauma, Amita integrated their narratives into one, finding a shared place for their experience of abuse alongside their hard work and well-deserved accomplishments.

After high school, Amita entered the School of Foreign Service at Georgetown University and carried the lessons from this group there, acting as a confidante to many friends who experienced their first encounters with trauma as college students.[29] Amita attended a Take

---

[29] One in five women are sexually assaulted while in college. *The Truth About Statistics of Sexual Assault in College*, The Hunting Group (June 25, 2019), www.thehuntinggroundfilm.com. A film exploring gender-based violence on college campuses is appropriately called "The Hunting Ground." *Id.*

Back the Night rally and listened to an Asian American incest survivor share her experience of rape by her brother.[30] When she was finished, the gathered crowd met her story with belief, support, and solidarity. Under the blanket of the dark sky, standing on the sidewalk of their college campus, Amita willfully and publicly shared their story, a moment that changed Amita's perception of themself. When Amita finished, Amita's world did not collapse; the university did not take back their college scholarship; fellow students did not shun them. Amita's story had become one narrative.

Amita was not able to attach emotions to their narrative until Amita had the distance that a semester abroad provided. Amita felt flooded by anger, fear, sadness, and disgust; feeling the hurt they had experienced while being raped while lacking the understanding of what was happening especially at this rather liberating time of their life. Amita had flashbacks of the abuse and started numbing the pain with alcohol. For the first time, Amita struggled in their studies, failed their classes, returned home, and engaged in counseling.

Amita was diagnosed with PTSD, now understood as complex PTSD resulting from repeated trauma. Through the safety of the therapeutic relationship, Amita began to grasp the damage the years of trauma had inflicted on their adrenal and limbic systems and neuro pathways that altered their brain and nervous system. Amita began identifying the emotions and flashbacks they felt as symptoms of complex PTSD, symptoms whose intensity lessened as Amita listened to them and integrated them into their trauma narrative. Amita took intentional and concrete measures to teach their body to "deactivate defensive maneuvers that once ensured their survival"[31] in order to learn that the "danger has passed and to live in the reality of the present,"[32] as Dr. Bessel van der Kolk described.

---

[30] The Take Back the Night foundation is committed to creating safe communities and respectful relationships through awareness events and initiatives in order to end sexual assault, domestic violence, dating violence, sexual abuse, and all forms of sexual violence. *Take Back the Night* (June 17, 2019), https://takebackthenight.org/about-us/. Take Back the Night rallies occur on college campuses as a way to grow visibility and support for those who have experienced sexual violence.

[31] van der Kolk, *supra* note 26, at 256.

[32] *Id.* at 85.

As an alchemist, Amita practices healing every day. If trauma inherently dissociates the mind from the body, even long after the trauma has passed, these practices reconnect the body with the mind and return natural rhythms and cadence to one's being. Now as a "truth-teller and magic warrior," Amita has learned to manage the chronic condition of complex PTSD, as Amita shared with their followers on social media,

> . . . I read a lot about the neurobiology of trauma, and follow a number of practices, everything from receiving acupuncture, myofascial release, meditations, and the use of plant-based medicines . . . I spend conscious time in nature. I have an emotional support dog. I engage in consensual, intimate, pleasurable, sober sex. I build my relationships with intentional and reciprocal access intimacy . . . Some of the symptoms . . . have gotten less acute for me since I was first diagnosed over 20 years ago. But what living with #CPTSD means for me is that if I don't pay attention to how my body-mind is feeling and go-go-go . . . I immediately relapse to all or most of these symptoms being acute again. It is not about me being "cured" (until and unless society gains better knowledge on brain healing), it's about me undoing my internalized ableism and respecting the fact that I live with an invisible disability that will flare if I deny to myself and others that I am a person who didn't survive as much trauma and violence as I actually did. However, the responsibility is a collective one—in order for me and others living with #CPTSD to be more honest about what we are feeling and how we need to move slower than non-traumatized people, we need workplaces and friendships and loverships, etc. that are trauma-informed. Given that more people have experienced repeated trauma and violence than those of who haven't, this SHOULD be a no-brainer . . .

Yet, as a gender-queer person of color, even when Amita heals a neural pathway from their childhood trauma, a new traumatized pathway can be created when harm comes from living at the intersections of racism, classism, homophobia, transphobia, and xenophobia. Healing, therefore, is not a destination but an iterative lifelong practice that state intervention must not hinder.

The Third Stage in the Alchemy of Healing: Reconnection

The third stage of healing is *reconnection*.[33] Having found safety and reckoning with the traumatic past, survivors face the task of creating their future. As they more actively engage with the outside, survivors discover who they now are. Helplessness and isolation turn into empowerment and reconnection as they understand the effect and purpose of their victimization. Survivors reconcile with themselves, integrating all aspects of self into the person they want to be, daring to define their wishes along the way. They recognize the value that may have evolved from the trauma while refraining from justifying the cost. Survivors also regain power by confronting danger, disclosing their pain to those who harmed them, and remaining open to the possibility of finding forgiveness within themselves independent of the outside response. Survivors reconnect outside of themselves. Many find a survivor mission, erasing the barrier between impacted and impactor. Culture and individual relationships can be robust sources of *reconnection,* the latch to which to connect.[34]

A source of both trauma and healing for Lenny Hayes, within his culture, lay his spirit of reconnection.

Reconnection of Spirit through Culture

Although Lenny Hayes lived in South Dakota on a reservation among members of his Sisseton-Wahpeton Oyate tribe hailing from the Great Sioux Nation, much of Lenny's life formed without the gift of spirituality and tradition. The little Lenny knew of his culture came from a story of creation his grandmother told him. By way of legend, each Dakota person began as a star in the sky. When a star's time came to enter the earth, each star would choose the parents through whom the star would gain personhood, forming a family,

---

[33] Herman, *supra* note 7 at chapter 10.

[34] The intersectionality of one's identity—the vast and varied characteristics, like race, gender, age, sexual orientation, religion, and class that form one's identity—are influenced by and informs the values of one's culture, which is contoured by the historical, social, and political events that shape life experiences. Kimberle Crenshaw, *Mapping the Margins: Intersectionality, Identity Politics, and Violence against Women of Color,* 43 STAN. L. REV. 1241, 1244 (1991).

thereby remaining circularly connected to the universe above. If the legend were true, Lenny would wonder, why, as a nascent star, would he have chosen parents who hurt him so much within a culture that bore such pain for those around him?

For generations, Lenny's culture had been endangered by outside forces, extinguishing aspects of Lenny's heritage that could have brought pride and comfort to a gay boy living in a home enraptured by violence. Traditionally universal among the diverse Native American tribes, had been the belief in the blurring between the natural and spiritual worlds; the existence of a soul in every aspect of Mother Earth's bounty. The most revered spiritual leaders and healers were Two-Spirit people or Winktas; those who identified as having both male and female spirits, as the duality they possessed enhanced their spiritual connections to their people, their land, and the universe. Two-Spirits were bestowed the honor of naming native babies in ways that connected the new life with flesh, earth, and spirit. Despite the strength of a people sewn to nature and the universe, European colonization and American infiltration destroyed their land, culture, language, and native identity through violence, trafficking, and assimilation. Two-Spirits were specifically targeted. Their differences led to their murder rather than reverence, extinguishing a tradition that embraced and esteemed variation. Due to being forced onto reservations and the intergenerational trauma of involuntary acculturation, reservation life was replete with poverty, addiction, disenfranchisement, struggling schools, and high rates of violence[35]—the scars of a people robbed of their universal connection to each other, their land, and their traditions.

In Lenny's childhood home, violence took the space where culture and spirituality could have been. His father's violence against his mother and both parents' alcoholism surrounded Lenny. Lenny's

---

[35] More than four in five American Indian and Alaska Native women (84.3%) have experienced violence in their lifetime and more than four in five American Indian and Alaska Native men (81.6%) have experienced violence in their lifetime. Dr. André B. Rosay, *National Institute of Justice Research Report, Violence Against American Indian and Alaska Native Women and Men, 2010 Findings from the National Intimate Partner and Sexual Violence Survey*, U.S. Department of Justice, Office of Justice Programs, National Institute of Justice (May 2016), https://www.ncjrs.gov/pdffiles1/nij/249736.pdf.

mother rejected her son because she perceived that he was different but not in a way that made him special and tormented him. As a young boy, Lenny's mother forced him to wear a dress and sat him on a chair in their front yard so that neighborhood boys and passerby could laugh at him. One afternoon when he was drunk, his father took a ball and chain and threatened to "beat the gay out" of Lenny.

The tribal child welfare court became involved with Lenny's family, and from ages six to ten, Lenny was repeatedly removed and returned to his mother. Every time he was sent home, he ran again, becoming a chronic runaway. Finally, when it was clear he was not going to stop running, the tribal court made him a ward of the court where the lack of safety became ever-present.

Reservations are governed by their own set of laws and court systems, including child welfare systems and juvenile courts. For Native American children not living on a reservation, however, the Indian Child Welfare Act (ICWA) offers specified safeguards.[36] ICWA is a federal law passed in 1978 in response to the systematic removal of Native and Alaskan children from their families and tribes.[37] Under ICWA, the child's tribe must be notified of the child welfare proceeding, can request that the case be transferred to the tribal court, or can participate in the state court proceeding.[38,39] ICWA also requires native children to be placed with extended families, a family in their tribe, or another native family,[40] aiming to preserve children as resources for the tribe and the cultural traditions as resources for children.[41]

Rather than fostering cultural connection, Lenny's time in foster care was laden with more abuse, prejudice, and disconnection, long

---

[36] Indian Child Welfare Act, 25 U.S.C. § 1901 (1978).

[37] For instance, the Indian Adoption Project administrated by the Child Welfare League of America and funded by the Bureau of Indian Affairs and the Children's Bureau, removed Native American children from their tribes and placed them with adoptive white families in order to assimilate children into "civilization," such that by 1960, one in four Native children were living apart from their families. STOLEN CHILDHOODS (KFAI 2016); *See,* DAWNLAND (UPSTANDER PROJECT 2018).

[38] Indian Child Welfare Act, 25 U.S.C. § 1911 (1978).

[39] Indian Child Welfare Act, 25 U.S.C. § 1912 (1978).

[40] Indian Child Welfare Act, 25 U.S.C. § 1915 (1978).

[41] Indian Child Welfare Act, 25 U.S.C. § 1901 (1978).

delaying his healing until adulthood. Lenny was moved from group homes to foster homes to boarding schools to detention centers and jails. Lenny's experience in out-of-home placements mirrored that which he endured at home. In a boarding school at age ten, Lenny was gang-raped by fellow students. In a Catholic children's home, Lenny was punished for uncertain offenses (likely spurred by discrimination against his vice of being gay) by kneeling on rice. Lenny was forced to see a psychiatrist who was more concerned with him being gay than the trauma he had endured.

In one of his many placements, Lenny was sent to live with a Native American family who practiced native culture and spirituality, providing Lenny with his first exposure to his traditions. Sanctifying the voluntary essence of native spirituality, the family gave Lenny the choice to participate in their traditions. Lenny chose to sit outside of the sweat lodge during a purification ceremony as he did not yet grasp the significance of his culture and the healing connection it could provide. Lenny's distinct memory of his first exposure to a sweat lodge ceremony remained in his mind's background as Lenny continued to struggle.

Eventually, Lenny's mother's rights were terminated. When his caseworker told him that he no longer had a legal relationship with his mother, the message Lenny heard was "I am nothing." He felt lost, lonely, sad, and confused; trauma piling atop trauma. Likely out of placement options, the tribal juvenile court system emancipated Lenny at the age of seventeen. Not yet even an adult, Lenny was now on his own without the necessary life skills or supports. Lenny aged out of foster care without a family; the permanence the child welfare system aspired to provide remained elusive for Lenny.

The tribal child welfare system failed Lenny not because it was involved in his life nor because it removed him from a home that was unsafe, but rather because it perpetuated more trauma and did not help him heal. Lenny's experience in the tribal system was punctuated with transience, devoid of stability and predictability, replete with continued physical assaults and emotional unsafety, barren of connection to culture (save for one foster home), and lacking in support to meet his needs, all of which impeded, rather than enhanced, his ability to heal. These failings layered atop the decimation of resources that native reservations had endured depleting the traditional and cultural safety nets and sources of resilience that could have supported Lenny's family without systemic intervention.

Lenny moved from the reservation in South Dakota to the city of Minnesota. There he searched to be loved by giving his body to other men and drinking to dull the years of unhealed preceding and ongoing pain, culminating in a near-fatal attempt to end his life. Faced with the choice of life or death, Lenny sought out therapy for the first time.

Lenny began the hard work of his healing journey. Lenny found *safety*, recognizing that hehimself was now the greatest threat to his own well-being. Lenny *remembered and mourned* the painful trauma he had experienced. Through the therapeutic process, Lenny uncovered experiences stored in inaccessible compartments of his mind. As memories resurfaced, Lenny spent months in therapy trying to accept the reality that his mother had also sexually abused him and that he had been molested by several relatives in his mother's home. He began constructing the narrative of his past as a gay man who, as a boy, was emotionally, physically, and sexually abused by those who were supposed to care for, love, and accept him.

To further heal by embarking on the third stage of *reconnection*, Lenny's therapist suggested he connect with an elder in his native community. Remembering the sweat lodge ceremony he observed while in foster care, Lenny recalled the transformative impact the ritual seemed to impart on the participants. The elder performed a healing ceremony for Lenny. She sang an ancient Ojibwa healing song and spoke to him of the child within him. She guided Lenny by saying, "Become one with that little boy. Take his hand. That little boy taught you to survive, even when it was bad and hard. Thank that little boy for taking care of you and tell him that is it now your time to take care of him." Lenny listened and cried. The elder said, "Our creator gave us tears for a purpose. Tears cleanse our spirit."

Thus began Lenny's journey connecting with his culture, heritage, and tradition through relationships, spirituality, ceremony, and ritual, ushering in that which had been historically taken from his people as a source of strength and rebirth for himself and his community. A Dakota Two-Spirit woman took Lenny into his first sweat lodge as an adult. She taught Lenny about the purifying and renewing purposes of the sweat lodge ceremonies, how to carry the rocks in, care for the fire, and what to do before and after entering the lodge. He learned to pray first for his people and then for himself. He learned that tobacco, cedar, sweetgrass, and sage are traditional, powerful, healing medicines in his tribe and across many native cultures. He learned how to smudge himself by rolling sage into a ball, lighting it, and rubbing the fragrant smoke around his head and heart, ending with a prayer of gratitude. Lenny learned the history of Two-Spirited people. She taught Lenny how to properly carry himself first as a Dakota male and then as a Two-Spirit, imbuing Lenny with pride about the historical role of Winktas in their culture. *Reconciling with himself* after years of rejection and self-loathing, Lenny started embracing himself as Two-Spirited. In *crafting his present narrative*, decolonizing his way of thinking, and reconnecting with culture and spirituality, Lenny identified, "First, I am a Winkta. This is a term given to me by my people. Second, I am a Two-Spirit male person. And lastly, I am a gay man."

Slowly as Lenny connected to these daily rituals and beliefs, his culture and spirituality influenced his view of himself in the world. Embracing these traditions enabled Lenny to embrace himself, thereby embodying the native keystone that compassion for others begins with compassion within. As an integrated self, Lenny *deepened his connection to others.* Lenny created friendships that were based upon appropriate trust, realistic expectations, and reciprocal mutuality. Lenny found a committed partner with whom to share his life.

Lenny dedicated himself to reviving and continuing the Two-Spirit tradition as a healer and helper in finding his *survivor mission.* After completing college, Lenny received a Master's degree in counseling and psychotherapy to become a mental and chemical health therapist and formed a consulting company called Tate Topa, meaning four winds/four directions in the Dakota language. Through his work with native individuals and tribal communities on local and national levels, Lenny focuses his counseling, education, advocacy, and training on breaking the silence around the trauma that native people are experiencing, especially boys, Two-Spirits, and the LGBTQ+[42] native community. Lenny connects his people with the healing traditions of

[42] LGBTQ+ is the acronym for lesbian, gay, bisexual, transgender, queer or questioning, and more. The "+" captures the spectrum of sexual orientations and gender identities without excluding identifications.

their heritage in order to interrupt the historical intergenerational trauma his people have survived.

Lenny also advocated and assisted in the creation of the first Two-Spirit Support Group in Minneapolis with the goal of creating a safe space for Two-Spirit people to discuss and heal from trauma. Through shared experiences of being shunned in their home and communities, denied education about culture and spirituality, and excluded from traditional ceremonies, the group members access their culture and spirituality as a source of healing from rejection, self-degradation, and prejudice. Lenny also leads a Circle of Elders that focus on their loss and grief from carrying centuries-old trauma alongside lifetimes of trauma. In a talking circle formation, the elders pass a stone amongst themselves, infusing power in the hands of those speaking. By putting words to their own pain, the elders regain their role in their communities as leaders and healers, thereby helping others in return. Walking alongside his elders as they heal in communion has been the honor of Lenny's life. Lenny always carries with him the talking circle stone, along with a ball of sage, so when he is reminded of his past, he can touch the evidence of his strength. Lenny has found meaning in his suffering by believing that the creator sent him to help his people, and by giving back to the universe, Lenny heals himself through a connection to others and his culture.

As a healer to his people, his native community nominated Lenny to testify in front of the U.S. Attorney General's Committee on Violence Against Native Children in 2013. Lenny wrote his testimony from the perspective of his six-year-old self. After he finished, a Democratic Senator from North Dakota responded to Lenny, "Rest assured, Mr. Hayes, your story has been heard." The act of sharing and being heard relieved Lenny of lingering shame he did not realize he still held. Later, Lenny then shared his speech with a Two-Spirit elder whom he respected and loved. The Two-Spirit elder transformed the speech into a poem, with a particular stanza capturing Lenny's healing journey:

> . . . One day, I saw the little boy that suffered and still suffers,
> I stretched out my hand, and reached out to that little boy.

He looked up at me, sideways at first,
as if seeing a bright light that was too much to take in.
He reaches back to me and I give him my healing hand.
He gives me his pained heart.
Together we walked, talked, healed—well, healing . . .
On our path towards being a whole person.

Lenny received the gift of his own story in poetry from his beloved Two-Spirit elder. There was beauty in the poem, and there was honesty. Through that honesty, Lenny was better able to see the beauty in himself.

Lenny Hayes is an inauspicious and undistinguished name for a person whose native identity now defines his place in the world. When Lenny was born, no Two-Spirit Winkta bestowed Lenny with a native name. Now, Lenny hopes to be welcomed into a naming ceremony to receive a native name so that when he passes on, the spirits will know him by name and call out to him as he journeys from this world to the next. When Lenny does pass on to the spirit world, he will ask the creator why, as a young star, he chose parents and a family who would hurt him. For now, he will act upon the answer to his own question by continuing to give back to the universe by helping others heal in ways that took half of a lifetime for Lenny to experience.

• • •

In addition to cultural connection, *reconnection* can also predominate through human relationships.

Reconnection Through Reparation

One of the middle children of seventeen siblings, Johnny Rice "J.R." and members of his family left the racism and oppression of South Carolina in the 1950s seeking opportunity and acceptance that Maryland appeared to promise. Plentiful World War II-related jobs and the promise of greater equality spurred the great migration from the impoverished rural and segregated South to the burgeoning industrial North.[43] In Maryland, the Rice family confronted a northern

[43] Even before the Rice family arrived, Baltimore had the highest proportion of Blacks in the country's ten biggest cities, a fifth of the city. Alec MacGillis, *The Third Rail*, PLACES (April 28, 2019), https://placesjournal.org/article/the-third-rail

brand of discrimination as they looked for their new home. In outward pandering to equality yet subliminal adherence to the fallacy that separate is equal, the Rices' were prohibited from living in the new garden suburbs and initially settled in a crowded West Baltimore neighborhood. With the majority of Blacks squeezed into one and a half square miles of the city, the oppression of prejudice and racism swelled in buses, restaurants, and shops all the same, yet was disguised in the mutual benefit of avoidance. The overt hate of the South became a veiled prejudice in Baltimore.

J.R. came of age amidst this Baltimorean variety of racism and oppression. Raised among a strong southern-transplant culture valuing family, food, song, celebration, and religious reverence amidst a painful history of slavery, fragile and often precarious freedom, and societal messages of inferiority, J.R. had a dynamic personality. Upon high school graduation, J.R. married his high school sweetheart, a young woman who aspired to be a librarian. A daughter and a son, Johnny Rice II, were born upon J.R.'s return from his draft service in the Vietnam War. J.R. started a small business, a stake in the northern soil his family applauded far from their southern plantation and working-class roots.

As a young boy, Johnny experienced two sides of his father. Johnny liked when his father took him to work, admired his ability to make each person feel important, and enjoyed their engaging conversations about local politics and the latest headlines. While Johnny felt loved by his father, he also dreaded the first of each month when J.R. would take his Veteran Affairs benefits to the bar and drink from Friday through Sunday. By Sunday night, he came crashing home. Johnny watched his mother nurse his father so he would be ready for work come the start of the week. On those weekends and then during the week too, his father screamed at his mother, and many times when he hit her, Johnny or his sister would call the police. The law enforcement response of the 1970s offered little protection. Stretches of time would pass with the lights shut off in their house or with barely any food in the refrigerator next to the beer bottles. J.R.'s mother dropped out of college when managing J.R. became

---

/?gclid=EAIaIQobChMIjc21r6Pz4QIVl7bACh3CewiXEAAYASAAEgIiLPD_BwE.

unmanageable. Johnny began to love and hate his father at the same time, and eventually, the respect Johnny had cultivated for his father dissolved.

Despite the chaos and unpredictability that was often felt inside their home, Johnny's mother ensured her children arrived on time for school every day. The counterweight to his father, Johnny's mother wrapped her children in her plumage of love, support, calm, and sureness, while also making certain that other feathers fluttered around them—Boy and Girl Scouts, church and youth groups, and refuge to the Eastern Shore with their grandmother.

When Johnny was thirteen-years-old, his mother left his father. Johnny, his mother, and his sister stayed for three days in one of the first battered women's shelters in Baltimore in the late 1970s. From the shelter, the three went to stay with a relative. While they had stayed with cousins and aunts in the past, this separation became longer and ultimately the last. Johnny's parents never divorced but remained apart ever after.

As Johnny approached high school, his mother encouraged and supported him in applying to the elite Baltimore City College. Accepted, Johnny celebrated his success as a young African American man who overcome the odds in Baltimore and excelled at "City." Yet, when Johnny entered college, he chose to live with his father rather than his mother, embracing the leniency he thought his father would grant him.

The distractions in his father's homemade attending college and working two jobs overwhelming for Johnny. His father's nights were filled with alcohol, gambling, and women, and Johnny decided to move out. The evening Johnny intended to retrieve his belongings from his father's apartment, J.R., who was intoxicated, stood at the top of the stairs and shot a handgun toward his son, striking the angled ceiling inches above Johnny's head. Johnny called the police, and J.R. was arrested. The state dropped the case, and Johnny dropped his relationship with his father throughout his remaining years of college.

To commemorate his college graduation, Johnny's extended family attended a service at church, and to Johnny's surprise, J.R. was present and stood up in front of the entire congregation, and spoke:

> As my son graduates college, I need to apologize to him and my family in front of all of you. For years, I mistreated my wife, the mother of my children. Many of you have thought of me as a hardworking man who loved his family and friends. I was only partly that person. I also drank, cheated, and gambled. I hurt my wife both physically and emotionally, and my children lived in a home they feared. The harm I have caused almost destroyed my family. The choices I made were wrong. Today, my son has reached this milestone in spite of me. To my son, my daughter, and their mother, I am sorry. I have changed and will be different. To all of you, I am sorry to have added to the challenges that our community faces.

Interwoven in J.R.'s words were the processes of accountability and healing. Johnny severing ties was his father beckoned J.R.'s self-reckoning. J.R. was driven by a desire to be a better father to his son. Despite ongoing barriers such as racism and discrimination, J.R. felt more in control of his ability to make healthy and sound choices, and without the grip of alcoholism, he felt *safer.* Within this sense of safety, J.R. was able to view himself as a person who had both harmed and helped, caused trauma, and felt traumatized by his mistakes, thus incorporating an integrated, multifaceted, and truthful *self-narrative*. Providing public testimony of his truth, J.R., in front of his congregation, *renounced* the use of violence and control and vowed to stop abusing others. He took *responsibility* for the choices he made and the harm those choices caused. J.R. became a person that others sought when they needed help, and J.R. continued to heal as he helped others through their struggles. As he wove gospel into regular discourse, faith in his lasting transformation emerged from friends and family. *Reconnecting* with others through a greater *mission,* J.R. stood ready to *repair* the relationships he had damaged.

Following college, Johnny chose a career dedicated to public service, got married, and had children. He was a foster care worker in the child welfare system, worked in prisons interacting with men who used violence, and held a position at a residential treatment facility for at-risk youth. Johnny then became involved in the domestic violence movement at the Center for Urban Families (CFUF). Johnny and his colleagues developed fatherhood programs for men who used violence. Lonna Davis (discussed in chapter 8) invited Johnny to present at a conference focused on children exposed to domestic violence hosted by Futures Without Violence. After years of approaching his work from the outside, as Johnny listened to the presenters, he was hit with a realization—for the first time, he saw himself in the profiles of the children being discussed. He had never seen himself as a survivor of domestic violence, or anything for that matter. He saw himself as a child growing up in Baltimore who had a tumultuous upbringing like so many others. The experience of being exposed to domestic violence as a child now became a part of his *personal narrative* of both trauma and triumph, and the honest place from which to start *reconnecting* with his father.

Repairing their relationship became the source of Johnny's *reconnection.* J.R. and Johnny spoke about the past, both *remembering and mourning* the trauma and the resounding pain. Johnny shared his anger at feeling robbed of the childhood that he was now giving to his children. J.R. acknowledged the harm he caused and demonstrated his commitment to nonviolent and egalitarian choices through his words and actions. And, Johnny forgave his father. As Dr. Judith Herman described, "true forgiveness cannot be granted until the perpetrator has sought and earned it through confession, repentance, and restitution."[44] Johnny's offering of acceptance and reconciliation was a gift of salvation to his father, and J.R.'s reparative accountability that made the reconnection possible was the gift of healing to his son. An invitation to be a part of a documentary together on healing from violence produced by the Institute on Domestic Violence in the African American Community at the University of Minnesota was an opportunity to help others. Sharing that change is possible and that from deep accountability invaluable connections can be reborn, together J.R. and Johnny lived a shared *mission* as father and son to guide others toward healing.

Johnny's professional path took him from direct service to systems work. He worked for the Maryland Department of Human Services and served as the Victims of Crime Act and Family Violence Services Program administrator for the State of Maryland. Through his work, he witnessed that many families resisted accessing systems—law

---

[44] Herman, *supra* note 7, at 482.

enforcement, civil, criminal, social services, child welfare—because of the social control, and therefore, the lack of safety that often accompanies social help. Upon reflection, he recognized the scarcity of systems involvement when his family was living with violence and wondered if his family was better off untouched by systems. Had the calls to the police led to child welfare Hotline calls, would Johnny and his sister have maintained the closeness with their mother that they needed and avoided additional abuse if they were in foster care? If the violence happened again, would the family have reached out for help again knowing the great costs of such outreach? Would systemically imposed restrictions on contact with his children have stripped his father of motivation to change? Ultimately, would increased systems involvement have strengthened or weakened the connections that were necessary to his family's ability to heal?

Johnny spent the last three days of his father's life at his side in hospice care. As he comforted his father, Johnny thought of people who died before they had time to change. With time and commitment comes the hope that change can help repair connections that enable the hurting to heal. When his father died, Johnny was deeply grateful that his father chose to use his time to mend what he had broken.

Alchemists

Along with Lenny and Johnny whose mission drives them to help others and make communities heal and become stronger, Amita uses the art of writing and storytelling to assist others in the practice of healing. Deepening Amita's own healing, practicing reconnection steers Amita's own survivor mission, becoming an alchemist for others so they can find their own alchemy. As Amita blogged, accessing the power of words in the act of writing to formalize a narrative:

> . . . is healing, in the sense that my poetry and essay writing help me put words to violence that was unwitnessed, unspoken, unacknowledged for many years. By vomiting it up (to paraphrase James Baldwin), I am allowing others to see those most isolated and violated parts of myself, and to connect with me through my wounds. I am also allowing myself to feel my

> own emotional response to memories that I have kept at bay for decades, finally integrating them so that I may be freer and more whole.[45]

Harkening to the testimonial power that occurred within feminist collectives, Amita has created two artistic platforms in which sharing and witnessing enhance the healing of others while simultaneously archiving a concert of voices that secure the existence of trauma into the collective conscious. *Secret Survivors* was an off-Broadway performance of survivors of sexual violence who shared their stories in front of a live audience. Then through Mirror Memoirs, sixty Black, indigenous, or people of color (BIPOC) across fifteen states who identify as LGBTQ+ and who were raped or sexually assaulted as children shared their narratives on a recording. The "Mirror Memoir" interviews not only reveal the prevalence, the commonness through frequency, of childhood experiences of domestic and sexual violence but also point to systems failure and often state violence that existed in many of their lives.[46] Stories of compounded traumas—sexual assaults in schools, foster care, police stations, detention facilities, mental health hospitals—unify so many of these shared experiences. Both Secret Survivors and Mirror Memoirs serve the universal need to be witnessed, especially after trauma that "invariably involves not being seen, not being mirrored, and not being taken into account."[47]

This age-old healing tradition of storytelling that Amita recreated—speaking and hearing, recounting and reconnecting—now have explanations in neurobiology. When people tell their story *and* the listener is trustworthy, affirming, and expresses belief, mirror neurons are activated in the listener and in the storyteller alike, creating parallel physiological responses. Activated mirror neurons produce empathy in the listener and release dopamine in the storyteller's brain, which is a healing hormone to the traumatized brain. As such, the response

---

45 Amita Swadhin, *Hematopoiesis press* (June 25, 2019), http://hematopoiesispress.com/amita-swadhin.

46 At the time of this book's publication, Amita was in the process of publishing a report about the findings from Mirror Memoirs.

47 van der Kolk, *supra* note 26, at 185.

of the listener can actually trigger conditions for healing. Therefore, sharing one's narrative, the fundamental request of the child welfare system must be met with the safety of shared power, control, predictability, and responsive connection grounded in respect and nonjudgment. Unlike what Amita experienced, every interaction of a child welfare intervention is capable of mirroring healing, thereby countering the trauma and aspiring higher. Trauma-informed, strength-based, family-centered, and equity-focused child welfare interventions are the golden alchemy of enhancing the safety, stability, well-being, and healing of children and families.

Recently, Amita attended a restorative justice circle in prison with men who have committed rape or murder. Of the twelve men in the circle, nine of them spoke. Each man who spoke had been raped as a child between ages two and five. Like Amita's own father, this history does not condone the choices they made, the reactions they had that irreparably changed people's lives. But, how would their lives and the lives of their victims have been different had they experienced a healing intervention that interrupted the intergenerational perpetuation of violence? If the child welfare system enraptures families, the intervention must provide the opportunity for healing. But until then, if hurting people may hurt others, healing people help others to heal.

on the eve of
the season of grief
i weep for a world
in which more children
are treated as chattel
than as creatural
and, worse, taught to believe
they are the only ones.
i call circle with my kindred.
every breath we take
an affirmation,
every word we speak
a mirror.
our love is a force
like the fall:
alchemize despair

shed isolation
change it all.

-ritual @amitaswadhin

• • •

On September 28, 2019, in Porcupine, South Dakota, Lenny was given his Native name in a naming ceremony facilitated by an elder surrounded by his Two-Spirit community of friends, his family. Lenny received the name of Tunkan Wanagi Luta. With power in each word, this name sealed Lenny's healing journey, his spirit forever his, together unbroken to his past, present, and future. As Red Stone Ghost, Lenny's spirit feels whole.

11

No Wrong Door or No Door at All: From Fragmentation to Coordination, From Stagnation to Transformation

Families experiencing domestic violence can become involved in many systems through many different doors. No matter which door the family enters, the systemic response must provide the family with what they need. Currently, no right door exists. Child welfare interventions are still aspiring to be trauma-informed, strength-based, family-centered, and equity-focused, are surrounded by other systemic responses that are not effectively meeting the needs of families, and all of the systems responding to families experiencing domestic violence are fragmented from each other. While one system alone is typically not able to fully and sufficiently meet the needs of families experiencing domestic violence, no wrong door should exist either. In order to enhance the safety, stability, well-being, and healing of children and families, child welfare interventions must occur within a context of coordinated trauma-informed, strength-based, family-centered, and equity-focused responses to families experiencing domestic violence while also investing in responses outside of traditional systemic interventions.

The Message Behind Each Systemic Door

Isabel Rodriguez's interactions with systems only just began when she answered the door to the knocks of the child welfare investigator. Before reaching the age of twenty-five, Isabel had experienced the systems of child welfare, law enforcement, social service, criminal justice, and immigration and was cognizant of her likely involvement in civil family court at some point during Nathan's childhood. Each of these systems had its own message to Isabel about whether her experience of domestic violence deemed her blameless or blameworthy for the abuse she endured and viewed the legal significance of Nathan's exposure to domestic violence differently. A walk through each of these systemic doors with Isabel demonstrates the topography of inconsistencies in responding to families experiencing domestic violence as well as the harmful impact of systemic fragmentation.

The Child Welfare Door

By indicating Isabel for neglecting her son, the message the child welfare system sent was that the domestic violence automatically rendered Nathan a neglected child and held Isabel responsible. Nathan was deemed a victim and Isabel a perpetrator of child neglect. By ignoring Nathan's father, Isabel's choice in an abusive partner was treated as more blameworthy than Jason's choice to perpetrate abuse.

The Law Enforcement Door

Throughout the duration of Jason's abuse, Isabel did not call the police. Due to her undocumented status, calling the police could have resulted in her arrest, detention, and eventual deportation, leaving behind her U.S. citizen son.[1] And, Isabel feared Jason's

---

1 *See, Meg Townsend, Dana Hunt, Sarah Kuck, & Caity Baxter,* Law Enforcement Response to Emergency Domestic Violence Calls for Service, Final Report, Prepared for the National Institute of Justice 6-7 (Feb. 1, 2005), https://www.ncjrs.gov

retaliation.[2] Isabel's first interaction with the police occurred after she had left Jason when she went to the police station to report Jason's confession of killing their dog. Isabel told the police exactly where Jason said he had deposited Bella's severed parts; the police discovered Bella's remains, frozen in the snow. Isabel also reported to the police the physical and sexual abuse Jason committed against her. The police department did not have a specialized domestic violence or sexual assault response unit nor a partnership with a domestic violence agency. The officers did not communicate with the child welfare investigator to strategize ways to mitigate the risk of Jason's retaliation against Isabel and Nathan. Isabel felt treated like an informant rather than a teenager and a young mother who had endured trauma, victimization, and countless crimes, yet Isabel was not criminalized.[3] The police

---

/pdffiles1/nij/grants/215915.pdf. ("Battered women of immigrant status often face the additional burden of legal and social barriers to reporting. In a national survey, 67% of officials said that immigrants report crimes less often than other victims and that domestic violence was the least often reported.")

2 Isabel's resistance to calling the police is consistent with studies that identify the following reasons that domestic violence victims do not report to the police: the incident is considered private; fear of involving authorities; feelings that the police would not be able to do anything about the incident; fear of reprisal; perception of the incident as a minor crime; avoiding creating an embarrassment to family; cultural unacceptance; distrust or unfamiliarity with the criminal justice system; economic or psychological dependence; past poor interactions with the police; and impact of PTSD. *Id.* at 6.

3 Child endangerment statutes have been used to hold adult survivors criminally liable for "failing to protect" their children. Karen D. McDonald, *Michigan's Efforts to Hold Women Criminally and Civilly Liable for Failure to Protect: Implications for Battered Women*, 44 Wayne L. Rev 289, 297 (1999); *see* Massachusetts v. Lazarovich, 574 N.E.2d 340 (Mass. 1991)*;* Leticia Sierra, *Representing a Battered Women Charged with Crimes for Failing to Protect Their Children from Abusive Partners* (Sept. 1996). (unpublished manuscript, on file with the National Clearinghouse for the Defense of Battered Women). For instance, at nineteen-years-old Tondaloa Hall was convicted of "enabling child abuse" based upon the premise that she "failed to protect" her children from the man who harmed her and her children, and was sentenced to thirty years of incarceration while the person who inflicted the harm was not. Aimee Ortiz, *Mother is Freed After 15 Years in Prison for Father's Abuse,* New York Times (Nov. 8, 2019). On November 8, 2019, Ms. Hall was freed from prison after serving fifteen years behind bars. *Id.* As Ms. Hall's attorney from the American Civil Liberties Union stated "[Ms. Hall's] case, while horribly unjust, is not unique. There are still countless other women incarcerated for failing to stop the crimes of their male partners" and some of whom

did not include Nathan's exposure to domestic violence in their criminal investigation.[4]

The Criminal Justice Door

Isabel walked through the criminal justice door that remained open for four years. Following the police investigation, the state's Attorney charged Jason with four felonies: animal torture (Class 3 felony), aggravated cruelty to animals (Class 4 felony), aggravated criminal sexual assault (Class X felony), and aggravated domestic battery (Class 2 felony). Despite the innumerable times Jason physically and sexually assaulted Isabel over their relationship, Jason was charged with one count of rape and one count of strangulation—a five-year history of trauma distilled down to two prosecutable moments. Jason was in custody for twenty-three months, plead guilty to the animal cruelty charges, and received a two-year prison sentence but was released due to the time he had already served. Upon release, the judge issued a plenary Order of Protection protecting both Isabel and Nathan and prohibiting Jason from having "any contact by any means" with them.

---

received longer sentence terms than their actual abuser, a "pervasive problem" in some states. *Id.* Although criminal law is based on the delineation of roles—a defendant is not a victim and the victim is not a defendant—child endangerment statutes blur the lines between holding a victim of a crime responsible for a separate crime that is directly related to the crime that victimized her.

4 Children's exposure to domestic violence is relevant to some states' criminal codes. For instance, committing domestic violence in the presence of children can lead to enhanced sentences as a statutorily-recognized, aggravating, sentencing factor or can trigger mandatory minimum penalties. *See,* Arkansas, Arizona, California, Florida, Hawaii, Idaho, Illinois, Oklahoma, Oregon, Washington. *See also* Brown v. State, 21 S. 3d 108 (Fl. Dist. Ct. App. 2009) (because the charged acts of aggravated domestic battery and aggravated domestic assault were committed in the presence of children, the court applied a multiplier on sentencing to increase the length of the defendant's prison sentence). Prior bad acts of domestic violence are also relevant as aggravation at sentencing. *See,* People v. Reyes, 160 Cal.App.4th 246 (Cal. Ct. App. 3d Dist. 2008); People v. Brown, 77 Cal.App.4th 1324 (Cal. Ct. App. 1st Dist. Div. 2 2000); People v. Jennings, 81 Cal.App.4th 1301 (Cal. Ct. App. 1st Dist. Div. 3 2000); People v. Johnson, 77 Cal.App.4th 410 (Cal. Ct. App. 3 Dist. 2000); People v. Hoover, 77 Cal.App.4th 1020 (Cal. Ct. App. 4 Dist. Div. 2 2000); Commonwealth v. Oberle, 69 N.E.3d 993 (Mass. 2017). In Delaware, Georgia, and Utah, committing domestic violence in the presence of children is a separate crime.

While free from incarceration, the felonies for the crimes against Isabel were still pending. Even with the Order of Protection, it was hard for Isabel to feel safe because she lacked control over the course of the criminal case. As occurs across the country, she was merely a "complaining witness" and source of evidence, and the outcome was in the hands of the judge. As part of a specialized domestic violence prosecutorial unit, the assistant state's attorney and a victim-witness advocate worked with Isabel in preparation for the trial.[5] The trial took place over three days during the summer of 2018, nearly three-and-half years after Jason had been arrested. Jason waived his right to a jury trial. For the first time, Isabel would have to speak about the trauma she experienced in front of the person who inflicted that trauma, and she did so with dignity and courage. During the trial, the prosecutor asked Isabel about her undocumented status and her intentions to obtain a U-visa to live legally in the United States. At the end of the trial, the judge found Jason guilty but not of the felonies upon which he was charged. Instead, he found Jason guilty of one count of Class A misdemeanor sexual assault, expressing reluctance to find Jason guilty of an offense that required lifetime registration on the sexual offender registry. Following the judge's verdict, Jason's attorney filed a motion for a new trial based upon the reference to the U-visa in the trial. The judge granted the motion. The guilty finding was null and void.

Surmising that the judge would find Jason guilty at the second trial in the winter of 2019, Jason plead guilty to aggravated domestic battery, a Class 2 Felony. At the sentencing hearing, Isabel read a Victim Impact Statement. Standing in front of the judge, she had not been that close to Jason in four years. This time, her freedom was not at Jason's mercy. She used the power of her words—her story—to promote a pathway for change and growth, rather than to hurt him as he had hurt her. When she finished, the judge turned to Isabel and said, "Ms. Rodriguez, I have listened to you twice and both times, I believed you." The judge then sentenced Jason to two years of sexual

[5] The guiding philosophy of victim-witness programs is that victims should be afforded their place in the system, informed about the status of the case, supported as the legal case proceeds, and referred to outside agencies when additional help is needed.

offender probation. Even though Jason received a more restrictive sentence for killing an animal than nearly killing a human, Isabel viewed the sentence as a pathway to accountability if Jason chose to walk through that open door. The criminal justice system deemed Isabel a victim, focused on Jason, and, otherwise ignoring their son, protected him under the Order of Protection.

The Immigration Door

Isabel is a DREAMer—a young undocumented immigrant who was brought to the United States as a child, who has lived and gone to school here, and who identifies as a Mexican-American.[6] Isabel would have been eligible for Deferred Action for Childhood Arrivals (DACA) status,[7] but the program's short lifespan covered the years of Jason's abuse when Isabel's focus was monopolized by surviving and parenting.[8] Although the DACA door had closed, Isabel's cooperation in the criminal justice system opened the door to another immigration remedy.

Created by the Victim of Trafficking and Violence Protection Act of 2000, a U-visa provides lawful status to noncitizen crime victims who assist or are willing to assist with investigating or prosecuting the crimes committed against them.[9] On the day Jason was sentenced,

---

6 The term DREAMer originated from the DREAM Act—Development, Relief, and Education for Alien Minors Act—which was introduced to but never passed in Congress. The DREAM Act would have granted permanent legal status to qualifying people who came to the United States as children and who made their lives here.

7 DACA's more limited program provided temporary relief to nearly 800,000 individuals, many of whom hailed from Mexico, to obtain work authorization, apply for financial aid for college, and be protected from deportation for two years. *DACA and Dream Act 101*, World Relief (Sept. 7, 2017), https://worldrelief.org/blog/daca-and-dream-act-101?gclid=EAIaIQobChMI5PuC842I5QIVj8DACh1q_g3_EAAYASAAEgLrD_D_BwE.

8 The DACA program was started by President Barak Obama's administration on June 15, 2012. Eligible immigrants who were born on or after June 16, 1981, arrived in the United States before the age of sixteen, and have lived in the United States since June 15, 2007. On September 5, 2017, President Donald Trump announced the termination of DACA.

9 The main purpose of the U-visa is to encourage undocumented crime victims to help law enforcement investigate and prosecute crimes without fear of being deported. *Legal Information-Federal-Immigration*, National Network to End Domestic

Isabel was finally able to submit her U-visa application to the U.S. Citizenship and Immigration Services, the law enforcement certification signed by the criminal judge in hand. If granted, Isabel could become a lawful permanent resident, a Green Card holder.

The U-visa process assigned Isabel the status of a crime victim worthy of only conditional permission to stay in this country. Crossing illegally into the United States when Isabel was four-years-old could deem Isabel ineligible. Processing Isabel's U-visa application could take up to five years or more and there is a 10,000 cap on U-visa issuances per year.[10] Isabel lacks any legal status while her application is pending and cannot legally work. For at least five more years, Isabel will face the uncertainty of being detained or deported, the fear of being separated from her son reoccurring.

The Protection Order Door

The Order of Protection requiring Jason to stay away from Isabel and Nathan would be in effect for two years following the closure of the criminal case.[11] Nathan was a protected party without needing to show particularized past abuse, harm, or risk to him.[12] Only the respondent, like Jason, can violate the orders that restrict his behavior, and violating the Order of Protection could result in a separate criminal offense. The petitioner, such as the survivor of domestic violence like Isabel, cannot violate the Order of Protection. Although a protective order is only a piece of paper, Isabel believed that the order would deter Jason from contacting her or Nathan.[13] Isabel felt safer,

---

Violence (Oct. 6, 2019), https://www.womenslaw.org/laws/federal/immigration/u-visa-laws-crime-victims/basic-info-and-definitions. *Id.*

10 As of January 2018, U.S. Customs and Immigration Services were reviewing U-Visa applications filed in August of 2014. *Id.*

11 Such orders vary by name across the states. Judges can issue Orders of Protection as part of a criminal case or existing civil case, and survivors can seek a civil Order of Protection as a separate proceeding. A restraining order is often conflated with Orders of Protection, but they are separate remedies with their own set of eligibility and relief.

12 *See*, Rodriguez v. Zavala, 398 P.3d 1071 (Wash 2017) (The mother was awarded a domestic violence protection order for herself and her children, even though one child was not present during the father's assaults against the mother).

13 The decision to seek an Order of Protection should rest with the person who has experienced abuse. Deciding to pursue an Order of Protection involves thoughtful consideration of the benefits and costs of both petitioning and obtaining an Order

even though Orders of Protection are inconsistently enforced[14] and law enforcement agencies are not held liable for failing to enforce their requirements.[15]

The Social Services Door

Isabel first connected with a domestic violence agency that specifically served Latinx women. Although Isabel identifies as Mexicana, the cultural foundation and values that this organization ascribed to felt too traditional to Isabel, and the door to her healing journey did not open there. Isable was determined to find a pathway to overcome the trauma she endured, Benefiting from the richness of resources in the dense urban environment in which she lived, Isabel's school counselor referred her to another domestic violence agency. There Isabel found a connection with her counselor, also a Latina. Feeling safe through counseling, Isabel created a self-narrative of both pain and triumph.

The Domestic Relations Door

Hoping to prolong the inevitable, Isabel resisted applying for public benefits because the state would initiate child support proceedings against Jason. When the criminal case closes, Isabel anticipates that Jason may take legal action to see his son, thus ushering Isabel and

---

of Protection. The survivor may feel that the Order of Protection will likely deter future abuse and provide her and her children with needed remedies. The survivor may also fear retaliation or escalated abuse as a result of taking this action against the person who committed the qualifying "abuse."

[14] The Illinois Coalition Against Domestic Violence issued a report documenting that the "promise of safety and security provided by Orders of Protection are consistently and uniformly broken across the state." *Survivors' Access to Safety is Not Fully Available,* Illinois Coalition Against Domestic Violence (Fall 2019), http://cm20-s3ilcadv1.s3.amazonaws.com/ResourceFiles/cf448aa84ab44ced9f617de885a4f5d2SurvivorAccessToSafetyNotFullyAvail.Sept2019.pdf.

[15] The U.S. Supreme Court held that the police department that did not respond to the requirements of a protective order did not violate the constitutional rights of Jessica Gonzalez and her three deceased daughters, who were kidnapped and killed by their father who was prohibited from coming within one hundred feet of them except during designated visits; Justices Ruth Bader Ginsberg and John Paul Stevens dissented from the 7-2 decision. Town of Castle Rock v. Gonzalez, 545 U.S. 748 (2005). Castle Rock v. Gonzalez, Oyez (Oct. 7, 2019), https://www.oyez.org/cases/2004/04-278; *See* Home Truth (Adequate Images, Independent Television Service, Latino Public Broadcasting 2017).

Nathan into the domestic relations system. There, Isabel would face gender bias that infiltrates domestic relations proceedings such as the expectation of perfectionism from mothers that causes them to fall from grace for choosing an abusive partner yet rewards abusive fathers for expressing interest in their children.[16] In practicality, if Jason successfully completes probation, including the sex offender program, and when the Order of Protection expires, he likely will be allowed contact with his son. The existence of domestic violence alone is often not enough to restrict or condition visitation. Instead, a specific finding that Jason endangered or poses a risk to Nathan would be required.[17] Although Nathan was never harmed, Isabel is prepared to advocate for therapeutic visitation or visitation at a supervised visitation center to ensure Nathan's safety and well-being, along with her own.

No Right Door

As systemic doors opened and closed, Isabel's family received mixed messages. As Isabel, Nathan, and Jason experienced,adult and child survivors and those who use violence and coercive control are often viewed inconsistently depending upon which systemic door they enter. Isabel was deemed a perpetrator in the child welfare system, a victim in the criminal system, in need of protection through the Order of protection, quasi-deserving in the immigration system, and likely the lesser of two evils in the domestic relations system. Nathan's exposure to Jason's violence constituted per se neglect in the child welfare system, justified protection with an Order of Protection without particularized harm, and did not impact the criminal case, yet to place conditions on Jason's future contact with Nathan, a domestic relations judge would have to find that Jason endangered Nathan. Jason was ignored in the child welfare system, was designated as a perpetrator of abuse in the criminal case, was the subject of restrictions through the Order of Protection, and has low hurdles to overcome if he wants to see his son.

---

16 Melissa L. Berger, *The (In)Visibility of Motherhood in Family Court Proceedings*, 36 N.Y.U. Rev. L. & Soc. Change 555, 555 (2012).

17 Massachusetts 208 § 31A; *See* Montana § 40-4-218; North Dakota § 14-09-29; Oklahoma 43 § 112.2; Texas § 153.004; Pennsylvania § 5323.

Harm has and could further befall Isabel's family from these contradictory messages that led to splintered responses.[18] The requirements of the U-visa caused a mistrial in the first criminal trial against Jason where Isabel bravely testified. Isabel will have to contend with the indicated finding of neglect if Jason files a petition for custody or visitation in the domestic relations system. Most of these systemic responses impeded Isabel's healing in some way. The child welfare intervention caused her additional trauma by being threatening and punitive, stripping her of control, and deeming her a "bad" mother. The criminal system was a lengthy process that forced her to encounter the person who abused her nearly every month for four years and over who she also had little control. The immigration system generates a fear of deportation as she waits. None of the systems were trauma-informed, family-centered, strength-based, or equity-centered in philosophy or practice. Throughout four years of systems involvement, the Order of Protection did make Isabel feel safer, and she was proud of herself for using her voice in the criminal case against Jason. The system that brought Isabel the most healing was the social service system by partnering with her to meet her needs as a survivor and as a mother. Nathan's needs continue to be met in the most immediate concentric circles around his life—his family, his extended family, and his community. So far, none of the systems have become pathways for Jason's accountability.

As Isabel stands at the conclusion of closed systemic doors and at the potential precipice of future systemic involvement, she has constructed her own interpretation of her experiences, shifting the systemic messages she has received. As she tells herself, she was harmed but is a strong, capable, and dedicated mother; she has the ability to enable Nathan to ascend above and through the adversity of his young life; she and her son are deserving of the safety, stability, well-being,

---

[18] Lawyer, professor, and Director of the Domestic Violence Clinic at Georgetown Law, Deborah Epstein further captured the reality of Isabel's system odyssey when she described, "fragmented court systems are especially devastating for victims of domestic violence because they are often involved in many different proceedings in different courts stemming from a single incident or pattern of abuse, leading to a time-consuming, confusing, and overwhelming process. In this system, it is unlikely that victims will receive the necessary protection or services because of the numerous obstacles." Deborah Epstein, *Effective Intervention in Domestic Violence Cases: Rethinking the Roles of Prosecutors, Judges, and the Court System*, 11 YALE J.L. & FEMINISM. 3, 25 (1999).

and healing she has ushered into their lives, and she believes in the potential of change such that Jason is neither a demon nor a saint, but rather someone who can decide to make healthy and loving choices with the opportunity to learn and grow. Coordinated responses to domestic violence grounded in trauma-informed, strength-based, family-centered, and equity-focused principles and practice could translate these self-told messages into systems involvement that contributes to, rather than detracts from, the safety, stability, well-being, and healing of adult and child survivors of domestic violence, and the accountability of those who use violence and coercive control.

Strategies to Creating No Wrong Doors or No Doors at All

The intersection of domestic violence and child welfare does not exist in a vacuum. If healing from domestic violence needs reconnection, then so too must responses to families require connection within healing systems and to communities. Child welfare interventions that are trauma-informed, strength-based, family-centered, and equity-focused can lead by example for other systems, and surrounding systems that are not effective dilute the impact of child welfare interventions that are striving to meet the needs of families. Because complete and seamless systemic and community coordination around domestic violence seems illusory, infusing systems with trauma-informed, strength-based, family-centered, and equity-focused elements is a manageable step toward better meeting families' needs of safety, stability, well-being, and healing. One strategy alone will not solve the problem of systemic fragmentation nor will the simultaneous implementation of all the strategies eliminate systemic inconsistencies. Rather, communities can engage with one or more of the following strategies, all relevant to the child welfare system, as ways to enhance the coordination of the community's response to domestic violence, thereby reinforcing the benefits of effective child welfare interventions. These recommendations would be considered harm-reducing efforts by striving to reduce the negative impact on families while aspiring higher.

It is also critical to consider ways to shrink systemic interventions that have caused grave harm historically and contemporaneously. Strategizing ways to minimize child welfare interventions must coincide with an investment in resources outside of traditional systems and within families and communities. These strategies find alignment with abolitionist approaches to the child welfare system.

Systemic reform and radical transformation find moments of opportunity based upon the social, political, and historical climates both nationally and locally in which they arise. A one-size-fits- all approach will not work, just as it has never worked for the families themselves. Reform and transformation will vary from north to south, east to west, and everywhere in between. As such, both harm-reductionist and abolitionist-leaning strategies are shared here to provide possibilities for communities. Tackling centuries of patriarchy, burdened histories, and entrenched practice can begin with smaller, less daunting yet significant steps toward greater cohesion that fuse trauma-informed, strength-based, family-centered, and equity-centered elements between systems—the movement toward greater integration, to less broken responses, to no wrong doors for families to open or enter, or to not opening systemic doors at all. Some of the suggested strategies may feel at odds with another, some may appear to grow systems rather than reduce them, but all of these strategies are options, none inferior to the other, that communities can consider in isolation or in a tiered approach to reform and radical transformation of the child welfare system and its surroundings.

Harm Reduction through Greater Coordination

A Consistent Approach to Child Advocacy

Adults often become the mouthpieces for children, thereby contributing to the field of child advocacy.[19] That which is conveyed on behalf of children is determined by the assigned role of the child advocate and framed by what the child wishes, what is determined to be in the child's best interest, or both. No matter the framework, all child advocacy in any system should be grounded in family and community advocacy.

---

[19] Appointed counsel for children began in 1967 as a result of the U.S. Supreme Court case of *In Re Gault. In re Gault,* 387 U.S. 1 (1967). This decision provided attorneys for youth involved in juvenile delinquency proceedings. Ever since *Gault,* child advocates have grappled with the complexities of representing children.

Stacey Platt is a public interest lawyer who has been a child advocate in her decades-long legal career.[20] In working with families, including those experiencing domestic violence across systems, Stacey has anchored her child advocacy work in family and community advocacy. Child advocacy as family and community advocacy does not ignore the specific needs of children. Rather, Stacey's orientation as a child advocate sources children's needs in the places in which their needs should be met—in their families and communities—and strives to support children in families and communities with services and resources without overstepping. Child advocacy rooted in family and community advocacy, as demonstrated by the breadth and consistent approach of Stacey's career, can be a bridge between systems, a common element that decreases divergence, preserves a child's connection to that which they need for safety, stability, well-being, and healing and better meets of the needs of families.

A Uniform Framework for Domestic Violence Decision-Making

Because domestic violence inconsistently impacts systemic responses, a uniform framework for domestic violence decision-making is needed. Through the Battered Women's Justice Project,[21] Loretta Frederick and Gabrielle Davis have created a promising tool that could streamline decision-making about domestic violence among systems.[22] The SAFeR tool was born from the concerns of domestic violence advocates that adult survivors were losing custody of their children in private court cases and to the state through child welfare

[20] Stacey Platt is currently a clinical professor in the Civitas ChildLaw Center at Loyola University Chicago School of Law.

[21] The Battered Women's Justice Project (BWJP) began in 1994 as a federally created resource center on domestic violence, remains the national resource center on civil and criminal justice responses to intimate partner violence, and partners with the National Clearinghouse for the Defense of Battered Women to provide assistance to intimate partner violence victims charged with crimes and their defense teams. *About the Battered Women's Justice Project,* BATTERED WOMEN'S JUSTICE PROJECT (Oct. 13, 2019), https://www.bwjp.org/about-bwjp.html.

[22] The SAFeR approach has not yet been studied in the domestic relations context nor for its efficacy in other systems, yet the West Virginal Coalition Against Domestic Violence is piloting a version of SAFeR to be used by child welfare workers.

cases. In 2009, upon the request of the Office of Violence Against Women, Loretta and Gabrielle created a tool that would enable systems players to "think smarter" about domestic violence.

Central to making "smarter" decisions about domestic violence is bridging the gap between the lived experiences and institutional lives of families. In that way, systems become less of paternalistic impositions and more of partnered conduits toward greater safety, stability, well-being, and healing. The SAFeR approach also responds to the shortcomings of bright-line rules and presumptions that have not served adult and child survivors as intended and rather encourages information gathering, critical thinking, and problem-solving.[23]

The four parts of SAFeR include Screening, Assessing, Focusing on the Effects, and Responding to the Abuse. The tool includes detailed worksheets to guide systems players in answering the following questions:

Is abuse an issue here?
What is actually going on?
Why does it matter?
What can be done about it?[24]

The SAFeR approach does not dictate what decisions should be made but rather guides thinking, building individual and systemic capacity to think smarter about families experiencing domestic violence and their cases. Utilizing a tool to situate an understanding of people's real lives will lead to more effective decisions and if used across systems, will contribute to increased coordination and consistency.

Unified Family Courts with One-Judge to One-Family

Judge Katherine Tennyson centered her judgeship on helping people solve problems because in solving problems, peoples' needs are

[23] In the 1990s, many states became convinced about the harm that domestic violence posed to children and amended their domestic relations laws to implement presumptions against sole and joint custody for fathers who perpetrated domestic violence against the children's mothers. As an unintended consequence, domestic relations judges became reluctant to find the existence of domestic violence if it required them to presume the father should not be custodial.

[24] SAFeR, Battered Women's Justice Project (2017), https://www.bwjp.org/safer-worksheet-combined-113018.pdf.

met. Judge Tennyson was able to do so in a unified family court. A unified family court is a single court system with comprehensive subject-matter jurisdiction over all cases involving children and families, including family law, child welfare, delinquency, probate, and domestic violence. Existing in jurisdictions in at least eighteen states,[25] one door exists for families to open. Within a unified family court, a "one-family, one-judge" approach is considered best practice by the American Bar Association[26] and the National Council of Juvenile and Family Court Judges because one judge hears all of the issues related to a family over the life of their systems involvement with a holistic and longitudinal perspective.[27,28] Being in front of one judge in a system that can resolve cases more efficiently reduces the trauma associated with repeatedly coming to court, regularly facing the person who caused pain and fear, the unpredictability of different courtrooms, and repeating one's story.[29] Unified family courts with one-family, one-judge models decrease fragmentation amongst systems because many of the systems have come together in one courtroom with a singular judge.

Because Judge Tennyson would remain with a family from "cradle to grave," preserving judicial integrity, impartiality, knowledge, training, and the level of practice is increasingly important. As the assigned judge, Judge Tennyson fostered a culture of learning that continually sought new ways to meet the needs of families.[30] By being

---

25 Andrew Schepard & James W. Bozzomo, *Efficiency, Therapeutic Justice, Mediation, and Evaluation: Reflections on a Survey of Unified Family Courts*. 37 Fam. L.Q. 3, 333-359 (2003).

26 The American Bar Association started the Unified Family Court Coordinating Council in 2002. Herbert J. Belgrad, *An Introduction to Unified Family Courts from the American Bar Association's Perspective,* American Bar Association 37 Family Law Quarterly 329 (Fall 2003).

27 *Project ONE Key Principles,* National Council of Juvenile and Family Court Judges (July 2012), http://www.ncjfcj.org/sites/default/files/Project_ONE_Key_Principles_July_2012.pdf. Project ONE advances the use of effective multi-system holistic responses to youth and families.

28 By 2008, twelve states employed a one-family, one judge method. Barbara A. Babb, *Reevaluating Where We Stand: A Comprehensive Survey of America's Family Justice Systems*, 46 Fam. Ct. Rev. 230, 234 (2008).

29 *See* Jessica Pearson, *Court Services: Meeting the Needs of Twenty-First-Century Families,* 33 FAM. L.Q. 617, 629 (1999).

30 For instance, through the Family Court Enhancement Project of the National Council of Juvenile and Family Court Judges, Judge Tennyson and her colleagues

able to get to know the parties, Judge Tennyson was able to identify areas of strength and promise that were often masked by the struggles that brought them into the courthouse. From her comprehensive vantage, Judge Tennyson was able to identify both gaps in services and existing supports that warranted additional investment, using her judicial leadership to ensure that what families needed was available in their communities.[31] In doing so, unified family courts can incarnate and generate therapeutic justice.

Unified Human Services and Child Welfare Agencies

Being a door that meets the needs of families is challenging when the child welfare system is separated from other human service supports. Unified governmental departments that control both human services and child welfare agencies can enable families to seamlessly obtain the resources and services they need. In many jurisdictions, child welfare is administratively housed within the same agency that operates a variety of other concrete human services (e.g., public benefits) such as Temporary Assistance to Needy Families (TANF), Medicaid, Supplemental Nutrition Assistance Program (SNAP), child care supplements, and employment supports. At the same time, families eligible for human services are able to receive support that mitigates

received technical assistance in crafting custody and visitation orders involving families who experience domestic violence. The judges also received training on the intersection of domestic violence and child welfare that was guided by the Greenbook principles and recommendations.

31 Judges, for instance, can attend Domestic Violence Coordinating Council meetings in order to discuss conflicts they have observed between probation requirements and the rules of batterer intervention programs, or begin a task force to explore implementing a co-location program of domestic violence advocates in child welfare offices. Judges and state court systems can also create resources and services, like the New York State Courts that created a literacy program for children or the Spokane County Courthouse's free child-care clinic for families at court hearings. Press Release, New York State Unified Court System, NY Launches Nation's First Court-Based LiteracyProgram (Dec. 18, 2000), https://www.nycourts.gov/ip/justiceforchildren/PDF/projectliteracy.pdf; *See also,* Municipal Court of Seattle, *Court Resource Center, at* https://www.seattle.gov/courts/programs-and-services/community-resource-center (last visited Oct. 16,2019); Spokane County Washington, *Children's Waiting Room, at* https://www.spokanecounty.org/471/Childrens-Waiting-Room (last visited March 16, 2021).

the likelihood of becoming child welfare involved. Director David Berns was able to achieve significant reform in El Paso County, Colorado through integrated human and child welfare services. David orientated himself in the philosophy that poverty, the work of human services, and safety, the work of child welfare, were connected.

In March 1997, David became the director of the struggling El Paso County Department of Human Services (DHS), which oversaw public benefits and child welfare and passed money to social service agencies, structurally mirroring the common co-occurrence of poverty and struggles, like domestic violence, initiating child welfare involvement.[32] David observed that little difference existed between the families served in the economic assistance programs and in child welfare; instead what differed was the door through which they entered the system or which incident brought them to DHS' attention. Through either door, David's strategy put the client—the individual or the family—at the center, finding out what they needed, delivering on those needs, bolstering natural supports, and being as least intrusive as possible.

Practically, David harnessed the flexibility within DHS to invest in families in the front-end in ways they needed rather than in a one-size-fits-all approach at the back-end. TANF funds could be used for a wide range of needs and were used as the glue of child welfare family preservation services on which traditional child welfare funding could not be spent. No matter the door that initiated their involvement, a DHS-involved family would have one comprehensive plan that addressed issues related to poverty (i.e., stability) and safety, as well as well-being and healing. DHS created over seventy new initiatives within three months, including kinship services for grandparents, daycare assistance, substance abuse treatment, and domestic violence programs, thereby diverting families away from

[32] David was hired to reclaim a sinking ship. The county-run child welfare department was experiencing rising caseloads of children placed in foster care and a ballooning child welfare budget; families were not getting what they needed, and the county was spending a lot of money to fail. As David reflected, "If we could keep children safe, increase permanency and strengthen families, we would save money because good outcomes are cheaper than the bad outcomes they had come to expect." Esther Scott, *Child Welfare Services in El Paso County, Colorado: Where Human Services and the Courts Meet*, HARVARD UNIVERSITY, KENNEDY SCHOOL OF GOVERNMENT, CASE PROGRAM, C16-03-1702.0, 4 (2003).

nonvoluntary juvenile court involvement where flexibility was sacrificed for mandated compliance. Coordination evolved into integration such that, as David described, "DHS economic assistance programs became the primary prevention program for child welfare, and child welfare became an antipoverty program." Families could get what they needed without being involved in the protracted juvenile court system, and the child welfare system was no longer the only or last net available to catch families in need.

The reform of the El Paso County DHS received national attention and was further spotlighted as a selected Greenbook Demonstration site (discussed in chapter 3). As David opined, "It is hard to improve practice around domestic violence in child welfare systems when there is no foundation of flexibility, collaboration among systems and agencies, understanding that child safety is linked to adult safety and broader aspects of stability and well-being, and family-centered practice. Each of these components is necessary for improved child welfare practice with families experiencing domestic violence."

Family Justice Centers

During Isabel's systemic trek, she opened door after door of separated systems, cumbersomely traversing both the geography between and procedures behind each of those doors. Recognizing the burdens in navigating many systems, Casey Gwinn (discussed in chapter 4) as the Deputy City Attorney of San Diego observed that survivors of domestic violence could be better served by going to one place to access assistance.[33] Born of the idea for a co-located multi-disciplinary service model for domestic violence survivors, the first Family Justice Center opened in 2002 in San Diego, and now there are over forty Family Justice Centers across the country. Family Justice Centers provide one door as a gateway to multiple systems housed under one roof.

The largest, most comprehensive Family Justice Center is in Milwaukee, Wisconsin, and carries the name of the Sojourner Family

[33] *History,* Family Justice Center Alliance (Oct. 14, 2019), https://www.familyjusticecenter.org/about-us/history/. In 2003, President George W. Bush created the President's Family Justice Center Initiative, which allocated $20 million to create fifteen Family Justice Centers around the country. *Id.* The Family Justice Center Alliance began in 2006 to provide assistance to supporting and developing Family Justice Centers nationally and internationally. *Id.*

Peace Center. Sojourner is rooted in the theory of change that enhanced collaboration with partners and families that provide seamless, cohesive experiences that will promote optimal healing and well-being for children and adults impacted by violence.[34] Sojourner opened its doors in late 2015, and in 2017 served over 11,300 clients like Isabel, Nathan, and Jason.

Clients of Sojourner typically see an average of four partners within the building.[35] At Sojourner, Isabel could have met with the police, the prosecutor, someone from the Order of Protection clinic, a legal aid lawyer, and a domestic violence advocate. With Isabel's informed consent, all of the partners could have met together to share information, minimizing the repetition of Isabel telling her story over and over. Isabel could have attended individual and group domestic violence counseling and together with Nathan, they could have participated in the Child Witness to Domestic Violence program. She could have considered moving into the shelter with Nathan, where half of the fifty-four beds in twenty-one rooms are occupied by children. Isabel could have met with a nutritionist and practiced yoga and meditation to reconnect her mind and body. Jason could enter the building through a separate door and attend a batterer intervention program. If Jason was ever awarded visitation with Nathan, the visits could occur at Sojourner's supervised visitation center. Continually assessing the advantages and disadvantages of centralization, Sojourner includes the entire family in its dual mission of intervention and prevention of violence in families and communities through partnership with systems and families themselves.

Domestic Violence Coordinating Councils, Task Forces, and Multi-Disciplinary Teams

In 2013, the first symbol to create a powerful, visual way to express support for ending domestic violence and sexual assault was created and proffered by the NO MORE campaign—a blue circle with a

---

[34] Dr. Erin Schubert, *Hope Lives Here: Impact of the Family Peace Center*, SOJOURNER FAMILY PEACE CENTER 4 (Spring 2018).

[35] Sojourner chose not to co-locate Milwaukee County Child Protection Services because the founders did not want Sojourner to be a source of trauma, a place where children could be removed from their parents.

hole in the middle. NO MORE has become the largest public awareness campaign about domestic and sexual violence. Nearly 1,200 organizations and 75,500 individuals have joined NO MORE, over 300 schools have NO MORE groups, and over thirty local NO MORE initiatives have begun. Manifesting the visionary tagline of "together we can end domestic violence and sexual assault" requires the involvement and coordination of individuals and systems because domestic violence has both roots and solutions in communities.

Consistent with the NO MORE message, coordinating councils, task forces, and multi-disciplinary teams bring together a vast array of community stakeholders in the ecosystem of those who interact with families in order to both address domestic violence directly and incorporate domestic violence into the perspectives of other initiatives. Domestic violence- specific, coordinating councils exist in cities across the country such as in Baltimore, Kansas City, and San Diego.[36] Domestic violence has been incorporated into the priorities of the monthly, multi-focused Lake County Stakeholders Meeting in Illinois led by the director of a holistic child welfare program. Across states, domestic violence advocates have become involved in advocacy efforts to increase the minimum wage because enhanced employment viability has a tangible benefit for adult survivors of domestic violence. In Florida, the co-located domestic violence advocates with the Department of Children and Families convene multi-disciplinary teams that meet to discuss the specific needs of individual families when the child welfare system alone cannot meet the panoply of needs without the involvement of other community partners and access to concrete supports.

As captured by Alaska's NO MORE's post on social media, "Domestic violence is everyone's business. We are all part of the solution."

Domestic Violence Fatality Review

This book conveys the experiences of adults and children who have survived the perils of domestic violence. Yet survival is not the fate

[36] Sandra J. Clark, Martha R. Burt, Margaret M. Schulte, & Karen E. Maguire, *Coordinated Community Responses to Domestic Violence in Six Communities: Beyond the Justice System,* URBAN INSTITUTE (Oct. 1, 1996), http://www.urban.org/sites/default/files/publication/70271/406727-Coordinated-Community-Responses-to-Domestic-Violence-in-Six-Communities.pdf.

of all people victimized by domestic violence. Nearly half of female murder victims are killed by their intimate partners.[37] Seventy-two percent of all murder-suicides are perpetrated by intimate partners. Nearly 1,000 women are killed by their intimate partners each year in the United States, contributing to an average of 137 women killed *each day* across the world.[38] For every woman killed in the United States, nine, like Isabel, are almost killed.[39] Domestic violence not only predicts over half of the nation's mass shootings, but more than half of the mass shootings *are* domestic violence shootings.[40] Femicide, suicide-femicide, and familicide have become hallmarked casualties of domestic violence-related homicides. This book is dedicated to the memory of two such people behind these statistics, A.K. and V.K., a mother and child who lost their lives at the hands of an abusive partner and father.

Unable to consent post-mortem to the sharing of their experiences, the information conveyed here is in the public record. A.K. emigrated from Poland to the United States seeking a life of promise. She met M.K. and their romance was quickly filled with violence. They had a daughter, V.K. When V.K. was one-year-old, she was rushed from daycare to the hospital after having a seizure and becoming unconscious. The child welfare system removed V.K. from both of her parents, and she was placed in foster care. The person who caused her injuries remained unproven. A.K. and M.K. separated. After two years in foster care, V.K. was returned to her loving and devoted mother, and the juvenile court case closed shortly thereafter. A few years later, A.K. and M.K. reunited. In 2014, M.K. stabbed A.K. and V.K. to death, nearly decapitating A.K. and sending a knife through V.K.'s back. In

---

37 Olga Khazan, *Nearly Half of All Murdered Women are Killed by Romantic Partners*, The Atlantic (Jul. 20, 2017), https://www.theatlantic.com/health/archive/2017/07/homicides-women/534306/ (reporting on a 2017 report from the Centers for Disease Control, updating the previous understanding that one in three homicides of women are committed by intimate partners); *See*, *Domestic Violence*, National Coalition Against Domestic Violence https://assets.speakcdn.com/assets/2497/domestic_violence2.pdf (citing a study that one in three homicides of women are committed by intimate partners) (hereinafter "NACDV").

38 Caren Lissner, *US Domestic Violence Murder Rate Rise* (Oct. 11, 2018) https://www.ozy.com/acumen/us-domestic-violence-murder-rate-rises/89868/.

39 *Id.*

40 *Id.*

police custody, M.K. confessed to the murders as well as to causing V.K.'s injuries when she was a baby. What could have prevented this thirty-four-year-old mother and her seven-year-old daughter from becoming a statistic of domestic violence fatality?

Domestic violence fatality review aims to answer this question by focusing on improving systemic and community responses to domestic violence. Nearly 200 domestic violence fatality review teams (DVFRT) are in operation.[41] A DFVRT is a multiagency and multidisciplinary group that engages in the deliberative process of identifying domestic violence-related deaths (homicide and suicide) and near-deaths;[42] tracing prior systemic interventions to examine barriers to safety, justice, and self-determination; locating systemic and community gaps; considering alternate and more effective systemic responses in order to avert future fatalities; and developing recommendations for greater coordinated community prevention and initiatives to reduce the occurrence, frequency, and severity of domestic violence. The work of DVFRT is domestic violence prevention at its core. The state in which the lives and deaths of A.K. and V.K. occurred passed legislation in 2021 to begin a statewide domestic violence review initiative.[43]

Lessons learned from reviewing the fatalities of A.K. and V.K. could impact and save the lives of mothers like Isabel. For instance, a DVFRT may identify that nonsupportive child welfare responses contributed to the deaths of A.K. and V.K. The DVFRT may recommend against holding nonoffending parents neglectful in the child welfare system because inappropriately assigning responsibility to them without holding perpetrators solely responsible serves as a

---

[41] *A Wealth of Knowledge*, The National Domestic Violence Fatality Review Initiative (Oct. 13, 2019), https://ndvfri.org/resources/getting-started/.

[42] DVFRT membership should be inclusive and expansive, including: survivors, family members and friends, an attorney general, legislators, prosecutors, law enforcement, public benefits representatives, medical examiners/coroners, emergency medicine physicians, nurses, mental health service providers, victim advocates, judiciary/court personnel, animal control officers, public defender/defense attorneys, legal aid lawyers, employers/business community members, educators/school representatives, child welfare administrators, probation and parole officers, batterer intervention program professionals, housing authorities, substance abuse treatment specialists, faith leaders, researchers/evaluators, and community members.

[43] Domestic Violence Fatality Review Act, PA 100-0520 (2021).

license to escalate abuse and leaves adult survivors in a desert of support accentuating their isolation. Addressing a system's punitive response and refusal to offer support as fodder for increased violence and lethality would improve the child welfare system's subsequent responses to families like Isabel, Nathan, and Jason.

Reduction and Investment in the Direction of Abolitionism

The Threshold of Equity

An unbroken system must be equitable.

The overrepresentation and disparate treatment of communities of color,[44] women, and families living in poverty in the child welfare system is so ubiquitous as to lull us into expectance and so pervasive that gravity overwhelms remedy. Standstills, deadlocks, and perpetuation is the snare of inequality and inequity—it tricks us into believing that oppression is self-evident, that undoing itself unravels the fabric that keeps us intact. Indeed, the face of the "child welfare system is the reason Americans have tolerated its destructiveness."[45] The discriminatory intersection of race, poverty, and gender in the child welfare system exists in the context of white privilege, individual and systemic discrimination, and implicit bias. In the face of grave discrimination, overrepresentation, and disparity, we must be willing to open a door to a different reality.[46]

The disproportionality and disparity for families of color in the child welfare system demand specific attention. Disproportionality is the underrepresentation or overrepresentation of a racial or ethnic

---

[44] Professor Dorothy Roberts, in her seminal book *Shattered Bonds: The Color of Child Welfare* concludes that ". . . the system designed to protect children remains one of the most segregated institutions in the country." DOROTHY ROBERTS, SHATTERED BONDS: THE COLOR OF CHILD WELFARE (2002).

[45] *Id.* at 17.

[46] *See, upEND*, CENTER FOR THE STUDY OF SOCIAL POLICY, https://cssp.org/our-work/project/upend/. The upEND movement is about "ending the current child welfare system as we know it; it's about the abolition of child welfare through the creation of new, anti-racist structures and practice to keep children safe and protected in their homes. It is about changing our approaches to family poverty and instability so that we are working collectively to tackle the core stressors that make children vulnerable to unnecessary family separation.

group compared to its percentage in the total population.[47] Disparity is the unequal outcomes of one racial or ethnic group as compared to the outcomes for another racial/ethnic group.[48] The key indicators of structural racism and discrimination—disproportionality and disparity—are documented. Professor Dorothy Roberts captures the face of disproportionality when she describes that "Black children make up nearly half of the foster care populations, although they constitute less than one-fifth of the nation's children. In Chicago, 95 percent of children in foster care are Black."[49] The National Council of Juvenile and Family Court Judges surveyed all fifty states and found that "children of color are disproportionately represented in the U.S. foster care system."[50] Families of color are also over-represented in the services of domestic violence agencies and other systems with mandated reporters and thereby have an increased chance of being referred to child welfare agencies. Indeed, 50 percent of African American children will be the subjects of child abuse and neglect investigations before their eighteenth birthdays. The child welfare system is adroit at surveillance, investigation, and separation especially for children of color. Then, once removed from their homes, children of color remain in foster care longer, move more often, receive fewer services, less likely to be either returned home or adopted, and more likely to exist the child welfare system without permanency.[51]

Entering a door requires stepping over a threshold. When families experiencing domestic violence step through the doors of various systems, the thresholds they cross must be equitable *and*

---

47 *Racial Disparity in Child Welfare,* Child Welfare Information Gateway (Nov. 2006).

48 *Id.*

49 *Roberts,* supra note 44, at 8.

50 Shamini Ganasarajah, Gene Siegel & Melissa Sickmund, *Disproportionality Rates for Children of Color in Foster Care (Fiscal Year 2015), Technical Assistance Bulletin,* National Council of Juvenile and Family Court Judges (Sept. 2017), https://www.ncjfcj.org/sites/default/files/NCJFCJ-Disproportionality-TAB-2015_0.pdf. On average across the country, African American children are represented in foster care 2.5 times their rates in the general population (33% v. 14%), and Native American children have a disproportionality rate of nearly 1.5 to 3 times (3% v. 1%). Hispanic children are overrepresented 1.5 to more than 4 times their rates in the general population in seven states. *Id.* at 3, 15.

51 *Roberts,* supra note 44, at 8.

anti-discriminatory, including anti-racist.[52] An equitable child welfare system meets the needs of all children and families. An anti-discriminatory child welfare system then recalibrates so that race, class, and gender do not impact outcomes, unwinds the policies and practices that perpetuate harmful inequities,[53] and redistributes power and support to meet the needs of children, families, and communities. Leading with equity to be anti-discriminatory and anti-racist requires child welfare agencies in part to know their data, and provide training for individuals to confront their own implicit bias and moral constructions of race, class, gender, victimization, and violence create brave spaces for self-honesty, reflection and openness to growth, and advance specifically attuned efforts to undue harmful inequities and disparities. For abolitionists, the racism, too endemic, and the damage, too deep, renders the child welfare system beyond repair. What follows are concrete recommendations that can contribute to cementing the threshold of equity and anti-discrimination into the child welfare system and reduce the reach of the child welfare system for all families, including those experiencing domestic violence.

Differential Response

An unbroken system orientates away from breaking families apart.

When Isabel's school counselor called the Hotline because she was worried about Isabel and Nathan, the only option that the child welfare agency had to respond was to send an investigator to knock on Isabel's door and proceed with an intervention based upon finding

[52] The Center for the Study of Social Policy defines an anti-racist approach as the active process of identifying and challenging racism by changing systems, organizational structures, policies, and practices; redressing past injustices; meeting the needs of children and families of color; supporting the whole family; and serving all children and families in need. Elisa Minoff, *Principles for Anti-Racist Policymaking,* Center for the Study of Soc. Pol. (2020), https://cssp.org/wp-content/uploads/2020/12/Principles-for-Anti-Racist-Policymaking.pdf.

[53] The Annie E. Casey Foundation recommends that "using a racial equity impact assessment process and tool can help jurisdictions assess the actual or anticipated effect of proposed policies, institutional practices, programs, plans, and budgetary decisions." Annie E. Casey Foundation, *Race, Equity, and Inclusion Action Guide* (2015), https://www.aecf.org/resources/race-equity-and-inclusion-action-guide. The Center for the Study of Social Policy has created a race equity impact assessment that can be found at https://cssp.org/wp-content/uploads/2018/08/Race-Equity-Impact-Assessment-Tool.pdf.

fault and issuing investigative findings. This path inherently and as implemented fell devastatingly short of providing Isabel with the support she needed to continue parenting Nathan in safety and stability. In the end, this investigative intervention issued a finding that labeled Isabel as a neglectful mother to her son and implied that she was a danger to other children by retaining her name in the state's register of those who have harmed children. When the child welfare door opens in states such as Colorado, Arkansas, Nebraska, and Washington, however, more than one pathway exists for the case. Rather than initiating an investigation every time a case crosses the Hotline where child welfare agencies implement a differential response to families, the traditional investigative path exists along with an alternate response.

Thirty states have statutes or regulations that authorize differential response, with varying levels of implementation from policies on paper to statewide programs.[54] Most commonly, the investigative path is typically reserved for the most severe cases of physical and sexual abuse, involves the gathering of evidence, and making findings that are kept in the state central register.[55] The alternative response is often called the family assessment response and is usually the path for cases with concerns about neglect, such as those involving struggles with mental health, substance abuse, and domestic violence. The main tool of intervention is not removal or separation but rather family preservation and support. Ideally, family assessment caseworkers strive to develop a supportive, rather than adversarial role with the family, assess the families' needs with their input, and connect the family to services and provide concrete supports, all without needing to make a final determination or substantiation about whether abuse or neglect occurred. Child safety remains a focus of both tracks. If safety concerns arise or are made visible by being monitored, a case can jump from the family assessment track to the investigative track.

---

[54] *Differential Response in Child Protective Services, Analysis of State Legislative Provisions,* National Conference of State Legislatures (2019) https://www.ncsl.org/research/human-services/state-legislation-differential-response.aspx.

[55] *Differential Response: A Primer for Child Welfare Professionals,* Child Welfare Information Gateway (Oct. 2020), https://www.childwelfare.gov/pubPDFs/differential_response.pdf.

The family assessment track often leads to more favorable outcomes when compared to the investigative track.[56] The alternative path is more transparent for and engaging with families.[57] Children are equally as safe.[58] Families are less fearful in their interactions with child welfare. Children are less likely to be removed and placed in foster care. Families are more engaged in services.[59] Families have fewer subsequent reports of abuse or neglect.[60] Family assessment caseworkers report greater satisfaction than investigators, and retention is higher. The family assessment path costs less than the traditional approach in the long run.[61] While still opening the child welfare door and monitoring families, the alternative path defends against severing the value of children with their families even when struggles exist. Differential response is an attempt to shift paradigms and challenge historical orientations by focusing on strength-based partnerships with families instead of deficit-centered confrontation.

Blind Removals

An unbroken system mitigates the likelihood of unnecessarily removing children from their families.

Dr. Jessica Pryce, a former child welfare worker who now directs the Florida Institute for Child Welfare at Florida State University, poses a direct and simple question: Do we need to know the race of the family or where they live in order to decide if children should be

---

[56] John Fluke, Nicole Harlaar, Kurt Heisler, Adam Darnell, Brett Brown, & Lisa Merkel-Holguin, *Differential Response and the Safety of Children Reported to Child Protective Services: A Tale of Two Cities,* U.S. Dep't of Health and Human Services (2016), https://aspe.hhs.gov/sites/default/files/migrated_legacy_files//146476/DifferentialResponse.pdf.

[57] *Four Questions about Differential Response for Laura Carter-Beck,* Co4Kids Blog (Dec. 4, 2020), https://co4kids.org/blog/four-questions-about-differential-response-laura-carter-beck.

[58] *Differential Response, supra* note 56.

[59] *Id.*; *Nebraska IV-E Waiver Final Report,* The University of Nebraska-Lincoln, Center on Children, Families and the Law (Dec. 2019), https://dhhs.ne.gov/Documents/Nebraska%20IV-E%20Waiver%20Final%20Report.pdf.

[60] *Id.*

[61] *Id.*

removed from their home?[62] The answer should be in the negative, but practice reveals otherwise.

In Nassau County, New York, 57 percent of children in foster care were Black while they constituted only 10 percent of the general population,[63] resulting in a disproportionality rate of five times, more than double the average disproportionality rate across the country. Black children were five times more likely to be removed than white children experiencing similar circumstances. Yet within five years, the number of Black children in foster care decreased by more than half.

Blind removal meetings were responsible for reducing the number of Black children in foster care from 57 percent to 21 percent in Nassau County. Adhering to blind removals, before any decisions were made about whether to remove children from their families, the investigator presented to a removal committee withholding any identifying information, including the names, race, ethnicity, and neighborhood of the children and family. The investigator presented what was found, what happened, the family strengths, the relevant history, and the initial assessment of risk. The committee then decides if removal is necessary. As a child welfare administrator in Nassau County acknowledged, ". . . take the subjectivity of race and neighborhood out of it, and you might get different outcomes."[64] While disproportionality still remained in Nassau County, few programs targeting overrepresentation in the child welfare system have had such impact.[65]

Because implicit bias and structural discrimination, rather than actual harm or risk, led to the high rates of removal for children of color, keeping children from entering foster care did not jeopardize

---

62 Jessica Pryce, *Blind Removal Meetings—What are They?* (Sept. 25, 2018), https://medium.com/@jessicapryce/blind-removal-meetings-what-are-they-a21b7ee67830.

63 David Olson, *Nassau's White Population Below 60% in New Census Estimates,* News Day (June 20, 2019).

64 Jessica Pryce, To Transform Child Welfare, Take Race Out of the Equation, Presented at TED (May 2018), https://www.ted.com/talks/jessica_pryce_to_transform_child_welfare_take_race_out_of_the_equation.

65 Other states are considering the implementation of blind removals. For instance, in 2021 the California legislature considered a bill that would have authorized a blind removal pilot program. Jeremy Loudenback, *California Legislator Pauses Blind Removal Bill,* The Imprint (May 1, 2021).

their safety. As Dr. Pryce concludes, such innovation enables us to "imagine a child welfare system . . . that wants to make families stronger instead of pulling them apart."[66]

Leadership from Communities of Color and Survivors

An unbroken system looks to leadership from individuals and communities with lived experience and expertise.

Elevating holistic approaches and leadership from survivors and communities of color into child welfare agencies and collaborations are essential to increasing equity.[67] Instructively, the life work of Dr. Julia Perilla, the founder of Caminar Latino, rested on a simple philosophy: listen.[68] Dr. Perilla believed in the value, the greatest worth indeed, of the opinions of those impacted by violence. What she heard when she listed was a rejection of dichotomies between staying and leaving/good and bad and a need to holistically respond to families experiencing domestic violence.

The family and community are at the heart of Caminar Latino's holistic work, encompassing adult and child survivors of domestic violence and the person who uses coercive control and violence. For instance, Dr. Perilla heard women in programs say that they wanted their partners to receive domestic violence education at the same time they attended group counseling because it was easier for the family to find transportation to Caminar Latino once rather than twice per week.[69] Ruby White Starr (chapter 4), who leads the policy arm of Caminar Latino called Latinos United for Peace and Equity, recalls that Dr. Perilla would stand at the bottom of the stairs, pointing women upstairs for their program and men downstairs for theirs.

---

[66] Pryce, *supra* note 64.

[67] *The Activist Dialogues*, the compendium to the Greenbook, "recognizes the necessity for forming partnerships with a dynamic circle of people concerned with ending violence." Chic Dabby, Angela Autry, *Activist Dialogues: How Domestic Violence and Child Welfare Systems Impact Women of Color and Their Communities*, FAMILY VIOLENCE PREVENTION FUND (April 2005), https://www.futureswithoutviolence.org/userfiles/file/Children_and_Families/Activist.pdf.

[68] Our Founder, Julia Perilla, CAMINAR LATINO (Oct. 20, 2019), http://caminarlatino.org/profile-founder-julia-perilla/.

[69] Ruby White Starr, *Moving From the Mainstream to the Margins: Lessons in Culture and Power*, 33 J. OF FAMILY VIOLENCE 551, 553 (2018).

And in hearing from mothers that Caminar Latino's youth program was not reaching many children impacted by domestic violence, Caminar Latino developed a music program as an unexpected net that would inevitably reach and touch children who had experienced domestic violence.[70] Survivors and those from deeply impacted communities must lead because those closest to the struggles are also closest to the solutions.

Infusing holistic approaches into child welfare interventions should not result from merely pilfering ideas and practices, but rather by fostering genuine partnerships with and incorporating leadership from communities of color and survivors. In an article entitled "Moving from the Mainstream to the Margins: Lessons in Culture and Power", Ruby White Starr writes that partnerships with culturally specific organizations, like Caminar Latino, often consist of relationships based upon no more than "knowledge appropriation."[71] Instead, partnerships must result in a "more deliberate sharing of power," which "begins with a commitment to understand and resist structural racism as an explicit part" of the partnership's work.[72] Equity in structure spurs greater equity in practice aimed at holistically meeting the needs of families in their homes and communities.

Restorative Justice

Unbroken systems look toward alternative processes to heal individuals, families, and communities together.

Listening as families seek new doors to interrupt the cycle of violence, restorative justice aims to repair harm with the survivor, the person who caused harm, and the community together.

Restorative justice is a response to—and a reaction against—the didactic and adversarial traditional systemic and community responses to violence that consist of separate doors of healing and accountability without a role for the community. Restorative justice is premised on the belief that families and communities have the capacity to heal transgenerational harms through connection and support

---

[70] *Youth Programs*, Caminar Latino (Oct. 21, 2019), http://caminarlatino.org/programs/family-initiatives/youth-program/.

[71] Starr, *supra* note 69, at 553.

[72] *Id.*

and that justice can be healing by repairing the harm caused. Restorative justice brings together the centerpieces of holistic approaches to domestic violence by connecting the voice of the survivor, a belief in change, and the support of the community in narrating the impact of the harm and in discussion of how to repair.[73]

Disrupting conventional grassroots responses and cognizant of the need for survivor safety, communities of color have been leaders in implementing restorative justice practices involving people and communities experiencing domestic violence. Mimi Kim, a second- generation Korean American, founded Creative Interventions in 2004 as an alternative response to gendered violence that is not dependent upon punitive responses.[74] In collaboration with Mimi Kim, Sujatha Baliga directs the Restorative Justice Project at Impact Justice in California to provide opportunities to resolve and heal from domestic violence without state intervention.[75] Direct communication between those who cause harm, victims, family, friends, and community members occurs in programs such as Círculos de Paz in Nogales, Arizona. Adapted from the Navajo peacemaking process, peace circles are a central restorative justice practice.

Symbolically erasing power imbalances by sitting in the physical shape of a circle whose existence is continual without weighted sides,[76] those around the circle together address the tangible ways to repair the harm, bringing forth shared opportunities for healing and accountability.[77] Despite the systemic interventions that distanced

---

73 John Braithwaite & Heather Strang, Restorative Justice and Family Violence (2002).

74 Leah Sottile, *Abuser and Survivor, Face to Face,* The Atlantic (Oct 5, 2015).

75 Leah Sottile, *Abuser and Survivor, Face to Face,* The Atlantic (Oct 5, 2015).

76 Braithwaite and Strang, *supra* note 73, at 11.

77 Restorative justice practices reduce domestic violence recidivism *See, News Release, New Treatment for People Convicted of Domestic Violence Reduced Subsequent Arrests for All Types of Crimes, Study Finds*, New York University (Sept. 24, 2019), http://www.nyu.edu/about/news-publications/news/2019/september/DomesticViolneceStudy.html. A study evaluated a randomized control trial in Salt Lake City using circles of peace as the intervention in conjunction with batterer intervention treatment and the participation of willing survivors. Linda G. Millas, Briana Barocas, Robert P. Butters, & Barak Ariel, *A Randomized Controlled Trial of Restorative Justice-Informed Treatment for Domestic Violence Crimes,* Nature Human Behavior (2019), https://www.nature.com/articles/s41562-019-0724-1. Researchers found that when people convicted of a misdemeanor domestic

Isabel and Jason, if Isabel desired and if Jason were ready, they could listen to each other about the impact of the violence and understand the cause of harm in the presence of their community. Through this reparative process, parallel healing transpires as Jason's empathetic capacity grows, while Isabel's mind and body calibrate to a greater sense of safety. The community's participation would provide Jason with more pathways for change.[78] For instance, an elder from the community in attendance could offer that Jason study with him to learn the traditions of their culture, a middle-aged father present could share his own struggles to stop perpetrating violence and could offer to mentor Jason, or others could brainstorm ways for Jason to find meaning in community service such as by collecting donations for a local domestic violence shelter. The involvement of the community as a source of reparative solutions reinforces the importance of informal and formal community systems of care that warrant investment as well as community-designed responses that move away from state-sanctioned separation systems.

Restorative justice is a direct response to the injustice of violence and the injustice experienced in systemic responses. When used as an alternative to inequitable systemic responses or when restorative principles are incorporated into systems that traditionally result in disparate outcomes, restorative justice can increase equity for those who experience domestic violence by bringing forward natural supports and changing the cultural, social, and political conditions that support domestic violence.[79] Restorative justice contributes to responses surrounding therapeutically just child welfare interventions infused with gold that similarly meet the needs of families by making healing possible through promise and strength, connection and support.

Statutory Changes

An unbroken system must be willing to undo, redo, and change.

---

violence crime were randomly assigned to an intervention that included a component informed by restorative justice, arrests were reduced by 53%. Of the arrests that were made, the severity of the crimes was reduced by half in that same two-year window. *Id.*

[78] Braithwaite and Strang, *supra* note 73, at 18.

[79] Donna Coker, *Restorative Justice, Navajo Peacemaking, and Domestic Violence,* Theoretical Criminology 67 (Feb. 2006).

Federal and state statutes are responsible for setting the policies that become translated into child welfare interventions. Amending particular federal and state statutes would both reduce the reach of the child welfare system as well as decrease the harm it has caused to families.

Federally, repealing the Adoption and Safe Families Act (ASFA) would increase the likelihood that a family receives ample opportunity to reunify. Short of repeal, amending ASFA to remove the requirement to file a termination of parental rights petition if a child has been in foster care for fifteen out of twenty-two months would abolish the ticking clock that makes the chance of reunification for thousands of families more difficult. If ASFA retains the provision that provides a financial incentive to agencies to achieve permanency through adoption, an identical financial benefit should be statutorily instituted for cases that achieve permanency through reunification. Also, guardianship should not be deemed an inferior permanency goal to adoption. Instead, guardianship should be a preferred permanency goal over adoption, or at least a statutorily equivalent outcome.

Although great variation exists amongst state statutes, legislative reform at the state level would contribute to transforming the experiences of families at the intersection of domestic violence and child welfare in practice. Specifically, state statutes should be amended to remove domestic violence advocates from the list of mandated reporters of abuse or neglect. In California, Kansas, and Oregon, domestic violence advocates are not mandated reporters. Where domestic violence advocates are mandated reporters, many survivors of domestic violence are deterred from reaching out for help and resist being forthcoming about the full extent of help they need because of their well-founded fear that doing so would lead to a Hotline call that could result in being deemed neglectful or losing their children.[80] In addition, statue statutes that govern both child welfare operations, as well as the juvenile court process, should specifically address families experiencing domestic violence. State statutes should (1) codify

---

[80] *See,* Carrie Lippy, Connie Burk, & Margaret Hobart, *There's No One I Can Trust, The Impact of Mandatory Reporting on the Help-Seeking and Wellbeing of Domestic Violence Survivors,* The National LGBTQ DV Capacity Building Learning Center (2016).

that exposure to domestic violence is not per se neglect, (2) set a threshold that determines when exposure to domestic violence constitutes neglect, (3) presume that an adult survivor is not neglectful so long as she took precautionary measures to protect her children, even if those steps were not successful, and (4) explicitly define the required "reasonable efforts" to support adult and child survivors together and to foster avenues of accountability for the parent using violence and coercive control. Statutes consistent with these priorities are more likely to lead to interventions that avoid punitive responses to adult survivors, prioritize keeping children with the adult survivor, and cultivate opportunities for accountability, all of which contribute to the enhanced safety, stability, well-being, and healing of families.

Prevention

An unbroken system aims to not open its door.

The response of the child welfare system to families experiencing domestic violence should be one of last resort. Solutions for meeting the families' needs should be sourced in the family itself, then the community, and only in systems, especially those that are not uninvited, when gaps remain in the closer concentric circles surrounding families. Primary and secondary prevention, therefore, are needed to improve outcomes and prevent the inequity and disparity that systemic involvement has historically caused. Primary prevention targets the conditions that open the door to child welfare system involvement, like domestic violence. Any effort aimed at enhancing equity, decreasing oppression, addressing patriarchy, balancing power at the intersectionality of people's identities and experiences, ensuring opportunities to heal from trauma that stems the perpetuation of pain by pain-filled people, and strengthening individuals, families, and community can be considered domestic violence prevention. Secondary prevention strives to keep closed the child welfare door, and if opened, to curb the inequitable responses that sever the needs of children from their families and community through removal, foster-care placement, and long-term systemic involvement by instead providing concrete family preservations services upstream and financing community-based resources.

Long-overdue federal legislation in 2018 prioritized secondary prevention. Historically, Title IV-E of the Social Security Act, the principal source of federal child welfare funding, was only accessible to states as entitlement reimbursement for services provided to families with children in state custody, such as in foster care.[81] As the Pew Charitable Trusts posits, "Because more than half of all children in foster care eventually return home . . . it is logical to ask whether more children could safely remain with their families without the trauma of removal if services and supports were available to their families?"[82] This logic manifested into the bipartisan Family First Prevention Services Act that allows states to seek reimbursement from Title IV-E dollars to cover up to half of the costs of providing prevention or reunification services to children who are at imminent risk of entering or remaining in foster care and their families.[83,84] Not without limitations,[85] this federal priority on prevention and reunification has the potential to be the pendulum that fosters child welfare culture and practice that views families and communities as sources of strength rather than deficit, as solutions rather than problems, orientating toward preservation rather than removal. To do so, Family First must be intentionally implemented in order to distribute family preservation services equitably to families in their homes and communities. Family First must avoid being more of the

---

[81] Specifically, of the $7.2 billion in federal funds dedicated to child welfare in 2007, 90% supported children in foster care ($4.5 billion) and children adopted from foster care ($2.0 billion). Only 10% of dollars were allocated for family support services, such as prevention and reunification services. States were not restricted from spending additional money on prevention services but would not be able to seek federal reimbursement.

[82] *Time for Reform: Investing In Prevention: Keeping Children Safe At Home*, The Pew Charitable Trusts, 4 (2007).

[83] H. R. 1892 to the Bipartisan Budget Act of 2018.

[84] The Family First Prevention Services Act also reimburses prevention services to adoption and guardianships at risk of disrupting, pregnant or parenting foster youth, and kinship caregivers, as well as provides in part new licensing standards for relative foster family homes, takes steps to safely reduce the inappropriate use of congregate/group care for children, and extends the age eligibility of foster youth who are transition into adulthood to continue receiving services.

[85] Family First focuses narrowly on preventing children from being in foster care, and not on preventing child welfare system involvement at all. All programs delivering prevention or reunification services eligible for reimbursement meet certain stringent, evidence-based requirements approved by the California Evidence-Based Clearinghouse for Child Welfare such that effective programs that do not meet this threshold are not eligible for Family First dollars.

same—surveillance, regulation, punishment, and separation—under a different name. Nonetheless, Family First is opening a new door—a lift gate of sorts—whose impact remains to be written.

Investment

An unbroken system cares more about supporting families than about maintaining the institution itself.

The federal government is investing in secondary prevention through Family First. Primary prevention also requires investment. Primary prevention entails preventing families from coming to the attention of the child welfare system in the first place, not because they have evaded detection per se, but because they have the resources to address the struggles they may be facing within their own families and communities. Financial investment in families and communities is needed.

Spending on anti-poverty programs can substantially strengthen families, provide the resources needed to address struggles, and reduce child abuse and neglect (in both a universal sense and in the way abuse and neglect are currently defined). This directive has arisen from research conducted by a group of pediatricians. Their published article contains a charge for responding to families in need in a very different way than the call-to-action Dr. Kempe invoked decades earlier.[86] The study examined the relationship between the states' rates of child maltreatment and their annual spending, per person, in poverty on major benefit programs from 2010 to 2017.[87] Benefit programs included those providing cash, housing or material resources, child-care assistance, refundable earned income tax credits, and medical assistance programs such as Medicaid. The findings indicate that an increase of $1,000, or 13 percent, in annual spending on these programs per person living in poverty by all fifty states and Washington, DC, might be associated with approximately 181,000 fewer children being reported for maltreatment, 28,500 fewer victims, 4,100 fewer children entering foster care, and 130 fewer children dying every

---

[86] Henry T. Puls, Matthew Hall, James D. Anderst, Tami Gurley, James Perrin, & Paul J. Chung, *State Spending on Public Benefit Programs and Child Maltreatment,* 148 PEDIATRICS 5 (2021).

[87] *Id.*

year.[88] The results also suggest that reductions in child maltreatment might provide fiscal returns in the long-term for states and society.[89] The 13 percent increase in spending would amount to $46.5 billion nationally.[90] The research estimates these reductions might return $1.5 billion to $9.3 billion in avoided economic burdens associated with maltreatment in the short term but as much as $25.8 billion to $153.2 billion over the course of children's lives. In contrast, every $1 spent on foster care results in a negative return on the investment making it a more expensive response in the short term that leads to more costly outcomes in the long term.[91]

The investment in anti-poverty programs is not to say that families living in poverty are more likely to abuse or neglect their children nor does it support the proposition that the child welfare system is the appropriate system to intervene in the lives of families living in poverty. What the study does show is that often the intervention that has been created is not only harmful but is also not needed. All before the fateful photograph was taken, what if Mary Ellen Wilson's mother (chapter 2) would have received childcare assistance so she did not have to board her daughter in order to work as well as cash assistance so she did not have to place her daughter in an orphanage when she lost her job?

Investment in public benefits is not a panacea. Public benefits programs are still an arm of the state and often carry detriments of paternalism, surveillance, and mandates. To avoid these oppressive disadvantages, the investment in families can also occur by investing in areas that aspire higher beyond basic needs, such as in providing job training, fair market loans to begin] businesses, and financial aid for post-high school education or vocational schools. Investment must also ensure that the needs of a family can be met in their own community and by their own community members.

Community investment through public or private dollars should aspire to imbue communities with the resources their members need to create the resources the community demands. Each community,

---

88 *Id.*

89 *Id.*

90 *Id.*

91 *Id.*

like each family, will carry different needs but such resources could include food stores with fresh fruits and vegetables, childcare options, after-school arts programs, nonpredatory financial institutions, green spaces, affordable and safe housing, schools that address diverse learners, depots of culture, accessible transportation, language support, employment opportunities that pay a liveable wage, diverse food and cuisine, medical and mental health clinics, community centers with fitness and holistic programming, affordable legal representation, and religious and spiritual outlets. In doing so, the needs of families will be met within the closest concentric circles surrounding them, thereby, for the majority of families, buffering against and mitigating the opportunity for the child welfare system to be called or compelled to respond.

It is our collective responsibility to all families and communities to continue innovating better, more effective, even reimagined, equitable responses to families experiencing domestic violence, guided by that which we know is true—meeting the needs of safety, stability, well-being, healing, and accountability occurs amidst honest compassion, within a supportive partnership, and in connection with family and community, thereby preventing child welfare and surrounding systemic interventions from being additional traumas from which to heal.

• • •

Isabel Rodriguez. Molly McGrath Tierney. Susan Schechter. Jeffrey Edleson. Casey Keene. Ruby White Starr. Juan Carlos Areán. Darrell Jackson. Casey Gwinn. Sharwline Nicholson. Betsy McAlister Groves. Liz Roberts. Jacquelyn Campbell. Karen Johnson. Alessa Karadere. Judge Leonard Edwards. James Henderson. Heather Cantamessa. Lonna Davis. Shellie Taggart. Susan Hubert. Isa Woldeguiorguis. Tammy Mello. Katchi Lessard. Crystal Jackson. Andrew Rome. Sue Englaish. Barbara Price. Patricia Sevedo. Alejandra Sevedo. Judith Herman. Amita Swadhin. Lenny Hayes. Johnny Rice II. Stacey Platt. Judge Katherine Tennyson. David Berns. Loretta Frederick. Gabrielle Davis. A.K. V.K. Julia Parilla. Everyone present in this book has stood at the intersection of domestic violence and the child welfare system and had experiences that warranted reimagined responses, did something reimagined, or experienced and did both.

Unity exists among their actions and experiences that dare, that demand, to respond to families experiencing domestic violence in the child welfare system differently. That difference begins by both committing to what child welfare systems should not do and to the harder task of articulating what the system should do. Systems should not replicate the abuse of the person who uses violence and coercive control with the violence and control of the state. A valuable goal defined by avoidance, however, still creates dichotomies of good and bad, worthy and unworthy, them and us. The difference that is needed, then, is defining the goal of our child welfare systems in the positive, to enhance, rather than impede, the safety, stability, well-being, and healing of children and their families, children *with* their families, together, and to foster opportunities for sustainable accountability.

If we begin with this goal, we orient ourselves to the value in every family, to the family as the source of children's right-filled needs, to the need of connection for all children with their families even amidst dire struggles,

> struggles whose solutions are sometimes elusive or so fundamental that we disregard their lifeline importance;
>
> solutions that carry costs and benefits;
>
> fearful costs that derive from intervening too much and not intervening enough;
>
> benefits that arise from partnering with those who are in need;
>
> partnerships that begin on high and parallel on the ground that which can be universally desired;
>
> abidance by the universal needs to be heard, to be believed, to feel supported; and
>
> support that concretely strengthens promise and buffers risk.

Then, in the end, and all along the way, we will act in accordance with the promise to aspire higher by hoping that our actions, messages, and touch will struggle toward unbroken togetherness. An unbrokenness that those who experience domestic violence and the child welfare system may have realized with or without the outside response- a beauty and infragility made more likely now by spinning toward trauma's healing, resilient strength, centered connection, and nuanced support. A golden unbrokenness prevailing no matter come what may that reverberates through deferential admiration of and admirable deference to families, and as the now intrinsic grounding of our activism, our advocacy, our resolution. Together unbroken in the golden aura as individuals, as families, as communities, and as systems. Through the open door the line between those impacted and those who impact forever blurred, rendering all of us, in partnership and solidarity, together unbroken, in mutuality of purpose and aspiration.

• • •

A handful of years after graduating high school, Isabel received a call from Marta. Marta, Isabel's counselor in high school, who helped her develop a plan to leave Jason and who, fearing the worst, made a Hotline call when Isabel did not return to school with Nathan according to their plan. On the phone, Marta informed Isabel that county funding for the in-school medical and mental health clinic that both Isabel and Nathan accessed was in jeopardy. Isabel took a breath—both the clinic and Marta had been feathers that contributed to Isabel's wings. Seeking Isabel's assistance for the first time, Marta asked Isabel to testify at a public hearing on the need to save the clinic. Isabel did not hesitate.

On the day of the public hearing to save the clinic, Isabel stood with Marta and a current high school student who had accessed the clinic to heal from sexual abuse she endured as a child. The County Board of Commissioners numbered seventeen, only two of whom were women, and community members filled the remaining chairs along with hospital administrators and other public health officials whose funding was also at risk. Isabel's name was called, and she walked up to the podium. Once again, light graced her paper and cast dusky shadows onto the handwritten words in the notebook she grasped in her hands.

> *I am here today to talk about my experience in the school-based clinic at my former high school. Not only did I become a mother at a very young age, but I suffered greatly when unfortunately I became involved in a very abusive relationship with the father of my son. I was only fifteen years old at the time, trying to finish high school to give my son a better future. But I faced many challenges along the way. My counselor, Marta,*

> *who is here tonight, was the only support I had at the time. If it wasn't for Marta, I would have fallen too far behind to graduate, but she advocated for me many times by talking to my school dean to help me get back on my feet. How many of us would need someone to speak on our behalf when you feel like your whole world is crashing down? Marta had a very big impact on my life but that wouldn't have been possible if the clinic wasn't in the school. Besides my counseling, my son was also part of the children's center at the clinic so I did not have to miss school to take him to the doctor. Now here I am here today, a high school graduate. But none of my success would have been possible if the clinic had not been in the school. I know that there are many students who won't reach their full potential if the clinic is no longer in the school . . .*

When Isabel finished speaking, a well-known commissioner told her she was very brave. Although appreciative of the compliment, bravery did not propel Isabel. Rather, she had found her place, a fitting place to hold her experiences, both those of pain and growth, trauma and resilience, indispensable to where she now stood. She was safe in this room of strangers, just as she and her son were now safe in their own home. She shared her story, she conveyed her narrative, and the audience listened, mirroring healing back to her. She felt connected to the clinic, her school, and the community that encompassed both, and by her presence and commitment, Isabel connected herself to their needs. As Isabel stepped down from the podium, she was hopeful, believing in her ability to affect the experiences of the 3,500 students at her alma mater who may now have a chance to continue accessing this supportive clinic, in part, because of her words.

A month later, Marta called Isabel again, this time to tell her that funding for the clinic had been approved. Isabel felt appreciative to have had the opportunity to lend her voice, proud of her impact, and grateful that the clinic would survive to benefit thousands of students each year—another feather in her winged collection and theirs. The parts of Isabel that once felt broken brought her to a place in which she could advocate for the benefit of others, and those parts in need of ongoing and deeper healing became a little less fractured.

During both the good and hard days that inevitably come, Isabel often reminds herself of the words she spoke shortly before leaving the podium at the public hearing. In front of elected officials, former teachers, medical professionals, and her neighbors, Isabel declared, ". . . I look forward to becoming an advocate for domestic violence victims in hopes that maybe one day, I will be able to work with some of you here."

Intuiting that activism is the antidote to despair, Isabel completed the training to be a certified domestic violence professional in her state. Once she is able to access financial aid for college and legally work in this country, Isabel has committed to becoming a domestic violence advocate.

A few years later, Isabel, as a parent mentor, became a member of a coalition that focuses on collaborating with the very child welfare agency that once deemed her neglectful in order to work toward more effective interventions for families like hers.

Isabel is strong in the places that were once broken, and like those who strengthened her along her way, she will now help others impacted by domestic violence—individuals, families, communities, and systems—find strength in together

becoming

unbroken.

Epilogue: Stronger Together

Isabel Rodriguez and Sharwline Nicholson's voices have been heard together.

In the fall of 2021, Futures Without Violence,[1] Ujima,[2] Women Transforming Families,[3] and Latinos United for Peace and Equity,[4] organized a three-part series called "The Accountability Dialogues." The Susan Schechter Memorial Foundation sponsored this first-of-its-kind series.

The dialogues brought together policymakers and government leaders with survivors from communities of color who experienced domestic violence and had been re-victimized by the child welfare system in order to amplify their voices and circumstances. In centering on the truth and expertise of Isabel, Sharwline, and other mothers, survivors and policymakers together aimed to co-create innovative recommendations to boldly transform the child welfare system. Isa Woldeguiorguis moderated the dialogues while hundreds of people across the country listened.

In the first session entitled "Justice is Truth," Isabel, Sharwline, and three other survivors of domestic violence and the child welfare system shared space virtually together. Attendees were instructed to

---

1 Lonna Davis and Shellie Taggart from Futures Without Violence were involved in planning and executing *The Accountability Dialogues*.

2 Ujima: National Center on Violence Against Women in the Black Community.

3 Women Transforming Families in Communities of Color.

4 Ruby White Starr from Latinos United for Peace and Equity participated in *The Accountability Dialogues*.

engage in the "revolutionary act of listening."[5] Isabel and Sharwline spoke in dialogue together. Sharwline shared, "I was punished when all I needed was help and support. Afterward, I feared ever reaching out for help because the system took all that I had left, my children." Together in shared understanding despite the years between their experiences, Isabel acknowledged the impact of Sharwline's words and continued, "If we don't seek help or if we don't speak up, it's because we are scared. We are scared of the abuse *and* of our kids being taken away. The system needs to be healing, rather than traumatizing." Sharwline, Isabel, and the other courageous women told their truths. Their truths had power.

"Justice is Accountability" framed the second session. Policymakers, including judges, federal secretaries and commissioners, and community activists spoke directly to the survivors. Collectively they said, "We hear you. We see you. Together, we need to do better." Isabel and Sharwline together heard their words.

Vice President of the United States Kamala Harris opened the third session with a recorded statement delivered specifically for *The Accountability Dialogues* that became imprinted upon all who were moved when her calm and commanding face appeared on the screen. Isabel and Sharwline together received the words of one of the most influential women in the world when the Madame Vice President assuredly declared this to be a "transformative moment." The survivors and policymakers together then addressed the harm done to families and the means of aspiring higher because as the third session guided, "Justice is Prevention." The line between the impacted and the impactor became indistinct yet again, as the survivors and policymakers discussed together that the roots of child welfare transformation must be hope, love, and commitment to family preservation—the embodied humanity of what each person deserves, the encapsulation of strength amidst the struggle, the imperative to respond with the opposite. Amidst priorities placed on providing concrete supports and financial resources to families, an activist for families imparted the sober reminder that "the system is doing exactly what it was designed to do." From one mother, whose advocacy began years before, to another mother who is fulfilling the commitment she made

---

[5] Gloria Steinem, My Life on the Road (2016).

to herself to advocate for others, Isabel and Sharwline together spoke the same message through their individual words, "We are here to prevent what happened to us from happening to another family, another mother and her children. The opposite of our experiences in a broken system is a system that helps us heal together."

Justice is healing, a system together then unbroken.

Acknowledgements

Writing a book measures time differently. Minutes are measured by sentences. Hours by paragraphs. Weeks by pages. Months by chapters. A year of words. A journey with an intended message. Within those measures, gratitude abounds, without which the sentences, paragraphs, pages, chapters, and words would never have found life, found a voice. I share this book filled with endless thankfulness:

To the Loyola University Chicago School of Law and the Civitas ChildLaw Center and Fellowship program for providing me with philosophical orientation, doctrinal understanding, practical skills, and renowned mentors as the foundation for my legal career. I reflect on my time in law school as one of my most treasured experiences and am proud that my once-professors are now colleagues;

To the Skadden Fellowship Foundation for providing me with the opportunity to delve into the intersection of domestic violence and child welfare as a new lawyer, for continuing to support my work throughout my career, and for fostering a community of lawyers dedicated to public interest lawyering and social justice;

To my fellow family defenders at the Legal Assistance Foundation of Metropolitan Chicago (now Legal Aid Chicago) and The Family Defense Center (now Ascend Justice) for finding solidarity in the inherent value we regard in all families, for teaching and uplifting me, for partnering with me in zealously advocating for the families in which we wholeheartedly believe, for the strategic debates, the intellectual and honest discussions, and the times in which tears or a smile became a language of understanding. To Richard Cozzola, my first supervisor and mentor who unexpectedly passed away as this book was going to print, for the countless formative conversations filled with a little bit about work, a little more about family, and always with a lot of heart and humor. In Rich's memory and to honor his legacy, I will strive to emulate his empathy, gentle strength, generosity of spirit and mind, encouragement of others, creativity, and dedication to the practice of law for the benefit of those we serve. And to my former clients for your lessons of bravery, resourcefulness, and strength, for your unwavering dedication to your children, for being a role model of parenting for me, for motivating me to consciously grow to be a better person, lawyer, wife, mother, daughter, and community member, for your friendship, and for being conduits of essential change.

To the American Bar Association Commission on Domestic and Sexual Violence for identifying the need for this book and for inviting me to be the one to write it. And to the American Bar Association's publishing department for your patience, editorial guidance, deftness, and openness to the evolution of this book's journey and message;

To law students Theresa Barton, Cassandra Burns, Mehgan Keeley, and Brianna Steger. If your inestimable research assistance for this book is any indication of the lawyers you will become, you each will be invaluable additions to the field of law;

To the caseworkers, child welfare administrators, advocates, lawyers, judges, researchers, mental health professionals, and academics, many of whom shared their wisdom and insights here, who are devoted to working on behalf of and in partnership with families, who realize that we must work together in order to strive for cohesive and effective responses to family violence, and who spend their careers serving, trailblazing, and innovating approaches to supporting families by being sources of safety, stability, well-being, and healing;

To the Black Lives Matter movement that overlapped and will outlast the publishing of this book. Rising through the names that cannot be forgotten is widespread demand for change and the ultimate reminder that state power must be a harbinger of good, not breathless harm.

To my mom who was the first and last reader of every chapter (twice), providing feedback, edits, and encouraging comments about parts that particularly resounded, who—along with my dad—understood and supported the time and dedication that this book required and deserved, who have always cared about the issues that are important to their daughter, and who are the foundation for all that I do;

To my parents, in-laws, and siblings by blood and marriage for creating and contributing to homes in which love, kindness, and respect abound;

To my husband whose indoctrination into the world of feminism began years ago, who steadfastly supports and encourages my work on behalf of women, children, and families, who imparts the importance of fighting for families with friends and colleagues, who patiently tolerated the distractions from life that this book often caused, and who shares our deepest commitment to the importance of family;

To my two daughters, J and A, for being my forever inspiration. Over the past years, this book became our third child, your newest and youngest sister. You met the frequent motto of "Mommy is writing" with patience and acceptance. You showed interest when J asked, "Mommy, is your book going to include dialogue?" and showed enthusiasm when A exclaimed, "I am going to get a copy of your book!" I will always remember writing the last sentence of the book interrupted by A's question of what she should wear to picture day the next day. I am proud every day to be your mother, and I hope I have made you proud. May this book be a small contribution to moving our community, our society, and our world toward a place where girls, women, mothers, and families are safe, stable, and able to thrive;

The global pandemic intersected the editing of this book. The pandemic has both spotlighted the issues of this book as well as underscored the importance of the preached approaches. For many families on the brink of managing their struggles, the pandemic has disintegrated their thin safety net and detached them from their supports. Sheltering at home has been especially dangerous for adults and children experiencing abuse behind closed doors that have recently remained shut, breeding unfettered access without reprieve. The circumstances associated with the pandemic have been converted into tactics of violence and coercive control. Communities of color disproportionately impacted by the child welfare system have been disproportionately impacted in frequency and severity by COVID-19. Yet, one of the many lessons that have arisen from the pandemic's devastation is the importance—the vital need—of supporting families and communities. The pandemic has unraveled a modicum of the moral construction around families in need, as struggling and being in need has been more universally felt over the year (and counting) of the virus. Evaporating divisions between families and neighbors and connecting individual action with collective responsibility are the mantras I have chosen to hear that the pandemic has elevated. We *must* carry forward the value in every family and the universality of support that the pandemic is leaving in its wake, together unbroken.

And in parting gratitude:

To each person who shared your story, bore your soul, imparted your struggles, and demonstrated immeasurable strength, this book, the readers, and I are indebted to you. You are the heart and soul of this book without which the law, policy, and pathways toward healing are devoid of resonance and importance. My life will forever be enriched by knowing you, and it has been an honor of a lifetime to be entrusted with your experiences. I now carry your stories inside of me and feel incalculably fortunate to be a conduit for disseminating the power of hope and shared humanity that your stories emanate. Since writing this book's opening sentence, I have been reminded of the words of Holocaust survivor, psychiatrist, and neurologist Viktor Frankl. In grappling with his own experiences of trauma and loss personally, spiritually, culturally, and globally, he wrote, "In some ways, suffering ceases to be suffering at the moment it finds a meaning . . ."[1] A glimmer of meaning can be found in the impact your stories will have on the readers of this book and on the places—conversations, meetings, classrooms, courtrooms, and capital buildings—to which they will bring your teachings. You have changed hearts and minds, you have informed practice, and you have moved practitioners to rise to the standards you have demonstrated families deserve. Your voices have meaning. Your voices have been heard. We will continue listening to your lessons. Gracias. Dhanyavaad. Wopila. Thank you.

---

[1] Viktor E. Frankl, Man's Search for Meaning (1992).

About the Author

Sara B. Block has dedicated her career to supporting survivors of domestic violence and their children. Sara is the director of advocacy at Ascend Justice where she focuses on policy and systemic reforms that impact families experiencing domestic violence as well those involved in the child welfare system. Sara is an adjunct professor in the Masters of Jurisprudence in ChildLaw program at Loyola University Chicago School of Law, in which she teaches Child Welfare Law and Policy and Juvenile Justice Law Policy. Sara was a Skadden Fellow at the Legal Assistance Foundation of Metropolitan Chicago with a fellowship focusing on the intersection of domestic violence and child welfare. Sara has received the Chicago Metropolitan Battered Women's Network's Outstanding Partnership Award, the Family Defense Center's Major Litigation Award for her involvement in *Julie Q. v. DCFS,* and the Jewish United Fund's "36 Under 36" award. Sara received her JD, *magna cum laude*, from Loyola University Chicago School of Law in 2007, where she was a ChildLaw Fellow and the Features Editor of the *Children's Legal Rights Journal.* Sara received her BA degree with honors in American Studies from Northwestern University. She is most proud of her two spirited and strong daughters.

About the Author

Index

D

J

O

P

Q

R

S

T

U

V

W